Alfresco One 5.x Developer's Guide

Second Edition

G000065322

Discover what it means to be an expert developer by exploring the latest features available to you in Alfresco One 5.x

Benjamin Chevallereau
Jeff Potts

BIRMINGHAM - MUMBAI

Alfresco One 5.x Developer's Guide

Second Edition

First published: October 2008

Second edition: February 2017

Production reference: 1220217

Published by Packt Publishing Ltd.
Livery Place
35 Livery Street
Birmingham
B3 2PB, UK.
ISBN 978-1-78712-816-3

www.packtpub.com

Credits

Authors

Benjamin Chevallereau
Jeff Potts

Reviewer

Bindu Wavell

Commissioning Editor

Amarabha Banerjee

Acquisition Editor

Shweta Pant

Content Development Editor

Aditi Gour

Technical Editor

Anushree Arun Tendulkar

Copy Editor

Safis Editing

Project Coordinator

Ritika Manoj

Proofreader

Safis Editing

Indexer

Tejal Daruwale Soni

Graphics

Jason Monteiro

Production Coordinator

Melwyn Dsa

About the Authors

Benjamin Chevallereau is a French software architect, based in London, who has been working on Alfresco projects for the last 8 years and Ephesoft projects for the last 3 years. He implemented solutions for small companies and global organizations in different domains such as transport, finance, and government.

He has worked for different Alfresco-recognized partners in France, the UK, and USA, including Armedia LLC, Zaizi, Michelin / Wipro, and BlueXML. He is also one of the committers and PMC members of the Apache CMIS Chemistry project.

Jeff Potts is the founder of Metaversant Group, Inc., a consulting firm focused on content management, search, and workflow. Jeff brings over 20 years of Enterprise Content Management implementation experience to organizations of all sizes including the Fortune 500. Throughout his consulting career he has worked on a number of projects for clients across the media and entertainment, airline, consumer packaged goods, and retail sectors.

Jeff began working with and blogging about Alfresco in November of 2005. In 2006 and 2007, he published a series of Alfresco tutorials and published them on his blog, `ecmarchitect.com`. That work, together with other Community activity in Alfresco's forum, Wiki site, and JIRA earned him Alfresco's 2007 Community Contributor of the Year Award.

In the past, Mr. Potts has worked for Alfresco Software, Inc. as Chief Community Officer, Optaros as Senior Practice Director, and Hitachi Consulting as Vice President where he ran the ECM practice.

About the Reviewer

Bindu Wavell is the chief architect at Zia Consulting. He has been doing enterprise system integration consulting for the past 24 years. At Zia, Bindu provides guidance and mentoring around Alfresco architecture and design in addition to working hands on with customers. He develops processes and technologies to streamline onboarding new developers, delivers trainings for customer developers and provides support for implementations and delivered projects.

I would like to thank the whole team at Zia for providing an amazing environment for learning, discovery and excellence. I'd also like to thank everyone at Alfresco for delivering such a great content management platform and for continuing to focus on being the best in the industry.

www.PacktPub.com

For support files and downloads related to your book, please visit www.PacktPub.com.

Did you know that Packt offers eBook versions of every book published, with PDF and ePub files available? You can upgrade to the eBook version at www.PacktPub.com and as a print book customer, you are entitled to a discount on the eBook copy. Get in touch with us at service@packtpub.com for more details.

At www.PacktPub.com, you can also read a collection of free technical articles, sign up for a range of free newsletters and receive exclusive discounts and offers on Packt books and eBooks.

https://www.packtpub.com/mapt

Get the most in-demand software skills with Mapt. Mapt gives you full access to all Packt books and video courses, as well as industry-leading tools to help you plan your personal development and advance your career.

Why subscribe?

- Fully searchable across every book published by Packt
- Copy and paste, print, and bookmark content
- On demand and accessible via a web browser

Customer Feedback

Thanks for purchasing this Packt book. At Packt, quality is at the heart of our editorial process. To help us improve, please leave us an honest review on this book's Amazon page at `https://www.amazon.com/Alfresco-One-5-x-Developers-Guide-ebook/dp/1787128164`.

If you'd like to join our team of regular reviewers, you can e-mail us at `customerreviews@packtpub.com`. We award our regular reviewers with free eBooks and videos in exchange for their valuable feedback. Help us be relentless in improving our products!

Table of Contents

Preface

Alfresco is the leading open source platform for Enterprise Content Management. The evolution of the product has been quite impressive during the last 10 years. The first edition of this book has been published in 2008, and after 8 years, it really needed an update. This new book will give you some insights on the most advanced capabilities of the Alfresco platform. This book takes you through the process of customizing and extending the Alfresco engine, the out-of-the-box user interface Alfresco Share that will suit most of your requirements in terms of document collaboration. It uses a fictitious professional services company called "SomeCo" as an example. SomeCo has decided to roll out Alfresco across the enterprise. Your job is to take advantage of Alfresco's extension mechanism, workflow engine, and various APIs and SDKs to meet the requirements from SomeCo's various departments. Although many customizations can be made by editing XML and properties files, this book is focused on developers. That might mean writing Java code against the Alfresco API to implement an action or a behavior, maybe creating some server-side JavaScript to use as the controller of a RESTful web script, or perhaps implementing custom business logic in an advanced workflow. The point is that all but the most basic implementations of any ECM platform require code to be written. The goal of this book is to help you identify patterns, techniques, and specific steps that you can use to become productive on the platform more quickly. By the end of this book, you will have stepped through every aspect of the Alfresco platform. You will have performed the same types of customizations and extensions found in typical Alfresco implementations. You'll have discovered the Mobile Alfresco SDK and creates your own mobile application. Finally, you'll get a preview of the latest Alfresco Development Framework (ADF) based on Angular. Most importantly, when someone comes to you and asks, "How would you do this in Alfresco?", you'll have at least one answer and maybe even some source code to go with it.

What this book covers

Chapter 1, *The Alfresco Platform*, is for people new to the Alfresco platform. It walks you through the capabilities of Alfresco and gives some examples of the types of solutions that can be built on the platform. You'll also learn what tools and skills are required to implement Alfresco-based solutions.

Chapter 2, *Getting Started with Alfresco,* is about getting your development environment set up. Like preparing for a home improvement project, this is the trip to the hardware store to get the tools and supplies you'll need to get the job done. Throughout the book, you will be building and deploying changes. So just as in any software development project, it pays to get that process working up front. You'll also learn about the debugging tools that are available to you. The chapter includes a short and simple customization example to test out your setup.

Chapter 3, *Working with Content Models,* starts where all Alfresco projects should begin: defining the content model. You'll learn how to define the content model as well as how to expose the model to Alfresco Share. Once you've got it in place, you'll write some Java code that utilizes the CMIS API to test out the model. This will also be your first taste of the JavaScript API. The exercises set up the initial content model for SomeCo.

Chapter 4, *Handling Content Automatically with Actions, Behaviors, Transformers, and Extractors,* begins to show you the power of the repository by exposing you to some of the mechanisms or hooks that can be used to perform "hands off" operations on content. You'll learn about actions, behaviors, transformers, and metadata extractors. The exercises include implementing a rule action for SomeCo's Human Resources department to help manage HR policies, writing a custom behavior to calculate user ratings, and writing a custom metadata extractor to make Microsoft Project files indexable by SolR.

Chapter 5, *Customizing Alfresco Share,* takes you through Alfresco Share customizations. First, it establishes whether or not you should be customizing the user interface at all. Once that's out of the way, you learn how to add new menu or action items, how to create your own custom metadata template, how to develop new pages and dashlets, and how to define new dialogs to gather information from a user.

Chapter 6, *Creating an Angular Application,* shows you how to use the new Alfresco Development Framework (ADF) released in 2016. First, you start by discovering the new JavaScript library that you could include in any of your web applications. Then, you discover the new user interface implemented in AngularJS, and test all available current components. At the time of writing, this framework is only an early release and is not suitable for production. However, we are convinced that this framework will become an important component for any Alfresco developer.

Chapter 7, *Exposing Content through a RESTful API with Web Scripts,* focuses on the web script framework. Web scripts are an important part of the platform because they allow you to expose the repository through a RESTful API. The exercises in this chapter are about creating a set of URLs that can be called from the frontend web site to retrieve and persist user ratings of objects in the repository.

`Chapter 8`, *Advanced Workflows*, is about the embedded Activiti workflow engine, how it works and how to define your own workflows, including how to implement your own business logic. The chapter includes a comparison between the capabilities of Alfresco's simple workflow and advanced workflow so that you can decide which one is appropriate for your needs. By the end of the chapter, you will have built a workflow that SomeCo will use to review and approve Whitepapers for external publication.

`Chapter 9`, *Amazing Extensions,* shows you one of the most amazing extensions including the use of facets configured with the search manager. Then, you discover what are smart folders and how to use them. After, you create your own template for SomeCo Whitepapers. Finally, you even create your own mobile application connected to your Alfresco instance.

`Chapter 10`, *Security,* covers a variety of security-related topics. You'll learn how to define your own custom roles, and how to create users and groups with the API. Although not strictly developer-centric, you'll also learn how to configure Alfresco to authenticate and synchronize with an LDAP directory and how to implement Single Sign-On (SSO) between Alfresco and other web resources.

What you need for this book

To work through the examples in this book, you will need:

- Alfresco. Preferably Enterprise, but Community should work, except for some advanced chapters. The examples have been tested on Alfresco from 5.1
- Spring Tool Suite (STS)
- Apache Maven
- Vagrant (to create your virtual machines)
- Appcelerator (to create your mobile application)

There are other tools or libraries that you will need for certain exercises, which will be mentioned as necessary.

Who this book is for

This book will be most useful to developers who are writing code to customize Alfresco for their organization or who are creating custom applications that sit on top of Alfresco.

This book is for Java developers, and you will get most from the book if you already work with Java, but you need not have prior experience on Alfresco. Although Alfresco makes heavy use of open source frameworks such as Spring, Hibernate, no prior experience using these is assumed or necessary.

Conventions

In this book, you will find a number of styles of text that distinguish between different kinds of information. Here are some examples of these styles, and an explanation of their meaning.

Code words in text are shown as follows: "Let's clarify what's an AMP file or package. An AMP file is a `.zip` file with the `.amp` extension."

A block of code will be set as follows:

```
{
  "rating": {
    "average": 1.923,
    "count": 13
  }
}
```

When we wish to draw your attention to a particular part of a code block, the relevant lines or items will be made bold:

```
enableLookups="false"
disableUploadTimeout="true"
acceptCount="100"
scheme="https"
secure="true"
clientAuth="false"
sslProtocol="TLS"
keystoreFile="/root/.keystore"
keystorePass="changeit"
```

Any command-line input and output is written as follows:

```
service alfresco start
```

New terms and important words are shown in bold. Words that you see on the screen, for example, in menus or dialog boxes, appear in the text like this: "When users log in to Alfresco, the first thing that is usually displayed is the **My Dashboard** section."

 Warnings or important notes appear in a box like this.

 Tips and tricks appear like this.

Reader feedback

Feedback from our readers is always welcome. Let us know what you think about this book-what you liked or disliked. Reader feedback is important for us as it helps us develop titles that you will really get the most out of. To send us general feedback, simply e-mail feedback@packtpub.com, and mention the book's title in the subject of your message. If there is a topic that you have expertise in and you are interested in either writing or contributing to a book, see our author guide at www.packtpub.com/authors.

Customer support

Now that you are the proud owner of a Packt book, we have a number of things to help you to get the most from your purchase.

Downloading the example code

You can download the example code files for this book from your account at http://www.packtpub.com. If you purchased this book elsewhere, you can visit http://www.packtpub.com/support and register to have the files e-mailed directly to you.

You can download the code files by following these steps:

1. Log in or register to our website using your e-mail address and password.
2. Hover the mouse pointer on the **SUPPORT** tab at the top.
3. Click on **Code Downloads & Errata**.
4. Enter the name of the book in the **Search** box.

5. Select the book for which you're looking to download the code files.
6. Choose from the drop-down menu where you purchased this book from.
7. Click on **Code Download**.

Once the file is downloaded, please make sure that you unzip or extract the folder using the latest version of:

- WinRAR / 7-Zip for Windows
- Zipeg / iZip / UnRarX for Mac
- 7-Zip / PeaZip for Linux

The code bundle for the book is also hosted on GitHub at `https://github.com/PacktPubl` `ishing/Alfresco-One-5x-Developers-GuideAlfresco-One-5x-Developers-Guide`. We also have other code bundles from our rich catalog of books and videos available at `https` `://github.com/PacktPublishing/`. Check them out!

Downloading the color images of this book

We also provide you with a PDF file that has color images of the screenshots/diagrams used in this book. The color images will help you better understand the changes in the output. You can download this file from `https://www.packtpub.com/sites/default/files/down` `loads/AlfrescoOne5xDevelopersGuide_ColorImages.pdf`.

Errata

Although we have taken every care to ensure the accuracy of our content, mistakes do happen. If you find a mistake in one of our books-maybe a mistake in the text or the code-we would be grateful if you could report this to us. By doing so, you can save other readers from frustration and help us improve subsequent versions of this book. If you find any errata, please report them by visiting `http://www.packtpub.com/submit-errata`, selecting your book, clicking on the **Errata Submission Form** link, and entering the details of your errata. Once your errata are verified, your submission will be accepted and the errata will be uploaded to our website or added to any list of existing errata under the Errata section of that title.

To view the previously submitted errata, go to `https://www.packtpub.com/books/conten` `t/support` and enter the name of the book in the search field. The required information will appear under the **Errata** section.

Piracy

Piracy of copyrighted material on the Internet is an ongoing problem across all media. At Packt, we take the protection of our copyright and licenses very seriously. If you come across any illegal copies of our works in any form on the Internet, please provide us with the location address or website name immediately so that we can pursue a remedy.

Please contact us at `copyright@packtpub.com` with a link to the suspected pirated material.

We appreciate your help in protecting our authors and our ability to bring you valuable content.

Questions

If you have a problem with any aspect of this book, you can contact us at `questions@packtpub.com`, and we will do our best to address the problem.

1
The Alfresco Platform

This chapter introduces the Alfresco platform and answers the question, *"What can I do with this thing?"* A few examples will be provided to help answer this question from the *solving business problems* perspective. The chapter then skims over basic configuration and customization before introducing the advanced customization concepts covered throughout the book. The chapter concludes with a brief discussion on the different Alfresco editions that are available.

In this chapter, we will go through the following points:

- Examples of practical solutions built on Alfresco
- High-level components of the Alfresco platform
- Examples of the types of customizations that you will likely perform as a part of your implementation
- Technologies you will use to extend the platform

Alfresco in the real world

Alfresco will tell you that the product is a platform for **enterprise content management (ECM)**. But ECM is a somewhat nebulous and nefarious term. What does it really mean? It depends on who is saying it. ECM vendors usually use it as an umbrella term to describe a collection of content-centric technologies as follows:

- **Document management (DM):** This is used for capturing, organizing, and sharing binary files. These files are typically produced from office-productivity software, but the scope of the files being managed is unlimited.

- **Web content management (WCM)**: This is used for managing files and content specifically intended to be delivered to the Web. The key theme of WCM is to reduce the "web developer" bottleneck and empower non-technical content owners to publish their own content.
- **Digital asset management (DAM)**: This is used for managing graphics, video, and audio. You can think of this as DM with added functionality specific to the needs of working with rich media such as thumbnailing, transcoding, and editing. Like WCM, the intent is to streamline the production process.
- **Records management(RM)**: This is used for managing content as a legal record. Like DAM, RM starts with DM and adds functionality specific to the world of RM such as retention policies, records plans, and audit trails.
- **Knowledge management(KM)**: This is used for capturing knowledge from employees or customers and providing it in a form that others can use.
- **Case management(CM)**: This is used managing information related to a case, such as an insurance claim, an investigation, or personnel processing.
- **Imaging** : This includes capturing, tagging, and routing images of documents from scanners.

Most people will also include **collaboration**, **search,** and occasionally, **portals** as well.

Practitioners have a different perspective. They will say that ECM is less about the technology and more about how you capture, organize, and share information across the entire enterprise. For them, the *how* is more important than the *what*.

What's important to know from an Alfresco perspective is that Alfresco is a platform for doing all these things.

So rather than worrying about a concise definition of ECM, let's look at a few examples to illustrate how clients are using Alfresco today, particularly in Alfresco's sweet spots such as DM and WCM.

Basic document management

Alfresco started its life as a document management repository with some basic services for document management. Alfresco focused on this smart area initially for two reasons. First, it allowed Alfresco to establish a strong foundation and then build upon that foundation by expanding into other areas of ECM. Second, there is a huge market for systems that can manage unstructured content (aka "documents").

The market is so big because document management is a problem for everyone. All companies generate files that benefit from the kind of features document management provides such as check-in/check-out, versioning, metadata, security, full-text search, and workflow.

Examples of classic document management are often found in insurance, manufacturing, packaged goods, or other companies with large research and development divisions. As you can imagine, companies such as these deal with thousands of documents every day. The documents are in a variety of formats and languages, and are created and leveraged by many different types of stakeholders from various parts of the company.

The critical functionality required for basic document management includes things such as:

- **Easy integration with authoring tools:** If users can't get documents into and out of the repository easily, user adoption will suffer. This means users must be able to open and save documents to the repository from applications such as Microsoft Office, Microsoft Windows Explorer, and e-mail.
- **Security**: Many documents, particularly legal documents and anything around new product development, are very sensitive. Employees must be able to log in with their normal username and password, and see only the documents they have access to.
- **Library services**: This is a grouping of foundational document management functionality that includes check-in/check-out, versioning, metadata, and search. The ability to offer these library services is one of the things that sets a document repository apart from a plain filesystem.
- **Workflow**: Quite literally, workflow describes the "flow of work" or business process related to a document. Requirements vary widely in this area and not everyone will leverage workflows right away. Workflows can be used to streamline and automate manual business processes by letting the document management system keep track of who needs to do what to a document at any particular time.
- **Scalability/Reliability**: The system needs to scale in order to support several hundred or more users and hundreds of thousands or even millions of documents with some percentage of growth each year. Because the repository holds content that's critical to the business, it needs to be highly available.

- **Customizable user interface**: Alfresco is split into two web applications. The first one contains only the core engine capabilities that are required for all Alfresco installation. The second one is the out-of-the-box Alfresco Share client made for generic document management, which may be appropriate in many cases. Most clients will want to make at least some customizations to the web client to help increase productivity and improve user adoption. It's possible as well to develop your own frontend from scratch.

The following diagram shows an example of high-level architecture to understand how basic document management might be implemented:

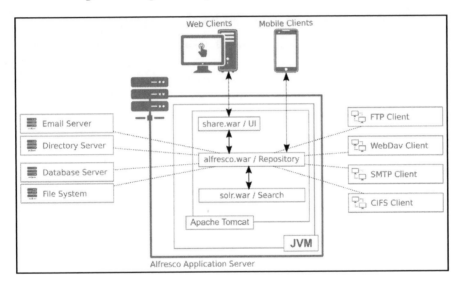

The diagram shows a single instance of Alfresco authenticating against a **Directory Server** (such as LDAP). Some content managers are using Alfresco Share via HTTP/S, while others are using Windows Explorer, Microsoft Office, and other *thick clients* to work with content via one or more protocols such as **CIFS**, **WebDAV**, **FTP**, or **SMTP**. As noted in the diagram, Alfresco stores metadata in a relational database and the actual content files on the filesystem.

Most of the techniques for customizing Alfresco for DM solutions apply to other ECM solutions such as WCM, RM, Imaging, and DAM. Of course, there are business concepts and technical implementation details specific to each that make them unique, but the details provided in this book apply to all because the specialized solutions are built as extensions to the core Alfresco repository. This books dedicates an entire chapter, Chapter 9, *Amazing Extensions*, to some very famous extensions as Alfresco Mobile and Alfresco Analytics.

Web content management

On the surface, WCM is very similar to document management. In both cases, content owners store files in a repository. Often, the content is assigned metadata, secured, indexed for search, and routed through a workflow. The most obvious difference between DM and WCM is that the content being managed is meant specifically to be published on a website or as part of a web application. Beyond that high-level distinction, there are several other differences that make WCM worthy of separate discussion. These include:

- Content authoring tools used to create content
- Separation of presentation from content
- Systematic publication or deployment of content

Let's briefly look at each of these.

Content authoring tools

The majority of document management solutions deal with files generated by an office suite. Of course, there are exceptions such as various types of graphics files, CAD/CAM drawing formats, and other specialized tools. But mostly, the files are generated by a small number of different tools and an even smaller number of different software vendors.

In the case of WCM, there is a wide variety of tools involved from text editors to **integrated development environments** (**IDEs**) to graphics programs with multiple vendors in each category. This means the WCM solution needs to be very flexible in the way it integrates with authoring tools. The alternative, which is forcing authors to give up their favorite tools in favor of a standard, can be a management nightmare.

Separation of presentation from content

WCM does not require the separation between content's appearance on the web site and its storage. But many implementations take advantage of this principle because it makes redesigning the site easier, facilitates multichannel publishing, and enables people to author content without web skills.

To understand why this is so, think about a website that has its content and presentation of that content merged together. When it is time to redesign the site, you have to touch every single web page because every page contains presentation markup. Similarly, content authoring is limited to people with technical skills. Otherwise, there is a risk that the content owner (for example, the person writing a press release or a job posting) will inadvertently clobber the page design.

One way to address this is to separate the content (the press release copy) from the presentation of that content. A common way to do that is to store the content as presentation-independent XML. The XML can then be transformed into any presentation that's needed. A redesign is as simple as changing the presentation in a single place, and then regenerating all of the pages.

The impact of separating content from presentation is three-fold. First, assuming the content consumers aren't interested in reading raw XML, something has to be responsible for transforming the content. Depending on the implementation, it may be up to the WCM system or a frontend web application.

Second, in the case of static content, any change in the underlying content has to trigger a transformation so that the presentation will be up-to-date, keeping in mind that there may be more than one file affected by the change. For example, data from a job posting appears in the job posting detail as well as the list of job postings. If the posting and the job posting index are both static, the list has to be regenerated whenever the job posting changes.

Third, content authors lose the benefit of **WYSIWYG (What You See Is What You Get)** content authoring because the content doesn't immediately look the way it will as soon as it is published to the web site. The WCM system, then, has to be able to let content authors *preview* the content as they author it, preferably in the context of the entire site.

Systematic publication or deployment

A document management system is a lot like a relational database in the sense that it is typically an authoritative, centralized repository. There are exceptions, but for the most part, content resides in the repository and is retrieved by the systems and applications that need it. On the other hand, a WCM system often faces a publication or deployment challenge. Files go into the repository, but must be delivered somewhere to be consumed. This might happen on a schedule, at the request of a user, as part of a workflow, or all of the above. Granted, some websites retrieve their content dynamically; but most sites have at least a subset of content that should be statically delivered to a web server.

Alfresco WCM example

Let's look at an example of a basic corporate website. Most companies have a mix of *About Us* content that probably doesn't change very often, *Press releases* or *News* sections that might get updated daily, and maybe some document-based content such as marketing slicks, product information sheets, technical specifications, and so on. There's also some content that is used to build the site such as HTML, XML, JavaScript, Flash, CSS, and image files.

It is likely that there are several different teams with several different skill sets, all collaborating to produce the site. In this example, suppose the *About Us* and *News* pages come from the marketing team, the site is built by the web team and the document-based content can come from many organizations within the company.

Alfresco WCM sits on top of the core Alfresco product to provide additional WCM-specific functionality. An important distinction between Alfresco WCM and other open source **content management systems (CMS)** is that Alfresco is a *decoupled* CMS while something such as Drupal is a *coupled* CMS. This means that Alfresco manages the website but does not concern itself with presentation unlike Drupal, which is both a repository and a presentation framework. This doesn't mean that Alfresco can only manage static sites. You can easily query the repository in any number of ways. It just means it is up to you to provide the frontend from the ground up.

Custom content-centric applications

Content-centric applications are those in which the primary purpose of the application is to process, produce, archive, collaborate on, or manage unstructured or semi-structured content.

The Alfresco Share client is an example of a content-centric application, although it is meant for a very general, all-purpose use case. When solutions are very close to basic document management, Alfresco Share can be customized as previously discussed. At some point, it makes more sense to build a separate custom application with Alfresco as the backend repository for that application.

Consider the sales process within a company, for example. Sales people create proposals. Those proposals are usually routed internally for review and approval, and then are delivered to the client. If the client accepts the proposal, a contract is drawn up and the product is delivered. The out-of-the-box Alfresco Share could be used to manage these documents, assign metadata, manage the review process through workflows, and make it all searchable. But the sales team might be even more productive if it used a purpose-built user interface. For this solution, a frontend built on top of NodeJS and Angular, a custom Spring web application, or even a **custom mobile application** might be a good option. Alfresco would provide the document management services. The frontend would talk to Alfresco via CMIS or RESTful services.

Another example is using Alfresco in a digitization project. More and more companies are trying to reduce the use of paper-based process for many different reasons. Alfresco can be integrated with various scanning solutions as Ephesoft via CMIS, or Kofax via the connector supported by Alfresco. Documents can be ingested and processed by the scanning solution and exported to Alfresco. Alfresco will be responsible to store, index and secure the scanned documents. Using the integrated Activiti framework, Alfresco can automatically start a process depending of the document type. If an invoice has been scanned, Alfresco will start a review process for the financial team. If it's a job application, Alfresco will start a new process for the HR team to track the different stages of this application.

As discussed previously, Alfresco provides two out-of-the-box web applications. The first one is the Alfresco repository engine. The first one provides only administration capabilities from a user interface point of view. The second one is the default web interface Alfresco Share. Many clients appreciate this separation because it gives them complete freedom with regard to how they build the frontend. Depending of your use case, you may want to use the standard Alfresco Share user interface; or including some customizations; or even build the frontend from scratch.

Alfresco Share provides many different options if you need customizations. The basic level is to configure some forms and pages to display your custom metadata. If you need further customization, you may want to customize an existing Dashlet or to develop a new one to add on the user or site dashboard. You may need to create custom actions in the use interface. If it's not enough, it's even possible to create new pages within Alfresco Share reusing the entire UI framework. Finally, if it's not sufficient, Alfresco can be integrated to any frontend using CMIS or REST API.

We'll see in one of the following chapters how Alfresco created tools to generate Angular applications from scratch:

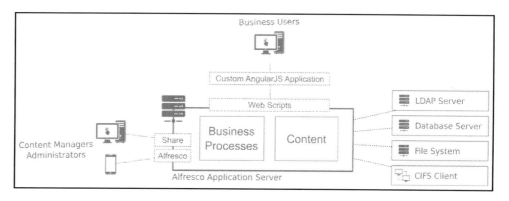

The openness of the Alfresco repository, particularly its ability to be easily exposed as a set of services, makes Alfresco an ideal platform for content-centric applications. As the examples have shown, custom content-centric web applications use Alfresco as the backend. As a result, they have complete flexibility in frontend technology choices from portals to lower-level frameworks to no framework at all.

Example used throughout this book

In this book, we'll assume we are rolling out Alfresco throughout a consulting firm. Professional services firms make great examples because they tend to generate a variety of different documents. The other reason is that document and content management is usually a big challenge, which is the core to the business. But the examples should be applicable to any business that generates a significant amount of documents.

The example firm, SomeCo, wants to leverage document and content management throughout the organization to make it easier to find important information, streamline certain business processes, and secure sensitive documents.

SomeCo's company organization is pretty standard. It consists of operations, sales, human resources, marketing, and finance/legal. Examples of the different types of content each department is concerned with are shown in the following table:

Department	Example document types	Format and process notes
Finance/legal	Client proposals for project work Statements of work Master services agreements Non-disclosure agreements	• Microsoft Word and Adobe PDF. • Several iterations between the firm and the client before a *final* version is completed. • Some documents may require internal review and approval.
Marketing	Case studies Whitepapers Marketing plans Marketing slicks/promotional material	• Microsoft Word, Microsoft PowerPoint, Adobe PDF, and Adobe Flash. • Mostly single-author content. • Some content may come from third parties. • Some content may need to be published on the website.
Human resources	Job postings Resumes Interview feedback Offer letters Employee profiles /Biographies Project reviews Annual reviews	• Microsoft Word, Adobe PDF, and HTML. • Single-author content with consumers being spread throughout the company. • Some content formats are unpredictable (such as resumes). Some are very standard and could be templatized (such as offer letters). • With the exception of job postings, none of this content should go near the Web. • Some content needs strict internal permissions.
Sales	Forecast Presentations Proformas	• Microsoft Excel and Microsoft PowerPoint. • Some business process and automated document-handling possibilities such as forecast. • *Searchability* of presentations is important.
Operations	Methodology Utilization reports Status reports	• All Microsoft Office formats. • Some opportunity for integration into enterprise systems such as time tracking and project management.

Examples throughout the rest of the book will show how Alfresco can be implemented and customized to meet the needs of the various organizations within SomeCo. During a real implementation, time would be spent gathering requirements, selecting the appropriate components to integrate with the solution, finalizing architecture, and structuring the project. There are plenty of other books and resources that discuss how to roll out content management across an enterprise and others that cover project methodologies. So none of that will be covered here.

Alfresco architecture

Many of Alfresco's competitors (particularly in the closed-source space) have sprawling footprints composed of multiple, sometimes competing, technologies that have been acquired and integrated over time. Some have undergone massive infrastructure overhauls over the years, resulting in bizarre vestigial tails of sorts. Luckily, Alfresco doesn't suffer from these traits. On the contrary, Alfresco's architecture shows the following characteristics:

- It is relatively straightforward
- It is built with state-of-the-art frameworks and open source components
- It supports several important content management and related standards

Let's look at each of these characteristics, starting with a high-level look at the Alfresco architecture.

High-level architecture

The following diagram shows Alfresco's high-level architecture. By the time you finish this book, you'll be intimately familiar with just about every box in the diagram:

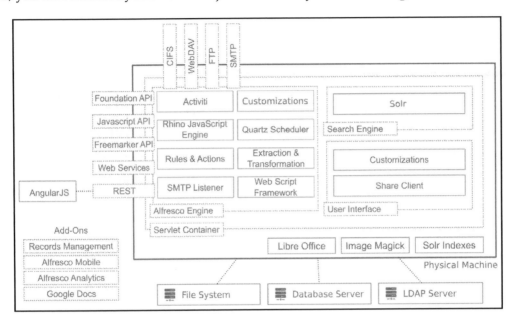

The important takeaways at this point are as follows:

- There are many ways to get content into or out of the repository, whether that's via the protocols (for example CIFS on the diagram) or the APIs on the left.
- Alfresco runs as a web application within a servlet container. From Alfresco 5.x, this web application doesn't provide anymore a user interface for end users. It includes only an administration console. If you need a user interface, you'll need to deploy the Alfresco Share web application (in the same container or not) and an extension package in the Alfresco web application to provide all web scripts required by Alfresco Share. You can as well implement your own user interface on top of your Alfresco repository.
- Customizations and extensions run as part of the Alfresco repository or Share web application. An extension mechanism separates customizations from the core product to keep the path clear for future upgrades.

- Metadata resides in a relational database. In a typical Alfresco installation, content files are usually stored in a different server than Alfresco itself (as compared to filesystem). Solr indexes needs to be located in the system as the Solr web application that can reside in a dedicated server too.

Add-ons

The add-ons are pieces of functionality not found in the core Alfresco distribution. If you are working with the binary distribution, it means you'll have additional files to download and install on top of the base Alfresco or Share installation.

Add-ons are provided by Alfresco, third-party software vendors, and members of the Alfresco community such as partners and customers. Alfresco makes several add-on modules available such as **Records Management**, **Google Docs**, **Office Services** or **Kofax** integration. Members of the Alfresco community create and share add-on modules via the **Alfresco add-Ons** (https://addons.alfresco.com/), a website set up by Alfresco for that purpose. At the time of writing, this website contains 444 different add-ons compatible with Alfresco Enterprise and/or Community.

Open source components

One of the reasons Alfresco has been able to create a viable offering so quickly is because it didn't start from scratch. The Alfresco engineers assembled the product from many finer-grained open source components. Why does this matter? First, instead of reinventing the wheel, they used proven components. This saved them time, but it also resulted in a more robust, more standard-based product. Second, it eases the transition for people new to the platform. If a developer already knows Spring, for example, many of the customization concepts are going to be familiar. Alfresco uses **Surf**, a Spring framework extension for building or extending MVC applications. And besides, as a developer, wouldn't you rather invest your time and effort in learning standard development frameworks rather than proprietary *development kits*?

The following table lists some of the major open source components used to build Alfresco:

Open source component	Use in Alfresco
Apache Solr (http://lucene.apache.org/solr/)	Full-text and metadata search
Hibernate (http://www.hibernate.org/)	Database persistence
FreeMarker (http://freemarker.org/)	Web script framework views, custom views in the web client, web client dashlets, email templates
Mozilla Rhino JavaScript Engine (http://www.mozilla.org/rhino/)	Web script framework controllers, server-side JavaScript, actions
OpenSymphony Quartz (http://www.quartz-scheduler.org/)	Scheduling of asynchronous processes
Spring ACEGI (http://projects.spring.io/spring-security/)	Security (authorization), roles, and permissions
Apache Axis (http://ws.apache.org/axis/)	Web services
LibreOffice (http://www.libreoffice.org/)	Conversion of office documents into PDF
Apache FOP (http://xmlgraphics.apache.org/fop/)	Transformation of XSL:FO into PDF
Apache POI (http://poi.apache.org/)	Metadata extraction from Microsoft Office files
Activiti (http://www.activiti.org/)	Advanced workflow
ImageMagick (http://www.imagemagick.org/)	Image file manipulation
GhostScript (http://www.ghostscript.com/)	Image file manipulation

Does this mean you have to be an expert in all open source components used to build Alfresco to successfully implement and customize the product? Not at all! Developers looking to contribute significant product enhancements to Alfresco or those making major, deep customizations to the product may require experience with a particular component, depending on exactly what they are trying to do. Everyone else will be able to customize and extend Alfresco using basic Java and web application development skills.

Major standards and protocols supported

Software vendors love buzz words. As new acronyms climb the hype cycle, vendors scramble to figure out how they can at least appear to support the standard or protocol so that the prospective clients can check that box on the **Request for proposal (RFP)**. Commercial open source vendors are still software vendors and thus are no less guilty of this practice. But because open source software is developed in the open by a community of developers, its compliance to standards tends to be more genuine. It makes more sense for an open source project to implement a standard than to go off in some new direction because it saves time. It promotes interoperability with other open source projects, and stays true to what open source is all about–freedom and choice.

Here, are the significant standards and protocols Alfresco supports:

Standard/protocol	Comment
HTTP	The main protocol used to access Alfresco content repository via for example the Alfresco REST APIs.
CMIS	CMIS is a standard allowing information sharing between different content management systems. Alfresco supports the version 1.0. and 1.1 of the CMIS standard.
FTP	Content can be contributed to the repository via FTP.
WebDAV	WebDAV is an HTTP-based protocol commonly supported by content management vendors. It is one way to make the repository look like a file system.
CIFS	CIFS allows the repository to be mounted as a shared drive by other machines. As opposed to WebDAV, systems (and people) can't tell the difference between an Alfresco repository mounted as a shared drive through CIFS and a traditional file server.
IMAP	IMAP protocol is used by any modern email clients. Directly from your client, you can connect to your Alfresco repository.
SMTP	It is possible to email content into the repository (InboundSMTP). A folder can be dedicated as an email target.
SPP	Enables Alfresco to act as a Microsoft SharePoint Server. Allows Microsoft Office users to access documents within the Alfresco repository.

Alfresco Office Services	Using **Alfresco Office Services** (**AOS**), you can access your documents directly via all Microsoft Office software. AOS replaces and improves the Microsoft SharePoint protocol available in the previous versions.
SOAP	The Alfresco Web Services API uses SOAP-based web services.
OpenSearch (http://www.opensearch.org)	Alfresco repositories can be configured as an OpenSearch data source, which allows Alfresco to participate in federated search queries.
XSLT, XSL:FO	Web form data can be transformed using XSL 1.0.
LDAP	Alfresco can authenticate against an LDAP directory or a Microsoft Active Directory server.

Customizing Alfresco

Alfresco offers a significant amount of functionality out of the box, but most *implementers* will customize it in some way. At a high level, the types of customizations typically done during an implementation can be divided into basic customizations and advanced customizations.

Basic customization

Many Alfresco customizations can be done without writing a single line of code. Some may be done even by end users through Alfresco Share. Others might require editing a properties file or an XML file. Let's look at some of them briefly here so that you can get an idea of what you don't have to code. Other customizations will be introduced in the Chapter 9, *Amazing Extensions*.

Dashlets

When users log in to Alfresco, the first thing that is usually displayed is the **My Dashboard** section. The dashboard is a user-configurable layout that contains dashlets. (If you are familiar with portals, think *portal page* and *portlet*). Users choose the layout of the dashboard (number of columns) as well as the specific dashlets they want displayed in each column.

There are a number of dashlets available out of the box, or you can develop your own and add them to the user-selectable list. Examples of out of the box dashlets include workflow-related dashlet such as **My Tasks** as well as content-related dashlets such as **My Documents**, **My Sites** or **My Activities**:

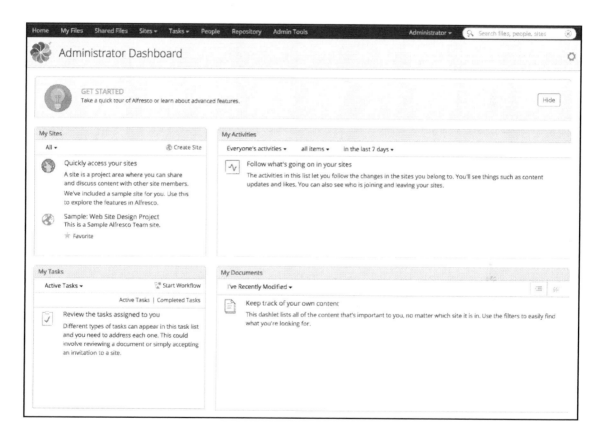

Currently most of these dashlets are **Spring Surf Dashlets** (`http://docs.alfresco.com/5.1/concepts/dev-extensions-share-surf-dashlets.html`), but they will eventually be converted to **Aikau Dashlets** (`http://docs.alfresco.com/5.1/concepts/dev-extensions-share-aikau-dashlets.html`). Aikau is the new UI framework developed by Alfresco, and available from Alfresco 4.2.Some of these existing dashlets allows you some configuration. Here are some examples:

- **RSS Feed**: By simply configuring the RSS Feed URL, it will display automatically the RSS items. The following screenshot shows a dashlet configured to display the latest tweets by `PacktPub`

  (`https://twitrss.me/twitter_user_to_rss/?user=packtpub`):

- **Saved Search**: This dashlet runs a specific search each time the dashboard is loaded:

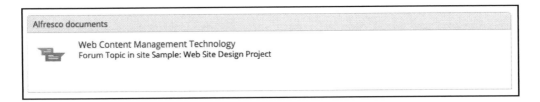

- **Web View**: This dashlet is used to display any website:

Obviously, developing custom dashlets is probably not something you'd let your business users do; but it is still considered a basic customization. It can be complex to develop new dashlet depending if you need to develop new web script for example.

Custom site configuration

The first concept that you'll discover using Alfresco Share is the concept of *site*. It's a secured area in the repository where a team, a project or a suborganization can share and manage any kind of contents, including documents of course. A site includes multiple pages, depending mainly of the type of content. Alfresco Share provides the following by default:

- A document library page
- A calendar page
- A Wiki page
- A forum page
- A data-list page
- A links page
- A blog page

In each site, you can configure and select only what is needed by the users.

Each Alfresco Share site contains as well a dedicated dashboard that you can entirely customize with all out-of-the-box dashlets already provided.

Rules and actions

A rule is something that says, *"When a piece of content is created, updated, or deleted, check these conditions. If these conditions are met, take these actions".* Conditions may check whether a piece of content is a particular mime type, or a specific content type. They may also check whether a piece of content has a specific aspect applied, or whether the content's name property matches a particular pattern. Rules can be defined on any folder in the repository. Child folders can inherit rules from their parent.

Rule actions are repeatable operations that enable us to do things similar to those that can be done using JavaScript or Java. Out-of-the-box actions include things such as check-in content, check-out content, move an item to another folder, specialize the type of the content, add an aspect to the content, transform content from one format to another, and so on.

Configuring folders to run rule actions is something non-technical users can do through Alfresco Share. In `Chapter 4`, *Handling Content Automatically with Actions, Behaviors, Transformers, and Extractors*, you'll learn how to write your own custom rule actions using the Alfresco API.

Simple workflow

Alfresco has two options for implementing workflow: simple workflow or advanced workflow. The good thing about simple workflows is that end users can configure them as needed without any technical skills or developer support.

Here's how it works. A user creates a rule to *add simple workflow* to a document when it is placed in the folder. When an item enters a folder with this type of rule applied, it will have additional UI action items available. The rule to specify the user actions and flow of the content between folders is configured in the repository action. When the step is invoked, the content can be copied or moved to another folder. It's also possible to add complexity to a simple workflow by creating rules for other folders and passing content around from location to location. For example, there might be folders called `Draft`, `In Review`, and `Approved`. The state of a document is determined by the folder in which it resides.

Simple workflows have obvious limitations:

- Workflows are limited to serial processes. Content can only move forward or backward, one step at a time.
- Content can only be in only one simple workflow state at a given time.
- Content must change physical locations to reflect a change in state.

- There is no opportunity for capturing (and acting on) process-related metadata.
- Tasks can't be assigned to individuals or groups. (Of course, you could limit folders to specific individuals or groups through permissions, which would have a similar effect to a task assignment. But you wouldn't be able to easily pull a list of tasks for a specific user across all simple workflows).
- Other than creating additional rules and actions for the folders used in a simple workflow, there is no way to add logic for decisions or other more complex constructs. If you need to implement specific behavior depending of the state, you have to implement additional action and rule attached to each folder.

Advanced customization

The basic configuration and customizations show that there is quite a lot of tweaking and tailoring that can happen before a developer gets involved. This is a good thing. It means a good chunk of the customization requirements can be dealt with quickly. In the case of simple workflows, they can be delegated to the end users altogether! Hopefully, this leaves more time for the more advanced (and more interesting) customizations required for a successful implementation.

Examples of advanced customizations

The advanced customizations are the customizations that are likely to require code. They are the focus of the book. To give you an idea of what's possible (and in an effort to provide an appetizer before the main meal is served), let's go over some of the areas of advanced customization.

Extend the content model

Alfresco's out-of-the-box content model can be extended to define your own content types, content aspects, content metadata (properties), and relationships (associations). The out-of-the-box model is very generic, and defines only a minimal subset of the metadata that will probably need to be captured with the content.

For example, SomeCo might want to capture different metadata for its marketing documents than for its HR documents. Or maybe there is a set of metadata that doesn't belong to any one content type in particular, but should rather be grouped together in an aspect and attached to objects as needed. These and other content modeling concepts will be covered in Chapter 3, *Working with Content Models*.

Perform automatic operations on content

There are several *hooks* or places where you can insert logic or take action to handle content automatically. These include rule actions, behaviors, content transformers, and metadata extractors. Rule actions have already been discussed. Behaviors are like actions but instead of being something that an end user can invoke on any piece of content, behaviors are tightly bound to their content type or aspect. Content transformers, as the name suggests, transform content from one format to another. Metadata extractors inspect content as it is added to the repository, and pull out data to store in the content object's properties. These tools for handling content automatically will all be covered in Chapter 4, *Handling Content Automatically with Actions, Behaviors, Transformers, and Extractors.*

Customize Alfresco Share

chapter 5, *Customizing Alfresco Share*, covers Share customization. Just about everything in the Share web application can be tweaked. In the document library, it's possible to configure the view of a content, or the edit form depending of the content type. It's possible as well to define a template renderer that changes the default view in the document list. Alfresco Share provides as well different views that you can customize, or even create new ones. And if you want more, you can even create your own page from scratch.

Create a RESTful API

Web scripts are one of the more exciting additions to the Alfresco architecture. The reason is that RESTful services are typically much easier to work with using scripting languages and AJAX toolkits than SOAP-based services, because they are invoked through plain old URLs.

The web script framework, based on the **Model-View-Control** (**MVC**) pattern, allows you to build your own RESTful API to the repository. It will be covered in detail in Chapter 7, *Exposing Content through a RESTful API with Web Scripts,* but the high-level summary is that URLs get mapped to a controller implemented as JavaScript or Java. The controller performs whatever logic is needed, then forwards the request to the view. The view is implemented as a **FreeMarker** template. The template could return anything from markup to XML to JSON. RESTful services via web scripts are the preferred way to integrate with the Alfresco repository.

Streamline complex business processes with advanced workflows

Advanced workflows provide a way to automate complex business processes. Alfresco's advanced workflows are executed by the embedded Activiti engine, which is a very powerful and popular open source workflow engine.

Rather than basic workflows, which are end-user configurable and limited to serial processes, advanced workflows offer the power of parallel flows, the ability to add logic to the process via JavaScript and Java, and much more.

A handful of advanced workflows are available out of the box. These are most useful as starting points for your own custom advanced workflows. Exactly how it has to be done will be covered in Chapter 8, *Advanced Workflows*.

Integrate with other systems

Most of the coding and configuration discussed so far can be divided into two parts:

- Customizations made to the core Alfresco repository
- Customizations made to Alfresco Share

There is a third bucket to be considered, which is coding and configuration related to integrating Alfresco with other solutions. Maybe Alfresco needs to authenticate against an LDAP directory. Maybe a portal will get its content from Alfresco, or perhaps some other third-party application needs to share content with Alfresco. Chapter 9, *Amazing Extensions*, discusses how to handle security and integration.

Dusting off your toolbox

Looking across both the basic and advanced customizations provides some idea about the extensibility of the platform. A commonly asked question at this point in the architecture discussion is, *Does Alfresco have an API*? Actually, it has several. Let's look at what APIs are available and where they are used. This should also give you some idea as to the tools and skills you'll need to have in your toolbox as you embark on your own projects.

The following table shows the APIs available and where they are used:

Alfresco API	Where Used	Comments
Foundation API	Rule actions, behaviors, Java-based web scripts, web client customizations, Activiti, standalone applications that embed the Alfresco repository.	As the name suggests, this is the core Alfresco API.
Alfresco One API	Web and non-web applications that need remote access to the repository.	The Alfresco One API was introduced with Alfresco 4.x, and is also present in the public cloud version of Alfresco. It provides the main remote API, and is the recommended API for developing remote client applications.
CMIS API	Web and non-web applications that need remote access to the repository.	CMIS provides a standardized set of common services for working with content repositories. Alfresco provides an implementation of CMIS Web service and RESTful bindings.
FreeMarker API	Custom views, mail templates, web script view logic.	FreeMarker is an open source templating engine.
Web script framework	Web and non-web applications that need to use REST to interact with the repository.	More of a framework than an API, web scripts implement a MVC pattern that relies on the JavaScript, FreeMarker, and Foundation APIs.

As the list of APIs shows, knowing Java will be the key to just about any successful customization effort. FreeMarker and JavaScript are important, but are easily picked up using Alfresco's code and online resources as references.

Understanding Alfresco's editions

Alfresco has three editions of its ECM products: **Alfresco One**, **Alfresco in the Cloud**, and **Alfresco Community Edition**. We won't describe the other BPM products offered by Alfresco, because they are not in the scope of this book.

Alfresco One is the package installable on premise supported by Alfresco. It provides hybrid capabilities with selective content-sync to the included SaaS Alfresco in the Cloud. Alfresco One provides as well different modules including content encryption, records management, analytics, and media management.

Alfresco in the cloud offers almost all out-of-the-box features provided by Alfresco Share without on-premises installation. It provides full mobile access and workflow for document review and approval. This product is well suited for smaller teams with multiple offices or branches that don't want to manage servers and don't require the full customization, extra modules or integrations offered by Alfresco One. This product can be used as well in a hybrid mode. Only documents that need to be shared with the outside world can be published into Alfresco Cloud. Content can be configured to synchronize between Alfresco Cloud and on premise Alfresco installations.

Alfresco community is intended for developers and technical enthusiasts who want the power of Alfresco in non-critical environments. However, some big organizations use Alfresco community in production. Be aware that Alfresco won't provide any support for this product. In terms of features, Alfresco community is usually the first product to receive the new features to allow the community to test. However, some features are provided only by Alfresco One including the administration console, the content encryption or the Activiti console.

Significant feature differences

At the time of this writing, the latest supported release from Alfresco is Alfresco One 5.1. The latest community release is **Alfresco Community 201605** (for May 2016).

What's used in this book

The vast majority of examples used in this book will work on both the Enterprise and Community editions (5.1 and 201605, respectively). Where a specific release is required, it will be noted wherever possible.

Summary

Hopefully, this chapter has given you several ideas about how Alfresco can be used to implement DM, WCM, and custom content-centric applications by walking through examples of each. The details may still be fuzzy, but the goal was to introduce the major components and capabilities of the Alfresco platform.

In this chapter, we discovered in which kind of use case Alfresco is a good fit. The potential and flexibility of Alfresco can be used to solve a variety of different content-related business problems. Then, we introduced the different configuration points that you can use in your organization without writing one line of code. Even if Alfresco provides you a lot of capabilities, we'll discover in the rest of the book how it can be customized and extended based on the fictitious consulting firm that we created called SomeCo. Next we covered the major open source components included in Alfresco, and the different protocols and standards that can be used to integrate Alfresco in your ecosystem.

2
Getting Started with Alfresco

Before you can customize Alfresco, you need to get your development environment in order. In this chapter, you'll learn how to install the **software development kit (SDK)**, how to build and deploy customizations, helpful debugging tips, and the cleanest and quickest way to *reset* your Alfresco sandbox. The chapter includes an example that shows how to package and deploy some extremely basic customizations just to get your feet wet. Specifically, you are going to learn:

- How to install Alfresco on your environment
- How to install and configure the software on which the SDK depends
- How to extend Alfresco without modifying the Alfresco source code or configuration
- How to package and deploy your customizations
- How to use the Eclipse debugger and log4j to troubleshoot problems
- How to start clean for testing or debugging purposes

This book will help you how to install Alfresco on your local by creating a virtual machine to host Alfresco. There are a lot of options to achieve this goal. In this chapter, we'll use Vagrant and VirtualBox.

It may seem odd to talk about deployment before you've learned how to create something worth deploying, but these techniques will be used in all subsequent chapters. So you might as well get everything set up and tested now so that you don't have to deal with it later.

Introduction to the Alfresco SDK

Alfresco is providing its SDK as a Maven based development kit. It provides a quick and easy approach to develop your own Alfresco extensions. You can use this SDK in any **integrated development environment (IDE)**, and even in the console. However, we'll use **Spring Tool Suite (STS)** in this chapter. With this SDK you can develop, package, test, run, document and release your Alfresco extension project. It is important to note that while previous versions of the Alfresco SDK were based around Ant, the latest versions of the SDK are based on Maven.

The Alfresco SDK includes three different Maven archetypes described below. These archetypes aim to provide a standardized approach to development, release, and deployment of Alfresco extensions.

Maven archetypes

There are three Maven archetypes that can be used to generate Alfresco extension projects. The following project types, and archetypes, are available:

- **Alfresco Repository AMP**: This archetype is used to create extensions for the **Alfresco repository web application** (alfresco.war) in the form of **Alfresco Module Packages** (**AMP**).
- **Alfresco Share AMP**: This archetype is used to create extensions for the **Alfresco Share web application** (share.war) in the form of AMPs.
- **Alfresco all-in-one** (**AIO**): This archetype is used to generate a project including an Alfresco and a Share module.It allows as well to run the full Alfresco platform embedded with all minimal components without installing anything like Solr. However, it doesn't include ImageMagick, LibreOffice.

Let's clarify what's an AMP file or package. An AMP file is a .zip file with the .amp extension. The default structure of AMP files is specified by Alfresco. They contain files that are overlaid on either the alfresco.war or share.war using the **module management tool (MMT)**. By default, the structure of an AMP file is not exactly the same as the structure of the WAR file, a file called file-mapping.properties can be placed in the root of the AMP to instruct MMT how to map files into the target WAR file. Additionally, a file called module.properties is placed in the root of the AMP file, this file includes the module name, version and dependency information. Alfresco is moving towards standard JAR packaging. This will be the default packaging format with the Alfresco SDK 3.0. AMP files can be used to package custom templates, custom models, web scripts, UI customizations, and can be used to implement extensive additions to the Alfresco functionality.

Alfresco, itself, uses the AMP to package and provides extensions to their customers. The typical example is records management. Alfresco provides two different AMP files, one for the repository engine (that will be deployed in the `alfresco.war` web application), the other one for web client (that will be deployed in the `share.war` web application). We'll see later how to package and deploy your custom module.

Before starting, be aware that there is a dependency between the version of your Alfresco instance and the SDK instance:

- You should use Alfresco SDK 2.2.x if you use Alfresco 5.1+ (which will be our case in this book)
- You should use Alfresco SDK 2.1.x if you use Alfresco 5.0+ but not 5.1+

For earlier version of Alfresco, we recommend to check the compatibility matrix in the Alfresco documentation

Install prerequisites

In the following sections, we'll discover how to install all prerequisites required to develop and package your customizations.

Spring Loaded

Spring Loaded is a JVM agent for reloading class file changes whilst a JVM is running. The Alfresco SDK's **rapid application development** (**RAD**) features uses Spring Loaded to see the effect of the change directly in a running Alfresco-Tomcat-JVM instance without having to rebuild JARs, AMPs, and WARs and redeploying them, saving you loads of time. However, at the time of writing, the Alfresco documentation states that Spring Loaded works only with the Share AMP archetype (`http://docs.alfresco.com/5.1/tasks/alfre sco-sdk-install-spring-loaded.html`).Be aware that the 3.0 Maven SDK is moving from Spring Loaded to JRebel.

You just need to download the JAR file and save it somewhere on your environment from this URL:

`https://github.com/spring-projects/spring-loaded`

At the time of writing, the latest version is 1.2.5. Save the file `springloaded-1.2.5.RELEASE.jar` in your home directory.

JDK

As explained, the Alfresco SDK is based on Maven which requires a JDK. This section explains you how to check that Oracle JDK 1.8 is installed, or install it if it's not the case.

To check if you have the right JDK installed on your environment, open a command console and type the following command:

```
javac -version
```

You'll see a message like this one if it's properly installed:

```
javac 1.8.0_45
```

If you get a message like `Command not found`, you need to follow the steps given here. Otherwise, you are good to jump to the following section:

1. If you need to install or to upgrade your JDK, the first step is to download it from the Oracle JDK website (`http://www.oracle.com/technetwork/java/javase/downloads/index.html`)and then follow the Oracle instructions. When it's completed, recheck the version of the Java compiler as explained. If you get the right version, you can check also your Java runtime version by typing:

   ```
   java -version
   ```

2. You should see a message like:

   ```
   java version "1.8.0_45"
   Java(TM) SE Runtime Environment (build 1.8.0_45-b14)
   Java HotSpot(TM) 64-Bit Server VM (build 25.45-b02, mixed mode)
   ```

3. When the JDK is installed, you need to be sure that the environment variable `JAVA_HOME` is properly set. Use a method suitable for your system. On Mac OS X and Linux system, just type the following command:

   ```
   env | grep JAVA_HOME
   ```

4. You should see a message like this one on Mac OS X systems:

   ```
   JAVA_HOME=/Library/Java/JavaVirtualMachines
        /jdk1.8.0_45.jdk/Contents/Home
   ```

5. If it's not the case, check the documentation of your system to set this environment variable.

Maven

Of course, we need to install Maven to be able to use the Alfresco SDK. Maybe you already installed it on your system.

1. To check, just type the following command:

   ```
   mvn --version
   ```

2. If you get an error or a `Command not found` message, you need to install Maven on your system. Be aware that you'll need to update your Maven installation if your version is less than 3.2.5. To install Maven, download it from the **Apache Maven project website** (`http://maven.apache.org/download.cgi`) and follow the platform-specific installation instructions provided by Maven. When everything will be installed properly, the preceding command will return a message as follows:

   ```
   Apache Maven 3.3.3 (7994120775791599e205a5524ec3e0dfe41d4a06;
           2015-04-22T12:57:37+01:00)
   Maven home: /opt/local/share/java/maven3
   Java version: 1.8.0_45, vendor: Oracle Corporation
   Java home: /Library/Java/JavaVirtualMachines/
           jdk1.8.0_45.jdk/Contents/Home/jre
    Default locale: en_US, platform encoding: UTF-8
   OS name: "mac os x", version: "10.11.5", arch: "x86_64",
       family: "mac"
   ```

   As you can see, I have the version 3.3.3 installed on my system, and it's connected to the JDK 8 installed previously.

3. The next step is to be sure that environment variables are properly configured, following the same procedure as `JAVA_HOME`. Use the following command on Mac OS X and Linux system:

   ```
   env | grepM2_HOME
   env | grepMAVEN_OPTS
   ```

   And you should see these messages:

   ```
   M2_HOME=/opt/local/share/java/maven3
   MAVEN_OPTS=-Xms2048M -Xmx2048M
           -javaagent:/Users/john/springloaded-1.2.5.RELEASE.jar
           -noverify
   ```

4. If it's not the case, check the documentation of your system to set this environment variable.

> Be aware that the Alfresco SDK will use Alfresco Community Edition artifacts by default. If you want to use Alfresco One (Enterprise) artifacts, you'll need to require access to the Alfresco Private Repository. When you have received a username and a password from Alfresco, you must add your credentials to the Maven configuration. This is usually done by adding an entry to the `settings.xml` file, located in your `.m2` directory. Check the Maven documentation to identify where should be located this folder in your system. For Linux and Mac OS X that will most likely be ~/`.m2`. When you have located this file, just add the following section:

```
<server>
        <id>alfresco-private-repository</id>
        <username>username</username>
        <password>password</password>
</server>
```

Install STS

Obviously, you can use any software development tool to create an Alfresco module. You can even use the Windows Notepad, but I wish you good luck. In this book, we'll use **Spring Tool Suite (STS)** based on Eclipse. Because Alfresco is based on the Spring framework, STS seems to be the best tool to develop.

To install STS, open the download page (`https://spring.io/tools/sts/all`) and download the version depending of your system. If you are working on Windows, you'll download a ZIP file. Otherwise, you'll download a TAR.GZ file.

When you have downloaded the file, you just need to unzip it. The first time that STS is loaded, you'll need to select a workspace:

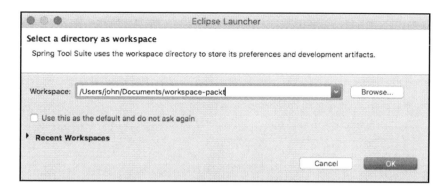

Then, we'll configure the Maven Central repository in STS. Open the STS **Preferences** window, and open **Maven | Archetypes**. Then, click on the button **Add Remote Catalog....**:

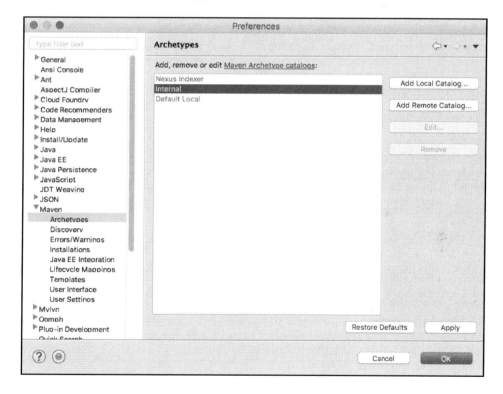

Provide the **Maven Central repository** (`http://repo.maven.apache.org/maven2/`) and add a description. By clicking on the **Verify...** button, you can see that this catalog contains **19779** archetypes. Validate by clicking on **Add**.

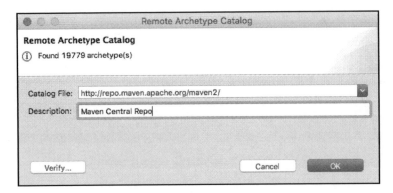

And that's it. You are now ready to create your first Alfresco application.

Create your first application

We'll first discover how we can use the Maven SDK and RAD to quickly create your own application. Even if we'll explore this option, we won't use it in the rest of the book. We'll use a more traditional approach that you'll be able to re-use in your own Alfresco projects.

Rapid application development

In this section, we'll take a small detour to talk about rapid application development. As explained before, Alfresco SDK provides three different archetypes. One of them is called the Alfresco AIO archetype. Using this archetype, you can easily implement all your customization in a unique STS project and run the full Alfresco platform. It means that you don't need to install Alfresco on your system and it provides a perfect starting point for full-blown Alfresco projects where the final artifacts should be the customized `alfresco.war` and `share.war`.

In a typical project, you want to develop a reusable module that should be distributed independently. To achieve this goal, we'll discover in the next sections how to install Alfresco on a CentOS system and create modules for Alfresco and Share.

To create your first RAD project, click on **File** | **New** | **Maven Project**. On this screen, let's keep the default configuration and click on **Next >**:

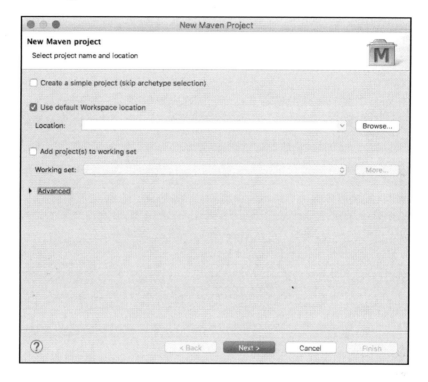

In the next window, limit the list archetypes by typing `org.alfresco` in the **Filter** field. Only three archetypes will be visible. In this book, we'll use the archetype `alfresco-allinone-archetype`. You can specify `enterprise` in the **Profiles** field, if you plan to use Alfresco Enterprise. If you don't, just leave it empty:

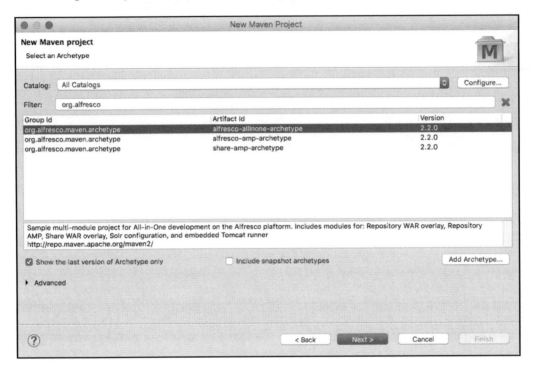

In the next screen, provide all information required to create your artifact and click on the button **Finish**:

- **Group Id**: `com.someco`
- **Artifcat Id**: `alfresco`

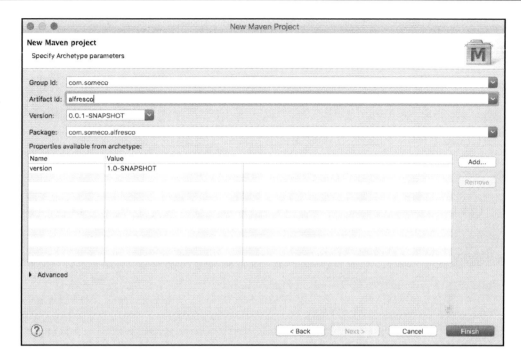

When the creation is completed, you should be able to see seven different projects:

- `alfresco`: This project is the parent project containing all six other projects.
- `alfresco-repo-amp`: This is a repository AMP project, demonstrating sample project structure and demo component loading
- `repo`: This is an `alfresco.war` aggregator project, overlaying the standard Alfresco WAR with the `alfresco-repo-amp` and any other AMPs and JARs that have been included as dependencies and configured in the overlay
- `alfresco-share-amp`: This is a Share AMP project, demonstrating sample project structure and demo Aikau page
- `share`: A `share.war` aggregator project, overlaying the standard Share WAR with the `alfresco-share-amp` and any other AMPs and JARs that have been included as dependencies and configured in the overlay
- `solr-config`: This project brings in the Apache Solr4 configuration files

- `runner`: A Tomcat plus H2 runner, capable of running the custom `alfresco.war`, custom `share.war`, and `solr4.war` for demo/integration-testing purposes

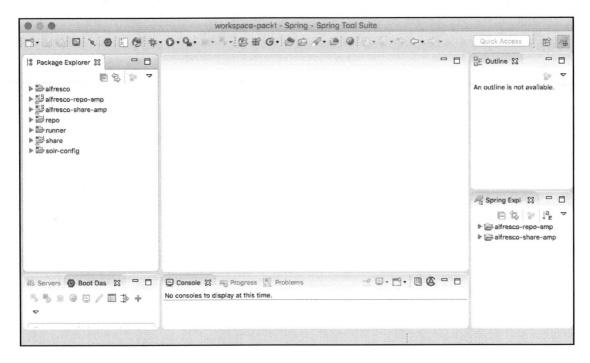

We are not going to explain how to customize Alfresco. We are just going to run Alfresco directly from STS (you can do it as well using a command-line tool):

1. Click on **Run | Run Configurations…**
2. Right click on the left-menu item called **Maven Build** and click on **New**.
3. Select the base directory as the project `alfresco`.
4. Specify the name `Run Alfresco`.
5. Specify the goals `clean install`.
6. But more importantly, specify the profile `run`.

7. Finally, click on the **Run** button and Maven will package, deploy and run a Tomcat instance:

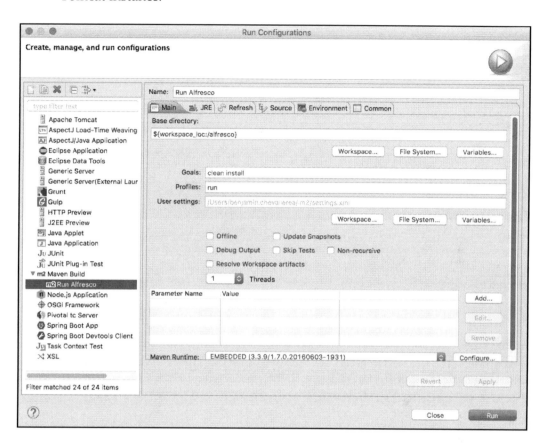

 If you get an `out-of-memory` error when Alfresco is starting, you may need to configure some JVM memory parameters to Maven. One way is to open the **Environment** tab, and create a new variable called `MAVEN_OPTS` and use the following value:
`-Xmx1024M -XX:MaxPermSize=512m`

When it's completed (and be patient because the process can be long for the very first time), just open a browser on `http://localhost:8080/` and you'll have access to the following page. On this page, you'll be able to open Alfresco, Share, Solr or the new REST API explorer:

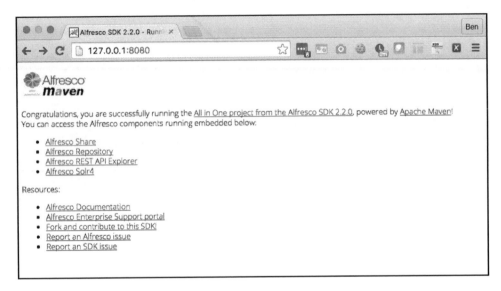

Alfresco is now running the Community edition. You can open Alfresco Share, log in using the credentials `admin` / `admin` and play will all out-of-the-box features.If you want to run the Enterprise edition, use the profile run, enterprise, instead of run. If you have an Alfresco license, you can add it to the following folder path:

`alfresco | repo | src | main | resources | alfresco | extension | license`

Traditional approach

As explained, you can use the AIO archetype for prototyping or if you need to provide WAR files for deployment, or start a new project. However, if you need to develop an add-on or reusable component that you want to distribute independently, the two other archetypes will need to be used. Let's start by deleting the previous project to avoid any confusion, or switch to another workspace if you want to keep both options in your system.

Following exactly the same approach as used before, we are going to generate two projects:

- Repository project:
  - Select the artifact: `alfresco-amp-archetype`
  - Group Id: `com.someco`
  - Artifact Id: `repo`
- Share project:
  - Select the artifact: `share-amp-archetype`
  - Group Id: `com.someco`
  - Artifact Id: `share`

When it's done, you should have two projects in your workspaces:

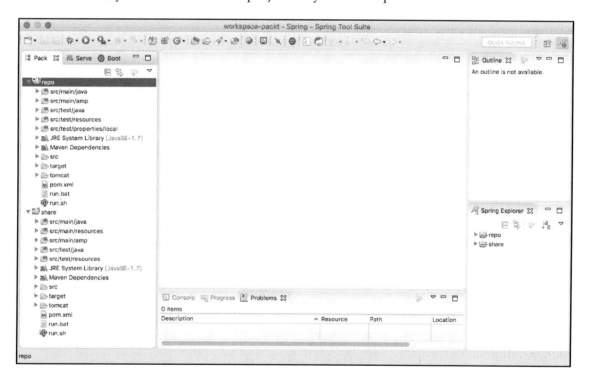

The `run` profile doesn't exist in these archetypes. Instead, these two archetypes includes a profile called `amp-to-war`. The first step that we need to do is to create the two Maven configurations by following the steps explained before:

1. Click on **Run | Run Configurations...**
2. Right click on the left-menu item called **Maven Build** and click on **New**.
    *   Name: `Run Alfresco`.
    *   Base directory: Click on the **Workspace...** button and select the **repo** project.
    *   Goals: `clean install`.
    *   Profiles: `amp-to-war`.
    *   Click on **Apply.**
3. Right click on the left-menu item called **MavenBuild** and click on **New**.
    *   Name: `Run Share`.
    *   Base directory: Click on the **Workspace...** button and select the **share** project.
    *   Goals: `clean install`.
    *   Profiles: `amp-to-war`.
    *   Because we don't want to run Share on the same Tomcat port, we need to change it. Open the tab **JRE**, and provide the following **VM argument**:
    *   `-Dmaven.tomcat.port=8181`
    *   Click on **Apply.**

If you execute these two configurations, the Alfresco repository will run on the port 8080 (`http://localhost:8080/alfresco/`) and Alfresco Share will run on the port 8181 (`http://localhost:8181/share/`). You can use the default admin/admin credentials to authenticate.

By default, it will be the Community edition. Following the same principles as the AIO artifact, you just need to add the profile enterprise to your list of profiles in the Maven configurations.

Now, we want to package our modules. In this case, I prefer to create two new Maven configurations:

1. Click on **Run | Run Configurations...**
2. Right click on the left-menu item called **Maven Build** and click on **New**
   - Name: `Package Alfresco Module`
   - Base directory: Click on the **Workspace...** button and select the `repo` project
   - Goals: `clean package`
   - Click on **Apply**
3. Right click on the left-menu item called **Maven Build** and click on **New**
   - Name: `PackageShare Module`
   - Base directory: Click on the **Workspace...** button and select the `share` project
   - Goals: `clean package`
   - Click on **Apply**

Now, you just need to run these two Maven configurations to generate the two AMP modules in:

- `/repo/target/repo-1.0-SNAPSHOT.amp`
- `/share/target/share-1.0-SNAPSHOT.amp`

Now, we need to figure out what to do with these AMP modules.

Install Alfresco

The goal of this book is to give you an entire prospective on developing an Alfresco project. The easy way is to use the AIO archetype that bundles Alfresco. However, it probably won't be the best option in this book. We want to show you as well how to install Alfresco from scratch. Most developers don't work on the same operating system as the one where Alfresco will be installed. Depending of your organization, some developers may develop on a Windows system, a Mac OS system or a Linux system. It may create some issues depending of the project. It's why we'll use virtual machines to test our development.

Download Alfresco

Alfresco provides different installers. In this book, we want to install both Alfresco and Share, so we'll use the Alfresco One installer. If you need to install only Alfresco or Share, you could use the Alfresco One platform or Alfresco Share installer. Depending of the version that you want to install, you are not following the same steps:

- If you want to install the Community version:
    - Open the following URL:
      `https://www.alfresco.com/alfresco-community-download`
    - Download the Linux edition
    - At the time of writing, the file of the current version is called
      `alfresco-community-installer-201605-linux-x64.bin`

- If you want to install the Enterprise version, be aware that you'll need an access to the support Alfresco system, and you'll need an Alfresco license:
    - Open the following URL: `https://support.alfresco.com`
    - Authenticate using the credentials provided by Alfresco
    - Open the **DOWNLOADS** tab
    - Click on the current version **Alfresco One 5.1.1**
    - Click on the link to download the Linux installer: `5.1.1 Alfresco One Linux 64 bit` installer
    - The name of the downloaded file will be: `alfresco-one-installer-5.1.1-linux-x64.bin`

Create your virtual machine

In this section, we'll use Vagrant and VirtualBox to replicate a real deployment environment. It's not the purpose of this book to explain deeply how these two tools work. Vagrant is a software that creates and configures virtual development environments. It can connect to different virtualization tool, but VirtualBox is free, available on every major platform, and has built-in support in Vagrant. To be able to follow the next steps, you'll need to install VirtualBox (`https://www.virtualbox.org/wiki/Downloads`) and Vagrant (`https://www.vagrantup.com/downloads.html`). However, feel free to use any virtualization method that you are used to.

Create a file called `Vagrantfile` and add this text:

```
Vagrant.configure(2) do |config|
config.vm.box = "box-cutter/centos72"
  # Redirect Tomcat Port
config.vm.network "forwarded_port", guest: 8080, host: 8080
  # Redirect JPDA Debugging Port
config.vm.network "forwarded_port", guest: 8000, host: 8000
  # Redirect Custom NodeJS port
config.vm.network "forwarded_port", guest: 9000, host: 9000
config.vm.provider "virtualbox" do |v|
v.memory = 4096
v.cpus = 1
  end
end
```

This Vagrant configuration file specifies that we'll create a new virtual machine based on Cent OS 7 with one virtual CPU and 4 GB of memory. This file contains as well a port forwarding rule to allow us to access the Alfresco repository UI and the Alfresco Share UI from the host system. It forwards as well the port 8000 that we'll use to do some JPDA debugging. The port 9000 is as well forwarded and will be used in the Chapter 6, *Creating an Angular Application*.

The next step is to create the virtual machine:

1. Open a command-line tool.
2. Go to the folder containing the Vagrant file.
3. Type `vagrant up`. This command will download the image of Cent OS 7 and we'll create the VM in VirtualBox.
4. When it's completed, the VM is available and you can login using SSH by typing `vagrant ssh`.

You are now logged in to your VM and ready to install Alfresco.

The first step is to transfer the previously downloaded installer into the VM:

- By using SCP:

    The virtual machine is listening on the port 2222 for SSH. You can use the `scp` command by typing:

    ```
    scp -P 2222 alfresco-one-installer-5.1.1.4-linux-x64
    .binvagrant@localhost:/tmp
    ```

The password for the vagrant user is vagrant.

- By using a FTP client. We'll use FileZilla as example:
    - Start FileZilla.
    - Create a new connection:
        - Host: localhost
        - Port: 2222
        - Protocol: SFTP - SSH File Transfer Protocol
        - Logon Type: Normal
        - User: vagrant
        - Password: vagrant
    - Click on **Connect**.
    - Then, you just need to drag and drop files between your system and the virtual machine.

The following installation notes are based on the Enterprise version of Alfresco. But the steps are exactly the same for the Community version. You just need to use the Community installer file name, instead of the Enterprise one:

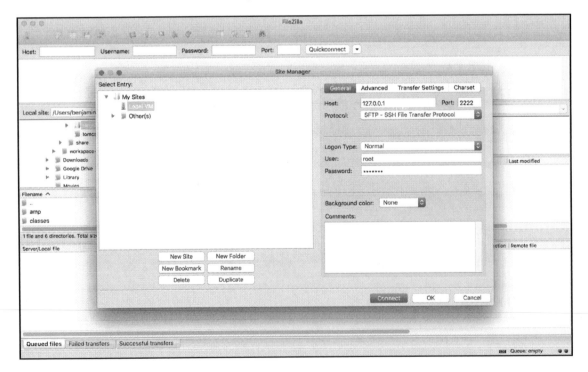

Now, we are ready to install Alfresco. We could install Alfresco using the root user. However, for security reasons, it's recommended to install Alfresco with another user. The downside of doing that is that Alfresco won't install the service for you, so we'll need it to do it manually:

1. Create the `alfresco` group :

   ```
   sudo groupadd alfresco
   ```

2. Create the `alfresco` user:

   ```
   sudo adduser-m -g alfresco alfresco
   ```

3. Define a password for the `alfresco` user:

   ```
   sudo passwd alfresco
   ```

4. Add the `vagrant` user to the `alfresco` group too:

   ```
   sudo usermod -a -G alfresco vagrant
   ```

5. Create the folder where we'll install Alfresco and give access to our newly created user:

   ```
   sudo mkdir /opt/alfresco
   sudo chown alfresco:alfresco /opt/alfresco/
   ```

6. Install some dependencies not bundled in the Alfresco installer:

   ```
   sudo yum -y install fontconfiglibSMlibICElibXrenderlibXext
      cups-libs libGLU
   ```

7. Create the Alfresco service file `/etc/init.d/alfresco` (by using vi, or nano if you installed it) and add the following content:

   ```
   #!/bin/sh

   RETVAL=0

   start () {
       /opt/alfresco/alfresco.sh start "$2"
       RETVAL=$?
       if [ -d "/var/lock/subsys" ]&& [ `id -u` = 0 ] &&
         [ $RETVAL -eq 0 ] ; then
             touch /var/lock/subsys/alfresco
       fi
   ```

```
}

stop () {
    /opt/alfresco/alfresco.sh stop "$2"
    RETVAL=$?
}
case "$1" in
    start)
        start "$@"
        ;;
    stop)
        stop "$@"
        ;;
    restart)
        stop "$@"
        start "$@"
        ;;
    *)
        /opt/alfresco/alfresco.sh "$@"
        RETVAL=$?
esac
exit $RETVAL
```

8. Make this script executable:

```
sudo chmod +x /etc/init.d/alfresco
```

9. Authenticate as alfresco:

```
sudo su alfresco
```

10. Make the installer executable:

```
chmod +x /tmp/alfresco-one-installer-5.1.1.4-linux-x64.bin
```

- Start the installation:

```
/tmp/alfresco-one-installer-5.1.1.4-linux-x64.bin
```

- First, let's select English as installation language:

```
Language Selection

Please select the installation language
[1] English
[2] French
```

```
[3]  Spanish
[4]  Italian
[5]  German
[6]  Japanese
[7]  Dutch
[8]  Russian
[9]  Simplified Chinese
[10] Norwegian
[11] Brazilian Portuguese
Please choose an option [1] : 1
```

- Accept the license (if you install the Enterprise version):

```
Read the following License Agreement.
You must accept the terms of this
agreement before continuing with the installation.

Press [Enter] to continue:
[...]

Do you accept this license? [y/n]: y
```

- The next step is to select the installation type: Easy or Advanced. To simplify we'll select the Easy installation type. It will install all required components including Java, LibreOffice, ImageMagick, PostgreSQL:

```
Installation Type

[1] Easy - Install using the default configuration.
[2] Advanced - Configure server ports and service properties.:
    Choose optional components to install.

Please choose an option [1] :1
```

- Specify that you want to install Alfresco in the /opt/alfresco folder:

```
Installation Folder
Choose a folder to install Alfresco One.
Select a folder: [/home/alfresco/alfresco-one]:/opt/alfresco
```

- Specify the admin password. By default, it's recommended to use the same password as the username:

```
Admin Password
Specify a password for the Alfresco administrator account.
Admin Password: admin
Repeat Password: admin
```

- You may receive a warning that the environment is not optimal because there are not enough resources. This is not critical, because it's just a development environment:

```
Warning

This environment is not configured optimally for Alfresco -
    review this list before continuing.

While these issues won't prevent Alfresco from functioning,
    some product features might not be available,
    or the system might not perform optimally.

Not enough CPUs (cores) available
(2+): 1

Not enough system RAM available
(4.0GB+): 3.70GB
SMTP TCP port in use: 25

Press [Enter] to continue:
```

- We are now ready to start the installation:

```
Setup is now ready to begin installing
 Alfresco One on your computer.

Do you want to continue? [Y/n]: Y
-----------------------------------------------------------
Please wait while Setup installs Alfresco One on your computer.

Installing
0% _____ 50% _____ 100%
########################################
```

- Finally, we don't want to read the Readme file:

```
Setup has finished installing Alfresco One on your computer.
View Readme File [Y/n]: n
```

- And we don't want to start Alfresco right now:

```
Launch Alfresco One[Y/n]: n
```

Be aware that Alfresco provides a **Day Zero configuration guide** that will help to check and to improve your Alfresco configuration for a production use http://docs.alfresco.com/5.0/concepts/zeroday-overview.html.

Deploy your modules

Before starting Alfresco, we want to deploy our new AMP modules in our virtual machines. Using your favorite method:

- Transfer repo-1.0-SNAPSHOT.amp to /opt/alfresco/amps
- Transfer share-1.0-SNAPSHOT.amp to /opt/alfresco/amps_share

The next step is to apply the AMP module to the alfresco.war and share.war files. Alfresco provides a tool called **Module Management Tool** (**MMT**). The MMT program, alfresco-mmt.jar, supports the following:

- Installation of AMP files including upgrades to later versions
- Uninstallation of installed modules
- Listing of currently installed module

This file is deployed in the bin directory of the Alfresco installation. In the same folder, Alfresco provides another program called apply_amps.sh on a Linux system. This executable script used the MMT tool to install AMP module to WAR files.

- Open the bin folder:

  ```
  cd /opt/alfresco/bin
  ```

- Apply the AMP modules:

  ```
  ./apply_amps.sh
  ```

- When it's installed, you can just start Alfresco:

  ```
  service alfresco start
  ```

You can track the startup of Alfresco by typing the following command:

```
less+F/opt/alfresco/tomcat/logs/catalina.out
```

You should see the following message that confirms that your Alfresco module is properly installed:

```
INFO [repo.module.ModuleServiceImpl] [localhost-startStop-1]
    Installing module 'repo' version 1.0-SNAPSHOT
```

When Alfresco is started, you should see the message:

```
INFO: Server startup in 136101 ms
```

Then, just open your browser on `http://127.0.0.1:8080/share/` and login as `admin/admin`:

The two modules that we just installed contains already some example of customization. For example, there is a new web script deployed in Alfresco. To test it, just opens the URL `http://127.0.0.1:8080/alfresco/s/sample/helloworld` (you should see a dialog box where you need to authenticate with the `admin` username):

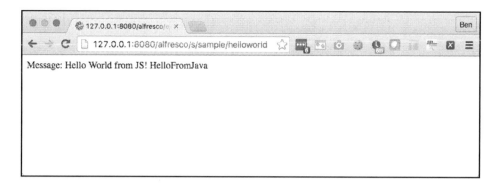

The Share module contains as well some customization. For example, it includes a new Aikau page. To test it, just open the URL `http://127.0.0.1:8080/share/page/dp/ws/simple-page` (you should see a login page where you need to authenticate with the `admin` username):

Check that your modules are installed

Alfresco Enterprise provides different way to check that your modules are installed properly. As shown previously, we can use the log file to check that the repository module is installed. As well, if you use the Enterprise edition, you can open the following URL `http://127.0.0.1:8080/alfresco/service/enterprise/admin/admin-systemsum mary` and in bottom right corner, you should see the list of installed modules:

Alfresco Share provides as well a page to check the list of installed modules. You just need to open the following URL

`http://127.0.0.1:8080/share/page/console/admin-console/module-package:`

Extending Alfresco

Alfresco provides an extension mechanism that keeps customizations separate from the files that are a part of the Alfresco distribution. It is important to keep your customizations separate from Alfresco's in order to help streamline future upgrades and to simplify troubleshooting.

Understanding the extension mechanism

When you implement Alfresco, you will inevitably identify things you want to tweak and potentially define an entirely new functionality that you would like to add to the platform. Because Alfresco is based on the Spring framework, you'll use the same approach with your own customizations. You will extend the existing or write new Spring beans, Java classes, Freemarker templates, and other files. The custom files are deployed as a part of the Alfresco or Share web application. The trick is to override or extend Alfresco with your own code, while keeping those extensions and customizations separate from the Alfresco core.

This means you have to know what goes where and the answer to that depends on what's being extended.

When implementing your solution, you are likely to create or customize one or more of the following types of files:

- Standard Java web application files
- Framework files (Spring beans and their associated configuration files)
- Alfresco configuration files (properties files and XML files)
- Solution-specific files (content models, business process definitions, web scripts, JavaScript, and Freemarker templates)

Let's look at how each of these areas is extended.

Standard Java web application files

Given that you probably have experience developing Java web applications, there is not much need to go into detail here. The Java classes you develop as a part of your customization will go into a JAR file. The JAR file will reside in the `WEB-INF | lib` folder of the Alfresco or Share web application. By default, the name of the JAR files is the same name as the AMP module.

Framework files

Alfresco makes heavy use of the Spring Framework and can be used for plenty of customizations. You'll discover in the next sections some customization that you can do.

Spring configuration files

Spring configuration files always end in `-context.xml`. That's how Spring knows to read them when the application starts up. Each repository module contains a file called `module-context.xml`. This is used to load the Spring configuration for the module. Usually, this context file loads other specific context models. If you open the file `repo|src|main|amp|config|alfresco|module|repo|module-context.xml`, you can notice that it loads three additional context files located in the sub-directory `context`. It allows to have one context file per component:

- `bootstrap-context.xml` that loads the two content models already defined
- `service-context.xml` that create the custom Java service
- `webscript-context.xml` that create the Java back-end webscript

Let's look at an example. Here's the Alfresco Spring bean that's used to tell Alfresco to load the default custom content models already existing in our module:

```
<bean id="repo.dictionaryBootstrap" parent="dictionaryModelBootstrap"
    depends-on="dictionaryBootstrap">
  <property name="models">
        <list>
              <value>alfresco/module/${project.artifactId}
                  /model/content-model.xml</value>
              <value>alfresco/module/${project.artifactId}
                  /model/workflow-model.xml</value>
        </list>
  </property>
</bean>
```

In the Share module, it's slightly different. The Share module contains a file called share-slingshot-application-context.xml that resides in the folder share|src|main|amp|config|alfresco|web-extension. Right now, this file is only used to load new messages"

```
<bean id="share.resources"
class="org.springframework.extensions.surf.util.ResourceBundleBootstrapComp
onent">
  <property name="resourceBundles">
        <list>
              <value>alfresco.web-extension.messages.share</value>
        </list>
  </property>
</bean>
```

Alfresco configuration files

Not all configurations are handled through standard frameworks such as Spring. Some configuration changes are made using properties files or Alfresco configuration XML. For example, the most commonly customized properties file is alfresco-global.properties. In the file located in <TOMCAT_HOME>|shared|classes, you can find things such as the username and password used to connect to the underlying relational database, the database driver, and the data directory file path. There are sample properties in the file called alfresco-global.properties.sample located in the same directory.

The full out of the box `repository.properties` file resides in the JAR file called `alfresco-repository-5.1.1.jar` located in `<TOMCAT_HOME>|webapps|alfresco|WEB-INF|lib`. To override any of the properties in that file, add custom values to a file called `alfresco-global.properties` in the `<TOMCAT_HOME>|shared|classes`directory or directly in the file included in the repo module in the directory `repo|src|main|amp|config|alfresco|module|repo`.

Solution-specific files

There are several types of files that, conceptually, sit on top of the Alfresco platform as a part of the solution you are implementing with Alfresco. These include files such as content models, business process definitions, web scripts, server-side JavaScript, and FreeMarker templates. Alfresco ships several of these with the product in the Alfresco repository and the Share web applications. Some are purely meant to be used as examples, while others are functional pieces of the platform. With the exception of content models that can import and extend Alfresco's out of the box content models, there is no need to extend these files directly. Instead, your custom versions of these types of files will sit alongside Alfresco's.

These files can live on the file system or in the repository. When they reside on the file system, they need to be on the classpath. So they should be placed in the **alfresco|extension** directory. When stored in the repository, each type of file has a designated folder within the **|Company Home|Data Dictionary** folder.

For example, suppose you write a JavaScript file to implement the business logic for an action. Ignoring the details on actions for the moment, you can choose to store that JavaScript file either on the file system, perhaps in a directory called **scripts** in the `alfresco|extension` directory, or in the repository within the Scripts folder under **Data Dictionary**.

Business process definitions can live on the file system and in the repository, but they can also be deployed directly to the Activiti engine. This will be discussed in the Advanced Workflow chapter.

Avoid Modifying Alfresco Code and Configuration

It may be tempting to make changes directly to the Alfresco web application. Avoid this temptation at all costs. "But this is open source," you may say, "Why can't I change it if I want to?". Yes, it is open source and, yes, you can change it to your heart's content. It will be up to you to figure out whether a problem is in your code or Alfresco's. You will also have to devote more time to upgrades than you would have, had you kept your customizations separate from Alfresco's code.

There are three situations when, try as you might, you may have to touch Alfresco's files. First, you may identify a bug in the Alfresco source as well as a fix. In this situation, the best thing to do is to put the fix in place as a temporary measure, file a JIRA ticket, and attach the fix to the ticket. Alfresco will confirm the bug and implement the fix (sometimes using your code unchanged and sometimes with its own). Enterprise customers can usually get a patch right away. Community users may have to run on their own fix until the problem is resolved in a future build.

The second situation is that sometimes (and this is increasingly rare) there may be a configuration change or customization that cannot be implemented through the standard extension mechanism. This is really no different than the previous scenario. If this happens, treat it like a bug. Make the change then file a ticket. Alfresco's intent is for the product to be extensible without the need to change the core installation, so anything less than that is a bug.

The third situation is that you might identify a product enhancement that cannot be implemented without modifying the source. In this case, it is a very good idea to talk to Alfresco (either your representative or via the forums) before you start coding, particularly if it is a big change. They might already be working on the same enhancement. Or, they might be able to gauge demand for the enhancement as well as provide implementation advice. If this enhancement is critical to your solution but no one else is interested in it, you'll have a hard decision to make because it may be a long time before the enhancement gets incorporated into the product. Moving forward without Alfresco's commitment to incorporate the enhancement into the product could mean supporting your own fork of the Alfresco source for the foreseeable future.

Troubleshooting

There are three primary troubleshooting tools you will become intimately familiar with: Log4j, your favorite Java debugger, and the Alfresco Node Browser. There are other, less-frequently used tools and techniques that will be discussed when the time is right.

Log4j

Most of you are already familiar with this common logging tool, so not a lot of discussion is needed. For everyone else, here are the basics. The verbosity of the log output, the specific classes being logged, and other logging settings are controlled by Log4J property file:

If you are looking at a temporary change, you can update the file `custom-log4j.properties` in the directory `<TOMCAT_HOME>|shared|classes|alfresco|extension`.

- Don't forget the JMX option. The JMX interface allows to access Alfresco Enterprise via a standard JMX console that supports JMX Remoting (JSR-160). It's a very useful tool to perform on-demand change at runtime without needing to restart the server.
- If you are looking for a more permanent configuration, you can use the `log4j.properties` file located in your module in `repo|src|main|amp|config|alfresco|module|repo`.

For example, if you are testing out some server-side JavaScript, you might want to change the JavaScript-related logger from error to debug like this:

```
log4j.logger.org.alfresco.repo.jscript=DEBUG
```

If you want to add your own logger for one of your own Java classes, add a new logger to the end of the file like this:

```
log4j.logger.com.someco=DEBUG
```

Then, within your class, call the logger's methods like this:

```
public class SetWebFlag extends ActionExecuterAbstractBase {
private static Logger logger = Logger.getLogger(SetWebFlag.class);
@Override
protected void executeImpl(Action action, NodeRefactionedUponNodeRef) {
if (logger.isDebugEnabled()) logger.debug("Inside executeImpl");
```

The call to `DebugEnabled()` isn't required, but it may help a bit with performance.

Step-by-step – debugging from within Eclipse

Like Log4j, stepping through the source code of a web application with a remote debugger will be familiar to many readers. Just in case it is new to you, this section walks you through the setup when using STS as your IDE and Alfresco running in a your virtual machine.

At a high level, what you are going to do is tell Tomcat to send debug information to a specific port. Then, you will tell STS to listen for that information using the same port. This setup will let you set breakpoints in the source code (both yours and Alfresco's), which will get tripped when the JVM processes a statement that has a breakpoint set.

Follow these steps to set this up:

1. In Tomcat's startup script located in `/opt/alfresco/tomcat/bin/startup.sh`, change the last line that invokes Catalina to include `jpda`. On Linux, this looks like:

   exec "$PRGDIR"/"$EXECUTABLE" jpda start "$@"

2. Start Alfresco.
3. In STS, go to the **Debug Configuration** dialog and create a new **Remote Java Application.** Browse to the project you want to debug. Take the defaults for everything else:

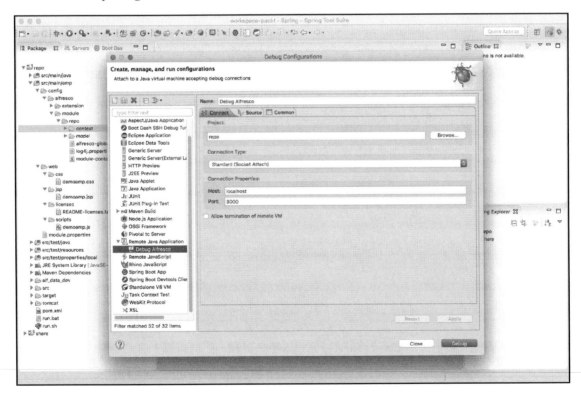

4. Click **Debug.**

You are now ready to debug. If you want to try this out on your own, try setting a breakpoint in the HelloWorld webscript. You can navigate to it in STS by going to the **repo** project, the source folder src|main|java, in the com.someco.repo.demoamp package. Once you've found the executeImpl method in the HelloWorldWebScript Java source, double-click the left margin to set a breakpoint. The checkmark that appears as part of the breakpoint indicates that this breakpoint is enabled and the class is loaded:

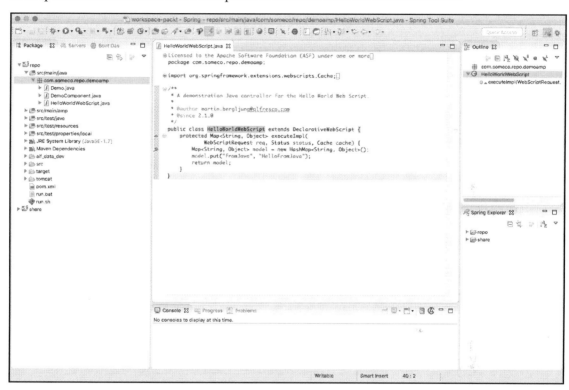

Now open the HelloWorld webscript URL
(`http://127.0.0.1:8080/alfresco/s/sample/helloworld`) in your browser. STS will
launch the Debugger perspective. You can then step through the source line by line using
the **bouncing arrow** icons or click the **green arrow** to continue to the next breakpoint:

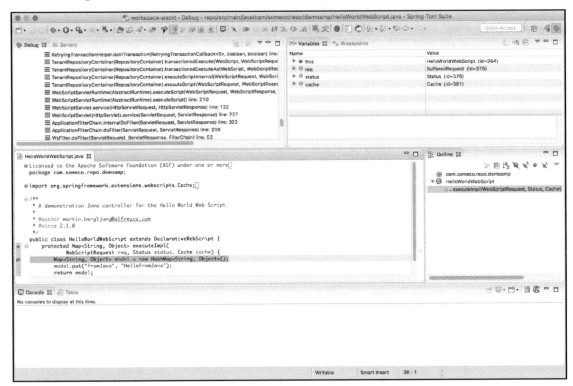

If you run Alfresco directly from Maven, you can use the command
mvnDebug to start Alfresco in DEBUG mode automatically:
`http://docs.alfresco.com/5.1/tasks/alfresco-sdk-rad-eclipse-remo`
`te-debugging.html`

Node browser

The Alfresco Node Browser is accessible via Alfresco or Share. If you want to use the one embedded in Alfresco (be aware that it's available only in the enterprise version):

- Open the Alfresco webapp (`http://127.0.0.1:8080/alfresco/`)
- Click on `Alfresco Administration Console (admin only)`
- In the left menu, click on `Support Tools|Node Browser`

If you want to use the one embedded in Alfresco Share:

- Open the Alfresco webapp (`http://127.0.0.1:8080/share/`)
- In the top menu, click on `Admin Tools`
- In the left menu, click on `Tools|Node Browser`

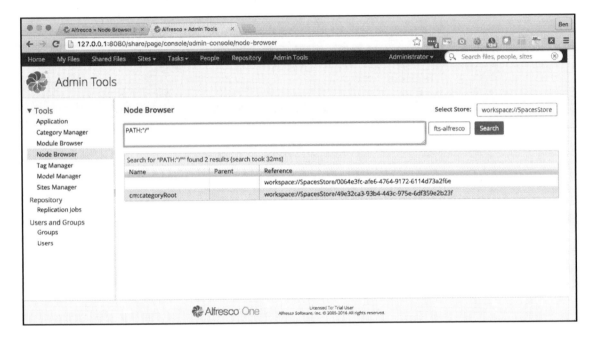

The Node Browser lets you navigate through the low-level representation of the repository. Even if you'll use mainly use the store `workspace://SpacesStore`, you'll be able to discover the other available stores. This browser displays useful information about each node such as its path, unique ID, node reference, type, list of aspects and properties. If you have an issue on a node, this will be THE tool that you'll need to investigate.

Besides being able to navigate the hierarchy, the Node Browser also provides a search box. If you know a node's reference, you can go right to it using the Node Browser's search tool. The search box is also handy for testing out Lucene, Xpath, CMIS SQL-like queries (and many more...).

Starting over

During development, it is quite common to have to start with a fresh repository. Usually this is because you've made a significant change to the model, and you'd rather blow everything away than clean up inconsistencies. The Alfresco repository is made up of three parts: the metadata stored in the relational database, the binary files stored on the file system and the Solr indexes. To clear out the repository, you have to clear out all three. If you delete the data directory but not the database, you will see a bunch of data integrity problems because the binary files that the database knows about are no longer there. Be sure that Alfresco is stopped.

Let's start by the database:

1. Start PostgreSQL: `service alfresco start postgresql`
2. Recreate the database:

   ```
   /opt/alfresco/postgresql/bin/psql -U postgres
   Password for user postgres: admin
   postgres=#DROP DATABASE alfresco;
   postgres=#CREATE DATABASE alfresco WITH OWNER alfresco;
   postgres=# \q
   ```

3. Then, let's delete the binary folders:

   ```
   rm -rf/opt/alfresco/alf_data/contentstore/*
   rm -rf/opt/alfresco/alf_data/contentstore.deleted/*
   ```

4. And finally, the Solr indexes:

   ```
   rm -rf/opt/alfresco/alf_data/solr4/*
   ```

You can now restart Alfresco and your instance should be the same as a fresh installation.

 If you run Alfresco directly from Maven, you can use the purge profile. Just type mvn clean -Ppurge and it will delete the database, the content stores, the index files and the log files:
`http://docs.alfresco.com/5.1/concepts/alfresco-sdk-cmd-reference -repo-amp.html`

Summary

This chapter was about getting your development environment ready to go, providing an overview of how the platform is extended, and understanding the debugging tools that are available. Specifically, you learned what is the Alfresco Maven SDK and which archetypes are available. We discovered how to install STS, and all-prerequisites to be able to use the Alfresco archetypes. Then, we did our first steps extending Alfresco without modifying Alfresco's source code or configuration. You learned the specific extension technique to use depending on the type of file being customized.

We learnt what to do when things inevitably go wrong. Familiar techniques such as log4j and remote debugging are available, just as they would be with any web application. In addition, the Node Browser can be a useful tool for inspecting the underlying data structure or testing out search queries.

And we terminated the chapter by understanding how to start clean for testing or debugging purposes. You learned that dropping and recreating the database as well as clearing out the data directory followed by a Tomcat restart will always give you a sparkling new repository to work with.

3
Working with Content Models

From setting up the initial content model to programmatically creating, searching for, and deleting content, how you work with the content in a content management system is a foundational concept upon which the rest of the solution is built. In this chapter, you'll learn:

- What a repository is and how it is structured
- How to make the underlying content model relevant to your business problem by extending Alfresco's out of the box model with your own content types
- What practices are the best for creating your own content models
- How to configure Alfresco Share to expose your custom content model via the user interface
- How to interact with the repository via the CMIS and JavaScript APIs

Defining SomeCo's content model

Recall from Chapter 1, *The Alfresco Platform*, that SomeCo is rolling out Alfresco across the organization. Each department has its own type of content to work with and different requirements for how it works with that content. SomeCo could just start uploading content into Alfresco. That would be better than nothing, but it doesn't take advantage of the full power of the platform, and makes for a really boring (and short) book. SomeCo would be better off formalizing the different types of content it works with by extending the Alfresco content model to make it SomeCo-specific.

Step-by-step – starting the custom content model with custom types

Let's start small and build the model up over successive examples. First, let's create a custom content type for Whitepapers, which are a type of marketing document. This is going to involve creating a content model file, which is expressed as XML, and then telling Alfresco where to find it using a Spring bean configuration file. The Alfresco repository Maven archetype already includes a custom content model. We are just going to re-use it.

 Be aware that Alfresco provides as well a Model Manger that allows you to create a custom content model (and the relevant forms) directly from Alfresco Share. However, we want to explain you in this book the underlying concepts of a content model, so we'll create the XML content model file manually. You can find more information about the Model Manager on this page:
http://docs.alfresco.com/5.1/concepts/admintools-cmm-intro.html

To start the content model, follow these steps:

1. Edit the file `bootstrap-context.xml` located in `repo` | `src` | `main` | `amp` | `config` | `alfresco` | `module` | `repo` | `context`. A custom model context file is a Spring bean configuration file. Spring bean configuration files were also discussed in `Chapter 2`, *Getting Started with Alfresco*. Remove the reference to the file `content-model.xml`, and replace it by `scModel.xml`. Your file should contain:

```
<?xml version='1.0' encoding='UTF-8'?>
<!DOCTYPE beans PUBLIC '-//SPRING//DTD BEAN//EN'
    'http://www.springframework.org/dtd/spring-beans.dtd'>
<beans>
    <!-- Registration of new models -->
    <bean id="repo.dictionaryBootstrap"
        parent="dictionaryModelBootstrap"
        depends-on="dictionaryBootstrap">

        <property name="models">
            <list>
              <value>
                  alfresco/module/${project.artifactId}
                  /model/scModel.xml
              </value>
              <value>
                  alfresco/module/${project.artifactId}
                  /model/workflow-model.xml
```

```
            </value>
          </list>
        </property>
      </bean>
    </beans>
```

2. Create a model file that implements the custom content model. We'll create it in the same folder as existing ones, that is `repo | src | main | amp | config | alfresco | module | repo | model`. Create a new XML file in the model directory called `scModel.xml` (this name matches the value specified in the `bootstrap-context.xml` file). The sample file called `content-model.xml` can be kept in the same folder. This one won't be loaded because it's not listed in the bean that we created previously.

3. Add the following XML that is used to describe the model, import other models that this model extends, and declare the model's namespace:

```
<?xml version="1.0" encoding="UTF-8"?>
<!-- Definition of new Model -->
    <model name="sc:somecomodel"
        xmlns="http://www.alfresco.org/model/dictionary/1.0">

        <!-- Optional meta-data about the model -->
        <description>Someco Model</description>
        <author>Optaros</author>
        <version>1.0</version>

        <!-- Imports are required to allow references to
            definitions in other models -->
        <imports>

            <!-- Import Alfresco Dictionary Definitions -->
            <import uri="http://www.alfresco.org/model
            /dictionary/1.0" prefix="d" />

            <!-- Import Alfresco Content Domain Model Definitions -->
            <import uri="http://www.alfresco.org/model
             /content/1.0" prefix="cm" />

        </imports>

        <!-- Introduction of new namespaces defined by this model -->
        <namespaces>
            <namespace uri="http://www.someco.com/model
             /content/1.0" prefix="sc" />
        </namespaces>
```

4. Next, add the types. A **whitepaper** is a type of marketing document that, in turn, is only one of several types of content SomeCo deals with. It's a hierarchy (summarized in next diagram). That hierarchy will be reflected in the model. Creating a base content type for a company is a really common and recommended pattern. Add this XML to the model file below the `namespaces` element:

```
<types>
    <!-- Enterprise-wide generic document type -->
    <type name="sc:doc">
        <title>Someco Document</title>
        <parent>cm:content</parent>

    </type>


    <type name="sc:marketingDoc">
        <title>Someco Marketing Document</title>
        <parent>sc:doc</parent>
    </type>


    <type name="sc:whitepaper">
        <title>Someco Whitepaper</title>
        <parent>sc:marketingDoc</parent>
    </type>

</types>
```

5. Be sure to close the model tag so the XML is valid.

```
</model>
```

6. Now, we need to package our module using Maven as explained in the previous chapter. If you want to package it quickly, you can skip the tests for the moment. You just need to run the following command: `mvn clean package - DskipTests=true`. When you created your file `repo-1.0-SNAPSHOT.amp`, you can move it to your virtual machine (using FileZilla for example).

 Before deploying on your virtual machine or any server, it's quite common that developers wants to run and to test their code in their local machine first. As explained in the previous chapter, you just need to use the profile `amp-to-war` (`http://docs.alfresco.com/5.1/concepts/alfresco-sdk-cmd-referenc e-repo-amp.html`) or just use the `run.sh` or `run.bat` file that will do it for you.

7. Stop Alfresco.

```
service alfresco stop
```

8. The final step is to deploy the changes and then restart Tomcat so that Alfresco will load the custom model. Copy the amp file `repo-1.0-SNAPSHOT.amp` to the folder `/opt/alfresco-one/amps`. Execute the bash script that install the AMP file.

```
sh /opt/alfresco-one/bin/apply_amps.sh
```

9. Restart Tomcat.

```
service alfresco start
```

Watch the log during the restart. You should see no errors related to loading the custom model. If there is a problem, the message usually looks something like `Could not import bootstrap model`.

With this change in place, the repository is now capable of telling the difference between a generic piece of content and SomeCo-specific pieces of content such as marketing documents and whitepapers.

You can easily check that your module is properly installed in your Alfresco repository, just open your browser on the following URL `http://localhost:8080/alfresco/s/api/dictionary`. This webscript lists all aspects and type definitions available in your repository. You'll find that the JSON object returns the following three types: **sc:doc**, **sc:whitepaper**, and **sc:marketingDoc**. You can as well use the following URL that will show you only the types defined in the SomeCo content model: `http://localhost:8080/alfresco/s/api/classes?nsp=sc`

Types

Types are like types or classes in programming languages. They can be used to model business objects, they have properties, and they can inherit from a parent type. "Content", "Person", and "Folder" are three important types defined out of the box. Examples include things such as "Expense Report", "Medical Record", "Movie", "Song", and "Comment".

Did you notice the names of the types you created in the example? Names are made unique across the repository by using a namespace specific to the model. The namespace has an abbreviation. The model you created for SomeCo defines a custom model, which declares a namespace with the URI of http://www.someco.com/model/content/1.0 and a prefix of sc. Any type defined as a part of the model will have a name prefixed with sc:. Using namespaces in this way helps to prevent name collisions when content models are shared across repositories.

Properties and property types

Properties are pieces of metadata associated with a particular class, both type and aspect are classes. In the following example, the property is the marketing campaign. The properties of a SomeCo Expense Report might include things such as "Employee Name", "Date submitted", "Project", "Client", "Expense Report Number", "Total amount", and "Currency". The Expense Report might also include a "content" property to hold the actual expense report file (maybe it is a PDF or an Excel spreadsheet, for example).

 You may be wondering about the sc:whitepaper type. Will we need to do anything special to make sure whitepapers can be tied to campaigns as well? Nope! In Alfresco, content types inherit the properties of their parent. The sc:whitepaper type will automatically have an sc:campaign property. In fact, it will have all sorts of properties inherited from its ancestor types. The file name, content property, and creation date are three important examples.

Property types (or data types) describe the fundamental types of data the repository will use to store properties. The data type of the sc:campaign property is d:text. Other examples include things such as dates (d:date and d:datetime), floats (d:float), booleans (d:boolean), and content that is the property type of the property used to store content in a node. Because these data types literally are fundamental, they are pretty much the same for everyone. So they are defined for you out of the box.

Constraints

Constraints can optionally be used to restrict the values that Alfresco will store in a property. In the following example, the `sc:campaign` property uses a LIST constraint. There are three other types of constraints available: REGEX, MINMAX, and LENGTH. REGEX is used to make sure that a property value matches a regular expression pattern. MINMAX provides a numeric range for a property value. LENGTH sets a restriction on the length of a string.

Constraints can be defined once and reused across a model. For example, out of the box, Alfresco makes available a constraint named `cm:filename` that defines a regular expression constraint for file names. If a property in a custom type needs to restrict values to those matching the filename pattern, the custom model doesn't have to define the constraint again. It simply refers to the `cm:filename` constraint.

Step-by-step – adding properties to types

The Marketing department thinks in terms of marketing campaigns. In fact, they want to be able to search by a specific campaign and find all of the content tied to a particular campaign. Not to hurt the Marketing team's feelings, but the HR, Sales, and Operations teams couldn't care less about campaigns.

You are going to address this by adding a property to the `sc:marketingDoc` type to capture the marketing campaigns the document is related to. You could make this property a text field. But letting users enter a campaign as free-form text is a recipe for disaster if you care about getting valid search results later because of the potential for misspelling the campaign name. Plus, SomeCo wants to let each document be associated with multiple campaigns, which compounds the free-form text entry problem. So, for this particular property it makes sense to constrain its values to a list of valid campaigns.

In a traditional use case, the list of campaigns may change quite a lot. So, using a list constraint won't be the best solution in this case. But we'll keep it like that in this book for an education purpose. A traditional list constraint would be a list of countries or regions per example. However, you can make your LIST constraint dynamic. You can create a Java class that inherits the Alfresco Java class `org.alfresco.repo.dictionary.constraint.ListOfValuesConstraint` and you could connect to a database to retrieve the list of active campaigns.

To allow the Marketing team to tag a piece of content with one or more campaigns selected from a list of valid campaign names, update the model by following these steps:

1. Edit the `scModel.xml` file in **repo|src|main|amp|config|alfresco|module|repo|model**. Replace the `sc:marketingDoc` type definition with the following:

```
<type name="sc:marketingDoc">
    <title>Someco Marketing Document</title>
    <parent>sc:doc</parent>
    <properties>
        <property name="sc:campaign">
            <type>d:text</type>
            <multiple>true</multiple>
            <constraints>
                <constraint ref="sc:campaignList" />
            </constraints>
        </property>
    </properties>
</type>
```

2. Now, define the campaign list constraint. Between the `namespaces` and `types` elements, add a new `constraints` element as follows (Be careful, the order that you define elements in the content model is very important:

```
<constraints>
    <constraint name="sc:campaignList" type="LIST">
        <parameter name="allowedValues">
            <list>
                <value>Application Syndication</value>
                <value>Private Event Retailing</value>
                <value>Social Shopping</value>
            </list>
        </parameter>
    </constraint>
</constraints>
```

3. Save the `model` file.
4. Stop Alfresco.
5. Package and move the module to your virtual Machine.
6. Deploy and restart Tomcat.

Here's an important note about the content model schema that may save you some time: Order matters. For example, if a type has both properties and associations, properties go first. If you get the order wrong, Alfresco won't be able to parse your model. There is an XML Schema file that declares the syntax for a content model XML file. It is called `modelSchema.xsd`, and it's packaged in the `alfresco-repository-5.x.jar` file (in the directory alfresco | model) that resides in the Alfresco web application under **WEB-INF|lib**.

Again, Tomcat should start cleanly with no complaints about the content model. You can use the two following URLs:

- To validate that the property has been added to the type:
  `http://localhost:8080/alfresco/s/api/classes/sc_marketingDoc`
- To validate that the constraint is properly defined:
  `http://localhost:8080/alfresco/s/api/classes/sc_marketingDoc/property/sc_campaign`

Step-by-step – relating types with associations

SomeCo has a generic need to be able to identify documents that relate to each other for any reason. A Whitepaper might be tied to a solution offering data sheet, for example. Or maybe a project proposal the Legal department has should be related to the project plan the Operations team is managing. These relationships are called **associations**.

Let's update the model file to include a related-documents association in the `sc:doc` type so that any SomeCo document can be related to any other.

To add assocations to the model, follow these steps:

1. Edit the `scModel.xml` file.
2. Add the following `associations` element to the `sc:doc` type. Notice that the target of the association must be an `sc:doc` or one of its child types. The association is not mandatory, and there may be more than one related document:

```
<type name="sc:doc">
    <title>Someco Document</title>
    <parent>cm:content</parent>
    <associations>
        <association name="sc:relatedDocuments">
            <title>Related Documents</title>
            <source>
```

```
                    <mandatory>false</mandatory>
                    <many>true</many>
                </source>
                <target>
                    <class>sc:doc</class>
                    <mandatory>false</mandatory>
                    <many>true</many>
                </target>
            </association>
        </associations>
    </type>
```

3. Save the `model` file.
4. Stop Alfresco.
5. Package and move the module to your virtual machine.
6. Deploy and restart Tomcat.

When you restart, watch the log for errors related to the content model. If everything is clean, keep going. You can as well use the following URL to check that your association is properly defined:
`http://localhost:8080/alfresco/s/api/classes/sc_doc`

Associations

Associations define relationships between types. Without associations, models would be full of types with properties that store "pointers" to other pieces of content. Going back to the expense report example, suppose each expense is stored as an individual object. In addition to an Expense Report type, there would also be an Expense type. In this example, associations can be used to tell Alfresco about the relationship between an Expense Report and one or more Expenses.

In the `sc:relatedDocuments` association you just defined, note that both the source and target class of the association is `sc:doc`. That's because SomeCo wants to associate documents with each other regardless of content type. Defining the association at the `sc:doc` level allows any instance of `sc:doc` or its children to be associated with zero or more instances of `sc:doc` or its children. It also assumes that SomeCo is using `sc:doc` or children of that type for all of its content. Content stored as the more generic `cm:content` type would not be able to be the target of an `sc:relatedDocuments` association.

Associations come in two flavors: Peer Associations and Child Associations. (Note that Alfresco refers to Peer Associations simply as "Associations", but that's confusing. So the book will use the "Peer" distinction.) Peer Associations are just that-they define a relationship between two objects, but neither is subordinate to the other. Child Associations, on the other hand, are used when the target of the association (or child) should not exist when the source (or parent) goes away. This works like a cascaded delete in a relational database: Delete the parent and the child goes away.

An out-of-the-box association that's easy to relate to is `cm:contains`. The `cm:contains` association defines a Child Association between folders (`cm:folder`) and all other objects (instances of `sys:base` or its child types). So, for example, a folder named `HumanResources` (an instance of `cm:folder`) would have a `cm:contains` association between itself and all of its immediate children. The children could be instances of custom types like Resume, Policy, or Performance Review. If you delete a folder, the folder's children are also deleted.

Another example might be a "Whitepaper" and its "Related Documents". Suppose that SomeCo publishes Whitepapers on its web site. The Whitepaper might be related to other documents such as product marketing materials or other research. If the relationship between the Whitepaper and its related documents is formalized, it can be shown in the user interface. To implement this, as part of the Whitepaper content type, you'd define a Peer Association. You could use `sys:base` as the target type to allow any piece of content in the repository to be associated with a Whitepaper, or you could restrict the association to a specific type. In this case, because it uses a Peer association, related documents don't get deleted when the Whitepaper gets deleted. You can imagine the headaches that would cause if that weren't the case!

Step-by-step – adding aspects to the content model

SomeCo wants to track the client name and, optionally, the project name for pieces of client-related content. But any piece of content in the repository might be client-related. Proposals and Status Reports are both project-related, but the two will be in different parts of the model (one is a type of legal document while the other is a type of operations document). Whether a piece of content is client-related or not, it transcends department-almost anything can be client-related. The grouping of properties that need to be tracked for content that is client-related is called an **aspect**.

Here's another example. SomeCo would like to selectively pull content from the repository to show on its web site. Again, any piece of content could be published on the site. So an indication of whether or not a piece of content is "webable" should be captured in an aspect. Specifically, content that needs to be shown on the web site needs to have a flag that indicates the content is "active" and a date when the content was set to active. These will be the aspect's properties.

Let's modify the content model to include these two aspects. To add the client-related and webable aspects to the content model, follow these steps:

1. Edit the scModel.xml file.

2. Add a new aspects element after the closing types tag to contain the new aspects. Add one aspect element to define the client-related aspect and another to define the web-related aspect. You'll notice that the syntax for the aspect element is identical to the type element:

```
<aspects>
    <aspect name="sc:webable">
        <title>SomecoWebable</title>
        <properties>
            <property name="sc:published">
                <type>d:date</type>
            </property>
            <property name="sc:isActive">
                <type>d:boolean</type>
                <default>false</default>
            </property>
        </properties>
    </aspect>
    <aspect name="sc:clientRelated">
        <title>Someco Client Metadata</title>
        <properties>
            <property name="sc:clientName">
                <type>d:text</type>
                <mandatory>true</mandatory>
            </property>
            <property name="sc:projectName">
                <type>d:text</type>
                <mandatory>false</mandatory>
            </property>
        </properties>
    </aspect>
</aspects>
```

3. Save the model file.

4. Stop Alfresco.
5. Package and move the module to your virtual machine.
6. Deploy and restart Tomcat.

Alfresco should start cleanly without making any model-related complaints. Using the two following URLs, you can check that the aspect have been created properly:

- `http://localhost:8080/alfresco/service/api/classes/sc_webable`
- `http://localhost:8080/alfresco/service/api/classes/sc_clientRel ated`

Aspects

To appreciate aspects, first consider how inheritance works and its implications on the content model. Suppose that SomeCo only wants to display a subset of the repository's content on the web site. (In fact, this is the case. The SomeCo write-up in `Chapter 1`, *The Alfresco Platform*, said that, except for job postings, HR content shouldn't go near the public web.) In the recent example, webable content needs to have a flag that indicates whether or not it is "active", and a date that indicates when it became active.

Without aspects, there would only be two options to model these properties. The first option would be to put the properties on `sc:doc`, the root object. All child content types would inherit from this root type, thus making the properties available everywhere. The second option would be to individually define the two properties only in the content types that will be published to the portal.

Neither of these is a great option. In the first option, there would be properties in each and every piece of content in the repository that may or may not ultimately be used. This can lead to performance and maintenance problems. The second option too isn't much better for several reasons. First, it assumes that the content types to be published to the portal are known when you design the model. Second, it opens up the possibility that the same type of metadata might get defined differently across content types. Third, it doesn't provide an easy way to encapsulate behavior or business logic that might be tied to the published date. Finally, property names must be unique across the model. So you'd have to modify the names of the properties in every type in which they were used, otherwise it would be a serious pain later when you try to run queries across types.

As you already know, the best option is to use aspects. Aspects allow "cross-cutting" of the content model with properties and associations by attaching them to content types (or even specific instances of content at runtime rather than design time) when and where they are needed.

In this case, SomeCo's webable aspect will be added to any piece of content that needs to be displayed on the web site, regardless of type.

Another nice thing about aspects is that they give you a way to have multiple inheritances. As you saw in the model, types can only inherit from a single parent. But you can add as many aspects to a type or object instance as you need.

Step-by-step – finishing up the model

Let's finish up the model by doing two things: First, the remaining departments need content types added to them. Second, there is an out of the box aspect that needs to be applied to all the content. It's called `generalclassifiable`. It allows content to be categorized. SomeCo wants all of its content to be classifiable as soon as it hits the repository. To make that happen, you need to define the aspect as mandatory. Because SomeCo wants it across the board, you can do it on the root type `sc:doc`, and have it trickle down to all of SomeCo's types.

To add the remaining departmental content types as well as make the `generalclassifiable` aspect mandatory, follow these steps:

1. Edit the `scModel.xml` file.
2. Add the the following types:

```xml
<type name="sc:hrDoc">
    <title>Someco HR Document</title>
    <parent>sc:doc</parent>
</type>

<type name="sc:salesDoc">
    <title>Someco Sales Document</title>
    <parent>sc:doc</parent>
</type>

<type name="sc:opsDoc">
    <title>Someco Operations Document</title>
    <parent>sc:doc</parent>
</type>

<type name="sc:legalDoc">
    <title>Someco Legal Document</title>
    <parent>sc:doc</parent>
</type>
```

3. Modify the `sc:doc` type to include `cm:generalclassifiable` as a mandatory aspect. Note that you can add as many mandatory aspects as you need:

```
<type name="sc:doc">
    <title>Someco Document</title>
    <parent>cm:content</parent>
    <associations>
        <association name="sc:relatedDocuments">
            <title>Related Documents</title>
            <source>
                <mandatory>false</mandatory>
                <many>true</many>
            </source>
            <target>
                <class>sc:doc</class>
                <mandatory>false</mandatory>
                <many>true</many>
            </target>
        </association>
    </associations>
    <mandatory-aspects>
        <aspect>cm:generalclassifiable</aspect>
    </mandatory-aspects>
</type>
```

4. Save the `model` file.
5. Stop Alfresco.
6. Package and move the module to your virtual machine.
7. Deploy and restart Tomcat.

Watch the log for content model-related errors. If everything starts up cleanly, you are ready to move on. You can check that everything is properly defined by opening this URL (`http://localhost:8080/alfresco/service/api/classes?nsp=sc`).In the next set of examples, you'll configure Alfresco Share so that you can work with your new model.

Manage property indexing

Directly in your content model, you can specify how your properties will be indexed by Solr. Below each property, you can add an index element like this one (that contains the default value):

```
<index enabled='true'>
    <atomic>true</atomic>
    <stored>false</stored>
    <tokenised>true</tokenised>
</index>
```

Here is the list of possible configuration:

- Change the enabled attribute to false to do not index this specific property. It means that you won't be able to search on it.
- Change the `atomic` property depending if you want properties to be indexed as part of the transaction commit (`true`), or indexed in the background (`false`). For example, the properties using `typed:content` are indexed in the background because some transformations need to be done before indexing.
- Change the `stored` property if you want to store the property value in the index. This property should never be changed in production. Set it to false only for debugging purposes.
- Change the `tokenised` property to control how values are tokenized in the index. If you use true, the string value will be tokenized before indexing. If you use false, the string value will be indexed as it is. If you use both, both forms will be used.

Configuring the indexing of your properties can be very useful and improve your system greatly. Just be very careful and sure to understand the consequences before deploying a change in production.

Modeling summary

A content model describes the data being stored in the repository. The content model is critical. Without it, Alfresco would be little more than a file system. Here is a list of key information that the content model provides Alfresco:

- Fundamental data types and how those data types should persist to the database. For example, without a content model, Alfresco wouldn't know the difference between a string and a date.
- Higher order data types such as "content" and "folder" as well as custom content types such as "SomeCo Standard Operating Procedure" or "SomeCo Sales Contract".
- Out-of-the-box aspects such as "auditable" and "classifiable" as well as SomeCo-specific aspects such as "rateable" or "client-related".
- Properties (or metadata) specific to each content type.
- Constraints placed on properties (such as property values that must match a certain pattern or property values that must come from a specific list of possible values).
- Relationships or "associations" between content types.

Alfresco content models are built using the following small set of building blocks:

- Types
- Properties
- Property Types
- Constraints
- Associations
- Aspects

When planning your Alfresco implementation, it may make sense to diagram the proposed content model just as you would a data model in a traditional web application.

The content model implemented in the examples could be diagrammed as follows:

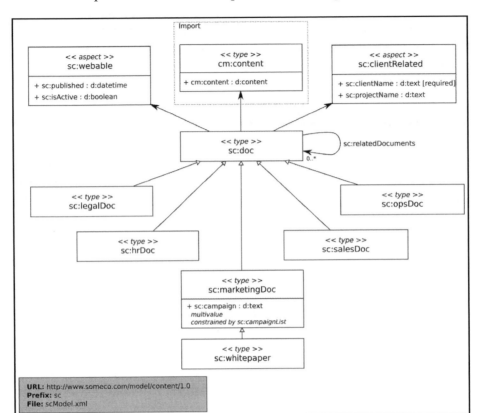

The Appendix contains similar diagrams for the out of the box content models for your reference.

Custom behavior

You may find that your custom aspect or custom type needs to have behavior or business logic associated with it. For example, every time an Expense Report is checked in, you might want to recalculate the total by iterating through the associated Expenses. One option would be to incorporate this logic into actions and rules in your Alfresco repository. But some behaviors are so fundamental to the aspect or type that they should really be "bound" to the aspect or type, and invoked any time Alfresco works with those objects.

Behavior really gets out of the realm of modeling and into "handling content automatically", which is the subject of `Chapter 4`, *Handling Content Automatically with Actions, Behaviors, Transformers, and Extractors*. For now, just realize that associating business logic with your custom aspects and types (or overriding out of the box behavior) is possible.

Modeling best practices

Now that you know the building blocks of a content model, it makes sense to consider some best practices. Here are the top ten:

1. *Don't change Alfresco's out of the box content model.* If you can possibly avoid it, do not change Alfresco's out of the box content model. Instead, extend it with your own custom content model. If requirements call for several different types of content to be stored in the repository, create a content type for each one that extends from `cm:content` or from an enterprise-wide root content type.

2. *Consider implementing an enterprise-wide root type.* Although the need for a common ancestor type is lessened through the use of aspects, it still might be a good idea to define an enterprise-wide root content type such as `sc:doc` from which all other content types in the repository inherit, if for no other reason, than it gives content managers a "catch-all" type to use when no other type will do.In the case that Alfresco is being deployed across multiple departments, it's possible to add a department-wide root type that extends from the enterprise-wide root type.

3. *Be conservative early on by adding only what you know you need.* A corollary to that is to be prepared to blow away the repository multiple times, until the content model stabilizes. Once you get content in the repository (that implements the types in your model), making model additions is easy, but subtractions aren't. A good practice is just to keep it in your content model file and add a comment saying that this property, type or aspect is deprecated. By following this practice, you are sure that Alfresco won't complain about "integrity errors" and may make content inaccessible when the content's type or properties don't match the content model definition.

4. *Take advantage of aspects.* In addition to the potential performance and overhead savings through the use of aspects, aspects promote reuse across the model, the business logic, and the presentation layer. When working on your model, you may find that two or more content types have properties in common such as `sc:webable` and `sc:clientRelated`. Ask yourself if those properties are being used to describe some higher-level characteristic common across the types that might be modeled better as an aspect.

5. *It may make sense to define aspect or types that have no properties or associations.* You may find yourself defining a type that gets everything it needs through either inheritance from a parent type or from an aspect (or both). In the SomeCo model `sc:marketingDoc` is the only type with a property. You might ask yourself if the empty type is really necessary. It should at least be considered. It might be worth it, just to distinguish the content from other types of content for search purposes, for example. Or, while you might not have any specialized properties or associations for the content type, you could have specialized behavior that's only applicable to instances of the content type.

6. *Remember that folders are types too.* Like everything else in the repository, folders are instances of types, which means they can be extended. Content that "contains" other content is common. In the earlier expense report example, one way to keep track of the expenses associated with an expense report would be to model the expense report as a sub-type of `cm:folder`.

7. *Don't be afraid to have more than one content model XML file.* When it is time to implement your model, keep this in mind: It might make sense to segment your models into multiple namespaces and multiple XML files. Names should be descriptive. Don't deploy a model file called `customModel.xml` or `myModel.xml`.

8. *Implement a Java interface that corresponds to each custom content model you define.* Within each content model Java class, define constants that correspond to model namespaces, type names, property names, aspect names, and so on. You'll find yourself referring to the qualified name (`Qname`, for short) of types, properties, and aspects quite often; so it helps to have constants defined in an intuitive way. The constants should be `QName` objects except in cases where the Web Services API needs to leverage them. The Web Services API doesn't have the `QName` class, so there will need to be a string representation of the names as well in that case. You can find an example for the default Alfesco content model here: `https://gitlab.alfresco.com/platform/alfresco-data-model/blob/master/src/main/java/org/alfresco/model/ContentModel.java`

9. *Use the source!* The out of the box content model is a great example of what's possible. The `forumModel`(`https://svn.alfresco.com/repos/alfresco-open-mirror/alfresco/HEAD/root/projects/repository/config/alfresco/model/forumModel.xml`) has some particularly useful examples. In the next section you'll learn where the model files live and what's in each. So you'll know where to look later when you say to yourself, "Surely, the folks at Alfresco have done this before".

This last point is important enough to spend a little more time on. The next section discusses the out of the box models in additional detail.

Out-of-the-box models

The Alfresco source code is an indispensable reference tool that you should always have ready along with the documentation, wiki, forums, and Jira. The out of the box content model files are written in XML and get deployed with the Alfresco engine. They can be found in the `alfresco-repository-5.x.jar` and `alfresco-data-model-5.x.jar` files deployed in the `alfresco.war` file in **|WEB-INF|lib**. You'll need to unzip the JAR file to be able to see all content models in the sub-directory **alfresco|model**. The following table describes several of the model files that can be found in the directory:

File	Namespaces*	Prefix	Imports	Description
dictionaryModel.xml	model|dictionary|1.0	d	None	Fundamental data types used in all other models like text, int, Boolean, datetime, and content. This is the only model packaged in alfresco-data-model-5.x.jar.
systemModel.xml	model|system|1.0 system|registry|1.0 system|modules|1.0	sys reg module	d	System-level objects like base, store root, and reference.
contentModel.xml	model|content|1.0 model|rendition|1.0 EXIF|exif|1.0 Audio|audio|1.0 WebDAV|webdav|1.0	cm rn exif audio webdav	d sys	Types and aspects extended most often by your models like Content, Folder, Versionable, and Auditable.
bpmModel.xml	model|bpm|1.0	bpm	d sys cm usr	Advanced workflow types like task and startTask. Extend these when writing your own custom advanced workflows.
siteModel.xml	model|site|1.0 model|sitecustomproperty|1.0	st stcp	d cm sys	Types and aspects related to collaboration sites

forumModel.xml	model|forum|1.0	fm	d cm	Types and aspects related to adding discussion threads to objects like forum, topic, and post

The table lists the most often referenced models. Alfresco also includes four other model files related to the calendar, blog, datalist, links pages. It contains as well some models to manage external integration with Facebook, Twitter, FlickR or Youtube. And many others...

In addition to the model files, the modelSchema.xsd file can be a good reference. It is located in **alfresco\|model** in the alfresco-data-model-5.x.jar file. As the name suggests, it defines the XML vocabulary Alfresco content model XML files must adhere to.

Configuring the UI

Now that the model is defined, you could begin using it right away by writing code against one of Alfresco's APIs that creates instances of your custom types, adds aspects, and so on. In practice, it is usually a good idea to do just that to make sure the model behaves as you expect. But you'd probably like to log in to Alfresco Share to see the fruits of your labor from the last section, so let's discuss what it takes to make that happen. By the end of this discussion, you will be able to use Alfresco Share to work with the SomeCo-specific content model to do things such as these:

- Display and update custom properties and associations
- Create instances of SomeCo-specific content types
- Configure actions that involve SomeCo types and aspects
- Use Advanced Search to query with SomeCo-specific parameters

Configuring the UI to expose the custom content model involves overriding and extending Alfresco's out of the box Share configuration. To do this, you'll use different extension points provided by Alfresco Share.

Step-by-step – configure Share forms

When a user opens the details page of a content stored as one of the custom types or with one of the custom aspects attached, the property sheet should show the custom properties. If there are associations, those should be shown as well:

In order to configure the properties sheet to show custom properties and associations, follow these steps:

1. In the `share` Eclipse project, create a new XML file called `share-config-custom.xml` in the directory `share | src | main | resources | META-INF | share-config-custom.xml`. Populate it with an empty `alfresco-config` element. You'll add child elements to it in the subsequent steps.

   ```
   <alfresco-config>
   </alfresco-config>
   ```

2. To display properties to property sheets, use the `aspect` evaluator for aspects and the `node-type` evaluator for content types. SomeCo has two aspects that need to be added to the properties sheet: `sc:webable` and `sc:clientRelated`. For `sc:webable`, add the following `config` element to `share-config-custom.xml` as a child of `alfresco-config`:

   ```
   <configevaluator="aspect"condition="sc:webable">
       <forms>
           <form>
               <field-visibility>
                   <show id="sc:published"/>
                   <show id="sc:isActive"/>
               </field-visibility>
               <appearance>
                   <field id="sc:isActive"read-only="true"/>
               </appearance>
           </form>
   ```

```
          </forms>
      </config>
```

3. Add the `config` element to show the properties for the `clientRelated` aspect on your own.

4. Add the following to display the `relatedDocuments` association for SomeCo documents and Marketing documents:

```
<config evaluator="node-type" condition="sc:doc">
    <forms>
        <form>
            <field-visibility>
                <show id="cm:name" />
                <show id="cm:title" force="true" />
                <show id="cm:description" force="true" />
                <show id="mimetype" />
                <show id="cm:author" force="true" />
                <show id="size" for-mode="view" />
                <show id="cm:creator" for-mode="view" />
                <show id="cm:created" for-mode="view" />
                <show id="cm:modifier" for-mode="view" />
                <show id="cm:modified" for-mode="view" />
                <show id="sc:relatedDocuments" />
            </field-visibility>
        </form>
    </forms>
</config>
<config evaluator="node-type" condition="sc:marketingDoc">
    <forms>
        <form>
            <field-visibility>
                <show id="cm:name" />
                <show id="cm:title" force="true" />
                <show id="cm:description" force="true" />
                <show id="mimetype" />
                <show id="cm:author" force="true" />
                <show id="size" for-mode="view" />
                <show id="cm:creator" for-mode="view" />
                <show id="cm:created" for-mode="view" />
                <show id="cm:modifier" for-mode="view" />
                <show id="cm:modified" for-mode="view" />
                <show id="sc:campaign" />
                <show id="sc:relatedDocuments" />
            </field-visibility>
        </form>
    </forms>
</config>
```

5. Do the same by yourself to create the same configuration for the Whitepaper documents using the Marketing document as example.

6. Do the same by yourself to create the same configuration for the HR, Sales, Operations and Legal documents using the SomeCo document as example.

7. Save the file.

Unfortunately, you don't have an easy way to test your new configuration yet. We need to follow the next section to be able to specialize a content.

In the previous code, the read-only attribute on the field element for `sc:isActive` prevents users from editing the property. It does not, however, prevent the property from being set through scripts or API calls. In this case, SomeCo wants it to be "read-only", so that it can be set through other means such as by actions or during an approval step in a workflow.

Step-by-step – adding types and aspects to Alfresco Share dropdowns

When a user uploads a document in Alfresco, it uses the default type `cm:content`. However, it's possible to change or to specialize the type through Alfresco Share. As well, when you want to configure a rule on a folder, you may want to apply it only on documents using specific content types or aspects. In the create rule screen, the dropdown list will include automatically your custom types.

Just as you did for custom properties and associations in the previous example, you have to override Alfresco Share configuration to get custom types and aspects to show up.

To add custom types and aspects to the appropriate dropdowns, follow these steps:

1. Edit `share-config-custom.xml`.

2. To add content types to the list of available types in the **change type** dialog, use the `string-compare` **evaluator** and the `DocumentLibrarycondition`.

```
<config evaluator="string-compare"
    condition="DocumentLibrary" replace="true">
</config>
```

3. As you can see below, the list of valid child types depends of the parent type. Add the following inside the `config` element:

```
<types>
    <type name="cm:content">
        <subtype name="smf:smartFolderTemplate" />
        <subtype name="sc:doc" />
        <subtype name="sc:marketingDoc" />
        <subtype name="sc:whitepaper" />
        <subtype name="sc:hrDoc" />
        <subtype name="sc:salesDoc" />
        <subtype name="sc:opsDoc" />
        <subtype name="sc:legalDoc" />
    </type>

    <type name="sc:doc">
        <subtype name="sc:marketingDoc" />
        <subtype name="sc:whitepaper" />
        <subtype name="sc:hrDoc" />
        <subtype name="sc:salesDoc" />
        <subtype name="sc:opsDoc" />
        <subtype name="sc:legalDoc" />
    </type>

    <type name="cm:folder">
    </type>

    <type name="trx:transferTarget">
        <subtype name="trx:fileTransferTarget" />
    </type>
</types>
```

4. To add aspects to the list of available aspects in the **manage aspects** dialog, use the same `config` element, just add the following after `</types>` (note that the addable and removable tags are empty, it means that we'll use the same list as the `visible` tag. It allows to avoid duplication):

```
<aspects>
    <visible>
        <aspect name="cm:generalclassifiable" />
        <aspect name="cm:complianceable" />
        <aspect name="cm:dublincore" />
        <aspect name="cm:effectivity" />
        <aspect name="cm:summarizable" />
        <aspect name="cm:versionable" />
        <aspect name="cm:templatable" />
        <aspect name="cm:emailed" />
```

```
            <aspect name="emailserver:aliasable" />
            <aspect name="cm:taggable" />
            <aspect name="app:inlineeditable" />
            <aspect name="cm:geographic" />
            <aspect name="exif:exif" />
            <aspect name="audio:audio" />
            <aspect name="cm:indexControl" />
            <aspect name="dp:restrictable" />
            <aspect name="smf:customConfigSmartFolder" />
            <aspect name="smf:systemConfigSmartFolder" />
            <aspect name="sc:webable" />
            <aspect name="sc:clientRelated" />
        </visible>
        <addable></addable>
        <removeable></removeable>
    </aspects>
```

5. Save the `share-config-custom.xml` file.
6. Stop Alfresco.
7. Package and move the module to your virtual machine. (As usual, feel free to run first the project from your machine using Maven to test.)
8. Deploy and restart Tomcat.

Now, let's finally test our configuration. You should be able to log in to Alfresco Share and upload a document. Open the details page of this document by clicking on the document name, and click on the **Change Type** action in the right toolbar. You should see this dialog:

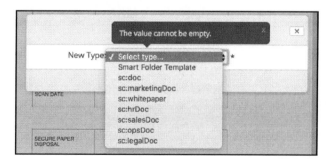

Select **sc:doc** and validate. Automatically, the panel **Properties** on the right side is updated and should display your custom association:

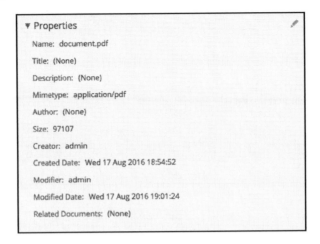

If you edit the properties, you'll be able to populate your association. Remember that you can only create association with `sc:doc` documents. If you want to test this feature, we recommend you to create multiple files and change the type to all of them to be able to test the association. Click on the **Change Type** action, and the new list of types should be shorter:

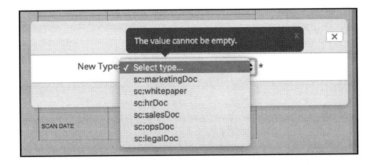

Select **sc:whitepaper**. Automatically, the panel **Properties** on the right side is updated and should display your custom property related to the campaign:

By clicking on the **Edit Properties** button, you should see a component that lets you choose the associated campaigns.

To test the aspect-related changes, click on the **Manage Aspects** action. At the bottom of the list, you should see the two SomeCo aspects:

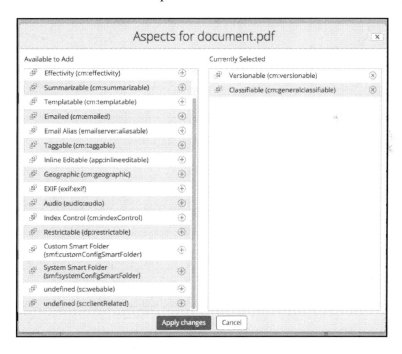

Select the two SomeCo aspects, and check the **Properties** panel. You should see four new properties displayed.

To test the changes related to rules, click on **Manage Rules** action on a folder and create a new one. If you want to use the type as criteria, you can use the SomeCo types:

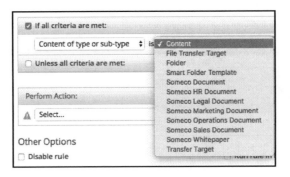

You can use as well the aspect as criteria:

Finally, you can check that you can use the SomeCo content types if you want to specialize a content in the **Perform Action** section. You can use as well the SomeCo aspects in the **Add Aspect** and **Remove Aspect** action.

Step-by-step – externalizing display labels

Note that some labels show the technical name. For example, the **Properties** panel displays properly the association by displaying **Related Documents**. However, it doesn't display properly the campaign property. The first reason is that we used the tag title on the association, and not on the campaign property. We could populate directly all titles in the content model. But a better practice is to externalize the string so that the interface can be localized if needed.

1. In the `share` Eclipse project, edit the file `share.properties` located in the directory `share | src | main | amp | config | alfresco | web-extension | message`. Add the following properties:

   ```
   type.sc_doc=Someco Document
   type.sc_marketingDoc=Someco Marketing Document
   type.sc_whitepaper=Someco Whitepaper
   type.sc_hrDoc=Someco HR Document
   type.sc_salesDoc=Someco Sales Document
   type.sc_opsDoc=Someco Operations Document
   type.sc_legalDoc=Someco Legal Document
   aspect.sc_webable=SomecoWebable
   aspect.sc_clientRelated=Someco Client Metadata
   ```

2. In the `repo` Eclipse project, create the file `scModel.properties` in the directory `repo | src | main | amp | config | alfresco | module | repo | messages`. Add the following properties:

   ```
   sc_somecomodel.type.sc_doc.title=Someco Document
   sc_somecomodel.type.sc_marketingDoc.title=Someco Marketing Document
   sc_somecomodel.type.sc_whitepaper.title=SomecoWhitepaper
   sc_somecomodel.type.sc_hrDoc.title=Someco HR Document
   sc_somecomodel.type.sc_salesDoc.title=Someco Sales Document
   sc_somecomodel.type.sc_opsDoc.title=Someco Operations Document
   sc_somecomodel.type.sc_legalDoc.title=Someco Legal Document
   sc_somecomodel.aspect.sc_webable.title=SomecoWebable
   sc_somecomodel.aspect.sc_clientRelated.title=Someco Client Metadata
   sc_somecomodel.association.sc_relatedDocuments.title=Related
   Documents
   sc_somecomodel.property.sc_campaign.title=Campaign
   sc_somecomodel.property.sc_published.title=Published date
   sc_somecomodel.property.sc_isActive.title=Active?
   sc_somecomodel.property.sc_clientName.title=Client Name
   sc_somecomodel.property.sc_projectName.title=Project Name
   ```

3. In the repo Eclipse project, locate the file `bootstrap-context.xml` in the directory `repo | src | main | amp | config | alfresco | module | repo | context`. Update the dictionary bootstrap by adding a new property:

```
<property name="labels">
  <list>
    <value>alfresco/module/${project.artifactId}
      /messages/scModel</value>
  </list>
</property>
```

4. Save these different files.
5. Stop Alfresco.
6. Package and move the modules to your virtual machine.
7. Deploy and restart Tomcat.
8. If you follow the same steps as explained in the previous *step-by-step* instructions, you should notice that all type, aspect and property titles are properly displayed.

Setting up additional locales

The whole point in externalizing the labels is that Alfresco Share can be localized to multiple languages. If you want to create a set of labels for a specific locale, you would create a file in the same directory called `scModel_[locale].properties` with the same keys and their localized values. For the share project, it's the same step. You need to create a file in the same directory called `share_[locale].properties` with the same keys and their localized values. Of course [locale] is just a placeholder for the locale identifier you are working one. If you want to create a message file containing the French values, the filenames will be `scModel_fr.properties` and `share_fr.properties`.

Step-by-step – adding properties and types to advanced search

When a user runs an advanced search, he or she should be able to restrict search results to instances of custom types and/or content with specific values for the properties of custom types. As before, this involves modifying `share-config-custom.xml`.

To add custom properties and types to the advanced search dialog, follow these steps:

1. First, we need to create a search form for each custom content type. Create a new `config` element with the `model-type` evaluator and the condition equals to the content type. Follow this template for the marketing document and whitepaper:

```xml
<config evaluator="model-type" condition="sc:marketingDoc">
    <forms>
        <form id="search">
          <field-visibility>
            <show id="cm:name" />
            <show id="cm:title" force="true" />
            <show id="cm:description" force="true" />
            <show id="mimetype" />
            <show id="cm:modifier" for-mode="view" />
            <show id="cm:modified" for-mode="view" />
            <show id="sc:campaign" />
            <show id="sc:relatedDocuments" />
          </field-visibility>
        </form>
    </forms>
</config>
```

2. Then, use the following templates for the other content types:

```xml
<config evaluator="model-type" condition="sc:hrDoc">
    <forms>
        <form>
          <field-visibility>
            <show id="cm:name" />
            <show id="cm:title" force="true" />
            <show id="cm:description" force="true" />
            <show id="mimetype" />
            <show id="cm:author" force="true" />
            <show id="size" for-mode="view" />
            <show id="cm:creator" for-mode="view" />
            <show id="cm:created" for-mode="view" />
            <show id="cm:modifier" for-mode="view" />
            <show id="cm:modified" for-mode="view" />
            <show id="sc:relatedDocuments" />
          </field-visibility>
        </form>
    </forms>
</config>
```

3. Finally, we need to enable these new search forms. In the same file, create a new
config element using the string-compare evaluator and the
AdvancedSearchcondition:

```
<config evaluator="string-compare" condition="AdvancedSearch">
    <advanced-search>
        <forms>
            <form labelId="type.sc_doc"
            descriptionId="search.form.label.sc_doc">
            sc:doc</form>
            <form labelId="type.sc_marketingDoc"
            descriptionId="search.form.label.sc_marketingDoc">
            sc:marketingDoc</form>
            <form labelId="type.sc_whitepaper"
            descriptionId="search.form.label.sc_whitepaper">
            sc:whitepaper</form>
            <form labelId="type.sc_hrDoc"
            descriptionId="search.form.label.sc_hrDoc">
            sc:hrDoc</form>
            <form labelId="type.sc_salesDoc"
            descriptionId="search.form.label.sc_salesDoc">
            sc:salesDoc</form>

            <form labelId="type.sc_opsDoc"
            descriptionId="search.form.label.sc_opsDoc">
            sc:opsDoc</form>
            <form labelId="type.sc_legalDoc"
            descriptionId="search.form.label.sc_legalDoc">
            sc:legalDoc</form>
        </forms>
    </advanced-search>
</config>
```

4. Save the share-config-custom.xml file.
5. Stop Alfresco.
6. Package and move the module to your virtual Machine.
7. Deploy and restart Tomcat.
8. To test out this change, log in to Alfresco Share and go to **Advanced Search**. The
SomeCo types should be listed in the **Look For** dropdown.

Working with content programmatically

Now the repository has a custom model and that model has been exposed to Alfresco Share. For simple document management solutions, this may be enough. But often, code will also be required as a part of your implementation. It might be code in a web application that needs to work with the repository, code that implements custom behavior for custom content types, code that implements Alfresco Share customizations, or code that implements a controller for a web script.

As mentioned in Chapter 1, *The Alfresco Platform*, there are several APIs available depending on what you want to do. Let's learn how to use code to create content, create associations between content, search for content, and delete content. You'll see a JavaScript example, several examples using the CMIS API with Java.

Step-by-step – creating content with JavaScript

The first example shows how to specialize some content and add aspects to that content using JavaScript. To specialize content, add aspects, and set properties using JavaScript, follow these steps:

1. Create a new file in **repo|src|scripts** called `createWhitepaper.js`.

2. Set up some variables you'll use later in the script. The `document` variable is a root object that is available when the script is executed against a document.

   ```
   var contentType = "whitepaper";
   var contentName = "wp-";
   var timestamp = new Date().getTime();
   var extension = document.name.substr(document
     .name.lastIndexOf('.') + 1);
   ```

3. Write code that will specialize the uploaded document.

   ```
   document.specializeType("sc:" + contentType);
   ```

4. Add a statement that uses the ScriptNode API to add the `sc:webable` aspect.

   ```
   document.addAspect("sc:webable");
   ```

5. Add code to set some properties. These properties include out of the box properties such as `cm:name` as well as SomeCo-specific properties. Notice the `contentName` and `timestamp` variables are being concatenated to make sure the name is unique on successive runs.

   ```
   document.properties["cm:name"] = contentName
       + " (" + timestamp + ")." + extension;
   document.properties["sc:isActive"] = true;
   document.properties["sc:published"] = new Date("07/31/2016");
   ```

6. Call save to persist the changes.

   ```
   document.save();
   ```

7. Test the script by uploading it to the repository and then running it against a folder. Using Alfresco Share, upload the file to the Data `Dictionary/Scripts` folder.

8. Create a new site called **Marketing**, open the **Document Library**, create a new folder called **Whitepapers**.

9. On this newly created folder, click on **Manage Rules**, **Create Rules**:

- **Name**: Create a new whitepaper
- **When**: Items are created or enter this folder
- **If**: Content of type of sub-type is Content
- **Perform Action**: Execute script `createWhitepaper.js`

10. Click on **Create.** Open the directory **Whitepapers**, and upload a new document.

The new document has been specialized to become a whitepaper. The name should be changed automatically, and you should notice the additional properties added to the document. Later in the book, you'll add a new UI action that makes executing scripts even easier.

Knowing when to save documents

Method calls that affect a node's properties require `save` to persist the changes. If in this example we were only adding an aspect, we wouldn't have to save the document because the change is persisted immediately.

Using JavaScript for batch manipulation

During projects you will often find that you need to perform batch operations on nodes in the repository. You might want to execute an action against all documents in all subfolders starting at a given path, for example. JavaScript is a quick way to perform such mass operations and doesn't require code to be compiled and packaged. Be aware that if you write such a script and run it on an important volume of documents in one shot, all of your changes will happen in a single transaction. This can be bad for performance of the script and can adversely affect index tracking.

Writing content to the content property

Properties store data about a node. The terms "metadata" and "attributes" are synonymous with "properties".

Content refers to the main unit of data being managed by the system—a file. A PDF file, for example, is a piece of content. Plain-text data such as XML, HTML, or JavaScript are also examples of content.

Content is stored as a property on the node. In Alfresco, the content is really stored on the file system, but as developers using the API, we don't care about where the content is physically stored. We could have created a whitepaper from scratch and populate the content of the document directly using Javascript.

Creating content with CMIS

JavaScript is fast to develop and very succinct, but it must run on the Alfresco server. CMIS API is one option to consider when you want to run code on a different machine than the Alfresco server. CMIS stands for Content Management Interoperability Services and has been created to improve the interoperability with different ECM solutions.

Let's do another example in this section. We'll try to create a Marketing document in Alfresco using the Java CMIS API. We'll create a new Maven project for this example.

1. An overview of the steps involved is: create a new Maven project, and add the CMIS dependency.
2. Authenticate to start a session.
3. Locate the document library and the marketing folder.
4. Create the **Marketing** folder if you didn't do it yet.
5. Create the new node with content.

The Apache Chemistry website (`https://chemistry.apache.org/`) provides already a lot of samples. First, let's create our new Maven project in STS. This time, we won't select any archetype. Don't forget to check **Create a simple project (skip archetype selection)**:

- Group Id: `com.someco`
- Artifact Id: `cmis`
- Click on **Finish**.

Then, let's open the `pom.xml` file and select the tab **Dependencies**. Click on **Add...**. Provide the following information:

- Group Id: `org.apache.chemistry.opencmis`
- Artifcat Id: `chemistry-opencmis-client-impl`
- Version: 0.13.0

That's it! We are ready to develop using CMIS. Create the Java class`com.someco.CmisClient` with a `main` method. The first thing that we need to do is to create a session to Alfresco:

```
SessionFactory factory = SessionFactoryImpl.newInstance();
Map<String, String> parameter = new HashMap<String, String>();
parameter.put(SessionParameter.USER, "admin");
parameter.put(SessionParameter.PASSWORD, "admin");
parameter.put(SessionParameter.ATOMPUB_URL,
"http://127.0.0.1:8080/alfresco/api/-default-/public/cmis/versions/1.1/atom
");
parameter.put(SessionParameter.BINDING_TYPE, BindingType.ATOMPUB.value());
parameter.put(SessionParameter.REPOSITORY_ID, "-default-");
Session session = factory.createSession(parameter);
```

Then, locate the document library folder of the Marketing Site that we created previously:

```
String path = "/Sites/marketing/documentLibrary";
Folder documentLibrary = (Folder) session.getObjectByPath(path);
```

In the document library, we try to locate the `Marketing` folder:

```
Folder marketingFolder = null;
for (CmisObjectchild :documentLibrary.getChildren()) {
    if ("Marketing".equals(child.getName())) {
        marketingFolder = (Folder) child;
    }
}
```

We have to consider that this folder may not exist. So, we need to create it on the fly:

```
// create the marketing folder if needed
if (marketingFolder == null) {
    Map<String, Object> properties = new HashMap<String, Object>();
    properties.put(PropertyIds.NAME, "Marketing");
    properties.put(PropertyIds.OBJECT_TYPE_ID, "cmis:folder");
    marketingFolder = documentLibrary.createFolder(properties);
}
```

Now, we are now ready to prepare the creation of our new document. The first step is to prepare the required properties:

```
// prepare properties
String filename = "My new whitepaper.txt";
Map<String, Object> properties = new HashMap<String, Object>();
properties.put(PropertyIds.NAME, filename);
properties.put(PropertyIds.OBJECT_TYPE_ID, "D:sc:marketingDoc");
```

Then, we can prepare the content. In this sample, we'll create a text file:

```
// prepare content
String content = "Hello World!";
String mimetype = "text/plain; charset=UTF-8";
byte[] contentBytes = content.getBytes("UTF-8");
ByteArrayInputStream stream = new ByteArrayInputStream(contentBytes);
ContentStreamcontentStream =
session.getObjectFactory().createContentStream(filename,
contentBytes.length, mimetype, stream);
```

Finally, we are ready to create the document:

```
// create the document
Document marketingDocument = marketingFolder.createDocument(properties,
contentStream, VersioningState.MAJOR);
```

Of course, you'll need to import all dependencies in your Java class. STS provides you a way of doing it quickly by clicking on **Source | Organize Imports**.

Step-by-step – run CmisClientClass to create content

To run the CmisTest class to create some content, follow these steps:

1. Right click on the project cmis.
2. Click on **Run As**, **Java Application**.

If everything is successful, you should be able to login to Alfresco Share, and locate your newly created document in the Marketing folder.

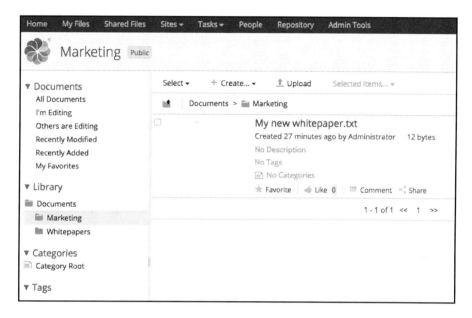

Creating associations

Now let's switch back to the CMIS API and look at how to create a related-documents association between two documents.

We'll just update the existing Java code that we wrote previously. The only missing information is the document that we want to create an association with. To achieve that, we'll look for a document in the Whitepapers folder.

Following the same principles that we used to locate the Marketing folder, we can retrieve all children of the document library and look for the right folder. In this case, we assume that this folder exists.

```
Folder whitepaperFolder = null;
for (CmisObjectchild :documentLibrary.getChildren()) {
    if ("Whitepapers".equals(child.getName())) {
        whitepaperFolder = (Folder) child;
    }
}
```

Then, we need to look for any whitepaper in this folder:

```
// look for a whitepaper
Document whitepaper = null;
for (CmisObjectchild :whitepaperFolder.getChildren()) {
    if (child.getType().getId().equals("D:sc:whitepaper"))
        whitepaper = (Document) child;
}
```

And finally, you can create the association:

```
properties = new HashMap<String, Object>();
properties.put(PropertyIds.NAME, "a new relationship");
properties.put(PropertyIds.OBJECT_TYPE_ID, "R:sc:relatedDocuments");
properties.put(PropertyIds.SOURCE_ID, marketingDocument.getId());
properties.put(PropertyIds.TARGET_ID, whitepaper.getId());
session.createRelationship(properties);
```

Re-execute the Java class. Before, you need to delete the file manually from Share. If you don't do it, you'll have an error indicating that a file already exists with the same name in the `Marketing` folder. If it's executed successfully, you'll be able that our marketing document is associated to one of the whitepaper that we created before. Alternatively, the Node Browser that is available in the Administration Console is a handy way to view associations.

Searching for content

Now that you have some content in the repository, you can test out the CMIS Search API. In this example, we'll look for all SomeCo documents available in the repository. And for each document, we'll display all properties available on each document.

We are going to encapsulate this into a new function:

```
private static void searchDocuments(Session session) {
}
```

Then, we need to query Alfresco:

```
ItemIterable<QueryResult> results = session.query("SELECT * FROM sc:doc",
false);
```

Finally, we just have to browse the list of results:

```
for (QueryResulthit : results) {
    for (PropertyData<?>property :hit.getProperties()) {
        String queryName = property.getQueryName();
        Object value = property.getFirstValue();
        System.out.println(queryName + ": " + value);
    }
    System.out.println("-------------------------------------");
}
```

In my repository, I have three documents, including 1 white papers and one marketing document. Here is an example of document:

```
alfcmis:nodeRef: workspace://SpacesStore/978751b1-7cc7-4be6-
aed9-2ff33f438df6
cmis:isImmutable: false
cmis:versionLabel: 1.0
cmis:objectTypeId: D:sc:whitepaper
cmis:description: null
cmis:createdBy: admin
cmis:checkinComment: null
cmis:creationDate: java.util.GregorianCalendar[...]
cmis:isMajorVersion: true
cmis:contentStreamFileName: wp- (1471536191073).pdf
cmis:name: wp- (1471536191073).pdf
cmis:isLatestVersion: true
cmis:lastModificationDate: java.util.GregorianCalendar[...]
cmis:contentStreamLength: 141120
cmis:objectId: 978751b1-7cc7-4be6-aed9-2ff33f438df6;1.0
cmis:lastModifiedBy: admin
cmis:secondaryObjectTypeIds: P:rn:renditioned
cmis:contentStreamId: store://2016/8/18/16/3/31dcb9be-4e50-4221-
b8d5-77deb3b044ac.bin
cmis:contentStreamMimeType: application/pdf
cmis:baseTypeId: cmis:document
cmis:changeToken: null
cmis:isPrivateWorkingCopy: false
cmis:versionSeriesCheckedOutBy: null
cmis:isVersionSeriesCheckedOut: false
cmis:versionSeriesId: 978751b1-7cc7-4be6-aed9-2ff33f438df6
cmis:isLatestMajorVersion: true
cmis:versionSeriesCheckedOutId: null
-------------------------------------
```

Deleting content

Now it is time to clean up after yourself by deleting content from the repository. In this sample, we'll delete all documents in the Marketing folder. Like that, you'll be able to execute a full cycle:

1. Create a new marketing document.
2. Confirm that it's created using the search API.
3. Delete the document created in the step 1.

We are going to encapsulate this into a new function:

```
private static void deleteDocuments(Session session) {
}
```

As previously, we need to look for the document library of the Marketing site:

```
String path = "/Sites/marketing/documentLibrary";
Folder documentLibrary = (Folder) session.getObjectByPath(path);
```

Then, we need to locate the Marketing folder:

```
Folder marketingFolder = null;
for (CmisObject child :documentLibrary.getChildren()) {
    if ("Marketing".equals(child.getName())) {
        marketingFolder = (Folder) child;
    }
}
```

Finally, we delete all children in this folder:

```
if (marketingFolder != null) {
    for (CmisObject child :marketingFolder.getChildren()) {
        session.delete(child);
    }
}
```

Note that this code deletes every matching object in the marketing folder. You would definitely want to *think twice and cut once* if you were running this code on a production repository!

Model manager

Alfresco provides an interactive tool to design your own custom model. It allows you to add custom types, aspects, and properties. On top of that, you can use the same tool to design the different forms for your content types and aspects. Open Alfresco Share and login as administrator, click on **Admin Tools**, click on **Model Manager**.

We are not going to discover how to use this tool but you'll notice that it follows exactly what we did to create our custom model manually. You could argue that it would have been easier to use this tool, instead of creating all these XML and properties file. However, I think that it's always important to really understand how it's configured and implemented from a pure technical point of view. Moreover, this tool doesn't cover all possibilities. For example, it's not possible to create association or child-association using this tool.

I would recommend this tool if you are looking for implementing a quick demonstration. But I don't think that it's the ideal tool for a real project, that you'll need to package and deploy in different environments. I recommend you to take a look and make your own opinion of it. Be aware that you can use the Model Manager first, then export the Alfresco content model and Share form configuration. You can refine these files manually after.

Summary

This chapter was about customizing Alfresco's content model, configuring Alfresco Share to allow end users to work with the custom content model via the user interface, and using the CMIS API to create, search, update, and delete objects in the repository. Let's recap what we specifically learned.

The Alfresco repository is a hierarchical collection of nodes.

The Alfresco content model defines the data types of nodes and properties, and the relationships between nodes.

Extending the content model to make it relevant to your business problem involves creating an XML file to describe the model, then telling Alfresco about it through a Spring bean configuration file.

The fundamental building blocks used to define the content model include: Types, Aspects, Properties, and Associations.

Best practices for creating your own content models include using aspects for re-usability, considering the use of a root content type, and leveraging the out of the box content model as a reference.

Configuring Alfresco Share to expose your custom content model via the user interface involves overriding configuration elements in the dedicated XML configuration file.

There are several options for interacting with the repository with code. Examples in this chapter included the CMIS API and the JavaScript API.

4

Handling Content Automatically with Actions, Behaviors, Transformers, and Extractors

Alfresco provides several types of hooks that can be used to perform interesting operations on content. Whether an operation is triggered by an end user, as is the case with Actions (sometimes called "**Rule Actions**"), or is handled automatically with Behaviors, Transformers, or Extractors. This chapter is about leveraging what is already available out of the box and, more importantly, how to develop your own when what is available doesn't meet your needs.

By the end of this chapter, you will know how to:

- Create your own actions using Java
- Bind Java- and JavaScript-based behavior to types and aspects
- Configure and extend metadata extractors
- Write custom content transformers

Encapsulating content operations in actions

As you might suspect, a repository action is a piece of code that can be executed against a piece of content. Actions are discrete units of work. Then, you have Share action representing an action that you can do in Alfresco Share. Some of the out-of-the-box Share actions are **Edit Online**, **Upload New Version**, **Edit Properties**, **Move to…**, **Copy to…**, **Start Workflow**, or **Delete Document**.

Most of the out-of-the-box Share actions are not linked directly to a repository action, most of them are linked to the Alfresco repository via webscripts. In this chapter, we will focus only on repository actions, and rules that can be configured in the UI and allow you to execute repository actions based on some criteria. Share actions will be covered in Chapter 5, *Customizing Alfresco Share*.

In the last chapter, SomeCo created some metadata related to publishing Whitepapers on the Web. The **sc:webable** aspect included a flag to identify whether or not a piece of content should show up on the Web as well as a published date that captures when the flag was set.

The **sc:isActive** flag was configured to be read-only, so SomeCo needs a way to set that flag. They might want to do it automatically when content is added to a folder, they might want to set it during a step in a workflow, or through a link in one of Alfresco Share menu. By using an action, you can write the code once and call it from all of those places.

Step-by-step – creating a basic action

At its most basic, a custom rule action requires three things:

- An action executer class.
- A Spring bean configuration file.
- A properties file to externalize action-related strings (this one is not required per se but is highly recommended)

Let's create an action to add the **sc:webable** aspect to a document, and set its **isActive** flag and publish date. By the end of these steps you will have an action that can be executed by an end user, a step in a workflow (and anywhere else Alfresco JavaScript can run), or a link in the user interface. Follow these steps:

1. The first class to create is SomeCoModel. This class will contain all Alfresco QName properties represented in our XML content model. Usually, you create this class at the same time you create the XML content model. Create a new class in your repo | src | main | java directory called com.someco.repo.common.SomeCoModel. Then, define the prefix and the model URI.

   ```
   public final static String SOMECO_MODEL_PREFIX= "sc";
   public final static String SOMECO_MODEL_URI =
        "http://www.someco.com/model/content/1.0";
   ```

2. Then, add all `QName` properties for the content types:

```
public final static QName TYPE_DOC =
    QName.createQName(SOMECO_MODEL_URI, "doc");
public final static QName TYPE_MARKETINGDOC =
    QName.createQName(SOMECO_MODEL_URI, "marketingDoc");
public final static QName TYPE_WHITEPAPER =
    QName.createQName(SOMECO_MODEL_URI, "whitepaper");
public final static QName TYPE_HRDOC =
    QName.createQName(SOMECO_MODEL_URI, "hrDoc");
public final static QName TYPE_SALESDOC =
    QName.createQName(SOMECO_MODEL_URI, "salesDoc");
public final static QName TYPE_HRPOLICY =
    QName.createQName(SOMECO_MODEL_URI, "hrPolicy");
public final static QName TYPE_LEGALDOC =
    QName.createQName(SOMECO_MODEL_URI, "legalDoc");
```

3. Then, add all `QName` properties for the aspects:

```
public final static QName ASPECT_WEBABLE =
    QName.createQName(SOMECO_MODEL_URI, "webable");
public final static QName ASPECT_CLIENTRELATED =
    QName.createQName(SOMECO_MODEL_URI, "clientRelated");
```

4. Then, add all `QName` properties for the properties and the association:

```
public final static QName PROP_CAMPAIGN =
    QName.createQName(SOMECO_MODEL_URI, "campaign");
public final static QName PROP_PUBLISHED =
    QName.createQName(SOMECO_MODEL_URI, "published");
public final static QName PROP_ISACTIVE =
    QName.createQName(SOMECO_MODEL_URI, "isActive");
public final static QName PROP_CLIENTNAME =
    QName.createQName(SOMECO_MODEL_URI, "clientName");
public final static QName PROP_PROJECTNAME =
    QName.createQName(SOMECO_MODEL_URI, "projectName");
public final static QName ASSOC_RELATEDOCUMENTS =
    QName.createQName(SOMECO_MODEL_URI, "relatedDocuments");
```

5. You are probably fluent in Java, and you know that you need to import some Java references. So far, you need only one reference:

```
import org.alfresco.service.namespace.QName;
```

6. Then, we are ready to create the Java class representing the action. Create a new class in your repo | src | main | java directory called com.someco.repo.action.executer.SetWebFlag. The class extends ActionExecuterAbstractBase, which means there are two methods that need to be implemented: executeImpl and addParameterDefinitions. The skeleton of your Java class should look like:

```java
package com.someco.repo.action.executer;

import java.util.List;
import org.alfresco.repo.action
    .executer.ActionExecuterAbstractBase;
import org.alfresco.service.cmr.action.Action;
import org.alfresco.service.cmr.action.ParameterDefinition;
import org.alfresco.service.cmr.repository.NodeRef;

public class SetWebFlag
    extends ActionExecuterAbstractBase {

    @Override
    protected void
      executeImpl(Action action, NodeRef actionedUponNodeRef) {
    }

    @Override
    protected void
      addParameterDefinitions(List<ParameterDefinition>
paramList) {
    }

}
```

7. First, let's start by defining the static variable representing the only parameter:

```java
public final static String PARAM_ACTIVE = "active";
```

8. Start implementing the executeImpl method. We could add a first check if the node exists or not, but to minimize our code in this exercise, we'll assume that the node exists. This code expects a parameter containing the flag indicating how the isActive property should be set. For now, the parameter is optional. So if it is null, default it to true.

```java
boolean activeFlag = true;
if (action.getParameterValue(PARAM_ACTIVE) != null)
  activeFlag = (Boolean) action.getParameterValue(PARAM_ACTIVE);
```

9. Setting the properties appropriately is a two-step process. First, grab the current properties from the node. (The `nodeService` is a dependency that will get set through a Spring bean configuration. The corresponding variable is created in the step 15.)

```
Map<QName, Serializable> properties =
    nodeService.getProperties(actionedUponNodeRef);
```

10. Then add the new property value to the properties map.

```
properties.put( SomeCoModel.PROP_ISACTIVE, activeFlag);
```

11. If the `activeFlag` is being set to `true`, set the published date property to the current date.

```
if (activeFlag) {
    properties.put( SomeCoModel.PROP_PUBLISHED, new Date());
}
```

12. Next, check for the aspect. If the aspect has already been added, just set the properties. Otherwise, it needs to be added. The aspect can be added and the properties can be set in one step.

```
// if the aspect has already been added, set the properties
if (nodeService.hasAspect(actionedUponNodeRef,
    SomeCoModel.ASPECT_WEBABLE)) {
        nodeService.setProperties(actionedUponNodeRef, properties);
} else {
    // otherwise, add the aspect and set the properties
    nodeService.addAspect(actionedUponNodeRef,
    SomeCoModel.ASPECT_WEBABLE, properties);
```

13. Save the class.

14. Now implement the `addParameterDefinitions` method. This method defines the parameters our action uses. The method is implemented as follows.

```
paramList.add(new ParameterDefinitionImpl(PARAM_ACTIVE,
        DataTypeDefinition.BOOLEAN,
        false,
        getParamDisplayLabel(PARAM_ACTIVE)));
```

15. The last step is to create the local variable for the `nodeService` and the associated setter method. The fastest way to do this is to simply add the local variable and then use STS to generate the setter methods. The class also has a couple of constants, shown below, to make it easier for others to work with the action class.

```
protected NodeService nodeService;
public final static String NAME = "set-web-flag";
```

16. Here is all references that you'll need to add:

```
import java.io.Serializable;
import java.util.Date;
import java.util.List;
import java.util.Map;

import org.alfresco.repo.action.ParameterDefinitionImpl;
import org.alfresco.repo.action.executer.ActionExecuterAbstractBase;
import org.alfresco.service.cmr.action.Action;
import org.alfresco.service.cmr.action.ParameterDefinition;
import org.alfresco.service.cmr.dictionary.DataTypeDefinition;
import org.alfresco.service.cmr.repository.NodeRef;
import org.alfresco.service.cmr.repository.NodeService;
import org.alfresco.service.namespace.QName;

import com.someco.repo.common.SomeCoModel;
```

17. Save the class.

18. Now write a Spring bean configuration file. Call it `action-context.xml` and save it in the directory `repo | src | main | amp | config | alfresco | module | repo | context`. The content of the config file is shown here:

```
<?xml version='1.0' encoding='UTF-8'?>
<!DOCTYPE beans PUBLIC '-//SPRING//DTD BEAN//EN'
    'http://www.springframework.org/dtd/spring-beans.dtd'>
<beans>
    <bean id="set-web-flag"
        class="com.someco.repo.action.executer.SetWebFlag"
        parent="action-executer">

        <property name="nodeService" ref="NodeService" />
            <property name="publicAction">
            <value>true</value>
        </property>
    </bean>
    <bean id="someco.actionResourceBundles"
```

```
        class="org.alfresco.i18n.ResourceBundleBootstrapComponent">
    <property name="resourceBundles">
      <list>
          <value>
              alfresco.module.${project.artifactId}
                .messages.action-config
          </value>
      </list>
    </property>
  </bean>
</beans>
```

19. Then, edit the file `module-context.xml` located in the `repo | src | main | amp | config | alfresco | module | repo` directory. You just need to add the following import:

    ```
    <import resource="classpath:alfresco/module
        /${project.artifactId}/context/action-context.xml" />
    ```

20. Create the I18N properties file `action-config.properties` that will contain the different labels in the `repo | src | main | amp | config | alfresco | module | repo | message` directory. Be careful to follow the naming convention that you'll easily understand:

    ```
    <ACTION NAME>.title=...
    <ACTION NAME>.decription=...
    <ACTION NAME>.<PARAMETER NAME>.display-label=...
    In our case, we'll have:
    set-web-flag.title=Sets the SC Web Flag
    set-web-flag.decription=This will add the sc:webable aspect
        and set the isActive flag.
    set-web-flag.active.display-label=Active?
    ```

21. Stop Alfresco.
22. Package and move the module to your virtual machine.
23. Deploy and restart Tomcat.

if you try to create a rule on a folder, you should see your new action:

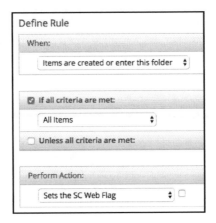

When the rule will be applied to the documents moved or uploaded into this folder, the aspects and properties will be properly set. At this stage, you can't execute this action by just clicking on a Share action. We'll cover that in the following chapter.

Hiding the action from end users

The `publicAction` parameter in the actions Spring bean configuration (`action-context.xml`) tells Alfresco whether or not to include the action in the dropdown list. For now, the flag is set to true. In the next chapter, you'll learn how to trigger the action from a UI action link. You will be able to make the UI Action Link hide or disappear based on logic (such as whether or not the current user is a member of a particular group). At that point, you'll set the flag to false to keep end users from running the action via the Manage Rulesscreen.

Creating actions that require user-specified parameters

In the previous example, an end user does not need to specify any parameters for the action to run successfully. But some actions can be reused much more broadly if they are set up to allow an end user to specify parameters.

For example, imagine that SomeCo's Human Resources department wants to store HR policies in the repository. Suppose they have a three-folder system for keeping track of **Draft**, **Active**, and **Archive** policies. Policies often replace or supersede existing policies. The HR department would like to tag a draft policy with the policy it replaces (a policy sitting in the **Active** folder). The HR Department will move policies from the **Draft** folder to the **Active** folder. When the draft policy is moved into the **Active** folder, the policy it replaces should automatically move from the **Active** folder to the **Archive** folder:

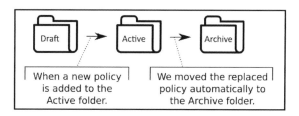

The code that moves the old policy from the **Active** folder into the **Archive** folder can be implemented as an action. The action can be called by a rule that fires when a document is added to a folder. The action's job is to figure out whether or not the incoming document is replacing another document in the same folder. If it is, the action needs to move the replaced document to a target folder. In this case, the target folder is the **Archive** folder. Without letting the user set the parameter, the target folder would have to be hardcoded. Instead, you'll create this action with a parameter so that if the target folder ever changes (from **Archive** to **Old Policies**, for example), or if someone else wants to use the action with their own set of folders, it won't require a code change.

Step-by-step – creating an action configurable in Alfresco Share

Before starting, think about similar code that might already exist within Alfresco that you could leverage for the new action. Alfresco is open source. So it would be a shame to ignore the source and end up recreating a functionality that already exists. Plus, following the same pattern to implement our customization will make it easier for someone to support and share our code with others.

It turns out that there is already an out-of-the-box **Move** action. The out-of-the-box Move action moves the node against which the action is running to a target folder specified as a parameter. The difference between Alfresco's Move action and the new custom action is that the node that needs to be moved isn't the node the action is running against; it's the node containing the old policy.

The action can get to the old policy because the new policy document has a *replaces* relationship with the old policy document. So the action will look to see if the newly arrived document has a *replaces* relationship. If it does, it will grab the target of that relationship (the document being replaced) and move it to the target folder.

The previous example consisted of an Action Executer class, its Spring bean configuration file, and a properties file. To create an action that accepts parameters, you will be creating a UI to set the destination folder, which requires the same ingredients as a basic action.

To create a new action that accesses parameters, follow these steps:

1. There isn't anything in the SomeCo model related to HR policies. So update `repo | src | main | amp | config | alfresco | module | repo | model | scModel.xml` with a new type called `sc:hrPolicy` that is a child of `sc:hrDoc`:

```
<type name="sc:hrPolicy">
  <title>Someco HR Policy</title>
        <parent>sc:hrDoc</parent>
</type>
```

2. Alfresco has a `cm:replaceable` aspect available out of the box that will work perfectly for this. All HR policies are replaceable. So make the aspect a mandatory aspect of the new type by adding the following immediately after the parent element of the `sc:hrPolicy` type:

```
<mandatory-aspects>
  <aspect>cm:replaceable</aspect>
</mandatory-aspects>
```

3. Although the aspect is available out of the box, it isn't configured to show in the UI by default. So add the following to `share-config-custom.xml`:

```
<config evaluator="aspect" condition="cm:replaceable">
    <forms>
        <form>
            <field-visibility>
                <show id="cm:replaces" />
            </field-visibility>
        </form>
    </forms>
</config>
```

4. Don't forget to add cm:replaceable to the list of visible aspects in the same file. And configure the list of types to make available our new type sc:hrPolicy.

5. Don't forget to add the new type `sc:hrPolicy` to the list of valid childtypes for `cm:content`, `sc:doc` and `sc:hrDoc` in theshare-config-custom.xml file.

6. And of course, update the Java class SomeCoModel by adding a reference for our new type:

```
public final static QName TYPE_HRPOLICY =
    QName.createQName(SOMECO_MODEL_URI, "hrPolicy");
```

7. Open the `share.properties` file in the share project and add this line:

```
aspect.cm_replaceable=Replaceable aspect
```

8. Before we start the Java code, let's update the scModel.properties by adding the I18N display label:

```
sc_somecomodel.type.sc_hrPolicy.title=Someco HR Policy
```

9. That's all for the model-related changes. Now let's work on the action executer class. Create your Java class into **repo|src|man|java** and call it `com.someco.repo.action.executer.MoveReplacedActionExecuter`. The class extends `ActionExecuterAbstractBase`, which means we need to implement the two same methods as previously: `executeImpl` and `addParameterDefinitions`. Just as in the previous example, the heavy lifting is done in the `executeImpl` method. You should have something like that:

```
package com.someco.repo.action.executer;

import java.util.List;
import
org.alfresco.repo.action.executer.ActionExecuterAbstractBase;
import org.alfresco.service.cmr.action.Action;
import org.alfresco.service.cmr.action.ParameterDefinition;
import org.alfresco.service.cmr.repository.NodeRef;

public class MoveReplacedActionExecuter extends
ActionExecuterAbstractBase {

    @Override
    protected void executeImpl(Action ruleAction,
      NodeRef actionedUponNodeRef) {
      }
```

```
   @Override
   protected void
     addParameterDefinitions(List<ParameterDefinition> paramList) {
     }

}
```

10. It's the first time that we are going to define a logger in this book. Of course, it's highly recommended to define loggers in all Java code. Add the following `logger` in your class:

```
private static Logger logger =
    Logger.getLogger(MoveReplacedActionExecuter.class);
```

11. Then define the static variable representing the only parameter:

```
public static final String PARAM_DESTINATION_FOLDER =
    "destination-folder";
```

12. Let's start by implementing the `executeImpl` method. The first thing to do is to create the `QName` object for the `replaces` association, and check if some association are defined on the current object:

```
QName assocReplacesQname = QName.createQName(
NamespaceService.CONTENT_MODEL_1_0_URI, "replaces");
List<AssociationRef> assocRefs = nodeService.getTargetAssocs(
actionedUponNodeRef, assocReplacesQname);
if (!assocRefs.isEmpty()) {
  [...]
}
```

13. Then, in the `if` statement, we need to browse all associated items:

```
NodeRef destinationParent = (NodeRef)
ruleAction.getParameterValue(PARAM_DESTINATION_FOLDER);
for (AssociationRef assocNode : assocRefs) {
  try {
  [...]
  } catch (Exception e) {
   logger.error("Error moving the document: " +
     assocNode.getTargetRef());
  }
}
```

14. Finally, we need to process each association:

```
NodeRef replacedDocument = assocNode.getTargetRef();
if (nodeService.exists(replacedDocument) == true) {
  fileFolderService.move(replacedDocument,
    destinationParent, null);
```

15. We need to define the parameter to specify the destination folder:

```
protected void
  addParameterDefinitions(List<ParameterDefinition> paramList) {
    paramList.add(
      new ParameterDefinitionImpl(PARAM_DESTINATION_FOLDER,
        DataTypeDefinition.NODE_REF,
        true,
        getParamDisplayLabel(PARAM_DESTINATION_FOLDER)));
}
```

16. Don't forget to define the few constants and variables that we need:

```
private NodeService nodeService;
private FileFolderService fileFolderService;
public static final String NAME = "move-replaced";
```

17. By your own, use STS to generate the required setters for the two Alfresco Java services that we need and the different required imports.

18. That's it for the Java code. Now it is time to tie it all together with the appropriate Spring bean configuration and properties files. Declare the action executer class and point to the resource bundle. Edit the file action-context.xml. Add the following:

```
<bean id="move-replaced"
class="com.someco.repo.action.executer.MoveReplacedActionExecuter"
parent="action-executer">
    <property name="nodeService" ref="NodeService" />
    <property name="fileFolderService" ref="FileFolderService" />
</bean>
```

19. Update `action-config.properties` with:

```
move-replaced.title= Move replaced document to folder
move-replaced.description=
    This will move the target node of a replaces
    association to a specified folder.
```

20. We completed everything for the repo project. Now, let's switch to the Alfresco Share configuration. Unfortunately, Alfresco Share is not really easy to configure in this case. We'll need to override some files provided by Alfresco Share. The first thing is to create the Javascript file that will handle the displaying of the rule in the **Manage Rules** screen. Create the file someco-action.js in the directory share│src│main│amp│web│js│someco. We are not going to explain step by step how to create this file, but only focus on important steps. The goal is to create a new Javascript object SomeCo.RuleConfigActionCustom that will replace the default object. To achieve that, we'll extend the Alfresco Javascript object that contains all rules:

```
YAHOO.extend(SomeCo.RuleConfigActionCustom,
  Alfresco.RuleConfigAction,
 {
  customisations : {
    [...]
  }
});
```

21. Then, we'll add the rule for our new rule, and we'll use the Move action as example:

```
MoveReplaced : {
   text : function(configDef, ruleConfig, configEl) {
     this._getParamDef(configDef, "destination-folder")._type =
       "path";
     return configDef;
   },
   edit : function(configDef, ruleConfig, configEl) {
     this._hideParameters(configDef.parameterDefinitions);
     configDef.parameterDefinitions.splice(0, 0, {
       type : "arca:destination-dialog-button",
       displayLabel : this.msg("label.to"),
       _buttonLabel : this.msg("button.select-folder"),
       _destinationParam : "destination-folder"
     });
     return configDef;
   }
}
```

22. Now, we need to override Alfresco to specify with Javascript object should be instantiated for the **Manage Rules** screen. Create the directory share|src|main|amp|web|WEB-INF|classes|alfresco|site-webscripts|org|alfresco|components|rules|config. Then, copy the file rule-config-action.get.config.xml from Alfresco share (located in **WEB-INF|classes|alfresco|site-webscripts|org|alfresco|rules|config**) in this directory. The first change that we need to do is to change the component that should be used:

```
<component>SomeCo.RuleConfigActionCustom</component>
```

23. Then, we need to match the MoveReplaced customization object defined in Javascript, and the move-replaced action defined in Alfresco. Just add the following line in the customise tag:

```
<action name="move-replaced">MoveReplaced</action>
```

24. There is one last change to do in Alfresco Share. We need to be sure that our Javascript file will be properly loaded in the **Manage Rules** screen. Copy the file rule-edit.get.html.ftland rule-details.get.html.ftlfrom Alfresco share in the directory share|src|main|amp|web|WEB-INF|classes|alfresco|site-webscripts|org|alfresco|components|rules. In each file, identify the markup tag with the idequals to jsand add the dependency as shown below:

```
<@markup id="js">
<#-- JavaScript Dependencies -->
  [...]
<@script src="${url.context}/res/js/someco
/someco-action.js" group="rules"/>
    [...]
</@>
```

25. Stop Alfresco.
26. Package and move the modules to your virtual machine.
27. Deploy and restart Tomcat. Note that from now on, when you call the apply_amps.sh script to install the AMP modules, you'll need to add the option "-force". It's because we override some Alfresco configuration files.

You have just created a new type, `sc:hrPolicy`, which has a mandatory `cm:replaces` aspect. That means that HR policies can point to other policies in the repository that they will replace once approved. You can also now configure the custom Move Replaced action against a folder. When setting up the action, the web client will allow the user to specify a target folder for the replaced document.

To set up a test, follow these steps:

1. Log in to Alfresco.
2. Create a new site called **Human Resources**. In the Document Library, create a folder called **Policies**.
3. Within **Policies**, create folders for **Draft**, **Approved**, and **Archived**.

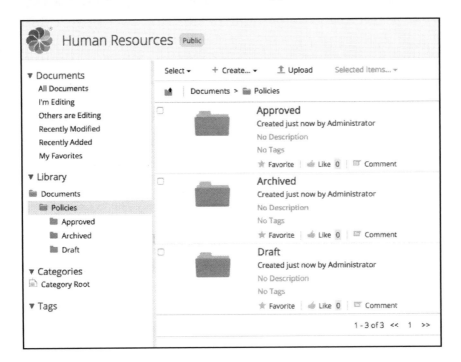

4. Create a rule on the Policies folder that specializes all documents to **Someco HR Policy** and that should apply to subfolders.

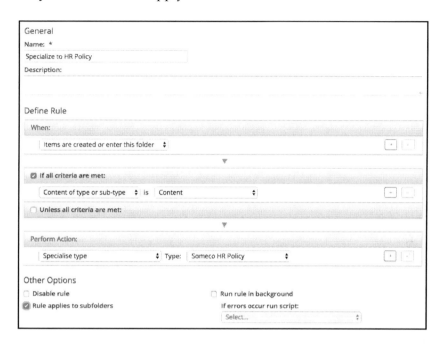

5. Upload a document in the **Approved** folder that will represent an **existing policy**, and another document in the **Draft** folder that will represent the new policy. Edit the **replaces** property of the new policy to point to the **Existing Policy** document.

6. Create an inbound rule in the **Approved** folder that runs the **Move Replaced** action:

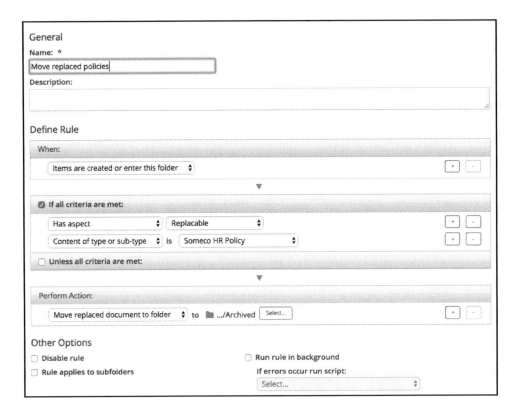

7. Now move the **New Policy** document into the **Approved** folder. The action should automatically trigger, moving the **Existing Policy** into the **Archived** folder:

Specifying parameters when code executes an action

In this example, the end user is specifying the destination folder when the action is configured through Alfresco Share. Parameters can also be specified when executing actions from Java and JavaScript. For example, here is a JavaScript snippet that invokes the `addfeatures` action to add an aspect. The `addfeatures` action takes one parameter, which is the name of the aspect to add:

```
var aspectName = "sc:clientRelated";
var addAspectAction = actions.create("add-features");
addAspectAction.parameters["aspect-name"] = aspectName;
addAspectAction.execute(document);
```

Executing actions from code is very common, especially when you need to run an action against a number of documents at once. Suppose SomeCo's HR department was already using Alfresco and you are just coming up with this "Move Replaced" idea. You would need to add the `cm:replaces` aspect to all existing HR policies. You could write JavaScript similar to the snippet above that would execute the `addfeatures` action against all of the results in a search query to save you the trouble of doing it manually for each existing document.

Be aware that actions are usually executed synchronously. It means that they will be executed in the same transaction. But it's possible to execute an action asynchronously.

Binding logic to custom types with behaviors

So far, you've seen how to write code that works with custom content types, properties, aspects, and associations. But the code wasn't tightly coupled to the objects on which it operated. With an action, the business logic is triggered by something-an item in the user interface, a schedule, or a workflow-rather than being bound to the content type or aspect.

As you know, a repository action is a piece of code that can be performed against a node. You don't have one good way of implementing your project. Some argue that the best place to develop your business logic is within repository actions. It's a good approach because it means that you can trigger your action using a rule, via a webscript, or via a Javascript code. I'll go a bit further and I'd say that a repository action should never contain business logic. All the business logic should be encapsulated in a Java service that is called by a repository action, or a webscript. It allows to share and re-use your business logic in your project. In this case, the Java service needs to do some check before executing any code like checking if the content type of the node is the right one.

But there are times when you want code to be tightly coupled to a content type because you need to be sure it gets executed, rather than leaving it up to a rule on a folder that triggers an action or a workflow that does the same. Fortunately, Alfresco provides just such a mechanism; it's called **behaviors**.

Step-by-step – writing a simple behavior in Java

Suppose you want to execute some code every time something happens to a particular type of node. You could write a rule action to do this and then configure a folder to execute the action. But what if the content you want to hook this code to is scattered across the repository? What you need is a behavior. Let us create a simple behavior that binds itself to a few different policies so you can see when a behavior is triggered based on what's happening to the content. To create this simple behavior, you'll need:

- A Java class to implement the behavior
- A Spring bean configuration file to configure the behavior
- A type to bind the behavior to
- A modified log4j.properties file to see debug messages

By the end of these steps, you'll be able to see the policies that get fired when you create, read, update, and delete content.

To create the policy logger behavior, follow these steps:

1. Create a new Java class in **repo|src|main|java** called
   com.someco.repo.behavior.PolicyLogger.

2. You're going to bind your behavior to the OnCreateNode, OnContentRead, OnContentUpdate, OnUpdateNode, and OnDeleteNode event policies. So the class needs to implement the appropriate interfaces as follows:

```
public class PolicyLogger
  implements ContentServicePolicies.OnContentUpdatePolicy,
             ContentServicePolicies.OnContentReadPolicy,
             NodeServicePolicies.OnCreateNodePolicy,
             NodeServicePolicies.OnUpdateNodePolicy,
             NodeServicePolicies.OnDeleteNodePolicy {
```

3. Next, set up some local variables. You'll need a logger to log messages when the policies are fired, Behavior objects (note the British spelling in the code), and a `PolicyComponent` bean:

```
private Logger logger = Logger.getLogger(PolicyLogger.class);
   //   Behaviours
    private Behaviour onContentRead;
    private Behaviour onContentUpdate;
    private Behaviour onCreateNode;
    private Behaviour onUpdateNode;
    private Behaviour onDeleteNode;
   // Dependencies
    private PolicyComponent policyComponent;
```

4. Create an `init` method that creates the behaviors:

```
public void init() {
  if (logger.isDebugEnabled())
    logger.debug("Initializing policy logger behaviour");
  // Create behaviours
  this.onContentRead = new JavaBehaviour(this,
    OnContentReadPolicy.QNAME.getLocalName(),
    NotificationFrequency.TRANSACTION_COMMIT);
  this.onContentUpdate = new JavaBehaviour(this,
    OnContentUpdatePolicy.QNAME.getLocalName(),
    NotificationFrequency.TRANSACTION_COMMIT);
  this.onCreateNode = new JavaBehaviour(this,
    OnCreateNodePolicy.QNAME.getLocalName(),
    NotificationFrequency.TRANSACTION_COMMIT);
  this.onUpdateNode = new JavaBehaviour(this,
    OnUpdateNodePolicy.QNAME.getLocalName(),
    NotificationFrequency.TRANSACTION_COMMIT);
  this.onDeleteNode = new JavaBehaviour(this,
    OnDeleteNodePolicy.QNAME.getLocalName(),
    NotificationFrequency.TRANSACTION_COMMIT);
}
```

5. Then, bind the behaviors to Alfresco's policies for the SomeCo HR Policy type (it could be any type, but use this one for this example) by adding the following code to the `init` method:

```
// Bind behaviours to node policies
this.policyComponent.bindClassBehaviour(
  OnContentReadPolicy.QNAME,
  SomeCoModel.TYPE_HRPOLICY,
  this.onContentRead);
this.policyComponent.bindClassBehaviour(
```

```
    OnContentUpdatePolicy.QNAME,
    SomeCoModel.TYPE_HRPOLICY,
    this.onContentUpdate);
this.policyComponent.bindClassBehaviour(
    OnCreateNodePolicy.QNAME,
    SomeCoModel.TYPE_HRPOLICY,
    this.onCreateNode);
this.policyComponent.bindClassBehaviour(
    OnUpdateNodePolicy.QNAME,
    SomeCoModel.TYPE_HRPOLICY,
    this.onUpdateNode);
this.policyComponent.bindClassBehaviour(
    OnDeleteNodePolicy.QNAME,
    SomeCoModel.TYPE_HRPOLICY,
    this.onDeleteNode);
```

6. Now implement the behaviors. In this case, you're just going to log a message:

```java
@Override
public void onContentUpdate(NodeRef nodeRef, boolean flag) {
    if (logger.isDebugEnabled())
        logger.debug("Content update policy fired");
}
@Override
public void onContentRead(NodeRef nodeRef) {
    if (logger.isDebugEnabled())
        logger.debug("Content read policy fired");
}
@Override
public void onUpdateNode(NodeRef nodeRef) {
    if (logger.isDebugEnabled())
        logger.debug("Node update policy fired");
}
@Override
public void onCreateNode(ChildAssociationRef childAssocRef) {
    if (logger.isDebugEnabled())
        logger.debug("Node create policy fired");
}
@Override
public void onDeleteNode(ChildAssociationRef childAssocRef,
 boolean isNodeArchived) {
    if (logger.isDebugEnabled())
        logger.debug("Node delete policy fired");
}
```

7. Create a setter method for the `PolicyComponent` dependency and add all import statements (a quick way to do that? *Ctrl + Shift + O*)

```
public void setPolicyComponent(
    PolicyComponent policyComponent) {
        this.policyComponent = policyComponent;
}
```

8. That's all for the Java class. Create a new Spring bean configuration file in **repo|src|main|amp|config|alfresco|module|repo|context** called `behavior-context.xml`. Add the following to register the new bean:

```
<?xml version='1.0' encoding='UTF-8'?>
<!DOCTYPE beans PUBLIC '-//SPRING//DTD BEAN//EN'
'http://www.springframework.org/dtd/spring-beans.dtd'>
<beans>
    <bean id="policyLogger"
    class="com.someco.repo.behavior.PolicyLogger"
    init-method="init">
        <property name="policyComponent"
            ref="policyComponent" />
    </bean>
</beans>
```

9. Update your `module-context.xml` by adding:

```
<import resource="classpath:alfresco
/module/${project.artifactId}/context
/behavior-context.xml" />
```

10. Confirm that your `log4j.properties` file (located in **repo|src|main|amp|config|alfresco|module|repo**) has:

```
log4j.logger.com.someco=DEBUG
```

11. Now deploy, restart, and test. When the server starts up, you should see:

```
DEBUG [repo.behavior.PolicyLogger]
[localhost-startStop-1] Initializing policy logger behaviour
```

Notice that you've bound the behavior to the HR Policy type. That means the behavior code will get executed any time Alfresco takes an action against an instance of the type that matches one of the policies you've bound to. To see this in action, log in to Alfresco and create, update, and delete a couple of HR Policies. Watch the Tomcat log as you do so. You'll see that those policies get fired multiple times during a typical transaction.

Binding to multiple types/aspects

In this example, we bound only to the HR Policy type. But there is nothing specific to any particular type in the class you just wrote. If you had behavior logic that was common to multiple content types or aspects, you could bind them to this behavior as well. For example, add the following to the init method:

```
this.policyComponent.bindClassBehaviour(
    OnContentReadPolicy.QNAME,
    SomeCoModel.ASPECT_CLIENTRELATED,
    this.onContentRead);
```

Now in addition to Operations Document instances, the onContentRead behavior code will fire when reading any content of any type that has SomeCo's client-related aspect.

As a best practice, you should only do this when the behavior is truly common. If you had behavior unique to Operations Documents and the client-related aspect, those should be broken into two different classes.

Frequency

Notice that the constructor included a frequency argument. This declares how often your behavior should be triggered. In the PolicyLogger example, you specified **TRANSACTION_COMMIT**. The other two choices are **FIRST_EVENT** and **EVERY_EVENT**.

Figuring out to which policies to bind

There are many out of the box policies to which your behavior can be bound. To find out what's available, you need to look only as far as the Javadoc. The latest Javadoc is always available at

http://dev.alfresco.com/resource/docs/java/overview-summary.html.

To make it easier to read the table, the inner interface that follows the pattern of `<method-name>Policy` is omitted. For example, the `onContentUpdate` method is a method of the inner interface `OnContentUpdatePolicy`:

Interface	Method

org.alfresco.repo.content.ContentServicePolicies
`http://dev.alfresco.com/resource/docs/java/org/al`
`fresco/repo/content/ContentServicePolicies.html`
	onContentUpdate
	onContentRead
	OnContentPropertyUpdate

org.alfresco.repo.copy.CopyServicePolicies
`http://dev.alfresco.com/resource/docs/java/org/al`
`fresco/repo/copy/CopyServicePolicies.html`
	onCopyNode
	onCopyComplete
	beforeCopyPolicy

org.alfresco.repo.node.NodeServicePolicies
`http://dev.alfresco.com/resource/docs/java/org/al`
`fresco/repo/node/NodeServicePolicies.html`
	beforeCreateStore
	onCreateStore
	beforeCreateNode
	onCreateNode
	onMoveNode
	beforeUpdateNode
	onUpdateNode
	onUpdateProperties
	beforeDeleteNode
	onDeleteNode
	beforeAddAspect
	onAddAspect
	beforeRemoveAspect
	onRemoveAspect
	onCreateAssociation
	beforeDeleteAssociation
	onDeleteAssociation
	onCreateChildAssociation
	beforeDeleteChildAssociation
	onDeleteChildAssociation
	beforeArchiveNode
	beforeMoveNode
	beforeSetNodeType
	onSetNodeType
	onRestoreNode

org.alfresco.repo.version.VersionServicePolicies `http://dev.alfresco.com/resource/docs/java/org/al fresco/repo/version/VersionServicePolicies.html`	beforeCreateVersion afterCreateVersion onCreateVersion calculateVersionLabel afterVersionRevert onRevertVersion
org.alfresco.repo.coci.CheckOutCheckInServicePolicies `http://dev.alfresco.com/resource/docs/java/org/al fresco/repo/coci/CheckOutCheckInServicePolicies.h tml`	beforeCancelCheckOut onCancelCheckOut beforeCheckIn onCheckIn beforeCheckOut onCheckOut

Note that there are some other less common available policies in Alfresco. Use the Javadoc if you are interested by all policies (`http://dev.alfresco.com/resource/docs/java/org/alfresco/repo/policy/ClassPolicy.html`).

Step-by-step – writing a simple behavior in JavaScript

You've seen how to implement a simple behavior in Java. But what if you wanted to implement the behavior using JavaScript instead? Behaviors can be implemented in JavaScript and bound to policies through Spring. Let's create an additional behavior using JavaScript; and we'll bind to the same content type.

The ingredients are the same as in the Java example, except that we'll be creating a JavaScript file instead of a Java class. This involves:

1. Creating a server-side JavaScript file that implements the behavior.
2. Creating a Spring bean to bind the JavaScript-based behavior to the appropriate policies.
3. Modifying `log4j.properties` to set the server-side JavaScript log level to DEBUG.

To create a JavaScript version of the `PolicyLogger`, do the following:

1. In your Eclipse project, create a `scripts` directory under the `repo | src | main amp | config | alfresco | extension` folder, and add a file called `onUpdateNode.js` with the following content:

```
var scriptFailed = false;
// Check the arguments
if (behaviour.args == null) {
  logger.log("The args have not been set.");
  scriptFailed = true;
} else {
  if (behaviour.args.length == 1) {
    var actedOnNode = behaviour.args[0];
    logger.log("You just updated:" + actedOnNode.name);
  } else {
    logger.log("The number of arguments is incorrect.");
    scriptFailed = true;
  }
}
```

2. Edit the `behavior-context.xml` file. Java behaviors bind themselves to policies. JavaScript behaviors, on the other hand, use the Spring bean configuration to bind to policies. Add the following bean to the file:

```
<bean id="onUpdateHrPolicy"
  class="org.alfresco.repo.policy
  .registration.ClassPolicyRegistration"
  parent="policyRegistration">

    <property name="policyName">
      <value>{http://www.alfresco.org}onUpdateNode</value>
    </property>
    <property name="className">
      <value>{http://www.someco.com/model
        /content/1.0}hrPolicy</value>
    </property>
    <property name="behaviour">
        <bean class="org.alfresco.repo.jscript
        .ScriptBehaviour" parent="scriptBehaviour">
          <property name="location">
            <bean class="org.alfresco.repo
            .jscript.ClasspathScriptLocation">

              <constructor-arg>
                <value>alfresco/extension
                /scripts/onUpdateNode.js</value>
```

```
            </constructor-arg>
          </bean>
        </property>
      </bean>
    </property>
  </bean>
```

3. Edit the `log4j.properties` file (located in
   repo|src|main|amp|config|alfresco|module|repo). Set
   `log4j.logger.org.alfresco.repo.jscript.ScriptLogger` to `DEBUG`.
4. Now deploy and test.

To test the JavaScript behavior, create a new HR Policy and watch the log. You should see multiple JavaScript logger messages.

Binding behavior to child types

In this example, you bound the `onUpdateNode.js` to the `onUpdateNode` policy of the SomeCo HR Policy type. Remember that HR policy is a child of HR Doc. So what will happen if you bind the policy to the HR Document content type? Children inherit the behaviors of their parents.

Step-by-step – writing a user ratings calculator

So far, the behaviors you've written have just written log messages, which isn't terribly exciting. SomeCo's Marketing department has a requirement to consider, though. Marketing wants to let website users rate Whitepapers on a scale of one to five. They then want to show the average rating for a given Whitepaper. Once this is in place, they'll be able to call their website 2.0, which will be a big win for everybody.

You're reading an Alfresco book, so let's assume the decision has been made to persist those ratings to Alfresco, though in real life that may or may not be the best thing to do (it might make more sense to store ratings and other user-generated content in a database).

A new type, `sc:rating`, will be created to store an individual rating. A new aspect, `sc:rateable`, will be created to attach to Whitepapers to identify them as something that can be rated and to store the summary statistics for the Whitepaper. Ratings will be associated with Whitepapers through child associations. That way, if the Whitepaper goes away, so will the ratings, which is what we want.

A Whitepaper's rating needs to be recalculated either when a new rating is created or when a rating is deleted. One possibility would be to bind the behavior to the `NodeService` policy's `onCreateChildAssociation` and `onDeleteChildAssociation` methods for the Whitepaper node. But that would mean the behavior would constantly be inspecting the association type to see if it needs to take any action because there could be other child associations besides ratings. Instead, the behavior will be bound to the rating node's `onCreateNode` and `onDeleteNode` policies. Any time a ratings node is created, the behavior will re-calculate the Whitepaper's summary statistics.

Here is what you're going to need to do:

1. Extend the SomeCo model with a rateable aspect and a rating type (and perform all of the UI configuration steps that go with it).
2. Write the custom behavior class and bind it to the appropriate policies.
3. Configure a Spring bean to initialize the behavior class and pass in any dependencies.
4. Build, deploy, restart, and test. In a later chapter, you'll work on the frontend that will create ratings via web scripts. In this example, you'll create some server-side JavaScript to create a few ratings to test out the behavior.

Let's get started. To create a behavior class that calculates the average rating across child rating objects, follow these steps:

1. Edit the `scModel.xml` in **repo|src|main|amp|config|alfresco|module|repo|model**. Add the new rating type:

```
<type name="sc:rating">
<title>Someco Rating</title>
<parent>sys:base</parent>
<properties>
  <property name="sc:rating">
        <type>d:int</type>
        <mandatory>true</mandatory>
  </property>
  <property name="sc:rater">
        <type>d:text</type>
        <mandatory>true</mandatory>
  </property>
</properties>
</type>
```

Note that `sc:rating` inherits from `sys:base`. That's because there won't be any content stored in a rating object; it only has properties. This is sometimes called a "content-less object".

2. Now add the `sc:rateable` aspect. The rateable aspect has one property to store the average rating, one to store the number of ratings, and one to store the sum of the ratings. The aspect also defines the child association that keeps track of the content's related ratings:

```
<aspect name="sc:rateable">
<title>Someco Rateable</title>
<properties>
    <property name="sc:averageRating">
        <type>d:double</type>
        <mandatory>false</mandatory>
    </property>
    <property name="sc:totalRating">
        <type>d:int</type>
        <mandatory>false</mandatory>
    </property>
    <property name="sc:ratingCount">
        <type>d:int</type>
        <mandatory>false</mandatory>
    </property>
</properties>
<associations>
    <child-association name="sc:ratings">
    <title>Rating</title>
    <source>
        <mandatory>false</mandatory>
        <many>true</many>
    </source>
    <target>
        <class>sc:rating</class>
        <mandatory>false</mandatory>
        <many>true</many>
    </target>
    </child-association>
</associations>
</aspect>
```

3. In the list of imports, don't forget to add the system definition model:

```
<import uri="http://www.alfresco.org/model/system/1.0"
  prefix="sys" />
```

4. Save and close the `scModel.xml` file.

5. Edit `share-config-custom.xml` in **share|src|main|resources|META-INF**. The rateable properties and associations need to show up on property sheets for objects with the aspect. So add the following:

```
<config evaluator="aspect" condition="sc:rateable">
<forms>
    <form>
      <field-visibility>
        <show id="sc:averageRating" read-only="true" />
        <show id="sc:ratings" />
      </field-visibility>
    </form>
</forms>
</config>
```

6. The rateable aspect needs to show up on the **add aspect** list. So add the rateable aspect to the list of visible aspects in `share-config-custom.xml`.

7. Update the `scModel.properties` file in the repo project by adding:

```
sc_somecomodel.aspect.sc_rateable.title=Someco Rateable
sc_somecomodel.property.sc_averageRating.title=Average Rating
sc_somecomodel.property.sc_totalRating.title=Total Rating
sc_somecomodel.property.sc_ratingCount.title=# of Rating
sc_somecomodel.association.sc_ratings.title=Ratings
```

8. Update the `share.properties` file in the share project by adding:

```
aspect.sc_rateable=Someco Rateable
```

9. Modify `com.someco.repo.common.SomeCoModel` to include new constants for the type, aspect, properties, and association that we just added to the model:

```
public final static QName TYPE_RATING =
  QName.createQName(SOMECO_MODEL_URI, "rating");
public final static QName ASPECT_RATEABLE =
  QName.createQName(SOMECO_MODEL_URI, "rateable");
public final static QName PROP_RATING =
  QName.createQName(SOMECO_MODEL_URI, "rating");
public final static QName PROP_AVERAGERATING =
  QName.createQName(SOMECO_MODEL_URI, "averageRating");
```

```
public final static QName PROP_TOTALRATING =
    QName.createQName(SOMECO_MODEL_URI, "totalRating");
public final static QName PROP_RATINGCOUNT =
    QName.createQName(SOMECO_MODEL_URI, "ratingCount");
public final static QName ASSOC_RATINGS =
    QName.createQName(SOMECO_MODEL_URI, "ratings");
```

10. Create a new class called `com.someco.behavior.Rating`. Let's worry about how to handle new ratings first and deletions later. Given that, the class declaration is:

```
public class Rating
    implements NodeServicePolicies.OnCreateNodePolicy {
```

11. The class has two dependencies that Spring will take care of. One is the `NodeService`, which will be used to produce the summary statistics, and the other is the `PolicyComponent`, which is used to bind the behavior to the policies. Add the two local class variables for the dependencies as well as one for the `onCreateNode` behavior:

```
// Dependencies
private NodeService nodeService;
private PolicyComponent policyComponent;
// Behaviours
private Behaviour onCreateNode;
```

12. Add the `init` method to create and bind the behaviors:

```
public void init() {
  this.onCreateNode = new JavaBehaviour(this,
    OnCreateNodePolicy.QNAME.getLocalName(),
    NotificationFrequency.TRANSACTION_COMMIT);
  this.policyComponent.bindClassBehaviour(
    OnCreateNodePolicy.QNAME,
    SomeCoModel.TYPE_RATING,
    this.onCreateNode);
}
```

13. In the `onCreateNode` behavior method, call a method that knows what to do when ratings are added:

```
@Override
public void onCreateNode(ChildAssociationRef childAssocRef) {
  addRating(childAssocRef);
}
```

14. Add the `addRating` method. It grabs the running total and rating count from the parent, adds the rating to the total, increments the count, and computes the new average:

```
public void addRating(ChildAssociationRef childAssocRef) {
  // get the parent node
  NodeRef parentRef = childAssocRef.getParentRef();
  NodeRef childRef = childAssocRef.getChildRef();

  Integer total =
    (Integer) nodeService.getProperty(parentRef,
    SomeCoModel.PROP_TOTALRATING);
  if (total == null)
    total = 0;
  Integer count =
    (Integer) nodeService.getProperty(parentRef,
    SomeCoModel.PROP_RATINGCOUNT);
  if (count == null)
    count = 0;
  Integer rating =
    (Integer) nodeService.getProperty(childRef,
    SomeCoModel.PROP_RATING);
  if (rating == null)
    rating = 0;

  Double average = 0d;
  total = total + rating;
  count = count + 1;
  average = total / new Double(count);

  // store the average on the parent node
  nodeService.setProperty(parentRef,
    SomeCoModel.PROP_AVERAGERATING, average);
  nodeService.setProperty(parentRef,
    SomeCoModel.PROP_TOTALRATING, total);
  nodeService.setProperty(parentRef,
    SomeCoModel.PROP_RATINGCOUNT, count);
}
```

15. Add the setters for the NodeService and PolicyComponents:

```
public void setNodeService(NodeService nodeService) {
  this.nodeService = nodeService;
}
public void setPolicyComponent(
PolicyComponent policyComponent) {
  this.policyComponent = policyComponent;
}
```

16. Configure the behavior class as a Spring bean. Edit `behavior-context.xml` in the **repo project**. Add the following bean:

```
<bean id="ratingBehaviour"
  class="com.someco.repo.behavior.Rating"
  init-method="init">
    <property name="nodeService" ref="nodeService" />
    <property name="policyComponent" ref="policyComponent" />
</bean>
```

17. Deploy, restart, and test.

Step-by-step – testing the new rating behavior

In the previous chapter, you used Java to test out the model by writing code against the CMIS API. This time, create server-side JavaScript you can use any time you need to create some test rating nodes for a piece of content. To do that, follow these steps:

1. Create a new Javascript file named `addTestRating.js` in the repo | src | scripts directory (create this folder if it does not exist yet) with the following content:

```
// add the aspect to this document if it needs it
if (document.hasAspect("sc:rateable")) {
  logger.log("Document already as aspect");
} else {
  logger.log("Adding rateable aspect");
  document.addAspect("sc:rateable");
}
// randomly pick a num b/w 1 and 5 inclusive
var ratingValue = Math.floor(Math.random() * 5) + 1;
var props = new Array(2);
props["sc:rating"] = ratingValue;
props["sc:rater"] = person.properties.userName;
// create a new ratings node and set its properties
```

Handling Content Automatically with Actions, Behaviors, Transformers, and Extractors

```
var ratingsNode = document.createNode("rating"
 + new Date().getTime(),
   "sc:rating", props, "sc:ratings");
ratingsNode.save();
logger.log("Ratings node saved.");
```

2. Log in to the Alfresco Share and upload this Javascript file in Data Dictionary
   | Scripts.

3. Open the **Marketing** site, click on **Document Library**, create a new folder called
   Test Rating, create a new rule on this folder:

   - Name: Execute addTestRating.js
   - When: Items are created or enter this folder; Items are updated
   - Perform Action: Execute Script addTestRating.js

4. When the rule is created, upload a document in this newly created folder.
   Automatically, you should see that a new rating has been added automatically:

5. On the same document, just upload a new version, and a new rating should be
   added:

```
▼ Properties                                                    ✎

     Name:  MyDoc.pdf

     Title:  (None)

     Description:  (None)

     Author:  (None)

     Average Rating:  4

     Ratings:    ▢  rating1471941446713    ▢  rating1471941589319

     Mimetype:  Adobe PDF          Size:  95 KB
     Document

     Creator:  admin               Created Date:  Tue 23 Aug 2016
                                    09:37:26

     Modifier:  admin              Modified Date:  Tue 23 Aug 2016
                                    09:39:49
```

Every time you create a new version, a new rating (with a random value) will be created as a child node of that content. If you look at the properties, the average rating should be updated too.

The default out of the box display for associations is simply a list of paths to the associated content. That's not helpful, in this case, if you want to see an individual rating value. Right now, the easiest way is to use the node browser.

Handling deleted ratings

If you edit the properties, you'll notice that each rating has a remove icon. If you delete a rating, the rating will go away. But you didn't bind `onDeleteNode` to a behavior, so the average will not get recalculated. Let's see how we can fix that.

To handle deleted ratings, you're going to edit `com.someco.repo.behavior.Rating` to add a new behavior for `onDeleteNode` that will call a method to recalculate the rating stats. Follow these steps:

1. First, the class now needs to implement the `OnDeleteNodePolicy`, so update the class declaration:

```
public class Rating
  implements NodeServicePolicies.OnDeleteNodePolicy,
            NodeServicePolicies.OnCreateNodePolicy {
```

2. Update the `init` method with the appropriate logic to instantiate and bind the `onDeleteNode` behavior:

```
this.onDeleteNode = new JavaBehaviour(this,
   OnDeleteNodePolicy.QNAME.getLocalName(),
   NotificationFrequency.TRANSACTION_COMMIT);
this.policyComponent.bindClassBehaviour(
     OnDeleteNodePolicy.QNAME,
   SomeCoModel.TYPE_RATING, this.onDeleteNode);
```

3. Add the `onDeleteNode` method. The method calls a method used to recalculate the rating statistics:

```
@Override
public void onDeleteNode(ChildAssociationRef childAssocRef,
  boolean isNodeArchived) {
    if (childAssocRef != null &&
     nodeService.exists(childAssocRef.getParentRef()))
    recalculateAverage(childAssocRef.getParentRef());
  }
```

4. Finally, implement the `recalculateAverage` method. The method knows how to iterate over a node's children to calculate the total rating, rating count, and average. The reason why it can't use a running total approach like `addRating` is that by this point, the rating has already been deleted:

```
public void recalculateAverage(NodeRef parentRef) {
    if (logger.isDebugEnabled())
      logger.debug("Inside recalculateAverage");
   // check the parent to make sure it has the right aspect
    if (nodeService.hasAspect(parentRef,
        SomeCoModel.ASPECT_RATEABLE)) {
      // continue, this is what we want
    } else {
      if (logger.isDebugEnabled())
        logger.debug("Rating's parent didn't have rateable aspect.");
      return;
    }
    // get the parent node's children
    List<ChildAssociationRef> children = nodeService
      .getChildAssocs(parentRef);
    Double average = 0d;
    int total = 0;
    // This actually happens when the last rating is deleted
    if (children.size() == 0) {
      // No children so no work to do
      if (logger.isDebugEnabled())
```

```
        logger.debug("No children found");
    } else {
        // iterate through the children to compute the total
        for (ChildAssociationRef child : children) {
            if (nodeService.getType(child.getChildRef())
                .equals(SomeCoModel.TYPE_RATING)) {
              int rating = (Integer) nodeService.getProperty(
                  child.getChildRef(), SomeCoModel.PROP_RATING);
               total += rating;
            }
        }
        // compute the average
        average = total / (children.size() / 1.0d);
        if (logger.isDebugEnabled())
          logger.debug("Computed average:" + average);
    }
    // store the average on the parent node
    nodeService.setProperty(parentRef,
      SomeCoModel.PROP_AVERAGERATING, average);
    nodeService.setProperty(parentRef,
      SomeCoModel.PROP_TOTALRATING, total);
    nodeService.setProperty(parentRef,
      SomeCoModel.PROP_RATINGCOUNT, children.size());
    if (logger.isDebugEnabled())
      logger.debug("Property set");
}
```

5. Don't forget to define the few constants and variables that we need:

```
private static Logger logger =
Logger.getLogger(Rating.class);
private Behaviour onDeleteNode;
```

6. Now save, deploy, restart, and test.

To summarize, each time that you delete a rating from Alfresco Share, it will recalculate the average rating. However, we configured a rule on the same folder that create a random rating each time that the document is updated. It means that, even if you delete all ratings from the edit form, a new rating will be automatically added.

Extracting metadata from files

Many authoring tools provide a mechanism for capturing metadata within the authoring tool user interface. If certain pieces of metadata are already stored as part of the file, why force content contributors to re-key the metadata when they add the content to the repository? Alfresco can use metadata extractors to inspect the file, extract the metadata, and save the metadata in the node's properties.

A metadata extractor is a Java class configured as a Spring bean that either gets called when content is created in the repository, or when the extractor is invoked by a rule action. Alfresco knows which extractor to use for a given piece of content because metadata extractors declare the MIME types they support.

Metadata extractors have a default mapping that identifies which pieces of file metadata should be stored in which node properties. The property mapping can be overridden by pointing to a custom mapping in the Spring bean configuration.

Customizing metadata extractors

SomeCo would like to set the `sc:clientName` property with the value of the keywords property in Word files. Alfresco already provides extractors for Word. The Word extractor knows how to retrieve the keywords from a Word file, but it is not mapped by default.

Step-by-step – customizing the metadata mapping

Let's customize the metadata mapping for the Office extractor so that when SomeCo adds Office documents to the repository, the keywords property gets stored in the `sc:clientName` property. This is just a matter of overriding the default mapping file. To do that, follow these steps:

1. Create a new Spring context file in **src|main|amp|config|alfresco|module|repo|context** within the `repo` project called `extractor-context.xml`.

2. Then, edit the extractor-context.xml file that overrides the out-of-the-box extracter.Poi bean, and points to a custom mapping file:

```xml
<?xml version='1.0' encoding='UTF-8'?>
<!DOCTYPE beans PUBLIC '-//SPRING//DTD BEAN//EN'
'http://www.springframework.org/dtd/spring-beans.dtd'>
<beans>
<bean id="extracter.Poi"
  class="org.alfresco.repo.content.metadata.PoiMetadataExtracter"
  parent="baseMetadataExtracter">
    <property name="inheritDefaultMapping">
        <value>false</value>
    </property>
    <property name="mappingProperties">
        <bean class="org.springframework.beans
        .factory.config.PropertiesFactoryBean">
            <property name="location">
                <value>classpath:alfresco
                /module/${project.artifactId}
                /extractor-mappings.properties</value>
            </property>
        </bean>
    </property>
</bean>
</beans>
```

3. As usual when we create a new Spring context file, we need to reference it in your module-context.xml file. You should be able to do it by your own now.

4. Create a new file in the src | main | amp | config | alfresco | module directory called extractor-mappings.properties. The custom mapping just needs to specify what to do with the keywords. The namespace for the property's content model also has to be declared. The entire contents of the properties file look like this:

```
namespace.prefix.cm=http://www.alfresco.org/model/content/1.0
namespace.prefix.sc=http://www.someco.com/model/content/1.0
    author=cm:author
    title=cm:title
    description=cm:description
    created=cm:created
    Keywords=sc:clientName
```

5. Sometimes, it may be tricky to know which extractor will be used by Alfresco. In my test, I'll use a `*.docx` document, and so I know that the `POIExtractor` will be used. To have more details, add these two lines to your `log4j.properties` (located in `repo | src | main | amp | config | alfresco | module | repo`):

```
log4j.logger.org.alfresco.repo.content
    .metadata=DEBUG log4j.logger.org.alfresco.repo.content
    .metadata.AbstractMappingMetadataExtracter=DEBUG
```

6. Deploy the change and restart Tomcat.

Now set up a test. When a document is added to SomeCo's Sales folder, three things need to happen: The document needs to be specialized to `sc:salesDoc`, the `sc:clientRelated` aspect needs to be added, and the metadata needs to get extracted. This is not completely true; you don't really need to add the aspect manually. The default behavior when you set a property from an aspect on a node via the Java API is that the aspect is added automatically. However, it makes your rule cleaner and makes more sense to add the aspect manually. One way to make sure that happens is to set up an inbound rule on the Sales folder. Let's do it:

1. Log in to Alfresco Share, and create a new site called **Sales**.
2. In the **Document Library**, create a new folder called **Public Document**.
3. Create a new rule on this newly created folder:
    - Name: Create Public Sales Document
    - When: Items are created or enter this folder
4. If all criteria are met:
    - Content of type or sub-type is Content

5. Perform Action:
    1. Specialise Type to Someco Sales Document
    2. Add Aspect Someco Client Metadata
    3. Extract common metadata fields

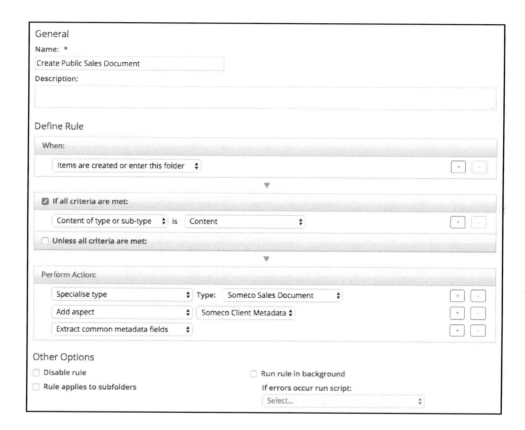

6. Save the rule.

7. Create a test Microsoft Office document. (You can use OpenOffice. Just save the file as one of the Microsoft Office formats). Use **File**, **Properties** to set the Keywords with a client name. Save the file.

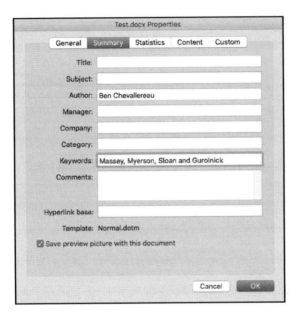

8. Add the file to the **Public Document** folder. In the properties panel, the **Client Name** property should default to the value you set using Office:

You can notice that the list of keywords appears in the **Description** and **Client Name** fields. The main reason is because Apache Tika populates the description automatically in this case (you can notice that in your log files by inspecting the Raw Properties generated by the extractor). To avoid this use case, we just need to edit the file extractor-mappings.properties and change the description mapping:

```
description=
```

If it doesn't work, it's probably because you are not customizing the right extractor. If you added the two lines in your log4j.properties, you should notice the following messages. The important message is the Get returning one that shows which extractor that will be used.

```
DEBUG [content.metadata.MetadataExtracterRegistry] [http-apr-8080-exec-4]
Get extractors for application/vnd.openxmlformats-
officedocument.wordprocessingml.document
DEBUG [content.metadata.MetadataExtracterRegistry] [http-apr-8080-exec-4]
Finding extractors for application/vnd.openxmlformats-
officedocument.wordprocessingml.document
DEBUG [content.metadata.MetadataExtracterRegistry] [http-apr-8080-exec-4]
Find supported:    extracter.TikaAuto
DEBUG [content.metadata.MetadataExtracterRegistry] [http-apr-8080-exec-4]
Find unsupported: extracter.PDFBox
DEBUG [content.metadata.MetadataExtracterRegistry] [http-apr-8080-exec-4]
Find supported:    extracter.Poi
DEBUG [content.metadata.MetadataExtracterRegistry] [http-apr-8080-exec-4]
Find unsupported: extracter.Office
DEBUG [content.metadata.MetadataExtracterRegistry] [http-apr-8080-exec-4]
Find unsupported: extracter.Mail
DEBUG [content.metadata.MetadataExtracterRegistry] [http-apr-8080-exec-4]
Find unsupported: extracter.Html
DEBUG [content.metadata.MetadataExtracterRegistry] [http-apr-8080-exec-4]
Find unsupported: extracter.OpenDocument
DEBUG [content.metadata.MetadataExtracterRegistry] [http-apr-8080-exec-4]
Find unsupported: extracter.DWG
DEBUG [content.metadata.MetadataExtracterRegistry] [http-apr-8080-exec-4]
Find unsupported: extracter.RFC822
DEBUG [content.metadata.MetadataExtracterRegistry] [http-apr-8080-exec-4]
Find unsupported: extracter.MP3
DEBUG [content.metadata.MetadataExtracterRegistry] [http-apr-8080-exec-4]
Find unsupported: extracter.Audio
DEBUG [content.metadata.MetadataExtracterRegistry] [http-apr-8080-exec-4]
Find unsupported: extracter.OpenOffice
DEBUG [content.metadata.MetadataExtracterRegistry] [http-apr-8080-exec-4]
Find unsupported: extracter.JodConverter
DEBUG [content.metadata.MetadataExtracterRegistry] [http-apr-8080-exec-4]
Find returning:
```

```
[org.alfresco.repo.content.metadata.TikaAutoMetadataExtracter@1b50ea6c,
org.alfresco.repo.content.metadata.PoiMetadataExtracter@3cf4021c]
DEBUG [content.metadata.MetadataExtracterRegistry] [http-apr-8080-exec-4]
Get supported:   extracter.TikaAuto
DEBUG [content.metadata.MetadataExtracterRegistry] [http-apr-8080-exec-4]
Get supported:   extracter.Poi
DEBUG [content.metadata.MetadataExtracterRegistry] [http-apr-8080-exec-4]
Get returning:   extracter.Poi
```

If metadata extraction is automatic, you may be wondering why we explicitly invoked it as part of the rule. It's a workaround for a little timing problem. Without the rule to explicitly invoke metadata extraction, Alfresco will perform the metadata extraction on its own because it recognizes the MIME type and it knows it has a metadata extractor configured for that MIME type. The problem is that it performs the metadata extraction before it has added the aspect. So in Alfresco Share, the clientName property doesn't default to the extracted metadata as you've specified. Using a rule to explicitly invoke the extraction forces Alfresco to add the aspect, then set the property. A side effect to this workaround is that the extractor gets invoked twice-once by Alfresco when the document is initially created, and a second time when the rule is fired.

Overriding the default mapping

Note that in this case, in the extractor POI Spring bean, inheritDefaultMapping, is set to false. This means that we redefine the entire mapping, that we can find in alfresco | metadata | PoiMetadataExtracter.properties packaged in the alfresco-repository-5.x.jar.

Leveraging out-of-the-box metadata extractors

There are several metadata extractors configured out of the box. These include:

- **Microsoft Office, OpenOffice.org, and Adobe PDF**: These extract summary information such as author, title, subject, and created date
- **HTML**: This extracts author, title, and description from META tags
- **MP3**: This extracts song, album, artist, year, track number, and several other fields from ID3 tags
- **XML**: This extracts Strings from XML using XPath expressions
- **Mail**: This extracts typical email information like sent date, originator or subject line.

When you add a piece of content matching any of these types to the repository, Alfresco invokes the metadata extractor and populates the node's properties as specified in the extractor's default mapping file.

A complete list of the out of the box metadata extractors, their class names, bean IDs, and the out of the box properties they extract is provided in the Appendix.

Transforming content from one format to another

A content transformer is used to transform content from one format to another. Content transformers are implemented as a Java class configured as a Spring bean. Alfresco finds the appropriate transformer based on source and target MIME type. There are two important use cases for transformers. The first is when an end user triggers a transformation, usually through an action. The most well-known out of the box example is converting Microsoft Office documents to PDF. Other out of the box transformers include:

- HTML-to-text
- Microsoft Excel-to-CSV
- Microsoft Word-to-text
- PDF-to-text
- Images-to-Images

See the Appendix for further details on the out of the box transformers.

The second key transformer use case involves the Solr full-text search engine. Solr indexes content when it is added to the repository. But the Alfresco Tracker code embedded in Solr only understands plain text. The Solr process sends queries every 15 seconds by default to Alfresco to get all changes in the Alfresco repository. After a binary file is added to the repository and need to be indexed in Solr, Alfresco looks for a transformer that can convert the file to plain text. The plain text is then sent back to Solr. If there is a content type that Alfresco doesn't know how to full-text index out of the box, the trick is to write a content transformer for it and you're in business.

Step-by-step – writing a custom transformer

SomeCo works a lot with Microsoft Project files. The project files have task and resource information that would be useful to search against. But Alfresco doesn't have a content transformer that deals with Microsoft Project files, so out of the box Microsoft Project files aren't full-text indexed. In order to rectify that situation, you're going to have to write a custom transformer that converts Microsoft Project files to plain text.

Content transformers extend `AbstractContentTransformer2`, which implements the `ContentTransformer` interface. At a minimum, all that is required for a custom content transformer is to implement twomethods. The `transformInternal()` method is used to actually perform the transformation. The `isTransformable()` method is used to specify if the transformer supports or not the transformation. Obviously, you'll also need an API that knows how to read the source format.

So, to do this task you'll need to:

1. Write a custom class that extends `AbstractContentTransformer2`.
2. Configure a Spring bean to declare the new transformer.
3. Tell Alfresco about the Microsoft Project MIME type.

To write a custom content transformer that uses MPXJ to convert Microsoft Project files to plain text, follow these steps:

1. Create a new class in `repo | src | main | java` called `com.someco.repo.transformer.ProjectToPlainText` that extends `AbstractContentTransformer2`.

2. Open your Maven `pom.xml` file in the repo project and add the following dependency:

```
<dependency>
    <groupId>net.sf.mpxj</groupId>
    <artifactId>mpxj</artifactId>
    <version>5.3.1</version>
</dependency>
```

3. Lets's start by the `isTransformable()` method to specify that we can transform from MSProject files to plain text files.

```
public boolean isTransformable(
    String sourceMimetype,
    String targetMimetype,
    TransformationOptions options) {
  if ("application/vnd.ms-project"
    .equalsIgnoreCase(sourceMimetype)
    && MimetypeMap.MIMETYPE_TEXT_PLAIN
    .equalsIgnoreCase(targetMimetype))
      return true;
      return false;
}
```

4. Next is the `transformInternal()` method. It does the bulk of the work, although the MPXJ library does the heavy lifting. The method uses the MPXJ library to iterate through the tasks and writes out the task information:

```
@Override
protected void transformInternal(
    ContentReader reader,
    ContentWriter writer,
    TransformationOptions options) throws Exception {
  Writer out = new BufferedWriter(
    new OutputStreamWriter(writer.getContentOutputStream()));

  ProjectFile mpp = new MPPReader().read(
    reader.getContentInputStream());
  ProjectProperties projectHeader = mpp.getProjectProperties();
  List<Task> listAllTasks = mpp.getAllTasks();
  List<Resource> listAllResources = mpp.getAllResources();

  out.write(projectHeader.getProjectTitle());
  for (Task task : listAllTasks) {
    out.write("ID:" + task.getID());
    out.write(" TASK:" + task.getName());
    if (task.getNotes() != null)
      out.write(" NOTES:" + task.getNotes());
    if (task.getContact() != null)
      out.write(" CONTACT:" + task.getContact());
    out.write("\r\n");
  }
  for (Resource resource : listAllResources) {
    out.write("RESOURCE:" + resource.getName());
    if (resource.getEmailAddress() != null)
      out.write(" EMAIL:" + resource.getEmailAddress());
```

```
      if (resource.getNotes() != null)
        out.write("  NOTES:" + resource.getNotes());
      out.write("\r\n");
    }

    out.flush();

    if (out != null) {
      out.close();
    }
  }
```

 The labels that get output in all caps ("NOTES", "CONTACT", and so on) don't do anything special. In fact, they add unnecessarily to the index. But if you actually want to try to read this output, it helps to have some markers in there. In a production implementation, it is probably best to leave them out.

5. That's all for the class. Now create a file in repo|src|main|amp|config|alfresco|module|repo|context called transformer-context.xml with the following:

```
<?xml version='1.0' encoding='UTF-8'?>
<!DOCTYPE beans PUBLIC '-//SPRING//DTD BEAN//EN'
'http://www.springframework.org/dtd/spring-beans.dtd'>
<beans>
</beans>
```

6. The bean to add declares the new transformer. The ID follows the Alfresco convention of starting with "transformer.":

```
<bean id="transformer.MSProject"
  class="com.someco.repo.transformer.ProjectToPlainText"
  parent="baseContentTransformer" />
```

7. Update the module-context.xml file in your repo project to include your newly Spring bean context file as usual.

8. Now, we need to define the supported MIME types. Edit the file alfresco-global.properties located in repo | src | main | amp | config | alfresco | module by adding these lines (be extremely careful, Alfresco is following strong rule to define the property names):

```
content.transformer.MSProject.priority=100
content.transformer.MSProject.extensions.mpp.txt.supported=true
```

9. Deploy, restart, and test.

To see what's going on with the out of the box content transformers, set
`log4j.logger.org.alfresco.repo.content.transform.Transfor merDebug` and
`log4j.logger.org.alfresco.repo.content.transform` equals to `DEBUG`.

To test the new content transformer, add a Microsoft Project file anywhere in the repository, then do a search for a piece of text contained within the file, but not in the file name. The test should return the Microsoft Project file. This would not have been possible prior to deploying the custom Microsoft Project-to-Plain Text content transformer. Another option is to create a rule that transform all Microsoft Project files to text files. Using this method, you can review exactly what Alfresco generates and indexes.

If you want to test, you can find a sample MS Project file in repo|resources that we downloaded from `http://www.techno-pm.com/p/sample-it-pro ject-plan.html`.

Summary

This chapter covered four different ways in which you can automatically process content as it is created, read, updated, and deleted. Specifically, you learned how to:

- Write custom actions both with and without action parameters, as well as how to invoke actions from JavaScript
- Bind logic to custom types using behaviors, including the logic that has a deal with the fact that it may have to wait until an existing transaction completes
- Extract metadata from binary files to reduce the amount of re-keying content contributors have to do when adding content to the repository
- Transform content from one format to another to facilitate full-text searching, or to simply provide a way for users to generate additional output formats from the same piece of content

When planning your own Alfresco implementations and Alfresco-based solutions, it is important to keep these hooks in mind. This is because the more code that can be moved into these areas, the more flexible and end-user configurable your solution will be.

5
Customizing Alfresco Share

Alfresco Share is an all-purpose user interface for general document management. As such, it may not be specific enough for the solution you are trying to implement. Or, you may have the opposite problem-too many choices can confuse the users. The good news is that Alfresco Share is easily configurable and can be extended.

By the end of this chapter, you will know how to:

- Add new action items to the Alfresco Share
- Show/hide menu items based on things such as permissions or arbitrary logic
- Create custom metadata template to change how Alfresco Share shows repository data
- Create custom dialogs to gather information from a user
- Create new pages into Alfresco Share
- Create new dashlets into Alfresco Share
- Assess whether the solution you are building should be based on a custom version of Alfresco Share or would be more appropriate as a custom application

 It is important to note that with the 4.2 release (and expanded with the 5.1 release), Alfresco introduced a new UI framework called **Aikau.**

There is always more than one option to implement something in Alfresco Share. Today, if you want to create a page or a dashlet, you have two main options: Aikau or Surf. This book will cover mainly the use of the Surf framework. The main reason is that Surf is a framework on the market for quite a while, and you'll find a lot of examples about it online. If you want to look for Aikau tutorials, Alfresco is providing as well a lot of information online in their documentation; `http://docs.alfresco.com/`

Knowing when to customize Alfresco Share and when to write your own

Before you set off on that big Alfresco Share customization project you've been dreaming of, it is important to ask yourself if the Alfresco Share is the right place for your customizations. The key consideration is how closely does your solution resemble the generic "document management" use case? If the answer is that it is quite close such that the list of substantial customizations is fairly small, then proceed. SomeCo's internal rollout is a good example of this. So far, everything SomeCo is looking to do with Alfresco has been about managing documents. The customizations have been small tweaks aimed at streamlining certain tasks for the end users.

However, if your solution is radically different from document management or is composed of several significant customizations, you should think twice about customizing Share. Instead, consider building a custom application loosely coupled to the repository through services. Here's why:

- At some point, it takes longer to customize Share to meet the requirements than it would have to build a custom solution on top of the repository. Solutions that stray too far from the "document management" use case end up wasting a lot of development effort removing or hiding Alfresco's out of the box features.
- Numerous and/or significant customizations present a heavy maintenance and upgrade burden, even when you stick to Alfresco's extension mechanism. As the number and complexity of the customizations increase, make sure what's left of the web client after you've customized it still adds enough value to compensate for the costs and overhead.
- If your solution could work without Alfresco Share, why lock yourself in? An n-tier solution leveraging Alfresco to provide "content as a service" will be much more flexible in the long run.
- Alfresco controls the future direction of Share. You can certainly influence Alfresco's product road map to a much greater extent than you can with proprietary vendors. But Alfresco, the commercial software company, still has ultimate control over Alfresco, the product. If you make significant investments in a solution based on a customized Share, you are risking future migration costs if and when Alfresco decides to change how Share is built.

All of this can be summarized with the old adage, "*Use the right tool for the right job*". If the customizations you are making seem natural and in line with how Share is "supposed" to be used, you are using the right tool for the right job. If, however, you are constantly "fighting" with Share features or metaphors, you may be pushing Share beyond what it was originally intended for. This may cause issues for you down the line.

Adding new menu items

Probably the simplest form of UI customization is adding new menu item in the header. In our use case, we'll add external URL.

Step-by-step – adding a simple menu item

Suppose SomeCo wanted to add a set of links to the Alfresco user interface. In this case, Alfresco Share is using the Aikauto display the header of the page. If you want to modify it, you'll need to use Aikau (and not Surf). To know where Aikau is used in Alfresco Share, you can check the following page
`http://docs.alfresco.com/5.1/concepts/aikau-intro.html` and scroll to the section *Aikau use in Share*.

Let's discover a bit more about Aikau. The main goal of the Aikau framework is to provide a library of widgets that can be re-used and assembled into a web application. Aikau won't replace Alfresco Share, but will be used more and more to move from its original Surf implementation. The main objectives of Aikau are:

- Maximize code re-use
- Build user interfaces faster
- Simplify greatly the customization of page

Don't believe that Aikau and Surf are completely decoupled. For example, an Aikau page is based on the Surf framework but it makes the composition of the page easier than pure Surf pages. However, as explained in the previous section, this book will mainly cover the Surf framework. If you are more interested by Aikau, the Alfresco documentation explains how to create menus, pages, dashlets and widgets using the Aikau framework on this page
`http://docs.alfresco.com/5.1/concepts/dev-extensions-share-extension-points-int roduction.html`.

Before starting the development, let's dig in the Surf Extension process which is the preferred way to customize Alfresco Share. If you open the Alfresco Share deployed web application, and if you look at the folder **WEB-INF | classes | alfresco**, you should find a lot of files ending by -config.xml, such as share-config.xml. These files contain configuration that are loaded into a Spring bean and used by Alfresco Share to define many aspects of its behavior. If you want to change this behavior, you won't update this file directly in the web application. You'll create a file called share-config-custom.xml that we'll introduce later in this chapter. This file will override the default configuration. Unfortunately, there is no easy way to modify this file if you don't have access to the server. Moreover, it's not really easy to split the configuration in different unites, name them, and version them. It's why Alfresco Share integrates the concept of *Spring Surf Extension Modules*. They enable dynamic control of the Share configuration at runtime. These modules can be deployed and un-deployed without restarting the server (but it will need a server restart if you install a new module).Instead of having everything in one long share-config-custom.xml file, configuration can now be named and kept in different modules so it is easy for an Administrator to deploy and un-deploy different configuration settings at runtime. We'll start by creating a new extension module file.

1. First, we need to create an Aikau extension module file. Create a new file called `someco-header.xml` in the directory where all extensions are defined **src | main | amp | config | alfresco | web-extension | site-data | extensions** located in the `share` project.

```
<extension>
  <modules>
    <module>
      <id> Add SomeCo links to header</id>
      <version>1.0</version>
      <auto-deploy>true</auto-deploy>
      <customizations>
        <customization>

<targetPackageRoot>org.alfresco.share.header</targetPackageRoot>
          <sourcePackageRoot>com.someco.header</sourcePackageRoot>
        </customization>
      </customizations>
    </module>
  </modules>
</extension>
```

2. As you can see, we configured the module to auto deploy. It means that you won't have to deploy it manually using the following page `http://localhost:8080/share/page/modules/deploy`.

3. If you check the customizations section, we ask Share to look for customizations in the folder **com|someco|header**, when awebscript located in the folder **org|alfresco|share|header** is called. What does it really mean? If you open the Share web application, and look into the folder **WEB-INF|classes|alfresco|site-webscripts|org|alfresco|share|header**, you'll find files starting by share-header. These files represent a web script that is called to render the Share header. What we need to do is to customize this webscript. To summarize, this extension mechanism is used to extend any webscriptin Alfresco Share. So, you can hook into the model object and modify it. Don't worry if it's not clear, it will be clarified in the following steps.

4. Then, we need to create the directories **com|someco|header** (related to the tag sourcePackageRoot in the previous step) in the folder **src|main|amp|config|alfresco|web-extension|site-webscripts**. As you can see, we are using the web-extension folder that is used to extend Alfresco Share. And the sub-folder site-webscripts because we want to override the default header webscript in Alfresco Share (we are mimicking the structure in the Share web application). Then, create the web script controller called share-header.get.js in this newly created folder. We just need to override the controller, and we want to keep all other artifacts unchanged. The first step is to retrieve the object representing the menu bar:

```
var headerMenu = widgetUtils.findObject(model.jsonModel, "id",
  "HEADER_APP_MENU_BAR");
if (headerMenu != null) {
  [...]
}
```

5. You have different way to find the widget id HEADER_APP_MENU_BAR. The first way is to look at the source code. If you look at the file WEB-INF|classes|alfresco|site-webscripts|org|alfresco|share|header|share-header.get.js in the Share web application, you should find two important information. The first one is that the list of widgets is computed by a function called getHeaderModel not present in this file.

```
{
  id: "SHARE_VERTICAL_LAYOUT",
  name: "alfresco/layout/VerticalWidgets",
config:
  {
    widgets: getHeaderModel()
  }
}
```

6. And at the top of the file, you can see that an external Javascript file is imported:

```
<import resource="classpath:/alfresco/site-webscripts
  /org/alfresco/share/imports/share-header.lib.js">
```

7. If you open the file listed above `WEB-INF|classes|alfresco|site-webscripts|org|alfresco|share|imports|share-header.lib.js`, you can find the function `getHeaderModel`, that contains a variable called `headerModel`, and you can finally see the following widget:

```
{
  id: "HEADER_APP_MENU_BAR",
  name: "alfresco/header/AlfMenuBar",
  align: "left",
  config: {
     widgets: headerMenus.appItems
  }
}
```

8. Another option is to use the debugger mode of your browser, and you should find the `widgetId` on the HTML tag:

```
<div class="alfresco-menus-AlfMenuBar"
  data-dojo-attach-point="containerNode"
  id="HEADER_APP_MENU_BAR"
   widgetid="HEADER_APP_MENU_BAR">
  ...
</div>
```

9. Then, we can define our new dropdown including three links:

```
headerMenu.config.widgets.push({
id : "HEADER_SOMECO_LINKS",
name : "alfresco/header/AlfMenuBarPopup",
config : {
id : "HEADER_SOMECO_LINKS",
label : "SomeCo Links",
widgets : [ {
   id : "HEADER_SOMECO_LINKS_GROUP",
   name : "alfresco/menus/AlfMenuGroup",
   config : {
   widgets : [ {
       id : "HEADER_SOMECO_LINKS_CORPORATE",
       name : "alfresco/header/AlfMenuItem",
       config : {
       label : "Corporate Website",
       targetUrl : "http://www.alfresco.com",
```

```
                targetUrlType : "FULL_PATH",
                targetUrlLocation : "NEW"
                }
            }, {
                id : "HEADER_SOMECO_LINKS_SEARCHENGINE",
                name : "alfresco/header/AlfMenuItem",
                config : {
                label : "Google",
                targetUrl : "http://www.google.com",
                targetUrlType : "FULL_PATH",
                targetUrlLocation : "NEW"
                }
            }, {
                id : "HEADER_SOMECO_LINKS_DOCUMENTATION",
                name : "alfresco/header/AlfMenuItem",
                config : {
                label : "Alfresco Documentation",
                targetUrl : "http://docs.alfresco.com",
                targetUrlType : "FULL_PATH",
                targetUrlLocation : "NEW"
                }
            } ]
        }
    } ]
    }
    });
```

10. All that we do in this step is to extend a JSON model that we retrieved in the previous step using the object widgetUtils. Our JSON object is first defining a menu bar popup (alfresco/header/AlfMenuBarPopup), that contains a menu group (alfresco/menus/AlfMenuGroup), that contains itself three menu items (alfresco/header/AlfMenuItem). You may wonder which properties you can use on each item. You can look at the Alfresco Share source code to find the inspiration. But, you can look at the Aikau Widgets documentation `https://dev.alfresco.com/resource/docs/aikau-jsdoc`.

11. Deploy, restart, and test.

You should now be able to log in and see the different links in the header:

---

[179]

Adding new action items

In the previous example, we just added some generic links in the header but there was no repository action behind that. In the previous chapter, we created some repository actions and we had to use some tricks to be able to test them. And now, in this section, we'll explain how to add a UI action related to the web flag on documents.

Step-by-step – adding an action item to set the web flag

Recall that a subset of SomeCo's Whitepapers will be available on the Web. Whitepapers that need to be published to the Web are identified by the `sc:webable` aspect, which contains an `isActive` flag. SomeCo employees can add or remove a Whitepaper to or from the Web by setting the flag to true or false. But SomeCo doesn't want just anybody to be able to set that flag. Alfresco doesn't have field-level security out of the box. So how can this be implemented?

One way to do this is to configure the property to be read-only in the interface and then use two actions, available only to the people who need it, to enable or disable this flag.

Let's do just that and let's start by Alfresco Share. All following changes will be done in the share project.

1. First, we need to create a new `config` element in the `share-config-custom.xml` file (located in `share|src|main|resources|META-INF`)with the condition attribute equals to `DocLibActions`:

```
<config evaluator="string-compare" condition="DocLibActions">
 <actions>
    [...]
 </actions>
</config>
We could have packaged that in a Surf Extension Module to be able to
enable/disable these actions. And it's highly recommended to do it in a
real life project. But to keep this section short and simple enough, we'll
define directly the configuration in this file. However, if you want to
create an extension instead. Just move the config element from the share-
config-custom.xml file, to a new XML file that you'll store in
src|main|amp|config|alfresco|web-extension|site-data|extensions.
<extension>
    <modules>
        <module>
```

```
            <id>Add SomeCo Document Library Actions</id>
            <version>1.0</version>
            <auto-deploy>true</auto-deploy>
            <configurations>
                <config evaluator="string-compare"
                condition="DocLibActions">
                    <actions>
                        [...]
                    </actions>
                </config>
            </configurations>
        </module>
    </modules>
</extension>
```

2. Then, we define the two actions using the type javascript. Other type exists like link or pagelink. Using the out-of-the-box Javascript handler onActionSimpleRepoAction, we just need to provide the identifier of the action within Alfresco. If we need to collect parameters from the user, we'll need to use the handler onActionFormDialog.

```
<action id="someco-web-enable" type="javascript" label="actions.someco-web-
enable" icon="someco-web-enable">
    <param name="function">onActionSimpleRepoAction</param>
    <param name="action">set-web-flag</param>
    <param name="active">true</param>
    <param name="successMessage">message.web-flag.enabled</param>
    <param name="failureMessage">message.web-flag.failure</param>
</action>
<action id="someco-web-disable" type="javascript" label="actions.someco-
web-disable" icon="someco-web-disable">
    <param name="function">onActionSimpleRepoAction</param>
    <param name="action">set-web-flag</param>
    <param name="active">false</param>
    <param name="successMessage">message.web-flag.disabled</param>
    <param name="failureMessage">message.web-flag.failure</param>
</action>
```

3. You can find the available list of parameters on this page http://docs.alfresco .com/5.1/tasks/dev-extensions-share-tutorials-add-action-doclib.html
.

4. In the same config element, define that you want to display these two actions in the browse and details pages:

```
<actionGroups>
    <actionGroup id="document-browse">
        <action index="400" id="someco-web-enable" />
        <action index="400" id="someco-web-disable" />
    </actionGroup>
    <actionGroup id="document-details">
        <action index="400" id="someco-web-enable" />
        <action index="400" id="someco-web-disable" />
    </actionGroup>
</actionGroups>
```

5. The index property is used to order the list of actions. If you look at the corresponding config element in the file WEB-INF|classes|alfresco|share-documentlibrary-config.xml, you'll see the index of all out-of-the-box actions.

6. Edit the file share.properties to define the different messages:

```
actions.someco-web-enable=SC Enable Web Flag
actions.someco-web-disable=SC Disable Web Flag
message.web-flag.enabled=Successfully enabled the SomeCo active flag
message.web-flag.disabled=Successfully disabled the SomeCo active flag
message.web-flag.failure=Error setting the SomeCo Web Flag
```

7. The two first lines defines the name of the action in Alfresco Share. The naming convention is easy to guess; it looks like that:

```
actions.<ACTIONID>=...
```

8. For the three last lines, we just re-use the keys that we defined in the step 2.

9. The last step is to add the icons. Create the directory components|documentlibrary|actions(to deploy our icons in the same folder as all other Alfresco Share ones) within the folder src|main|amp|web. Within this folder, create two icons called *someco-web-enable-16.png* and *someco-web-disable-16.png*.Be careful about the filename. As you easily understand, the filename must follow this convention:

```
<ACTIONID>-16.png
```

10. These icons have to be 16px square icons.

11. Deploy, restart, and test.

To test this, log in to Alfresco Share. On both the list of actions in the document list page and the details page, you should see the two new actions. By clicking on it, the sc:active tag should be updated automatically.

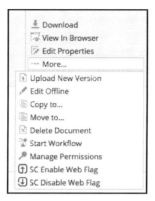

On the following screenshot, you can see how actions are displayed on the document detail page.

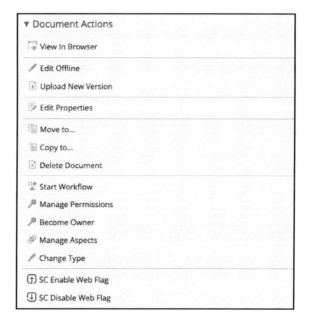

You can notice that these two actions are available to everyone and to all documents in the Alfresco repository. In the next section, we'll create some evaluator to display only these actions in relevant cases.

Restricting the action item by permission

For the next steps, you'll need to use another user than admin. By default, Alfresco contains another user called `abeecher` but is disabled by default. Use the **Admin Tools** section to re-enable `abeecher` and pick your own password. If you login using this new username, you can search for the **Marketing** site (if you keep the default visibility **Public**) and join it. This user becomes **Consumer** of the site and has only read-only permissions on documents. If you try to click on the two action items created previously, you should get an error. It's because thisuser has not been granted at least "write" permission on the test Whitepaper.

For each action item in the actions tag, add the following permission configuration:

```
<permissions>
    <permission allow="true">Write</permission>
</permissions>
```

If you re-deploy, you'll notice that the user `abeecher` can't see anymore these two actions, but they are still visible for the admin user.

> The permission elements that are part of the action's definition in `share-config-custom.xml` can use any of the permission groups Alfresco knows about. In this case you specified `Write`, which is a lower-level permission group. But you could also specify one of the higher-level groups such as `Coordinator` if it makes sense to do so for your solution. See the Appendix for information on the out of the box permission groups.

Writing action evaluators to show/hide UI actions

In the previous example, you set up two action items to enable and disable the `isActive` flag for a webable piece of content. The actions only show up if a user has the appropriate permissions. But what if SomeCo wants to give several different people or groups `Write` permission, but only wants a subset of those folks to be able to publish documents to the Web? Not only that, but isn't it a bit sloppy to show the **Enable** link when the `isActive` flag is already set to **True** (and **Disable** when it is already set to **False**)?

Both of these issues are easily addressed using Spring beans and out-of-the-box Alfresco Share evaluators. Evaluators are used to control if an action item should be displayed or not. If you don't find what you need in the standard evaluators, you can as well create your own evaluator coded in Java (more information here `http://docs.alfresco.com/5.1/tas ks/dev-extensions-share-tutorials-custom-evaluator.html`).

Step-by-step – evaluating whether or not to show the set web flag actions

SomeCo wants to create a group called "SomeCo'sPublisher" and populate it with the people and groups allowed to click the **Enable** and **Disable** Actions created in the previous example. Additionally, if the flag is set to **True**, the **Enable** Action should not be displayed. If the flag is set to **False**, the **Disable** Action should not be displayed. Finally, these actions should be available only for Whitepapers having the `sc:webable` aspect.

To make this happen, you are going to create someevaluators represented as Spring beans. And then you'll use them in the file `share-config-custom.xml`.

Follow these steps:

1. Edit the file `share-slingshot-application-context.xml`in the directory src|main|amp|config|alfresco|web-extension. This file contains all Spring beans evaluator. Add our first evaluator that checks if the user is member of the group SomecoPublisher.

```
<bean id="evaluator.doclib.action.isSomecoPublisher"
parent="evaluator.doclib.action.groupMembership">
    <property name="groups">
        <list>
            <value>GROUP_SomecoPublisher</value>
        </list>
    </property>
</bean>
```

2. For the identifier of the bean, you are free to use the one that you want. But it's good to keep the same rules and starts them by `evaluator.doclib.action` if it's an evaluator for an action. About the parent field, you can't guess it but you can find all available predefined evaluators here `http://docs.alfresco.com/5.1/concepts/doclib-predefined-evaluators-reference.html`.

3. Add the evaluator that checks the content type:

```
<bean id="evaluator.doclib.action.isSomecoWhitepaper"
parent="evaluator.doclib.action.nodeType">
    <property name="types">
        <list>
            <value>sc:whitepaper</value>
        </list>
    </property>
</bean>
```

4. Add the evaluator that checks the aspect:

```
<bean id="evaluator.doclib.action.isSomecoWebable"
parent="evaluator.doclib.action.hasAspect">
    <property name="aspects">
        <list>
            <value>sc:webable</value>
        </list>
    </property>
</bean>
```

5. Finally, we need to create the two evaluators that checks if the whitepaper is active or not. To simplify, we'll create the first evaluator that checks if the property sc:isActive is equal to true. The second evaluator will simply be the negation of the first one.

```
<bean id="evaluator.doclib.action.isSomecoWebActive"
parent="evaluator.doclib.metadata.value">
    <property name="accessor" value="node.properties.sc:isActive" />
        <property name="comparator">
            <bean
class="org.alfresco.web.evaluator.StringEqualsComparator">
                <property name="value" value="true" />
            </bean>
        </property>
</bean>
<bean id="evaluator.doclib.action.isSomecoWebInactive"
parent="evaluator.doclib.action.isSomecoWebActive">
    <property name="negateOutput" value="true" />
</bean>
```

6. We just defined all atomic evaluators that we need. We just need to combine them to properly displays the actions. For the action **SC Enable Web Flag,** we want to enable this action on whitepapers having the sc:webable aspect that are not active yet for SomeCo's publisher. And we want all conditions fulfilled:

```
<bean id="evaluator.doclib.action.isSomecoPublishable"
parent="evaluator.doclib.action.chainedMatchAll">
    <property name="evaluators">
        <list>
            <ref bean="evaluator.doclib.action.isSomecoPublisher" />
            <ref bean="evaluator.doclib.action.isSomecoWhitepaper" />
            <ref bean="evaluator.doclib.action.isSomecoWebable" />
            <ref bean="evaluator.doclib.action.isSomecoWebInactive" />
        </list>
    </property>
</bean>
```

7. For the action **SC Disable Web Flag,** we just need the same conditions except that the action will be available on active documents:

```
<bean id="evaluator.doclib.action.isSomecoUnpublishable"
parent="evaluator.doclib.action.chainedMatchAll">
    <property name="evaluators">
        <list>
            <ref bean="evaluator.doclib.action.isSomecoPublisher" />
            <ref bean="evaluator.doclib.action.isSomecoWhitepaper" />
            <ref bean="evaluator.doclib.action.isSomecoWebable" />
            <ref bean="evaluator.doclib.action.isSomecoWebActive" />
        </list>
    </property>
</bean>
```

8. We are ready to re-use our evaluators in our Share configuration. Edit the file share-config-custom.xml and update the two actions that we already defined previously:

```
<action id="someco-web-enable" type="javascript" label="actions.someco-web-
enable" icon="someco-web-enable">
    [...]
    <evaluator>
        evaluator.doclib.action.isSomecoPublishable
    </evaluator>
</action>
<action id="someco-web-disable" type="javascript" label="actions.someco-
web-disable" icon="someco-web-disable">
    [...]
    <evaluator>
```

```
            evaluator.doclib.action.isSomecoUnpublishable
        </evaluator>
    </action>
```

9. Deploy, restart, and test.

To test the new evaluator classes, log in as either admin or test user, and confirm that you cannot see either action. That means the group check is working because admin doesn't yet belong to the "Publisher" group. Once you've confirmed that the group check is functional, you can create a group called "SomecoPublishers" using the group identifier "SomecoPublisher" and assign both admin and your test user to the group. Only one action should be available, depending on the presence of the webable aspect and the value of the isActive flag. Note that you may need to re-login to be sure that the group evaluator is working as expected.

Now you have a relatively secure way to control who can make a document publishable on SomeCo's website. It's only relatively secure because anyone with write access can still change that flag through the API. We could change our Java code in our repository action to add more checks and avoid this kind of issues.

In addition to letting us secure the property, it gives publishers a quick way to set the publish status. They don't even have to edit the details. They can simply click on menu items.

From a support perspective, it is also pretty clean:

- If someone decides that they want to be able to set the flag from a different place in the UI, the existing UI action can be mapped to a different action group.
- If SomeCo wants to change who can set the flag, they can simply add or remove users and groups to and from the "Publisher" group.
- If the logic ever needs to change (suppose SomeCo wants to start tracking the date a piece of content was disabled for the Web instead of tracking only the publish date, for example), the code lives in one place: inside the rule action. The UI actions wouldn't have to be touched.

Changing how Share renders forms

The majority of the forms configuration are located in the share-config-custom.xml file. Alfresco provides form controls for most of the data types, but sometimes you want to customize it. A form control is implemented as a Freemarker template.

Let's look at a couple of basic examples that can at least get you pointed in the right direction. Suppose that SomeCo's Operations department wants to track status reports in Alfresco. Status reports will be written as documents and uploaded to the Operations space. Two properties will help the Operations team get a feel for the project's status: `statusSummary` will be a text property meant to capture a couple of sentences summarizing the status report, and `statusIndicator` will be a single-value select box consisting of color-coded statuses that are `Red`, `Yellow`, or `Green`.

Rather than creating a "status report" type, you will model the two status-related properties as part of a "status-able" aspect that will be applied as mandatory aspect on operational documents.

You've done enough modeling and Share wiring by this point to know what to do if these were the only requirements. So let's make it interesting. First, the standard text field that Alfresco uses to edit text properties isn't going to be very usable for typing a two-sentence summary. Second, the head of the Operations team is a very visual person. He or she doesn't want to see the words `Red`, `Yellow`, or `Green` to know a project's status, but wants to see a traffic light icon with the appropriate light lit up.

Both of these can be addressed through XML and Freemarkerchanges. In the case of the text area, Alfresco has provided a text area form control that accepts row and column arguments. You just need to configure the web client to use it. To display a traffic light depending on a property value, you'll need to create a new form control and then tell the web client to use it.

Step-by-step – using a text area field

SomeCo wants to track a status summary and a status indicator for its project status reports. They want the `statusSummary` property to be edited with a text area that is 50-columns wide and 5-rows tall. This will involve:

1. Updating the model with a new status-able aspect that contains the status summary and status indicator properties
2. Updating `share-config-custom.xml` with configuration settings that show the new aspect in the appropriate menus and identifying a new form control to use for the summary property

To make this happen, follow these steps:

1. Edit **repo|src|main|amp|config|alfresco|module|repo|model|scModel.xml**. Add a new aspect as follows.

```xml
<aspect name="sc:statusable">
  <title>Someco Status Tracking</title>
    <properties>
      <property name="sc:statusIndicator">
      <type>d:text</type>
      <mandatory>true</mandatory>
      <default>Green</default>
      <constraints>
        <constraint ref="sc:statusIndicatorList" />
      </constraints>
      </property>
      <property name="sc:statusSummary">
          <type>d:text</type>
          <mandatory>true</mandatory>
      </property>
    </properties>
</aspect>
```

2. The aspect refers to the LIST constraint that defines the possible values for the status indicator. Add the constraint definition to the existing constraints element.

```xml
<constraint name="sc:statusIndicatorList" type="LIST">
    <parameter name="allowedValues">
        <list>
            <value>Green</value>
            <value>Yellow</value>
            <value>Red</value>
        </list>
    </parameter>
</constraint>
```

3. Then the define our new aspect as mandatory aspect on our Operations document:

```xml
<type name="sc:opsDoc">
    <title>Someco Operations Document</title>
        <parent>sc:doc</parent>
        <mandatory-aspects>
        <aspect>sc:statusable</aspect>
        </mandatory-aspects>
</type>
```

4. Save and close the model file.

5. Update the scModel.properties properties to add the I18N messages:

```
sc_somecomodel.aspect.sc_statusable.title=Someco Status Tracking
sc_somecomodel.property.sc_statusIndicator.title=Status Indicator
sc_somecomodel.property.sc_statusSummary.title=Status Summary
```

6. Edit the fileshare-config-custom.xml **located** in the share project and find the config element with the evaluator attribute equals to node-type, and the condition attribute to sc:opsDoc. Add the two new fields in the list of visible fields. And, let's add an `appearance` element to specify that we want to use the text area form control for the status summary.

```
<config evaluator="node-type" condition="sc:opsDoc">
  <forms>
    <form>
      <field-visibility>
        [...]
        <show id="sc:statusIndicator" />
        <show id="sc:statusSummary" />
      </field-visibility>
      <appearance>
      <field id="sc:statusSummary">
      <control
template="/org/alfresco/components/form/controls/textarea.ftl">
            <control-param name="rows">5</control-param>
            <control-param name="columns">50</control-param>
      </control>
      </field>
      </appearance>
    </form>
  </forms>
</config>
```

7. You can find all control forms in your deployed Share web application in the folder WEB-INF | classes | alfresco | site-webscripts | org | alfresco | components | form | controls. For more details on how to configure them, you can check the following page: `http://docs.alfresco.com/5.1/references/forms-reference.html`.

8. Edit the share.properties file to externalize the aspect label.

```
aspect.sc_statusable=Someco Status Tracking
```

9. Package, deploy, restart, and test. Don't forget that you need to deploy both Alfresco and Share.

To test this change, you first need to create a new site called **Operations**.Then, you need to add a document to the **Document Library** and change the type to Someco Operations Document type. When you edit the properties, you should see that a text area of the size you specified is used for the **Summary**:

Step-by-step – changing the Status field on the Details page to display as a Stoplight indicator

SomeCo wants to show a graphical representation of the status indicator. Alfresco is using the standard components for displaying and editing the status indicator property. The edit is fine the way it is, but the display needs to change to show a traffic light. This involves:

- Updating `share-config-custom.xml` to specify the form control for the status indicator field
- Writing a new Freemarker file to implement the custom form control
- Finding or creating some traffic light icons

Ready? Let's get started. Follow these steps:

1. Edit the file **share-config-custom.xml** to specify that you want to use a custom template form control. We'll update the same config element as the previous section. We just need to add a new sub-element in the appearance element.

```
<field id="sc:statusIndicator">
    <control
template="/com/someco/components/form/controls/trafficlight.ftl">
        <control-param name="otpions">Green,Yellow,Red</control-param>
    </control>
</field>
```

2. This was the easy part! Now, we need to create the form control. Locate the directory **src|main|amp|config|alfresco|web-extension|site-webscripts** in the share project. Create the sub-directory **com|someco|components|form|controls** if it doesn't exist yet. We are not going to start from the scratch. We'll duplicate the selectone.ftl form control existing in the share web application (if you don't remember, this file is stored in the folder `WEB-INF|classes|alfresco|site-webscripts|org|alfresco|components|form|controls`). Just copy this file in your project and rename it to trafficlight.ftl.

3. You can notice that the form control manages the view and edit mode within the same file. In our case, we don't want to change the edit mode. We just want to display a traffic light in the view mode. Search for the following line:

```
<span class="viewmode-value">${valueToShow?html}</span>
```

4. And replace it by:

```
<span class="viewmode-value">
    <#if valueToShow == "Red">
        <imgsrc="${url.context}/res/components/form/images/trafficlight-
red-32.png"
        <#elseifvalueToShow == "Yellow">
        <imgsrc="${url.context}/res/components/form/images/trafficlight-
yellow-32.png"
        <#else>
        <imgsrc="${url.context}/res/components/form/images/trafficlight-
green-32.png"
```

```
    </#if>
</span>
```

5. The last step is to copy the traffic light images from the source code provided with this chapter into your `share` project under **src|main|amp|web|components|form|images**. We deploy these images to this folder, because we want to deploy in the folder **components|form|images** when the AMP module will be installed.

6. Deploy, restart, and test.

To test this, go take a look at the properties of the document you used to test the **Status** and **Summary** in the previous example. Now, instead of a boring text string, the status is shown using a visually striking traffic light metaphor:

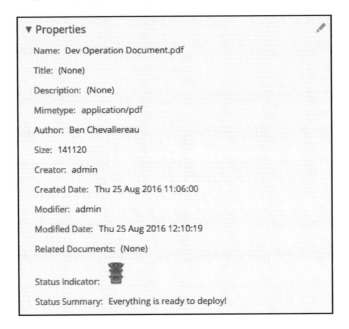

If you edit the properties, Alfresco should use its default list-constrained, single-value text field component, which is a drop-down selection list.

It is important to note that if you go back and remove the constraints from your model and try your test again, the component will still work. Of course, if the string you set for your status doesn't match any of the three colors, you won't see any traffic light.

Overriding and customizing components

You should now have a basic idea of how you can tweak forms and form controls. If you wanted to do something more complex-say for example you don't like the out of the box multi-value select behavior-you can override it. The steps are similar to what you've seen so far.

How to use indicators

The manager that asked to use traffic lights to have a quick understanding of the status complained that he/she has to click on each document to be able to see the status. To be more efficient, it seems that the indicator should be displayed directly in the document list. Hopefully, Alfresco provides the concept of indicators. A content in Alfresco can have one or more indicators and are used to reflect certain states. This will involve:

1. Create three evaluators to be able to differentiate the different states
2. Create three indicators for each possible state.

Step-by-step – creating indicators for the status indicator

1. The first step is to create indicators, as we do for the actions. Update the file share-slingshot-application-context.xml where you already created all indicators. We need to create one evaluator for each color of the traffic light:

```
<bean id="evaluator.doclib.action.statusIsGreen"
parent="evaluator.doclib.metadata.value">
    <property name="accessor" value="node.properties.sc:statusIndicator" />
    <property name="comparator">
        <bean class="org.alfresco.web.evaluator.StringEqualsComparator">
            <property name="value" value="Green" />
        </bean>
    </property>
</bean>
<bean id="evaluator.doclib.action.statusIsYellow"
parent="evaluator.doclib.metadata.value">
    <property name="accessor" value="node.properties.sc:statusIndicator" />
    <property name="comparator">
        <bean class="org.alfresco.web.evaluator.StringEqualsComparator">
            <property name="value" value="Yellow" />
```

```
            </bean>
        </property>
    </bean>
    <bean id="evaluator.doclib.action.statusIsRed"
    parent="evaluator.doclib.metadata.value">
        <property name="accessor" value="node.properties.sc:statusIndicator" />
            <property name="comparator">
            <bean class="org.alfresco.web.evaluator.StringEqualsComparator">
                <property name="value" value="Red" />
            </bean>
            </property>
    </bean>
```

2. That's it. Now, we can update the same file as usual, `share-config-custom.xml`. Locate the config element with the condition attribute equals to DocumentLibrary and add these evaluators as sub-element.

```
<indicators>
    <indicator id="trafficlight-red" index="100">
        <evaluator>evaluator.doclib.action.statusIsRed</evaluator>
    </indicator>
    <indicator id="trafficlight-yellow" index="110">
        <evaluator>evaluator.doclib.action.statusIsYellow</evaluator>
    </indicator>
    <indicator id="trafficlight-green" index="120">
        <evaluator>evaluator.doclib.action.statusIsGreen</evaluator>
    </indicator>
</indicators>
```

As you'll easily understand, the index field is used to prioritize the displaying order of the indicators.

Remember that all our Share customizations are implemented in the same share-config-custom.xml but you can easily make an extension module as described in the first examples of this chapter.

1. The last step is to copy the traffic light images from the source code provided with this chapter into your share project under **src|main|amp|web|components|documentlibrary|indicators**. By looking at the filenames, you'll easily guess the naming convention:

```
<INDICATOR ID>-16.png
<INDICATOR ID>-32.png
```

Why do we need a 16px and 32px square icons? Because, depending of the view that you select in Alfresco Share, it won't use the same icon size.

2. Deploy, restart, and test.

Now, you should be able to see a small traffic light next to each **SomeCo Operation Document** in the **Document Library**:

How to create metadata template

You just received a call from the same manager that works with the Operations document. The indicator is very useful; you can have a quick overview of the status of all documents. However, when the status is **Red**, the only way to get the status summary is to open the document details page. It would be very helpful if we can see the status summary directly in the document list. And this manger is proposing that we replace the documentation field, by the sc:statusSummaryfield. Hopefully again, Alfresco provides the concept of metadata template. You can define the list of metadata that you want to display depending of the content type.

Step-by-step – create a metadata template for Operations document

This configuration may be the easiest one in this book. We decided that we'll remove the description line and we'll replace it with the status summary. We are lucky, we already created the evaluator used to identify if the document is an Operation document.

1. This time, we are going to create an extension module to show you how it's possible. Just a reminder that we always have two ways to package Share customizations: (1) Integrate that to the module Share configuration file; (2) Create an extension module. Locate the directory **src | main | amp | config | alfresco | web-extension | site-data | extensions** in your share project. Create a file called `someco-metadata-template.xml` in this directory. And let's define our extension:

```
<extension>
    <modules>
        <module>
            <id>SomeCo Document Metadata Template</id>
            <version>1.0</version>
            <auto-deploy>true</auto-deploy>
            <configurations>
                <config evaluator="string-compare"
condition="DocumentLibrary">
                    <metadata-templates>

                    </metadata-templates>
                </config>
            </configurations>
        </module>
    </modules>
</extension>
```

2. We don't want to start from scratch, we just want to tweak the default template. Let's retrieve this template. Open the file `share-documentlibrary-config.xml` located in **WEB-INF | classes | alfresco** of the share web application. In this file, you should find a template element with the id attribute equals to default. Copy this template within the element metadata-templates. You don't want to override the default template, so you want to change the template id to somecoOperationalDocument.

```
<template id="somecoOperationalDocument">
    [...]
</template>
```

3. The next step is to provide an evaluator to identify only Operation Document. We can re-use the evaluator that we created previously.

```
<template id="somecoOperationalDocument">
    <evaluator>evaluator.doclib.action.isSomecoOperatonDoc</evaluator>
    [...]
</template>
```

4. And finally, we want to replace the line that contains the description. We are going to replace the line with the index attribute equals to 20 by the following line.

```
<line index="20" id="statusSummary"
view="detailed">{sc_statusSummaryproperty.sc_statusSummary}</line>
```

It may be a bit obscure at this point. The sc_statusSummary will be mapped to our custom model, and the following label is mapped to a property that we define just below in the I18N file.

5. The last step is to create the label for this new line. Open the share.properties file and add the following line.

```
property.sc_statusSummary=Status Summary
```

6. Deploy, restart, and test.

If you refresh your document list, and be sure to be in the **Detailed View**, you should be able to see the status summary for all **Operational** documents:

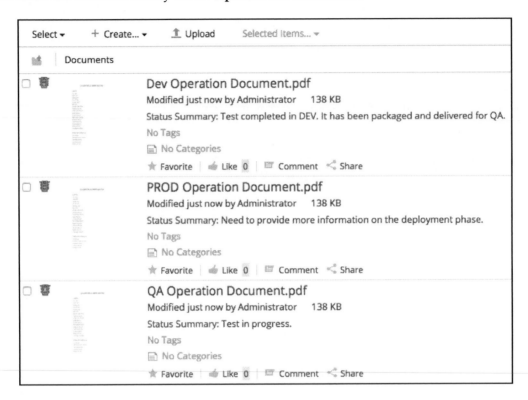

Creating custom dialogs

For the moment, the manager handling operational documents seems pretty satisfied by the solution that we implemented. We can work and satisfy another manager. If you remember our work on Whitepapers, we create two actions to enable and disable the Web flag. Each UI action calls the same action that we defined in the repository. Moreover, when we enable the Web flag, we update automatically the publish date with the current date. We want to improve this behavior. We want to be able to set the Web flag to true and to specify when should be the publish date. This feature will be very useful to plan the publication of the Whitepapers.

In this section, we'll:

- Update the Alfresco action to receive the publication date as parameter;
- Create a new form in Alfresco Share with an input field for the publication date;
- Update the action definition in Alfresco Share to use the new form.

Step-by-step – creating a dialog to publish Whitepapers

To develop the custom dialog, follow these steps:

1. First, we'll work on the existing Java class representing our action called `SetWebFlag` in the `repo` project. Update the method `addParameterDefinitions` and add the following line:

```
paramList.add(new ParameterDefinitionImpl(
  PARAM_PUBLISHED, DataTypeDefinition.DATE, false,
getParamDisplayLabel(PARAM_PUBLISHED))));
```

2. Add the following variable at the top of your class:
3. public final static String PARAM_PUBLISHED = "published";
4. Let's change how we populate the publication date. Locate the following statement in the `executeImpl` method:

```
if (activeFlag) {
properties.put(SomeCoModel.PROP_PUBLISHED, new Date());
    }
```

5. And replace it by:

```
if (activeFlag) {
  Date published = new Date();
  if (action.getParameterValue(PARAM_PUBLISHED) != null)
    published = (Date) action.getParameterValue(PARAM_PUBLISHED);
properties.put(SomeCoModel.PROP_PUBLISHED, published);
} else {
properties.put(SomeCoModel.PROP_PUBLISHED, null);
}
```

6. We are done with Alfresco. We can configure Alfresco Share. Open the file share-config-custom.xml located in the share project. Find the action tag with the id attribute equals to someco-web-enable. First, let's replace the function that will be used:

```
<param name="function">onActionSimpleRepoAction</param>
By:
<param name="function">onActionFormDialog</param>
```

7. Then, update the properties referencing the action:

```
<param name="action">set-web-flag</param>
<param name="active">false</param>
```

8. By:

```
<param name="itemKind">action</param>
<param name="itemId">set-web-flag</param>
<param name="destination">{node.nodeRef}</param>
<param name="mode">create</param>
```

9. You'll find on this page the meaning of all these parameters: http://docs.alfre sco.com/5.1/tasks/dev-extensions-share-tutorials-add-action-doclib.h tml.

10. Then, we are going to define the form that we'll be used of this action. Add the following config element that configures that we just want to see the published property in the form:

```
<config evaluator="string-compare"
    condition="set-web-flag">
    <forms>
      <form>
       <field-visibility>
       <show id="published" />
      </field-visibility>
      <appearance>
       <field id="published"
        label-id="property.sc_published"
        mandatory="true">
       <control
template="/org/alfresco/components/form/controls/date.ftl" />
       </field>
      </appearance>
     </form>
    </forms>
   </config>
```

11. Add the following I18N message to the share.properties file:

```
property.sc_published=Published
```

12. Deploy, restart and test.

After a successful restart, if you click on the action SC Enable Web Flag, you should see a new dialog. And you should be able to input the publication date:

Input the publication the date and clicking **OK** will execute the against the whitepaper and will set all properties:

Creating custom dashlets

Alfresco Share includes two special pages called Dashboard, which contains windows (think Portlets) of content called Dashlets. In the current version, most of these Dashlets are Spring Surf Dashlets. As I explained in the introduction, Alfresco Share provides two platforms or technologies to accomplish that: Surf and Aikau. But we'll use only Surf in this book (except for the menu customization because it's implemented using Aikau and we don't have other options).

As explained above, Alfresco provides two dashboard: user and site dashboard. Each dashboard can be customized by selecting a layout and add only the relevant dashlets. The user dashboard is customizable by each user, and the site dashboard available for each site is customizable by all Site managers.

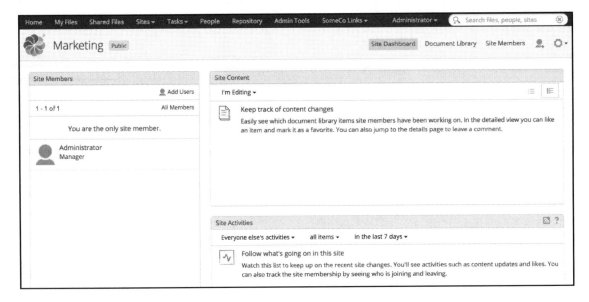

The following list displays all available dashlets by default in Alfresco.

Name	Description	User and/or Site Dashboard
My Activities	Tracks the most recent activities in your sites.	User Dashboard
My Meeting Workspaces	Displays all Meeting Workspace sit<ie>e</ie>s that you belong to (Meeting Workspaces are created in Microsoft Outlook)	User Dashboard
My Document Workspaces	Displays all Document Workspace sites that you belong to (Document Workspaces are created in Microsoft Word)	User Dashboard
My Tasks	Displays your tasks.	User Dashboard
Alfresco Add-ons RSS Feed	Displays the Newest Add-ons feed from the Alfresco Add-ons website by default.	User & Site Dashboard
Saved Search	Displays the results of a pre-configured search.	User & Site Dashboard

Content I'm Editing	Displays the last three library items, blog posts (drafts, not published posts), wiki pages, and discussion forum posts that you	User Dashboard
edited User Dashboard My Profile	Shows a summary of your personal details.	User Dashboard
My Discussions	Shows the most recent topics created in the discussion forums of your sites.	User & Site Dashboard
Site Search	Lets you search all the sites you belong to.	User & Site Dashboard
My Documents	Tracks your content in all site libraries.	User Dashboard
My Sites	Lists the sites you belong to.	User Dashboard
My Calendar	Displays upcoming events scheduled for your sites	User Dashboard
RSS Feed	Displays the Alfresco website feed by default.	User & Site Dashboard
Web View	Displays the website of your choice.	User & Site Dashboard
Site Calendar	Lists the upcoming events scheduled in this site's calendar.	Site Dashboard
Image Preview	Displays a thumbnail of all images stored in the site's library.	Site Dashboard
Site Data Lists	Lists this site's data lists.	Site Dashboard
Site Profile	Displays a summary of the site details.	Site Dashboard
Site Members	Displays the current members of this site (to a maximum of 100 members) and their assigned roles.	Site Dashboard
Site Activities	Tracks the most recent activities performed in this site such as content additions, edits, and deletions, as well as changes in site membership.	Site Dashboard
Site Links	Displays the web links compiled by site users.	Site Dashboard
Site Contributor Breakdown	Displays a breakdown of all site members contributing content to the site's library.	Site Dashboard

Site Content	Lists the library content that has been added or edited in the past seven days.	Site Dashboard
Site File Type Breakdown	Displays a detailed breakdown of all files stored in the site's library.	Site Dashboard
Site Notice	Displays a custom message posted by a site manager.	Site Dashboard
Wiki	Displays a selected page from the site wiki.	Site Dashboard

But sometimes, you need to implement your own dashlets that can be added to the user or site dashboard. For the moment, we want to create a dashlet that displays all whitepaper available in the repository. We want to make it available in any dashboard. For the moment, we'll display only basic information about the whitepapers, and no custom properties that we defined. The following picture illustrates the different connections:

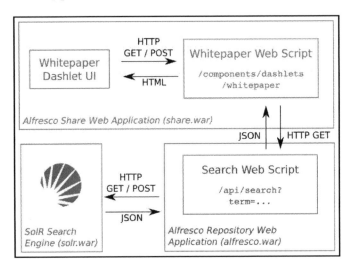

In our use case, we implemented the call to the Alfresco repository webscript to get a list of whitepaper in JSON format directly in the controller of the dashlet.

Step-by-step – creating a dashlet listing Whitepapers

To develop the dashlet, follow these steps:

1. In the share project, locate the folder **src|main|amp|config|alfresco|web-extension** and create the following directory **site-webscripts|com|someco|components|dashlets**. The first step is to create the file whitepaper.get.desc.xml that will describe the dashlet. Notice that we use the family `dashlet` (instead of `site-dashlet` or `user-dashlet`) to be able to use it on all dashboards.

```
<webscript>
    <shortname>List of whitepapers</shortname>
    <description>Display all available whitepapers</description>
    <family>dashlet</family>
    <url>/components/dashlets/whitepaper</url>
</webscript>
```

2. Then, create the Javascript controller `whitepaper.get.js` in the same directory that queries the Search API provided by Alfresco. We'll use the content type to be able to get all whitepapers. Then we'll populate the model object.

```
function main() {
    var query = "TYPE:sc\\:whitepaper"
    var result = remote.call("/slingshot/search?term=" +
encodeURIComponent(query));
        if (result.status == 200) {
        model.items = JSON.parse(result).items;
     }
    }
main();
```

Let's discover a bit this code. First, you can see the use of the object remote that allows you to make REST calls. In our case, we use it to send a search query and retrieve the items returned. Them we save the returned items in the model object that is passed to the Freemarker template for displaying. You can find all available root objects here: `http://docs.alfresco.com/5.1/references/APISurf-rootscoped.html`.

3. In the same directory, we'll create the Freemarker template whitepaper.get.html.ftl that will generate the HTML content. First, we need to declare the CSS dependency:

```
<@markup id="css">
<@link rel="stylesheet" type="text/css"
href="${url.context}/res/components/dashlets/whitepaper.css"
 group="dashlets"/>
</@>
```

We are just going to add one CSS rule to have a better displaying. Create the file share|src|main|amp|web|components|dashlets|whitepaper.css and just add the following code:

```
p.whitepaper {
    padding-left: 5px;
}
```

 You can find more information on the Freemarker syntax in the following page: http://docs.alfresco.com/5.1/concepts/dev-extensions-share-surf-dashlets.html.

4. Add the following code that will define the global structure of your dashlet. For the moment, your dashlet don't display anything.

```
<@markup id="html">
<@uniqueIdDiv>
<#assign id = args.htmlid?html>
<#assign dashboardconfig=config.scoped['Dashboard']['dashboard']>
  <div class="dashlet">
    <div class="title">${msg("someco.whitepaper.dashletName")}</div>
        <div id="${id}-whitepapers" class="body scrollableList" <#if
args.height??>style
        ="height: ${args.height?html}px;"</#if>>
    </div>
  </div>
</@>
</@>
```

5. Then, you are good to add the code that will generate the list of whitepapers. In our case, we just want to display the name of each document with a link to be able the details page of each document. Add the following code in the div element with the class body.

```
<#list items as item>
```

```
<p valign="top" class="whitepaper">
   <a href="${url.context}/page/site/${item.site.shortName}/document-
details?nodeRef=${item.nodeRef}">
   ${item.displayName}
   </a>
</p>
</#list>
```

> Be careful, the code above will work only if whitepapers are stored in Share sites. If you store them somewhere else, you'll have an error.

6. Finally, create the I18N property file whitepaper.get.properties in the same directory with the following line:

```
someco.whitepaper.dashletName=SomeCoWhitePaper List
```

7. Deploy, restart and test.

To be able to test, login to Alfresco Share and opens your dashboard or any site dashboard. Click on the configuration icon in the top right corner, and select **CustomizeDashboard**. Then, click on **Add Dashlets** and drag and drop the dashlet **List of whitepapers** into the **Column 1**:

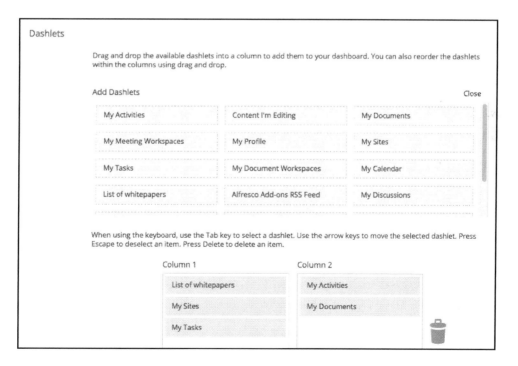

If you successfully added the dashlet, and you have some whitepapers already created in your repository, you should be able to see the following documents. If you click on each one, you should be able to open the details page of each document.

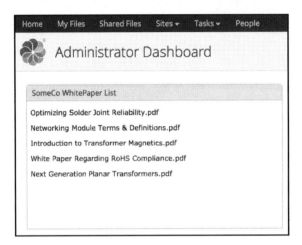

The Marketing manager is really happy to be able to find all whitepapers in the entire repository so quickly. However, it will be very nice if we could filter between active and inactive whitepapers. To accomplish that, we are going to refactor everything and re-use a component already developed by Alfresco called `Alfresco.component.SimpleDocList`. This component provides everything to display a list of documents based on filters.

Step-by-step – adding filters to your Dashlet

In this section, we'll update our dashlet to use the SimpleDocList component, and implement two filters to display active and inactive whitepapers. To update the dashlet, follow these steps:

1. Because we are going to re-use the Alfresco SimpleDocList component, we can remove the whitepaper.css that we created previously or you can just empty it.

2. Open the directory **src | main | amp | config | alfresco | web-extension | site-webscripts** and locate the presentation web service that you developed previously in **site-webscripts | com | someco | components | dashlets**. Then, create the XML file whitepaper.get.config.xml that list all available filters.

```
<config>
    <filters>
        <filter type="active" />
        <filter type="inactive" />
```

```
    </filters>
</config>
```

3. In the same directory, update the I18N properties file whitepaper.get.properties and add the two following lines.

```
filter.active=Active
filter.inactive=Inactive
```

4. In the same directory, we are going to update the Javascript controller whitepaper.get.js. You can just remove everything in this file. First, we need to import an Alfresco Javascript library that we'll use to retrieve the user preferences.

```
<import
resource="classpath:/alfresco/templates/org/alfresco/import/alfresco-
util.js">
```

5. Then, we can implement the first method getFilters() that will be in charge of retrieving all available filters from the XML file created in the step 2.

```
function getFilters()
{
var myConfig = new XML(config.script),
    filters = []
    for each (var xmlFilter in myConfig..filter)
    {
    if (xmlFilter.@evaluator.toString() === "" ||
runEvaluator(xmlFilter.@evaluator.toString()))
    {
    filters.push(
      {
      type: xmlFilter.@type.toString(),
      parameters: xmlFilter.@parameters.toString()
      });
    }
    }
    return filters
}
```

6. Add the following line that defines where is located the dashlet on the dashboard.

```
var regionId = args['region-id'];
```

7. Populate the `model` variable with the available filters and the user preferences. We didn't talk about the `model` variable. You'll discover more on the chapter dedicated to webscripts. To summarize, the model object is used to transmit variable between the controller and the Freemarker template. You could ask why do we need to get the user preferences. For example, if you selected inactive whitepapers, and then leave the page, we want to display inactive reports the next time that you open the same page. Append the following code to the Javascript file:

```
model.preferences =
AlfrescoUtil.getPreferences("org.alfresco.share.whitepaper.dashlet." +
regionId);
model.filters = getFilters();
```

8. Then, add the main() method that we'll define our dashlet, and we need to create as well a resizer object to allow users to change the size of the dashlet.

```
function main()
{
    var whitepaper = {
    id : "Whitepaper",
    name : "Alfresco.dashlet.Whitepaper",
    options : {
    filter :model.preferences.filter != null ? model.preferences.filter :
"active",
    regionId :regionId
    }
    };
    var dashletResizer = {
        id: "DashletResizer",
      name: "Alfresco.widget.DashletResizer",
    initArgs: [""" + args.htmlid + """, """ + instance.object.id + """],
    useMessages: false
    };
model.widgets = [whitepaper, dashletResizer];
}
```

You can find more information about the Alfresco Share client side Javascript API on this page. Unfortunately, it has not been updated with the 5.x version, but it's a very good source of information: http://sharextras.org/jsdoc/share/enterprise-4.0.0/.

Let's spend some time about the concept of widgets. In Alfresco Share, pages and dashlets are mainly processed by webscripts. But when client side processing is required (like CSS or Javascript), then we use the concept of widget. The Surf widgets use the YUI framework. In our case above, we instantiate two widgets that will inherit out-of-the-box widgets available in Alfresco Share. You'll see how to do that in the steps below.

1. Finally, add the very important following line:

```
main();
```

2. You just completed the Javascript controller. Let's switch to the Freemarker template whitepaper.get.html.ftl located in the same directory. You can empty this file too, and we can restart from scratch. Then, add the three following dependencies to the CSS file (even if it's empty, let's keep it if we need it), the Javascript file that will create the document list and finally the widget creation that will trigger the display of the document list.

```
<@markup id="js">
    <@script type="text/javascript" src="${url.context}/res/components
    /dashlets/whitepaper.js" group="dashlets"/>
</@>
<@markup id="css">
    <@link rel="stylesheet" type="text/css" href="${url.context}/res
        /components/dashlets/whitepaper.css" group="dashlets"/>
</@>
<@markup id="widgets">
    <@createWidgets group="dashlets"/>
</@>
```

 If you want to know more about the template markup for widgets, you can look at the following documentation: `http://docs.alfresco.com/5.1/concepts/dev-extensions-share-template-markup.html`.

3. Then, create the structure of the dashlet.

```
<@markup id="html">
    <@uniqueIdDiv>
        <#assign id = args.htmlid>
        <#assign prefFilter = preferences.filter!"active">
        <div class="dashlet whitepaper resizable yui-resize">

        </div>
    </@>
</@>
```

> You may ask why we should implement this kind of HTML and re-using these CSS classes. The best way to know what you need to use is to look at all dashlets out-of-the-box already available in Alfresco Share. And for that, you can check into the Share web application, in the folder WEB-INF|classes|alfresco|site-webscripts|org|alfresco|components|dashlets.

4. Locate the div element with the class dashlet, and add the HTML code representing the title.

```
<div class="title">${msg("someco.whitepaper.dashletName")}</div>
```

5. Then, append the HTML code that will display the list of filters. If you look carefully, the Freemarker code iterates over the variable filters that we initialized in the Javascript controller.

```
<div class="toolbar flat-button">
    <div class="hidden">
        <span class="align-left yui-button yui-menu-button" id="${id}-
filters">
        <span class="first-child">
            <button type="button" tabindex="0"></button>
        </span>
        </span>
        <select id="${id}-filters-menu">
        <#list filters as filter>
            <option value="${filter.type?html}">${msg("filter." +
filter.type)}</option>
        </#list>
    </select>
    <div class="clear"></div>
    </div>
</div>
```

6. And finally, append the HTML code that will represent the body of the dashlet that will contain the list of documents.

```
<div class="body scrollableList" <#if args.height??>style="height:
${args.height?html}px;"</#if>>
   <div id="${id}-documents"></div>
</div>
```

7. The dashlet is ready. We just need to create the Javascript file whitepaper.js in charge of the creation of the document list. This file should be in **share|src|main|amp|web|components|dashlets**. First, we are going to create the skeleton of the Javascript file.

```
(function() {
   var Selector = YAHOO.util.Selector;
   Alfresco.dashlet.Whitepaper = function Whitepaper_constructor(htmlId) {
         return
Alfresco.dashlet.Whitepaper.superclass.constructor.call(this, htmlId);
   };

   YAHOO.extend(Alfresco.dashlet.Whitepaper,
Alfresco.component.SimpleDocList, {
         [...]
   });
})();
```

You may find this start a bit scaring. The easiest way to start your new dashlet is usualy just to re-use an existing dashlet (following the same process as the Freemarker template. All Javascript files used in the out-of-the-box dashlets are located in components|dashlets in the Share web application.

8. As you see in the previous code snippet, our dashlet extends the Alfresco component SimpleDocList but we need to configure it. Insert the following code in the YAHOO.extend statement.

```
PREFERENCES_WHITEPAPER_DASHLET : "",
PREFERENCES_WHITEPAPER_DASHLET_FILTER : "",
onReady : function Whitepaper_onReady() {
   [...]
},
getParameters : function Whitepaper_getParameters() {
   [...]
},
getWebscriptUrl : function Whitepaper_getWebscriptUrl() {
   [...]
```

```
},
onFilterChange : function Whitepaper_onFilterChange(p_sType, p_aArgs) {
    [...]
}
```

 You can find more information about this Javascript component on this page: http://sharextras.org/jsdoc/share/enterprise-4.0.0/symbol s/Alfresco.component.SimpleDocList.html.

9. Now, we are going to populate each method. Let's start by getWebscriptUrl(). We are going to use the same webscript.

```
getWebscriptUrl : function Whitepaper_getWebscriptUrl() {
    return Alfresco.constants.PROXY_URI + "slingshot/search";
}
```

You may wonder where comes from the variable Alfresco.constants.PROXY_URI. This is one of the Javascript variable that is always available on every page. These variables are defined in the following freemarker file WEB-INF|classes|alfresco|site-webscripts|org|alfresco|components|head|resources.get.html.f tl in the Share web application. If you look at the source code of all Alfresco Share pages, you'll notice that this variable is defined.

10. Then, we populate the getParameters() method that will be called each time that the list of documents is loaded. We'll use the same query as previously, but we'll add a new filter on the property sc:isActive.

```
getParameters : function Whitepaper_getParameters() {
var param = "term=";
var query = "+TYPE:sc\\:whitepaper";
if (this.widgets.filter.value == "inactive")
    query += " +sc\\:isActive:false";
  else
    query += " +sc\\:isActive:true";
param += encodeURIComponent(query);
  return param;
},
```

11. Then, we need to populate the method onFilterChange() that will update the selected value, save the filter in the user preferences and reload the document list.

```
onFilterChange : function Whitepaper_onFilterChange(p_sType, p_aArgs) {
var menuItem = p_aArgs[1];
   if (menuItem) {
this.widgets.filter.set("label", menuItem.cfg.getProperty("text") + " " +
Alfresco.constants.MENU_ARROW_SYMBOL);
this.widgets.filter.value = menuItem.value;
this.services.preferences.set(this.PREFERENCES_WHITEPAPER_DASHLET_FILTER,
this.widgets.filter.value);
this.reloadDataTable();
   }
}
```

12. Finally, we'll work on the onReady() method which is the longest one. We'll go step by step. First, we populate the two global variables.

```
this.PREFERENCES_WHITEPAPER_DASHLET =
this.services.preferences.getDashletId(this, "whitepaper");
this.PREFERENCES_WHITEPAPER_DASHLET_FILTER =
this.PREFERENCES_WHITEPAPER_DASHLET + ".filter";
```

13. Then, we create the dropdown filter.

```
this.widgets.filter = Alfresco.util.createYUIButton(this, "filters",
this.onFilterChange, {
type : "menu",
menu : "filters-menu",
lazyloadmenu : false
});
```

You can check the following documentation to have more information on Alfresco.util: http://sharextras.org/jsdoc/share/enterprise-4.0.0/symbols/Alfresco.util.html.

14. We retrieve the current filter, and we update the widget properties. Then, we specify that we want to use the simple view mode of the document list.

```
var filter = this.options.filter;
filter = filter != null ? filter : "active";
this.widgets.filter.set("label", this.msg("filter." + filter) + " " +
Alfresco.constants.MENU_ARROW_SYMBOL);
this.widgets.filter.value = filter;
this.options.simpleView = true;
```

15. The toolbar is now created; we can remove the hidden CSS class to make it visible.

```
Dom.removeClass(Selector.query(".toolbar div", this.id, true), "hidden");
```

16. Then, we can call the parent method in the SimpleDocList component that will create the YUI2 datatable.

```
Alfresco.dashlet.Whitepaper.superclass.onReady.apply(this, arguments);
```

17. Unfortunately, the JSON returned by the Alfresco Search API doesn't match what's expected by the `SimpleDocList` component. For example, the filename is returned in a field called name, but the `SimpleDocList` component is expecting it in the field `fieldName`. Some minor other changes need to be done is the `onReady` function. To accomplish that, we'll bind the event `onDataReturnSetRows` provided by the YUI2 `DataTable` component (this DataTableYUI component is the one used by the `SimpleDocList` component).

```
var me = this,
dataTable = this.widgets.alfrescoDataTable.getDataTable(),
original_onDataReturnSetRows = dataTable.onDataReturnSetRows;

dataTable.onDataReturnSetRows = function
Whitepaper_onDataReturnSetRows(sRequest, oResponse, oPayload) {
  if (oResponse.results&&oResponse.results.length> 0) {
    for (var i = 0; i<oResponse.results.length; i++) {
oResponse.results[i].fileName = oResponse.results[i].name;
oResponse.results[i].location = {
        site: oResponse.results[i].site.shortName,
siteTitle: oResponse.results[i].site.title
      };
oResponse.results[i].permissions = {
userAccess: {
          create: false
        }
      }
    }
  }
  return original_onDataReturnSetRows.apply(this, arguments);
};
```

18. Deploy, package and test.

Login to Alfresco Share and check your dashboard, the new dashlet should be used automatically. In the list of filters, you should be able to select **Active** or **Inactive**. Automatically, the list of documents should be refreshed.

You can notice that we display more information now. We display the modified date, and we can see in which site the document is stored.

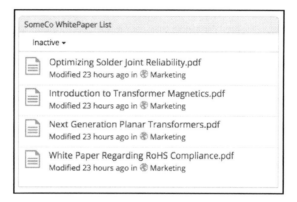

Finally, if you select the filter **Inactive** and then change pages, reload the page, or close your browser, the next time that the dashboard will be displayed, the last filter value should be used.

When you start to implement a dashlet, always check if one of the Alfresco out-of-the-box ones can't be used to meet your requirements. If it's not the case, you can take a look at `https://addons.alfresco.com/` that contains a lot of open-source extensions.

Create custom pages

You discovered in the Chapter 2, *Getting Started with Alfresco*, that Alfresco Share is based on the concept of pages. In each site, you can add or remove pages depending of the use of this site. Alfresco Share already provides out-of-the-box pages like **Document Library**, **Calendar**, **Wiki**, **Discussions**, **Blog**, **Links** or **Data Lists**. In the previous section, we discovered how to create new dashlets to your different dashboards to be able to display custom content. Sometimes, the use of dahslets is not sufficient, and you want to display more information and more features. In this case, you need to create a new Surf page.

In this section, we'll:

- Create a new page that you'll be able to add to any Share site;
- Use the CMIS 1.1 API directly from Alfresco Share;
- Create a simple Angular page to display all *webable* documents in a site.

Step-by-step – create a new page to list all Webable documents

In this section, we'll create a new Surf page addable to any Share site where the users will be able to list all webable documents in this site, and to filter quickly these documents. We'll introduce the use of the **Angular** Javascript framework. We won't go into details on how or why we use **Angular**. You'll get more information on this framework in the next chapter.

1. Let's start by the Surf page definition XML file. In the share project, locate the directory `src|main|amp|config|alfresco|web-extensions|site-data`. Create the sub-directory pages. In this directory, create the file `someco-webable.xml`.

```
<?xml version='1.0' encoding='UTF-8'?>
    <page>
        <title>SomecoWebable Documents</title>
        <title-id>page.someco.webable.title</title-id>
        <description>List all documents with the Webable
aspect</description>
        <description-id>page.someco.webable.description</description-id>
        <template-instance>someco-webable</template-instance>
    </page>
```

2. The template instance defined in this code has to match the filename listed in the next step.

3. Then, in the same site-data directory. Create the sub-directory template-instances. Create the template instance XML file someco-webable.xml that will define the path of the Freemarker template file.

```
<?xml version='1.0' encoding='UTF-8'?>
<template-instance>
    <template-type>com/someco/pages/webable</template-type>
</template-instance>
```

4. The template type in this case is the path where to find the Freemarker template that will be used for rendering.

5. Locate the directory `src|main|amp|config|alfresco|web-extensions|site-webscripts`. Create the sub-directory `com|someco|pages`. Then, create the Freemarker file webable.ftl that will generate the page. Add the following line that is the entry point to create a new Alfresco Share page:

```
<#include "/org/alfresco/include/alfresco-template.ftl" />
```

6. This Freemarker file (that you can find in the Share web application) will define the global structure of the HTML page. In the steps 4, 5 and 6, we'll just add the code that we want to add in the header, the body and the footer by using the Freemarker macros `templateHeader`, `templateBody` and `templateFooter`.

7. Use the `template-header macro` provided by Alfresco and include three new dependencies. The first one is the **Angular**Javascript framework; the second one is the Javascript file in charge of initializing the page and the third one is the CSS file that will use to make our page pretty.

```
<@templateHeader>
    <script
src="//ajax.googleapis.com/ajax/libs/angularjs/1.5.6/angular.min.js"></scri
pt>
    <script type="text/javascript" src="${url.context}/res/js/someco/page-
someco-webable.lib.js"></script>
    <@link rel="stylesheet" type="text/css"
href="${url.context}/res/components/someco-webable/someco-webable.css"/>
</@>
```

8. Then, let's use another macro provided by Alfresco too to generate the body of the page.

```
<@templateBody>
  <@markup id="alf-hd">
    <div id="alf-hd">
        <@region scope="global" id="share-header" chromeless="true"/>
    </div>
  </@>
  <@markup id="bd">
    <div id="bd">
    </div>
  </@>
</@>
```

 If you want to know more about templates and regions, you can look at this documentation: http://docs.alfresco.com/5.1/concepts/surf-te mplates-regions.html.

9. Finally, add the final macro that will generate the footer of the page.

```
<@templateFooter>
    <@markup id="alf-ft">
        <div id="alf-ft">
          <@region id="footer" scope="global" />
        </div>
    </@>
</@>
```

10. If you check carefully your code, you should find a DIV element with the id attribute equals to bd. This element will contain the HTML code of your page. First, we need to add a new DIV element that will be managed by our Angular application inside the DIV element with the id equals to bd.

```
<div ng-app="someco-webable" ng-init="init()" ng-
controller="SomecoWebableCtrl">

</div>
```

11. In this newly DIV element, we want to display a filter button to be able to select active, inactive or any webable documents.

```
<br />
<div class="set">
   <div class="set-bordered-panel">
      <div class="set-bordered-panel-heading">Filter(s)</div>
         <div class="set-bordered-panel-body">
           <div id="filter-menu"></div>
            <br />
         </div>
      </div>
   </div>
```

12. Below the list of filters, we just want to display the list of documents in a TABLE element containing one row per document. To accomplish that, we'll use the Angular variable documents that we will populate later, and we'll use as well the `filter` directive to be able to display only relevant documents.

```
<table>
   <tr ng-repeat="doc in documents | filter:filter" class="document">
   [...]
   </tr>
</table>
```

13. For each document, the first cell will be the thumbnail the document, and we'll reuse the same webscript used by Alfresco Share in the document library. We want as well to make the image clickable that will redirect the user to the document. Place the following code in the tr tag that we defined above.

```
<td>
  <span class="thumbnail">
   <a ng-
href="${url.context}/page/site/${(page.url.templateArgs.site!"")?url?js_str
ing}/document-details?nodeRef=workspace://SpacesStore/{{
doc.properties['d.cmis:objectId'].value.split(';')[0] }}">
     <img id="workspace://SpacesStore/{{
doc.properties['d.cmis:objectId'].value.split(';')[0] }}" ng-
src="${url.context}/proxy/alfresco/api/node/workspace/SpacesStore/{{
doc.properties['d.cmis:objectId'].value.split(';')[0]
}}/content/thumbnails/doclib?c=queue&amp;ph=true" >
   </a>
  </span>
</td>
```

14. The next and last cell will contain basic information like file name, version label, last modifier and last modification date. If we display an active document, we want to display the publication date, otherwise, we want display a message informing that the document is not published.

```
<td>
  <h3 class="filename">
    <a ng-
href="${url.context}/page/site/${(page.url.templateArgs.site!"")?url?js_str
ing}/document-details?nodeRef=workspace://SpacesStore/{{
doc.properties['d.cmis:objectId'].value.split(';')[0] }}">
{{ doc.properties['d.cmis:name'].value }}
    </a>
    <span class="document-version">{{
doc.properties['d.cmis:versionLabel'].value }}</span>
  </h3>
<div class="detail">
    Last Modified on {{ doc.properties['d.cmis:lastModificationDate'].value
| date:'medium' }} By {{ doc.properties['d.cmis:lastModifiedBy'].value }}
</div>
<div class="detail">
  <span ng-if="doc.properties['w.sc:published'].value">
    Published on {{ doc.properties['w.sc:published'].value | date:'medium'
}}
  </span>
  <span ng-if="!doc.properties['w.sc:published'].value">
    Not Published
  </span>
</div>
</td>
```

15. Let's populate the I18N message property file `share.properties` located in `src|main|amp|config|alfresco|web-extensions|messages` with the page title and description.

```
page.someco.webable.title=SomecoWebable Documents
page.someco.webable.description=List all documents with the Webable aspect
```

16. We need to make our new page available in the list of available pages for each site. Open the file `share-config-custom.xml` page located in `src|main|resources|META-INF`. Add a new config element using the evaluator string-compare and condition `SitePages`. We just copy the existing `config` element from the file share-config.xml in the `webappshare.war` and we add our new page.

```
<config evaluator="string-compare" condition="SitePages" replace="true">
    <pages>
        <page id="calendar">calendar</page>
        <page id="wiki-page">wiki-page?title=Main_Page</page>
        <page id="documentlibrary">documentlibrary</page>
        <page id="discussions-topiclist">discussions-topiclist</page>
        <page id="blog-postlist">blog-postlist</page>
        <page id="links">links</page>
        <page id="data-lists">data-lists</page>
        <page id="someco-webable">someco-webable</page>
    </pages>
</config>
```

17. Then, be sure to have a file named page-someco-webable-64.png in the folder **src|main|amp|web|components|images** that will be used to represent our new page. We are placing our image in the same folder used by Alfresco Share to store images for pages.

18. Let's add some CSS rules in the file someco-webable.css that you'll need to create in the directory src|main|amp|web|components|someco-webable.

```css
.thumbnail {
  cursor: pointer;
  display: block;
  height: 100px;
  overflow: hidden;
  position: relative;
  width: 100px;
}
.document {
  padding: 15px;
}
.detail {
  clear: left;
  line-height: 1.5em;
  min-height: 1.5em;
  padding-bottom: 0.2em;
  padding-left: 20px;
}
```

```
.filename {
  font-size: 131%;
  font-weight: normal;
  padding-bottom: 0.2em;
  padding-left: 20px;
  word-wrap: break-word;
}
```

19. The last missing piece is the Javascript file. In the directory
    src|main|amp|web|js|someco. Create the file page-someco-webable.lib.js.
    You could ask why we use the extension lib.js. The Alfresco Maven archetypes
    are pre-configured to minify Javascript files. During this process, some variable
    can be renamed to use shorter names. The problem is those changes are not
    compatible with Angular. To avoid any issue, we just use the extension lib.js
    because these files are not minified by Maven.First, let's create the Angular app.

```
var app = angular.module("someco-webable", []);
app.controller('SomecoWebableCtrl', SomecoWebableCtrl);

function SomecoWebableCtrl($scope) {

  $scope.documents = [];
  $scope.filter = {};

};
```

20. In the function SomecoWebableCtrl, create the init method and defined the url
    variable. You can notice that we'll use CMIS 1.1 to query the repository.

```
$scope.init = function() {

var url = Alfresco.constants.URL_CONTEXT + "proxy/alfresco-api/-default-
/public/cmis/versions/1.1/browser";
url += "?cmisaction=query";
url += "&statement=" + encodeURIComponent("SELECT d.*, w.* FROM
cmis:document AS d JOIN sc:webable AS w ON d.cmis:objectId =
w.cmis:objectId WHERE CONTAINS(d, 'PATH:"/app:company_home/st:sites/cm:" +
Alfresco.constants.SITE + "//*"')");

}
```

21. After that the url variable is initialized, we need to query Alfresco and we'll save
    the results in the the variable documents that is used in the Freemarker template.

```
Alfresco.util.Ajax.request({
method :Alfresco.util.Ajax.POST,
```

```
url :url,
successCallback : {
fn : function(response) {
    $scope.documents = response.json.results;
    $scope.$apply();
  },
scope : this
  },
failureMessage : "Error retrieving documents."
});
```

22. Finally, we need to add the following code in the init method to build the filters button.

```
var filterMenu = [ {
text : "Active and Inactive",
value : "all",
onclick : {
fn :updateFilter
  }
}, {
text : "Active",
value : "active",
onclick : {
fn :updateFilter
  }
}, {
text : "Inactive",
value : "inactive",
onclick : {
fn :updateFilter
  }
} ];

$scope.statusFilter = new YAHOO.widget.Button({
type : "menu",
label : "Active and Inactive",
name : "publishStatusSelect",
menu :filterMenu,
container : "filter-menu"
});
```

23. As you can see, I'm using a Yahoo UI button in this page. I'm doing that to be sure that I use the same UI framework in the entire Share web application. Like that, we are sure that the rendering of buttons is exactly the same in the entire application.

24. As you can see above, each time that we click on a filter, we'll call the function updateFilter. This filter will just populate the variable filter that is used in the directive that lists documents. Place the following function after $scope.init.

```
function updateFilter(p_sType, p_aArgs, p_oItem) {

var sText = p_oItem.cfg.getProperty("text");
  $scope.statusFilter.set("label", sText);

  if (p_oItem.value == "all")
    $scope.filter = {};
  else if (p_oItem.value == "active")
    $scope.filter = {
properties : {
        "w.sc:isActive" : {
value : true
        }
      }
    };
  else if (p_oItem.value == "inactive")
    $scope.filter = {
properties : {
        "w.sc:isActive" : {
        value : false
        }
      }
    };

  $scope.$apply();
}
```

25. Deploy, package and test.

To be able to test your new page, you need login and open a site where you are a Site Manager.

1. Click on the steering wheel in top right corner, and click on **Customize Site**.

2. Then, you new page should be displayed in the list of **Available Site Pages**.

3. Drag and drop the page to the list of **Current Site Pages**. Feel free to click on **Rename**, and give it the name that you prefer.

4. Click on **OK**, click on the name of the page in the top banner. You should be able to see the filter and all documents with the aspect sc:webable.

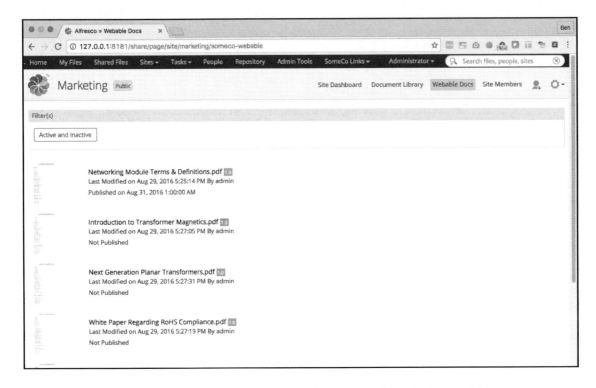

5. If you click on the filter and select **Active** or **Inactive**, the lists of documents should be refreshed to display only the relevant documents. You can re-apply the same steps in another site, and the list of documents will contain only items stored in the same Alfresco Share site.

Summary

In this chapter, you learned that the Alfresco Share is an all-purpose user interface for general document management. It can be easily extended using approaches that range from making XML configuration file changes to writing new Surf dashlets or pages.

Specifically, you learned how to:

- Add new menu items to the top bar menu
- Create new actions items using dialogs or not
- Show/hide action items based on things such as permissions or arbitrary logic
- Create custom metadata template to change how Share shows repository data
- Implement indicators in Share to reflect a status or an information on documents
- Create a new form control to interact differently with metadata
- Assess whether the solution you are building should be based on a custom version of Alfresco Share, or would be more appropriate as a custom application

We discovered in this chapter how you can configure and customize Alfresco Share for your use case. In the next chapter, we'll discover more about the new Alfresco Development Framework (ADF) to generate a full customized UI using Angular.

6
Creating an Angular Application

Depending on your use case, you may think that creating your own UI from scratch is what you need. And you may be right! Thanks to Alfresco APIs, you have a lot of options. In this chapter, we'll talk about the new **Alfresco Development Framework (ADF)** and how we can create a new Angular application.

By the end of this chapter, you will know how to do the following:

- Use the new Alfresco JavaScript library
- Create a new Angular application using Yeoman
- Discover all the out-of-the-box components provided by this framework

It is important to note that this chapter is based on the latest published version (at the time of writing) of the Alfresco Developer Framework, that is, 1.0.1. This version is not suitable for a production use. You may ask why it has been integrated into this book if we can't use it. Well, this is because I'm deeply convinced that this framework is going to be used by a very wide community. For this reason, I really believe that this book should give you the basics on how to use it, and how it works. Also, I just want to emphasize that this framework is only available on Alfresco Community, and from version 201606. The rest of the book is based on Alfresco Enterprise 5.1.x, so we'll provide you with a virtual machine and an installation script.

Understanding the framework

You may say "Oh, another way to create a UI integrated with Alfresco" and you are not completely wrong. However, this new framework will simplify the decoupling between Alfresco and the custom interface that you want to develop. Finding people with the required skills to do Share application development may not be easy. This new framework will help large companies to build better solutions by asking Alfresco experts to develop the core of your ECM, and UI experts with Angular experience to focus only on the building of application.

Components

This new framework is composed of four major components:

- The first component is the Alfresco JavaScript API. We know that developers spend a lot of time doing boilerplate code. The first main and basic example is to deal with authentication. To increase the efficiency of developers, Alfresco created a new JavaScript API not tied to any specific framework. You can use this API in any JavaScript-based application.
- The next component is a set of Angular components. They are based on the previous Alfresco JavaScript API, and they are completely reusable NG2 components. NG2 refers to Angular version 2.
- Another important component is an application generator that will help you create a new application in seconds.
- The final component is another generator to create custom component to integrate in your application.

Don't worry if it's still confusing for the moment, we'll go through all these components in the following section.

In summary, Alfresco provides four main ways to develop your own UI:

- Share customizations
- Angular applications (using the out-of-the-box NG2 components)
- Any JavaScript framework (using the Alfresco JavaScript API)
- Any application capable of using the CMIS protocol

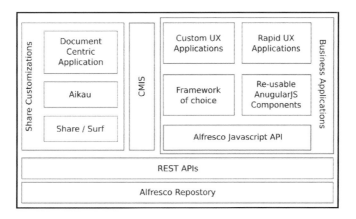

Prepare your environments

As explained earlier, the current version of the ADF is only available on Alfresco Community 201609 Early Access or newer (More details on this page `https://github.com/Alfresco/alfresco-ng2-components/blob/master/PREREQUISITES.m d`). We don't want you to spend too much time re-installing everything. To simplify this chapter, we'll provide you with the following:

- A `Vagrant` file to create a dedicated virtual machine
- A `bash` script that will install and configure everything to be able to use the ADF

The code that we'll develop in the later sections will be loaded from a different web server than the one Alfresco is running on. So we need to configure Alfresco to accept any request that comes in. So, we'll need to enable CORS.

Then, we'll deploy a REST API explorer developed by Alfresco. It's not a required component, but it will be very useful for your UI developers.

Before creating the virtual machine, we want to discuss and analyze the three files that you are going to use and we provide you:

- The `Vagrant` file, located in `vms|vagrant-ch6`, is very similar to the other one that you used to install Alfresco Enterprise. You can see few differences:
    - We are going to redirect port `8080` corresponding to the default *Tomcat* port, and port `9000`, which will be used by the Node.JS server that will be deployed in the same virtual machine:

```
# Redirect Tomcat Port
config.vm.network "forwarded_port", guest: 8080, host: 8080
```

- And you'll also notice an additional line at the end of the `Vagrant` file. This line asks `Vagrant` to execute the installation shell script that we are providing:

```
config.vm.provision "shell", path: "install-alfresco.sh"
```

- The file called `install-options.txt` contains additional options that will be used with the Alfresco installer. It allows us to run the installer without manual interaction. In this file, we just specify that we want to run the installer in **unattended** mode, and the admin user should be **admin**. You can find more details about silent install on `http://docs.alfresco.com/5.1/concepts/silent-alf-install.html`:

```
mode=unattended
alfresco_admin_password=admin
```

- The last file is the shell installations script called `install-alfresco.sh`. We are not going to review it in detail, but we are going to analyze this file step-by-step:

1. First, we need to login as `root` and go to the `/vagrant` folder, which is the default shared folder between the virtual machine and the host if you use Vagrant:

```
sudo su -
cd /vagrant
```

2. We are now installing some Alfresco prerequisites and useful tools:

```
echo "Installing pre-requisites..."
yum -y install fontconfig libSM libICE libXrender libXext
    cups-libs libGLU zip nano
```

3. Then, we are downloading Alfresco. Because we download the file from the `/vagrant` folder, the file will be stored on your computer and not inside the virtual machine. If you delete your virtual machine and recreate it, it won't redownload the file:

```
if [ ! -f alfresco-community-installer-201612-linux-x64.bin ];
then
  echo "  Downloading... (801M)"
  wget
http://dl.alfresco.com/release/community/201612-build-00014
      /alfresco-community-installer-201612-linux-x64.bin
  chmod +x alfresco-community-installer-201612-linux-x64.bin
else
  echo "  Installer already downloaded"
fi
```

4. The next step is to run the installer using the options file that we explained previously (we are installing Alfresco using the root user in this case, it's not something that you should do in production but it's acceptable in our case for a development environment):

```
echo "  Installing Alfresco..."
./alfresco-community-installer-201612-linux-x64.bin
      --optionfile install-options.txt
```

5. When the installation is completed, we'll enable CORS. We are just going to deploy a JAR file that will configure Alfresco to accept AJAX queries from other domains:

```
echo "  Enabling CORS..."
cd /opt/alfresco-community/modules/platform/
if [ ! -f enablecors-1.0.jar ];
then
  wget http://artifacts.alfresco.com/nexus/service/local
    /repositories/releases/content/org/alfresco
    /enablecors/1.0/enablecors-1.0.jar
else
  echo "  The CORS module is already installed."
fi
```

6. We are almost done. The last piece is the installation of the API explorer. We are just downloading version 1.1 from the Alfresco server and saving it in the webapps folder:

```
echo "  Installing API Explorer..."
cd /opt/alfresco-community/tomcat/webapps/
if [ ! -f api-explorer.war ];
then
  echo "  Downloading..."
  curl https://artifacts.alfresco.com/nexus/service/local
    /repositories/releases/content/org/alfresco
    /api-explorer/1.4/api-explorer-1.4.war > api-explorer.war
else
  echo "  Webapp already installed"
fi
```

7. Finally, the last step is to start Alfresco:

```
echo "  Starting Alfresco..."
service alfresco start
```

Be aware that this process can be quite long, depending on your Internet performance. On my machine, it took up to twenty minutes the first time, including downloading the Alfresco Community installer. You'll just need to be a bit patient.

Step-by-step – creating the new virtual machine

Follow these steps:

1. Download the ZIP file containing the code for this chapter, and unzip it.
2. Open a command-line console and go to the folder where you extracted the ZIP file.
3. Go to the subfolder called vm|vagrant-ch6 that contains the Vagrant file that we described above.
4. Be sure that your other virtual machine is suspended or shutdown.

5. Type the following command, which will create the virtual machine and install Alfresco Community. Remind you that it can take a bit of time to complete the process:

```
vagrant up
```

6. When it's completed, just wait few more minutes to let Alfresco start for the first time, and then `open http://127.0.0.1:8080/share/`. You should see the Alfresco Community login page:

7. You can also open the following URL and test the API explorer
   `http://127.0.0.1:8080/api-explorer/`:

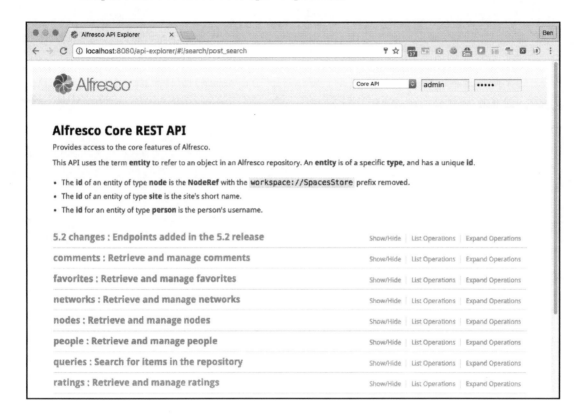

You can see in the top-right corner that you can enter the username and the password that you want to use for the authentication. Also, you have a drop-down list that allows you to select one of these APIs:

- **Core API**
- **Search API**
- **Authentication API**
- **Discovery API**
- **Workflow API**

Now that we have our new virtual machine installed, you can do the following things:

- Stop Alfresco
- Transfer the two modules that we developed (the Alfresco AMP file and the Share AMP file) into the virtual machine using FileZilla, SCP or your favorite tool
- Install your custom AMP files in Alfresco using the same instructions as before
- Restart Alfresco (you'll notice that your two modules are compatible with Alfresco Enterprise and Community)

When Alfresco is restarted and contains your new module, you need to create some documents to be able to test the Alfresco Development Framework:

1. Create a **Marketing** site.
2. Upload some documents that you'll transform to **whitepapers**.
3. Apply the **Someco Webable** aspect to those documents.
4. Create the group `SomecoPublisher` and add the user that you use to test as member.
5. Publish some documents using the **SC Enable Web Flag** action.

Now everything is ready to create our own custom JavaScript application.

Creating your first JavaScript application

In this section, we'll cover how to create a very basic screen using the new JavaScript API. The marketing chief wants us to develop a simple HTML page that displays all webable documents available in the Alfresco repository. For each of them, we need to display the name of the document, and the link to the **Document Details** page.

The Alfresco JavaScript API allows you to connect to the Alfresco API, and the Activiti REST API. In this chapter, we'll use only the Alfresco API. It's the only required to display webable documents. Let's quickly discover the available methods in this Alfresco JavaScript API:

- Authentication:
  - Login:

    Can be done against Alfresco (referenced as **ECM** in the documentation) and/or Activiti (referenced as **BPM** in the documentation).

Can use a username and a password, or an already existing ticket.

This method is monitored by three different events corresponding to success authentication, failed authentication, and logout:

- Logout
  - isLoggedIn
  - Get tickets: To retrieve the Alfresco and/or Activiti tickets after authentication

- Alfresco-related API (or ECM-related API):
  - **Get Node Information** using a node identifier
  - **Get Folder Children** using a node identifier
  - **Create Folder**
  - **Upload File** (this method is monitored by five events: in progress, successful upload, aborted upload, error during the upload, and unauthorized upload)
  - **Delete Node** using a node identifier
  - **Delete Node** permanently using a node identifier
  - **Get Thumbnail URL** using a node identifier
  - **Get Preview URL** using a node identifier
  - **Get Content URL** using a node identifier
  - **Custom Webscript Call** to send a query to any API available in Alfresco (out-of-the-box or custom)

We are not covering the Activiti-related API, but you can find all the details in the documentation (`https://github.com/Alfresco/alfresco-js-api`).

You can see that most of the APIs require a node identifier, but we don't have this information in our case (It's possible to use as well some special node identifier that are not relevant in our case like `-root-`, `-my-` or `-shared-`). Because we want to do a search and the JavaScript API don' provide a function to do that, we'll send a query to a webscript provided by the Alfresco Repository. This webscript is the same as the one used by Alfresco Share in the Advanced Search forms. To accomplish it, we'll use the custom webscript call listed in the latest bullet of the preceding list.

Step-by-step – develop your first custom UI using the JavaScript API

1. Open STS and create a new Dynamic Web Project. Click on **Next**:

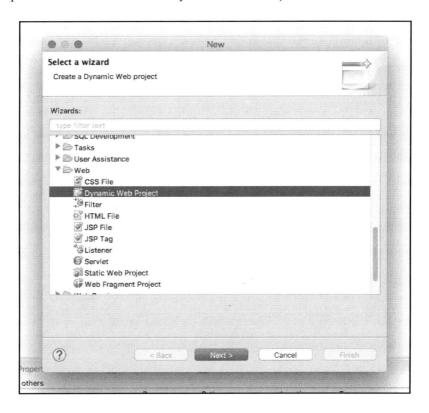

2. Name your project `webable-docs` and click on **Finish**:

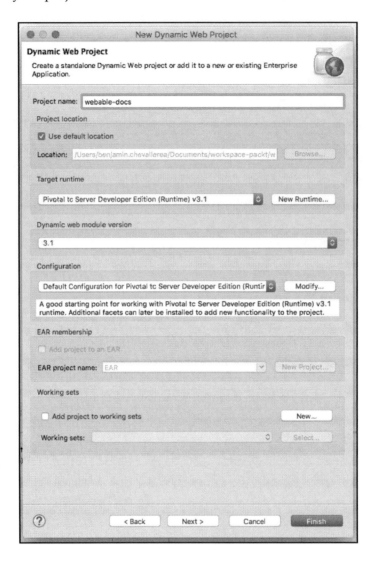

3. We need to download the JavaScript library and save it in our project. Open the GitHub project (`https://github.com/Alfresco/alfresco-js-api`) and open the folder called `dist`. You should find a file called `alfresco-js-api.js` (you can also find the minified version in the same folder). Click on this file, then on the **Download** button.

4. Create the `lib` folder in the `WebContent` subfolder of your newly created project and move the downloaded file in this folder.

5. Create a new file in the `WebContent` folder called `index.html` and add the basic following HTML code for your page:

```
<!DOCTYPE html>
<html>
    <head>
        <title>Published documents</title>
    </head>
    <body>
    </body>
</html>
```

6. Let's add a new reference in the `head` element for the Alfresco JavaScript API:

```
<script type="text/javascript" src="./lib/alfresco-js-api.js"
    charset="utf-8"></script>
```

7. And, finally let's add another reference to another JavaScript file that will send the query to Alfresco:

```
<script type="text/javascript" src="./index.js"
    charset="utf-8"></script>
```

8. And now, we need to create the JavaScript `index.js` file in the `WebContent` folder. Let's create the main structure first, that is, the authentication process. We'll use the username `admin`, with its default password `admin`:

```
this.alfrescoJsApi = new AlfrescoApi();
this.alfrescoJsApi.login('admin', 'admin').then(function(data)
{
    console.log('API called successfully Login ticket:' + data);
}, function(error) {
    console.error(error);
});
```

9. In the `then` function, we are going to create the query object that will use with the Search API to locate active whitepapers:

```
var q = {
    "prop_sc_isActive" : "true",
    "datatype" : "sc:whitepaper"
};
```

10. Then, we are going to use the JavaScript method that allows us to call any webscript provided by Alfresco:

```
this.alfrescoJsApi.webScript.executeWebScript ('GET',
    'slingshot/search?query='
    + JSON.stringify(q) ).then(function(data) {
    console.log('# of items received:' + data.numberFound);
        var items = data.items;
    }, function(error) {
        console.error(error);
});
```

11. And finally, we are going to create a table, with one row per document. On each row, we'll display the thumbnail, the document name with a link on the details page, and a download link. Add the following code below the definition of the variable `items`:

```
var html = "<table>";
for (var i = 0; i < items.length; i++) {
  var item = items[i];

  var nodeId =
    item.nodeRef.substring(item.nodeRef.lastIndexOf('/') + 1);

  html += "<tr>";

  html += "<td><img src='"
    +
this.alfrescoJsApi.content.getDocumentThumbnailUrl(nodeId)
    + "' ></td>";

  html += "<td>";

  html += "<a target='_blank'
    href='/share/page/document-details?nodeRef="
    + item.nodeRef + "'>" + item.displayName + "</a><br/>"

  html += "<a target='_blank' href='"
    + this.alfrescoJsApi.content.getContentUrl(nodeId)
    + "'>Download</a>"

  html += "</td>";
  html += "</tr>";
}
html += "</table>";
document.body.innerHTML += html;
```

12. Everything is ready. We can now package our mini project. To keep it simple, we are just going to create a new Tomcat web application and deploy it in the same Tomcat as Alfresco. Right-click on the `webable-docs` project and click on **Export** | **Export ....** Select `WAR file` in the `Web` category:

13. Click on **Browse** to select the export destination, and click on **Finish**:

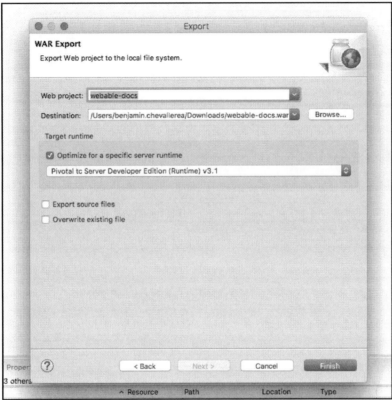

14. You are now ready to deploy your new web application into your virtual machine using FileZilla or SCP. You don't need to shutdown your Tomcat instance because it's configured in auto-deploy mode. Just drop your WAR file in the `/opt/alfresco-community/tomcat/webapps/` folder.

15. If you track the Alfresco log file, you should see those lines that means that Tomcat auto-deployed your WAR file:

```
Oct 09, 2016 7:01:46 PM org.apache.catalina.startup
.HostConfig deployWAR

INFO: Deploying web application
    archive /opt/alfresco-community/tomcat/webapps
    /webable-docs.war

Oct 09, 2016 7:01:46 PM org.apache.catalina.startup
```

```
.HostConfig deployWAR

INFO: Deployment of web application archive
    /opt/alfresco-community/tomcat/webapps/webable-docs.war
    has finished in 113 ms
```

16. Then, you can open your browser on
    `http://localhost:8080/webable-docs/` and see a list of documents. For
    each document, you should see the thumbnail, the document name with a link to
    the details page, and a **Download** link:

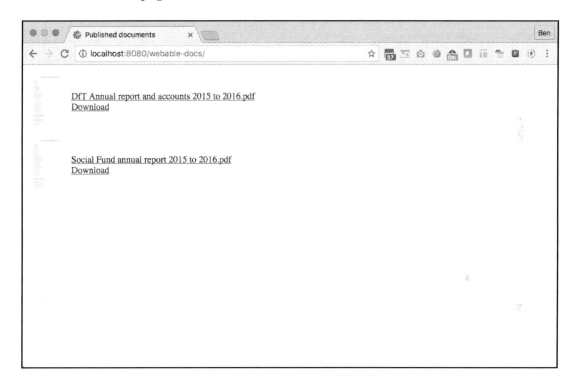

17. Feel free to create new whitepapers and enable them. The list should be automatically updated. However, be aware that Alfresco, and more especially Solr, needs few seconds to index your documents. Your newly uploaded documents may appear only five or ten seconds after the upload.

You just created your first JavaScript application using the Alfresco JavaScript API. You could have done the same using plain JavaScript or any other JavaScript framework providing methods to send AJAX queries. The Alfresco JavaScript API is just helping you by providing the basic mechanism required to build your own JavaScript application. It's time to switch to Angular.

Creating your first Angular web application

Let's start by a quick overview of an Angular application. We won't go into the details of the framework because it's not the purpose of this book. Angular is a framework for building web applications in HTML and JavaScript. It consists of multiple libraries, some of them core and other optional. You create an Angular application by writing HTML *templates* with Angularized markup, writing *component* classes to manage those templates, adding application logic in *services*, and boxing components and services in *modules*. Of course, there is more to it than this, and you can read more on the Angular website, `https://angular.io/docs/`.

Why Angular is so popular? From my point of view, the most relevant reasons are as follows:

- It's very easy to structure your code using the **MVC (Model-View-Controller)** pattern
- The two-way binding allows you to significantly reduce the amount of code to keep the model and the view synchronized
- The HTML and the JS code is very well decoupled, that allows to have designers and developers to work in parallel on the same screens
- Angular comes with all required libraries to build a complete data-based web application; there's no need to manually install any other framework

On top of Angular and the Alfresco JavaScript API, Alfresco has created seven components so far. This list is not closed; Alfresco will enrich it throughout the different versions. The list of components is as follows:

- `ng2-alfresco-core`: Core library used by the other components
- `ng2-alfresco-datatable`: Simple Document List component
- `ng2-alfresco-documentlist`: Advanced Document List component
- `ng2-alfresco-login`: Login component
- `ng2-alfresco-search`: Basic Search component
- `ng2-alfresco-upload`: Upload component
- `ng2-alfresco-viewer`: PDF previewer component using the library `PDF.js`

When we create our first application, you'll notice that all components are styled using a design guideline based on Google Material Design (`https://material.io/guidelines/`).

To help you to start quickly, Alfresco has created an app generator based on *Yeoman*. It is a generic scaffolding system allowing the creation of any kind of app. This generator will create all the boilerplate code required for an Angular web application.

Step-by-step – installing all prerequisites

An Angular web application can be packaged and deployed in any container. Alfresco decided to generate Node.JS application. To show that we can deploy in different servers the Angular web application and Alfresco, we'll install the Angular application directly in our computer. The following instructions should work on Mac OSX and UNIX systems. For each step, we'll point you to the relevant documentation to get details about your specific environment:

1. First, authenticate as root or Administrator
2. We need to install the latest Node.JS version in our system. (More details here: `https://nodejs.org/en/download/package-manager/`). The valid command for OSX is as follows:

```
curl "https://nodejs.org/dist/latest/node-
    ${VERSION:-$(wget -qO- https://nodejs.org/dist/latest/
    | sed -nE 's|.*>node-(.*)\.pkg</a>.*|\1|p')}.pkg" >
    "$HOME/Downloads/node-latest.pkg" && sudo installer
    -store -pkg "$HOME/Downloads/node-latest.pkg" -target "/"
```

3. Be sure that you use a Node.JS version higher than 5:

```
$> node -v
v6.7.0
```

4. Let's also check the npm version, which needs to be higher than 3:

```
$> npm -v
3.10.3
```

5. Then, we can install Yeoman:

```
npm install -g yo
```

6. And finally, install the Yeoman generator developed by Alfresco:

```
npm install -g generator-ng2-alfresco-app
```

Everything is now ready to create our first Angular application.

Step-by-step – creating your first Angular application

The following section will describe how you can create your first application using the application generator provided by Alfresco:

1. In STS, create a new **General** | **Project** called someco-app.
2. Open a command-line tool and go to the project folder that you just created in STS.
3. Create the Angular application:

```
yo ng2-alfresco-app
```

4. You will have to reply if you want to help Yeoman by providing them with information. Feel free to reply how you want:

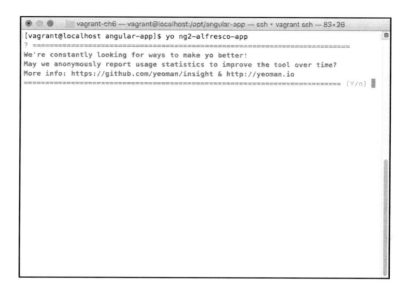

5. Then, reply to each question:

- What's the name of your App? `someco-app`
- How would you describe the app? `Someco Angular 2 Application`
- Author's Name: *Anything that you want*
- Author's Email: *Anything that you want*
- Author's Homepage: *Anything that you want*
- Package keywords (comma to split): `test,alfresco,someco`
- What is your Alfresco platform server URL? `http://127.0.0.1:8080`
- What is your Activiti platform server URL? `http://127.0.0.1:9999`
- GitHub username or organization: *Anything that you want*

- Do you want include the User info component? Yes
- Do you want include a drawer bar? Yes
- Do you want include a search bar? Yes
- Do you want include a Document List? Yes
- Do you want include Activiti BPM components? Yes
- Which license do you want to use? Apache 2.0

```
[vagrant@localhost someco-app]$ yo ng2-alfresco-app

              ,****.
          , .**. `*****   <-_
        *********  *****  ####
       $******* :*****  ####;
      _.`*_.`**  :*** #*####
    ,******  *::* .;##### @
    *********,' -#####',@@@
    ***' ,_  , ,. -@@@@@@@
     * /@@@@',@ @\ '@@@@@@@
     '@@@/ @@@ @@@\ ':#'
     !@@@@ @@@@ @@@@@@@@^
     @@@@ @@@@ @@@@@@@'
      `"$ '@@@@@. '##'
          '@@@;.'

      Welcome to the awesome
      Angular 2 app generator
           for Alfresco!

? What's the name of your App? someco-app
? How would you describe the app? Someco Angular 2 Application
? Author's Name Ben Chevallereau
? Author's Email benjamin.chevallereau@gmail.com
? Author's Homepage www.bataon.com
? Package keywords (comma to split) test,alfresco,someco
? What is your Alfresco platform server URL? http://127.0.0.1:8080
? What is your Activiti platform server URL? http://127.0.0.1:9999
? GitHub username or organization bchevallereau
? Do you want include a navigation bar? Yes
? Do you want include a drawer bar? Yes
? Do you want include a search bar? Yes
? Do you want include a Document List? Yes
? Do you want include a Tasks List? Yes
? Do you want include a sample dashboard? Yes
? Which license do you want to use? Apache 2.0
```

6. Then, it will generate all required files for our application. If files are not generated, try to run the generator in DEBUG mode: `DEBUG=yeoman:generator yo ng2-alfresco-app`

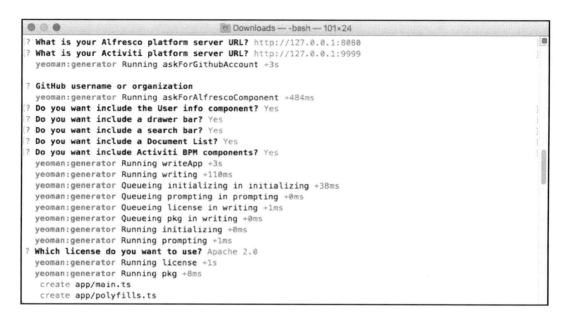

7. If you go back to STS, and refresh the project, you should see the entire folder structure:

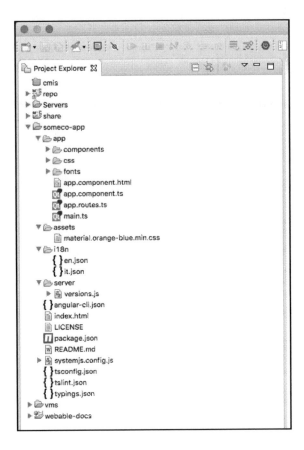

8. Now, let's install all dependencies (in the `node_modules` sub-folder) required by our application:

```
npm install
```

9. We can start the application now:

```
npm start
```

10. A browser should automatically open at `http://localhost:3000/`:

11. Authenticate as `admin`/`admin`. The application will open the dashboard.

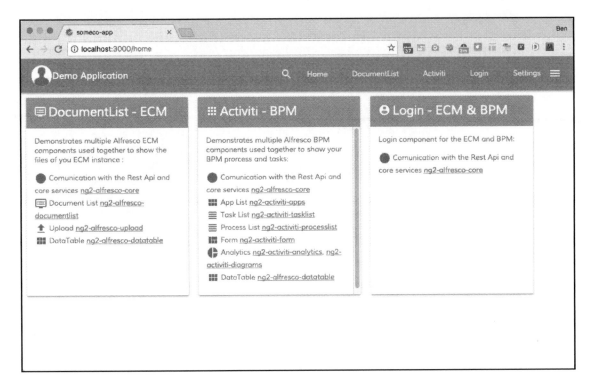

12. If you click on the **DocumentList** link in the top banner, it will show the folders and documents stored in the site **Sample: Web Site Design Project**:

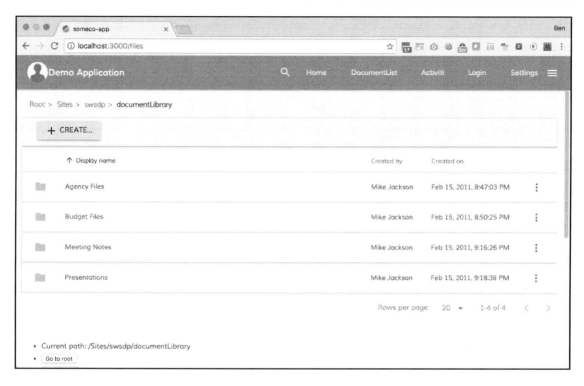

13. Click on the different **Go to** buttons and the list of documents will be directly refreshed. You can notice that we can implement some custom UI actions. Feel free as well to upload documents directly from this UI. You'll notice that you can just drag and drop documents into the page to upload documents.

14. If you click on **Activiti**, you'll be redirected to the login page because we don't have an Activiti server.

15. Finally, you can as well do some search in Alfresco. In the top banner, just type `ppt` and type on **Enter**. You should find these documents:

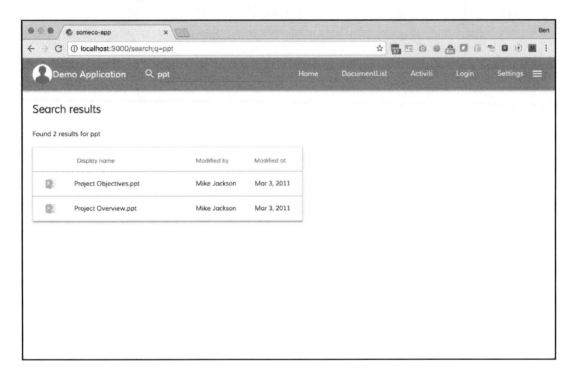

You'll notice that this application is functional but very basic for the moment. You have to keep in mind that the published version at the time of writing is only a way for Alfresco to demonstrate what they will provide in the future release with this Application Development Framework. I'm sure that you want to see a bit more. For that, you can re-use a demo shell available in GitHub.

Step-by-step – running the Alfresco demo shell

We are going to download the demonstration project from GitHub, run it and explore the additional components.

1. First, we assume that you have `git` installed on your computer.

2. Clone the GitHub repository of Alfresco Angular2 components:

```
git clone
https://github.com/Alfresco/alfresco-ng2-components.git
```

3. Go to the folder that just been created by the `git` command, and you should find a sub-folder called `demo-shell-ng2`:

```
$> cd alfresco-ng2-components/
$> ll
total 80
-rw-r--r--    1 ben   2380 Oct 10 17:49 INTRODUCTION.md
-rw-r--r--    1 ben   9724 Oct 10 17:49 LICENSE
-rw-r--r--    1 ben   4409 Oct 10 17:49 PREREQUISITES.md
-rw-r--r--    1 ben   4481 Oct 10 17:49 README.md
-rw-r--r--    1 ben   2852 Oct 10 17:49 appveyor.yml
drwxr-xr-x    6 ben    204 Oct 10 17:49 assets/
drwxr-xr-x   21 ben    714 Oct 10 17:49 demo-shell-ng2/
drwxr-xr-x   15 ben    510 Oct 10 17:49 ng2-components/
drwxr-xr-x   11 ben    374 Oct 10 17:49 scripts/
-rw-r--r--    1 ben   2554 Oct 10 17:49 tslint.json
```

4. Go to the `demo-shell-ng2` folder and install all dependencies:

```
cd demo-shell-ng2/
npm install
```

5. Start the demo shell:

   npm start

6. A browser should automatically open at http://0.0.0.0:3000/. It's very similar to your application (except that it contains more components):

7. Login as admin, click on the list icon in the header next to the **Settings** link, click on **DataTable**. It's a UI component that you can use to display items with advanced features, such as multiselect:

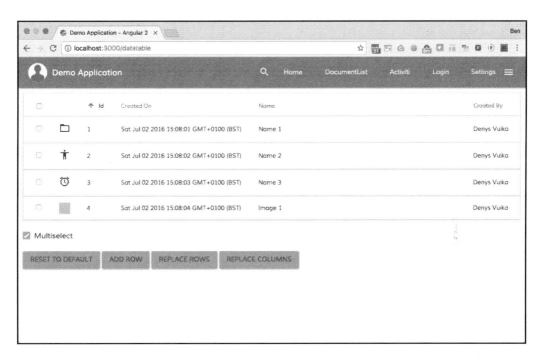

8. In the same list, click on the **Webscript** link. This page is developed to demonstrate that we can call any webscript provided by Alfresco, and we can display the results without reloading the page. Update the first field with this value:

```
sample/folder/Company%20Home/Sites/marketing/documentLibrary
```

9. It lists automatically the `Whitepapers` folder that you created using Alfresco Share:

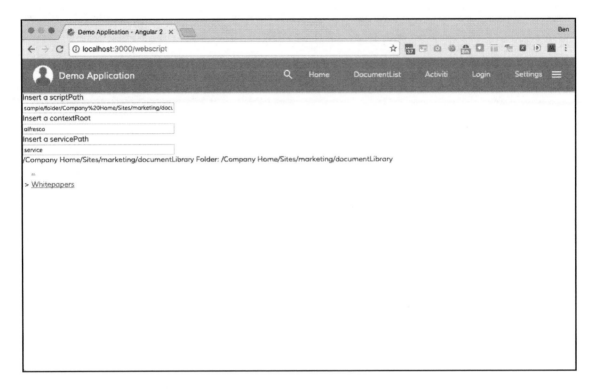

It's important to know that you can create your own custom components. Alfresco implemented another generator that you can find out on this page `https://github.com/Alfresco/generator-ng2-alfresco-component`. This page will explain you on how to install the generator and how to use it. If you want to re-use one of the components already developed by Alfresco, you can take a look at the following page `http://devproducts.alfresco.com/`.

Summary

In this chapter, you learned about the new Alfresco Development Framework that Alfresco is working on, including the new Angular2 components. By choice, we didn't cover the topic of creating a new component, or customizing an existing component. As already explained, this framework is not ready for a production use and is going to evolve very quickly in the next few months. I didn't want to provide information that maybe very quickly outdated.

Specifically, you learned how to do the following:

- Create a dedicated virtual machine for this chapter
- Create a new web project and deploy it in Tomcat using the Alfresco JavaScript API
- Configure your environment to create a new Alfresco Angular application
- Install the demonstration Angular application developed by Alfresco

7
Exposing Content through a RESTful API with Web Scripts

There are many ways to interact with the repository programmatically, one of which is via web scripts. Then why devote an entire chapter to the Web Script Framework? Web scripts allow you to define a REST API for the content in the Alfresco repository. REST stands for Representational State Transfer. In a nutshell, REST describes an architectural style of interaction based on simple URL-based requests and responses occurring over HTTP. Rolling your own RESTful API offers a huge advantage in terms of flexibility and implementation speed over other forms of web service, such as SOAP. Web scripts have quickly become the preferred integration method between the frontend and an Alfresco backend, particularly for portals and dynamic websites.

Specifically, in this chapter you will learn how to do the following:

- Write web scripts that create, read, and delete data in the backend repository and return responses in HTML, XML, and JSON
- Use both JavaScript and Java to write controller logic
- Make **Asynchronous JavaScript** (**AJAX**) calls to web scripts
- Create a rating service that centralizes all logic related to creating rating nodes

Introducing the Web Script Framework

Content-centric applications are becoming more and more componentized. This trend is turning traditional content management approaches inside out. Rather than having a single, monolithic system responsible for all aspects of a content-centric web application, loosely coupled subsystems are being integrated to create more agile solutions.

This approach requires that your **Content Management System (CMS)** has a flexible and lightweight interface. You don't want to be locked in to a presentation approach based on the content repository you are working with. In fact, in some cases, you might have very little control over the tools that will be used to talk to your CMS.

Consider the growing adoption of wikis and blogs within an Enterprise and the increasing popularity of mash-ups both inside and outside the Enterprise. These trends are driving implementations where the CMS is seen as a black-box component with the frontend (or perhaps many different frontends) interacting with the CMS and other components via REST. The shorthand way to refer to this is **content-as-a-service**.

Among open source ECMs, Alfresco is at the forefront of this trend, and the Web Script Framework is a key enabler of the product in the content-as-a-service world. Historically, there have been two approaches to interacting with Alfresco through services: SOAP-based web services and do-it-yourself REST. The SOAP approach is almost dead, but the implementation of your own RESTful API using Web Script is one of the preferred way to implement a content-as-a-service approach with Alfresco. The other approach is to use the CMIS API.

The Web Script Framework introduced in the 2.1 version essentially improves on the basic idea that started with URL addressability. Think of a web script as a chunk of code that is mapped to a human-readable URL. So, for example, a URL that returns expense reports that are pending approval might look like this:

```
/alfresco/service/expenses/pending
```

While a URL that returns expenses that are pending approval for a specific user might look like this:

```
/alfresco/service/expenses/pending/ben
```

In this URL, you could read the `ben` component of the URL as an implied argument. A more explicit way to provide an argument would be like this:

```
/alfresco/service/expenses/pending?user=ben
```

You might choose to treat the `pending` component of the URL as an argument as well, which tells the web script what status of expense reports to return. The point is that the Web Script Framework leaves the structure of the URL and how (and if) your URL includes arguments completely up to you.

Step-by-step – Hello World web script

Despite the fact that your repo module already contains a basic web script, we are going to create a new one from scratch. Let's implement the most basic web script possible: a HelloWorld script that echoes back an argument. You'll need one descriptor and one FreeMarker template. Do the following:

1. Log in to Alfresco Share.
2. Click on **Repository** in the top menu.
3. Navigate to **Repository** | **Data Dictionary** | **Web Scripts**.
4. Create an XML file called helloworld.get.desc.xml in the Web Scripts Extensions folder with the following content:

```
<webscript>
        <shortname>Hello World</shortname>
        <description>Hello world web script</description>
        <url>/someco/helloworld?name={nameArgument}</url>
</webscript>
```

5. Create a plain text file called helloworld.get.html.ftl with the following content:

```
<html>
    <body>
        <p>Hello, ${args.name}!</p>
    </body>
</html>
```

6. Go to http://localhost:8080/alfresco/service/index and press the **Refresh Web Scripts** button. You may be prompted to login. Click the **List Web Scripts** link-you should be able to find the web script you just defined.

7. Now point your browser to http://localhost:8080/alfresco/service/someco/helloworld?name=Ben. You should see this:

```
Hello, Ben!
```

You can notice that you have as well a folder called Web Scripts Extensions in the Data Dictionary folder. The Web Scripts folder is considered to store brand new web scripts, especially if you want to give a chance to extend it in the future. While the Web Scripts Extensions folder is used when you want to override a web script provided by Alfresco or another add-on. But nothing forbids you to store your brand new web scripts in the folder Web Scripts Extensions. What you need to understand is the priority order used by Alfresco. The Web Scripts Extensions folder will override the files in the Web Scripts folder, that will override the file in the extension folder in the classpath, that will override the file in the main Alfresco classpath. You can have more information on this page http://docs.alfresco.com/5.1/concepts/ws-component-place.html.

What just happened?

You invoked a URL in your web browser (specifically, you made a GET request over HTTP). The Alfresco web application is configured to map all requests matching the pattern /alfresco/service/* to the web script request dispatcher servlet. The servlet handed off the request to the Web Script Runtime to process the web script. The Web Script Runtime figured out which web script to execute by matching the remainder of the URL (someco/helloworld?name=Ben) to the URL pattern you declared in the web script's descriptor file, helloworld.get.desc.xml.

You didn't specify what kind of response you wanted from the web script, and the web script descriptor didn't declare a default, so the framework assumed HTML would be acceptable. It then used file naming convention to find a FreeMarker template to generate an HTML response for this web script. The FreeMarker template formatted a response to send back to the browser that included some HTML and the value of the name argument.

Following the Model-View-Controller pattern

The Web Script Framework makes it easy to follow the **Model–View–Controller (MVC)** pattern. You don't have to be a hardcore disciple of the Gang of Four to appreciate the value of the MVC pattern. In MVC, all business logic resides in the controller. It is completely separated from the presentation or view. This makes it possible to have as many views as you need without a big maintenance headache because the business logic isn't bundled together with the view. It is centralized in the controller. There is a clear separation of concerns.

In Alfresco's Web Script Framework, the controller is server-side JavaScript, a Java Bean, or both. The controller handles the request, performs any business logic that is needed, populates the model with data, and then forwards the request to the view. The view is one or more FreeMarker templates responsible for constructing a response in the appropriate format. The model is essentially a data structure passed between the controller and the view.

The mapping of URL to controller is done through an XML descriptor that is responsible for declaring the URL pattern, whether the script requires a transaction or not, and the authentication requirements for the script. The descriptor optionally describes arguments that can be passed to the script, as well as the response formats that are available.

Adding controller logic

The Hello World example consisted of one FreeMarker template and one descriptor XML file. The FreeMarker API is quite extensive, and many out-of-the-box examples rely solely on FreeMarker for light logic processing as well as rendering a response. Ideally, however, FreeMarker templates should be strictly focused on presentation. Logic, such as querying the repository, creating or updating content, executing actions, and so on, should be handled in the JavaScript or Java-based controller.

Try adding a simple controller to the Hello World example:

1. You should still be logged in to Alfresco Share.
2. Create a plain text file in **Repository** | **DataDictionary** | **Web Scripts** called `helloworld.get.js` with the following content:

   ```
   model.now = new Date();
   ```

3. Update your `helloworld.get.html.ftl` file with the following content:

   ```
   <html>
       <body>
           <p>Hello, ${args.name}!</p>
           <p><i>${now?datetime?string}</i></p>
       </body>
   </html>
   ```

4. Go to `http://localhost:8080/alfresco/service/index` and press the **Refresh Web Scripts** button. This is required because you added a controller that the web script runtime didn't know about.

5. Now go to your web browser and enter the same URL from the first example, which was
   `http://localhost:8080/alfresco/service/someco/helloworld?name=B en`. You should see this:

```
Hello, Ben!
Jan 15, 2017 4:06:05 PM
```

What's going on here is that the web script framework is executing the controller prior to rendering a response with the FreeMarker template. In the controller, you can do anything the Alfresco JavaScript API can do. In this case, you didn't leverage the JavaScript API at all. You just put some data into the model object. The model variable is a root variable Alfresco makes available to you to enable data sharing between the controller (JavaScript) and the view (FreeMarker).

In subsequent examples, the controller will have more work to do, and in one case, you'll use Java instead of JavaScript for the controller.

Configuring the Web Script Framework

The three most important settings for any web script are as follows:

- The HTTP method used to make the request to the web script
- The URL and any arguments the web script expects
- The response formats the web script supports

The web script framework defines conventions that make it easy to configure these settings.

Specifying the HTTP method

In the `Hello World` example, notice that the file names for the descriptor and the FreeMarker template include `get`. It tells the framework that when someone invokes the web script with a `GET`, those descriptors and FreeMarker files are applied. By differentiating the HTTP method (such as `GET`, `POST`, `DELETE`, and `PUT`), you can define multiple web scripts that get invoked depending on the method used to make the request.

Use the following to determine which HTTP method is appropriate for your web script:

- GET: Retrieves the representation of a resource or a list of resources. The URI should return the same resource no matter how many times it is called. Calling this URI should have no effect on the repository. A GET usually doesn't require a transaction.
- POST: Creates a new resource. The server decides on that resource's URI.
- PUT: Creates a new resource. But the client decides on the URI or updates an existing resource. Like a GET, the URI should update the same resource no matter how many times it is called.
- DELETE: Deletes a resource, or stops a resource from being accessible.

Specifying arguments

Arguments are declared as part of the url element in the web script's descriptor XML. There are two styles of arguments supported. The Hello World example used explicit arguments-argument names and placeholders appear in the URL as part of the query string:

```
<url>/someco/helloworld?name={nameArgument}</url>
```

The other style is to use implicit arguments in which the arguments are incorporated into components of the path:

```
<url>/someco/helloworld/{nameArgument}</url>
```

The Hello World example only had one argument, but you could add as many as you need. Using the explicit style, each argument is separated with an ampersand. Make sure you escape ampersands in a URL. Web script descriptors must always be valid XML:

```
<url>/helloworld?name={nameArgument}&amp;secondArg={anotherArg}</url>
```

How you choose to structure your URLs is a matter of preference, consistency, and, potentially, search engine friendliness (some search engines may have trouble indexing URLs that include a query string).

Specifying the response format

The response formats are mapped to FreeMarker templates through naming conventions. In the Hello World example, the FreeMarker template was named helloworld.get.html.ftl. So, Alfresco interprets that to mean "This is the template to use when someone asks for an HTML response for this web script."

One of the benefits of the MVC pattern is that you can have one set of controller logic with as many different views as you need because the controller logic and view logic are cleanly separated. For example, you could create a second FreeMarker template for the Hello World example named `helloworld.get.xml.ftl` that looks like this:

```
<helloworld>
    <message>Hello, ${args.name}!</message>
    <foo>${foo}</foo>
</helloworld>
```

The response format can be specified via URL as an extension on the script ID, like this:

```
http://localhost:8080/alfresco/service/someco/helloworld.xml?name=Ben
```

It could also be specified with an explicit `format` argument:

```
http://localhost:8080/alfresco/service/someco/helloworld?name=Ben&forma
t=xml
```

If a format is not specified, the default format will be returned. The default response format can be specified as part of the descriptor:

```
<format default="xml">any</format>
```

The content of the `format` element specifies the style in which the script expects the format to be provided. In the example, `any` specifies that either option is accepted. So it can be sent as extension (as used in the first example when you typed `helloworld.xml`) or as an argument (as used in the second example when you typed `?format=xml`).

If no default format is specified in the descriptor, Alfresco assumes a default of HTML.

Deploying web scripts

The descriptor, the JavaScript file, and the FreeMarker templates together make up the web script. These files can reside either in the repository or on the classpath. If a web script uses a Java Bean, the class must reside somewhere on the classpath. You can find in the following page all locations where a web script can be stored:

```
http://docs.alfresco.com/5.1/concepts/ws-component-place.html
```

Regardless of where they are deployed, updates can be picked up without an application server restart. After deploying a new or updated script, go to `http://localhost:8080/alfresco/service/index` and click on the **Refresh WebScripts** button.

Building solutions with the Web Script Framework

Now that you understand the basics, you may already be thinking of different ways you could leverage web scripts to build your own solutions. For example, you can use web scripts to achieve the following:

- Enable a frontend web application written in any language that understands HTTP to retrieve repository data in XML, JSON, or any other format
- Capture and persist user-contributed content/data
- Interact with a business process (for example, an Activiti workflow) through non-web client interfaces such as e-mail
- Create ATOM or RSS feeds for repository content or business process data

Alfresco Share is integrated to the Alfresco Repository via web scripts. If you look at the list of modules installed in your Alfresco repository using the Administration console (`http://localhost:8080/alfresco/s/enterprise/admin/admin-systemsummary`), you can easily see the `alfresco-share-services` module, which contains the web scripts required by Alfresco Share to run properly (Be aware that this module has been integrated recently. Before the Alfresco Repository was including all web scripts even if you didn't want to use Share following a more monolithic approach):

```
Module Packages

Currently Installed:
    alfresco-aos-module (version 1.1.3)
    org.alfresco.integrations.google.docs (version 3.0.3)
    alfresco-share-services (version 5.1.1)

Previously Installed:
```

You may recall from prior chapters that SomeCo would like to publish whitepapers on its website. In addition to making the whitepapers available on the Web, SomeCo wants to provide a way for website users to rate the whitepapers and display the aggregated ratings with each whitepaper. Earlier, you created a behavior that calculates the ratings summary. Now you are going to make whitepapers and ratings available via REST.

Planning the SomeCo whitepapers and ratings API

Before diving into the examples, let's plan the new API at a high level. The following table outlines the URLs, the HTTP methods, and the response formats for each:

URL	Method	Description	Response formats
/someco/whitepapers	GET	Returns a list of whitepapers	HTML, JSON
/someco/rating?id={id}	GET	Gets the average rating for a given whitepaper by passing in the whitepaper's nodeId	HTML, JSON
/someco/rating?id={id}&rating={rating}&user={user}	POST	Creates a new rating for the specified whitepaper by passing in a rating value and the user who posted the rating	HTML, JSON
/someco/rating?id={id}	DELETE	Deletes all ratings for a specified whitepaper	HTML

The API to create new ratings provides the option of passing the username as argument. From a security point of view, this is not ideal because you could provide any values. The ideal solution would be to retrieve the username from the authentication used when the web script is called. To simplify this chapter, we'll make unauthenticated queries to Alfresco. And we'll discover more about authentication and SSO in the final chapter.

When this API is in place, frontend developers can incorporate whitepapers and user-contributed ratings into the SomeCo website. The following screenshots show pages that use the API you're going to build to query for whitepaper and ratings data. Don't be too critical of my UI's capabilities:

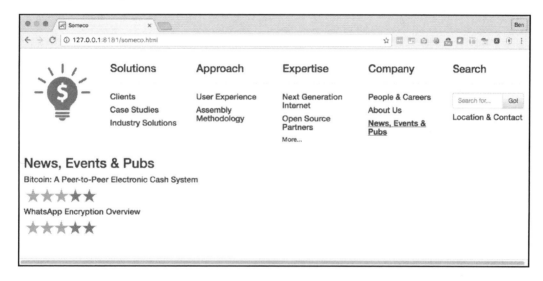

You can't tell from the screenshots, but the ratings widget (the row of five stars beneath each whitepaper title) is read-only in this case. When the whitepaper title link is clicked, the whitepaper detail is displayed as follows:

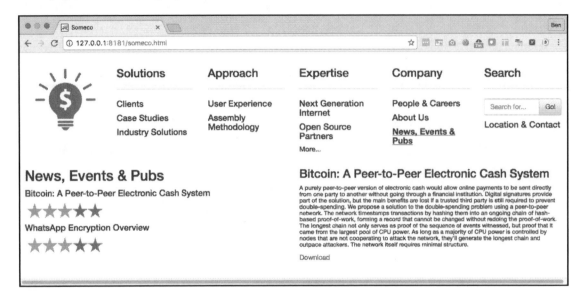

The **Download** link uses the standard Download URL to give the user direct access to the content.

By the end of the chapter, you will be able to deploy this web page and have it interact with your web scripts.

Retrieving data with web scripts

The first service that needs to be implemented retrieves the list of whitepapers enabled for publication. The web script needs to return the list of whitepapers in two formats: HTML and JSON. HTML will allow you to easily test the service and JSON will make it easy for code on the frontend to process the list. This will require four files: one descriptor, one JavaScript controller, and two FreeMarker templates-one for each format.

 New to JSON? It stands for JavaScript Object Notation. It is a way to describe JavaScript objects in plain text. The beauty of it is that it is extremely easy to create and consume, and it isn't as verbose as XML. For more information on JSON, see `http://www.json.org`.

Step-by-step – writing a web script to list whitepapers

We are going to create all our web scripts in the classpath. By choosing this option, we just package all our extensions in the same module that represent our solution. By just deploying our AMP file, everything will be installed and you won't have to deploy files manually in the repository. To create a web script that retrieves the list of whitepapers, do the following:

1. First, in your Eclipse project, create the descriptor file in **repo** | **src** | **main** | **amp** | **config** | **alfresco** | **extension** | **templates** | **webscripts** | **com** | **someco** | **whitepapers**. Name it `whitepapers.get.desc.xml` and give it the following content:

```
<webscript>
    <shortname>Get all whitepapers</shortname>
    <description>Returns a list of active whitepapers</description>
    <url>/someco/whitepapers</url>
    <!-- The 2 following lines are optional -->
    <url>/someco/whitepapers.json</url>
    <url>/someco/whitepapers.html</url>
    <format default="json">extension</format>
    <authentication runas="admin">guest</authentication>
    <transaction>none</transaction>
</webscript>
```

Be aware that we don't follow the best practices in the definition of the authentication mechanism. In this case, we define that you can call this web script being authenticated as a guest, but all actions will be executed under the username `admin`. The first issue is that you have to be sure that this username exists in Alfresco and includes all expected permissions.

2. Next, you need a controller to execute the query to find the whitepapers. Create a file in the same directory that you created the descriptor called `whitepapers.get.js`. The first thing you're going to do is import the `rating.js` JavaScript file. You're going to add a new function to that file in a moment:

```
<import resource="classpath:alfresco/extension/scripts/rating.js">
```

3. Now add code to execute a search for whitepapers. You can use a Lucene search string that grabs every whitepaper object and has the `isActive` flag set to `true`:

```
var whitepapers = search.luceneSearch("+TYPE:"sc:whitepaper"
+@sc\\:isActive:true");
```

4. If no whitepapers are found, an error message needs to be returned. Otherwise, build an array of whitepapers and store that array in the model:

```
if (whitepapers == null || whitepapers.length == 0) {
    logger.log("No whitepapers found");
    status.code = 404;
    status.message = "No whitepapers found";
    status.redirect = true;
} else {
var whitepaperInfo = new Array();
    for (i = 0; i<whitepapers.length; i++) {
        var whitepaper = new whitepaperEntry(whitepapers[i],
        getRating(whitepapers[i]));
        whitepaperInfo[i] = whitepaper;
    }
    model.whitepapers = whitepaperInfo;
}

function whitepaperEntry(whitepaper, rating) {
    this.whitepaper = whitepaper;
    this.rating = rating;
}
```

5. Save the JavaScript file.

6. The controller you just wrote imports a script called `rating.js`. Create this file, `repo | src | main | amp | config | alfresco | extension | scripts`, including the function called `getRating`, as shown here. The function is responsible for retrieving the rating summary statistics for a given node:

```
function getRating(curNode, curUser) {
    var rating = {};
    rating.average = curNode.properties["sc:averageRating"];
    rating.count = curNode.properties["sc:ratingCount"];
    rating.user = getUserRating(curNode, curUser);
    return rating;
}
```

7. The `getRating` function calls `getUserRating` to see if a specified user has already rated this whitepaper, and if so, retrieves the rating. Add the `getUserRating` function to the same JavaScript file as follows:

```
function getUserRating(curNode, curUser) {
    if (curUser == undefined || curUser== "") {
        logger.log("User name was not passed in");
        return 0;
    }

    var results = curNode.childrenByXPath("*//.[@sc:rater='"
        + curUser + "']");
    if (results == undefined || results.length== 0) {
        logger.log("No ratings found for this node for user: "
        + curUser);
        return 0;
    } else {
        var rating = results[results.length-1]
            .properties["{http://www.someco.com/model
            /content/1.0}rating"];
        if (rating == undefined) {
            return 0;
        } else {
            return rating;
        }
    }
}
```

8. Save the JavaScript file.
9. As you saw in the `Hello World` example, one FreeMarker template is needed for each response format. Let's create the HTML response template first. Create a new file in `repo` | `src` | `main` | `amp` | `config` | `alfresco` | `extension` | `templates` | `webscripts` | `com` | `someco` | `whitepapers` called `whitepapers.get.html.ftl`. The HTML response is for debugging purposes, so nothing fancy is needed. An HTML table showing the list of whitepapers will do fine. First, set up a date format variable and then start the table:

```
<#assign datetimeformat="EEE, dd MMM yyyyHH:mm:sszzz">
<html>
    <body>
        <h3>Whitepapers</h3>
        <table>
```

10. Now iterate over the array of `whitepaperEntry` objects to build the table:

```
<#list whitepapers as child>
    <tr>
        <td><b>Name</b></td>
        <td>${child.whitepaper.properties.name}</td>
    </tr>
    <tr>
        <td><b>Title</b></td>
        <td>
            <#if child.whitepaper.properties["cm:title"]?exists>
                ${child.whitepaper.properties["cm:title"]}
            </#if>
        </td>
    </tr>
    <tr>
        <td><b>Link</b></td>
        <td>
            <a href="${url.context}
              ${child.whitepaper.url}?guest=true">
                ${url.context}${child.whitepaper.url}
            </a>
        </td>
    </tr>
    <tr>
        <td><b>Type</b></td>
        <td>${child.whitepaper. mimetype}</td>
    </tr>
    <tr>
        <td><b>Size</b></td><td>${child.whitepaper.size} </td>
    </tr>
    <tr>
        <td><b>Id</b></td>
        <td>${child.whitepaper.id}</td>
    </tr>
    <tr>
        <td><b>Description</b></td>
        <td>
          <p><#if child.whitepaper
                .properties["cm:description"]?exists
              &&child.whitepaper
                .properties["cm:description"] != "">
          ${child. whitepaper.properties["cm:description"]}
          </#if></p>
        </td>
    </tr>
    <tr>
        <td><b>Pub Date</b></td>
```

```
        <td>
            ${child.whitepaper.properties["cm:modified"]
            ?string(datetimeformat)}
        </td>
    </tr>
    <tr>
        <td>
            <b><a href="${url.serviceContext}/someco/ rating.html
                ?id=${child.whitepaper.id}
                &guest=true"> Rating</a></b>
        </td>
        <td>
            <table>
                <tr>
                    <td><b>Average</b></td>
                    <td>${child. rating.average!0}</td>
                </tr>
                <tr>
                    <td><b>Count</b></td>
                    <td>${child. rating.count!0}</td>
                </tr>
                <#if (child.rating.user> 0)>
                    <tr>
                        <td><b>User </b></td>
                        <td>${child.rating.user}</td>
                    </tr>
                </#if>
            </table>
        </td>
    </tr>
    <#if !(child.whitepaper == whitepapers?last.whitepaper)>
    <tr><td colspan="2" bgcolor="999999"> </td></tr>
    </#if>
</#list>
</table>
</body>
</html>
```

11. Save the HTML response template.

12. Now create the JSON response template. Create a file called `whitepapers.get.json.ftl` in the directory in which you created the HTML template. The overall logic is exactly the same, but the output format is in JSON instead of HTML:

```
<#assign datetimeformat="EEE, dd MMM yyyyHH:mm:sszzz">

{"whitepapers" : [
 <#list whitepapers as child>
   {
        "name" : "${child.whitepaper.properties.name}",
        "title" : "<#if child.whitepaper.properties
              ["cm:title"]?exists>${child.whitepaper.properties
              ["cm:title"]?js_string}</#if>",
        "link" : "${url.context}${child.whitepaper.url}",
        "type" : "${child.whitepaper.mimetype}",
        "size" : "${child.whitepaper.size}",
        "id" : "${child.whitepaper.id}",
        "description" : "<#if child.whitepaper.properties
          ["cm:description"]?exists &&child.whitepaper.properties
          ["cm:description"] != "">${child.whitepaper.properties
          ["cm:description"]?j_string}</#if>",
          "pubDate" : "${child.whitepaper.properties
        ["cm:modified"]?string(datetimeformat)}",
          "rating" : {
             "average" : "${child.rating.average!0}",
             "count" : "${child.rating.count!0}",
             "user" : "${child.rating.user!""}"
          }
   }
     <#if !(child.whitepaper == whitepapers?last.whitepaper)>,
     </#if>
   </#list>
  ]
 }
```

13. Save the JSON response template.
14. Package, deploy, and restart Alfresco.
15. Open the following link to see all your available web scripts:
    `http://localhost:8080/alfresco/service/index/package/com/someco/whitepapers`.

Now, let's test our first web script Open the following URL and let's see the result
(`http://localhost:8080/alfresco/service/someco/whitepapers`). In my case, I
get a JSON file letting me know that I don't have any whitepapers:

```
{
    "status" :
    {
      "code" : 404,
      "name" : "Not Found",
      "description" : "Requested resource is not available."
    },

    "message" : "No whitepapers found",
    "exception" : "",

    "callstack" :
    [

    ],

    "server" : "Enterprise v5.1.1 (r128754-b138) schema 9,031",
    "time" : "Oct 19, 2016 10:02:00 AM"
}
```

It's correct, I destroyed my virtual machine before starting this chapter. So, my Alfresco
repository is completely clean. Let's open **Alfresco Share**, create a new **Marketing** site, open
the **Document Library**, create a new folder called whitepapers, and create a rule that will
do the following:

- Specialize any incoming document to Someco whitepaper
- Add the SomecoWebable aspect

- Add the SomecoRateable aspect
- Execute the `addTestRating.js` script:

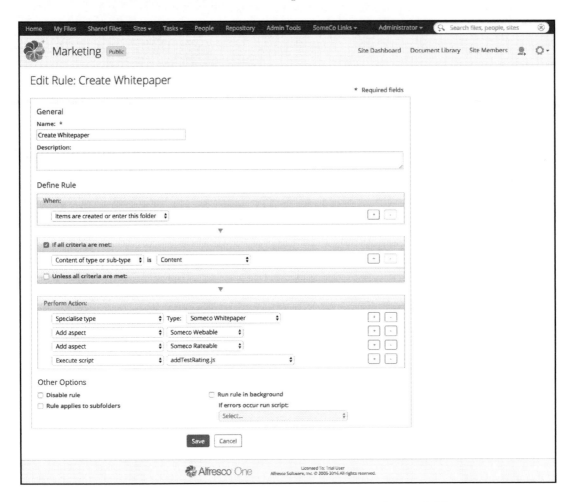

It means that you'll need the `addTestRating.js` script already available in your repository. If it's not the case, you can find it in **repo|src|scripts** and upload it to the **Repository | DataDictionary | Scripts** folder. Let's upload some documents in the whitepaper folder, and retry. Unfortunately, we have the same error, `No whitepapers found`. If you remember, we are looking for *Active* whitepapers. Just click on the **SC Web Enable** action to set the `isActive` flag to `true`. (Don't forget that your user needs to be member of the `SomecoPublisher` group to have access to this action).

Let's retry and I finally can see my whitepapers. But we are not done yet. Because the descriptor specifies that this script requires Guest access or higher, you'll need to either log in to Alfresco Share before running the script, authenticate with a valid user and password when the basic authentication dialog is presented, or append `?guest=true` to the URL. For now, use the guest approach, which means the URL should look like this:
`http://localhost:8080/alfresco/service/someco/whitepapers.html?guest=true`

If you forget the `html`, you'll get a JSON response because you set that as the default format in the descriptor. If you use this URL, you'll notice that it finds the same list of whitepapers, even if you are not authenticated. The reason is because we use the `runAs` parameter. Basically, the code is executed as a particular Alfresco content repository user, regardless of who initiated the web script.

If all goes well, you should see something similar to the following screenshot:

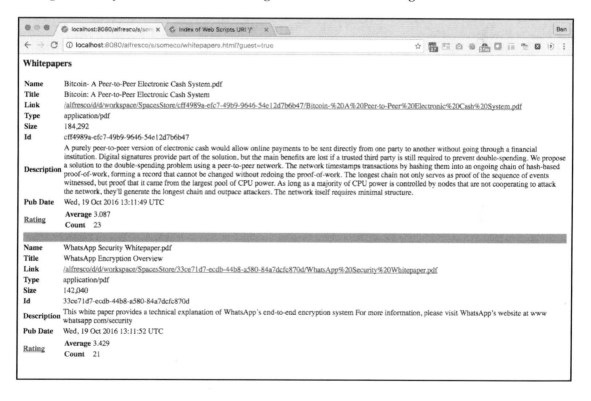

Debugging

Did your web script work? If not, it's time to debug. If you remember, you already enabled changed the logger level to DEBUG for the following logger:

`log4j.logger.org.alfresco.repo.jscript`

This means that you can see all the messages in the `catalina.out` file:

```
DEBUG [jscript.RhinoScriptProcessor.calls] [http-apr-8080-exec-9]
whitepapers.get.js Start
DEBUG [repo.jscript.Search] [http-apr-8080-exec-9]
query=+TYPE:"sc:whitepaper" +@sc\:isActive:true limit=none
DEBUG [repo.jscript.Search] [http-apr-8080-exec-9] query time: 23ms
DEBUG [repo.jscript.ScriptLogger] [http-apr-8080-exec-9] User name was not
passed in
DEBUG [repo.jscript.ScriptLogger] [http-apr-8080-exec-9] User name was not
passed in
DEBUG [jscript.RhinoScriptProcessor.calls] [http-apr-8080-exec-9]
whitepapers.get.js End 37 ms
```

Another tool you'll want to leverage is the web script list. You can use it to see whether Alfresco knows about your script and the version of the scripts the runtime knows about. The starting URL for the web script list is `http://localhost:8080/alfresco/service/index/`. From there, you can see a list of web scripts by package and by URL. You can also browse the configuration for a specific web script. For example, you can go to `http://localhost:8080/alfresco/service/script/com/someco/whitepapers/whitepapers.get` and Alfresco will dump the descriptor and all of the response templates.

The Node Browser can be helpful to debug problems as well. In this case, for example, you're running a Lucene query in the JavaScript controller to find whitepapers. If the controller doesn't find any whitepapers, even though you've created test data, try executing the query in the Node browser. If it doesn't return results, there could be something wrong with either your test data or the query syntax.

Fast facts

- The descriptor you created has multiple URL elements. There is one URL for each format plus a URL without a format. Because the URLs differ only in format, it isn't strictly required that they be listed in the descriptor. But it is a good practice to list all formats that your module supports. A better reason for using multiple URL elements would be if you wanted to use completely different URL formats for the same web script.

- The authentication element declares the lowest level of authentication required for this script. If your script touches the repository, you will want this to be Guest or higher. Other options are `none`, `user`, and `admin`. Authentication will be discussed shortly.

- The transaction element specifies the level of transaction required by the script. Listing whitepapers doesn't need a transaction so you specified**none**. Other possible values are `required` and `requires new` (http://docs.alfresco.com/5.1/references/api-wsdl-transaction.html).

- The ability to import a script from another script was added with release 2.1. The import tag also supports including scripts that reside in the repository. Note that the import tag is not native to the Rhino JavaScript implementation. Beware, though. Alfresco compiles all imported JavaScript files into a single file and gives that to Rhino. So, when there is an error, the line number Rhino reports is from the compiled set of JavaScript files, which could be hard to map back to the line number in the original JavaScript source.

- The controller builds a new array for the whitepaper search results. You could have just set `model.whitepapers`to the whitepapers variable that contains the query results, but in this case, you built a new array and set that to the model. You did that because you needed to incorporate a specific user's rating, if one exists, that isn't part of the whitepaper nodes in the query result set.

- The `getUserRating` function in `rating.js` looks for ratings specific to a particular user by querying the children using an XPath expression (shown as follows). XPath can be used to navigate through elements in a XML document. For more information on XPath, see https://www.w3.org/TR/xpath/. The expression asks for any child of the current node with the `sc:rater` property set to the name of the user passed in to the function:

```
var results = curNode.childrenByXPath("*//.[@sc:rater='"
  + curUser + "']");
```

- The FreeMarker template that renders the JSON response includes output that needs to be escaped. Both the title and the description could potentially contain characters that would make the JSON invalid (such as a quote). To address that, the code uses the FreeMarker built-in `js_string` to escape the string, as follows:

```
"title" : "${child.whitepaper.properties["cm:title"]?js_string}"
```

- The FreeMarker templates that renders both the JSON and HTML may generate errors if you don't have the rating aspect applied to them. It's why we added some default values if the property doesn't exist as follows:

```
${child.rating.average!0}
```

Organizing web scripts

The Web Script Framework allows you to organize script assets into a hierarchical folder or package structure. Just as it is with Java, it is a good idea to do this for all web scripts. That's because the number of web scripts your installation leverages is going to grow over time as you, Alfresco, and third parties add more functionality. Following a reverse domain name pattern is a good convention and is consistent with how Alfresco organizes its scripts. It's why we organized our web script in the folder com | someco | whitepapers.

Alfresco reserves certain package names for its own use. These may change over time, so consult the documentation website for the specific list. But if you steer clear of using `org/alfresco`, you'll probably be fine.

Overriding web scripts

Alfresco searches for web scripts in the following order:

1. In the repository under **Company Home** | **Data Dictionary** | **Web Scripts Extensions**.
2. In the repository under **Company Home** | **DataDictionary** | **Web Scripts**.
3. In the classpath under **alfresco** | **extension** | **templates** | **webscripts**.
4. In the classpath under **alfresco** | **templates** | **webscripts**.

If you want to override an existing web script, just make sure your web script is found first. In addition to overriding an entire web script, you can override components of a web script. For example, suppose a web script in the WebScripts folder has something in its JavaScript controller you want to override. You can add the controller to the WebScriptsExtensions folder in the same package folder structure to override the lower-level controller.

Choosing a URL

URLs can follow any pattern you want. Because the URL pattern must be unique to a given web application, it makes sense to use the package name partially or completely. For SomeCo, the convention will be to use someco in all URLs, assuming the default Alfresco web application name hasn't been changed. This means that when using HTTP, SomeCo's web script URLs will look like this:

```
/alfresco/service/someco/[web script name].[format]?[arguments]
```

They could also look like this (s is just a shortcut for service):

```
/alfresco/s/someco/[web script name].[format]?[arguments]
```

Within a web script, you can use ${url.serviceContext} to refer to the service context component of the URL to avoid hardcoding within references to other web scripts. Be aware that you have other prefixes as wcs and wcservice that are used mainly by if you use SSO.

Just like packages, Alfresco already has several URLs mapped to web scripts. Unfortunately, they don't follow a strict pattern. If your URLs don't incorporate a unique string, you may want to do a recursive search through the descriptor XML files in the source or browse the web script directory by URL (http://localhost:8080/alfresco/service/index/uri/) to make sure your URLs are easily distinguishable from Alfresco's.

Choosing between the repository and the classpath

You ran the Hello World web script out of the repository. The whitepaper listing ran out of the classpath. There are trade-offs to consider with each approach.

The advantage of using the classpath is that the web scripts that make up your solution can be deployed alongside your other extensions. This can be done using the same deployment tools without requiring the extra step of uploading them to the repository.

The trade-off is that it is a little more work to edit the web scripts when they need to be changed. If they are stored in the repository, they can be easily edited just like any other piece of content. If they are stored in your source code control system and deployed with the rest of your customizations, it's a little more work to make a change. Whether or not you consider this an advantage or a disadvantage depends on the team supporting the solution and the development processes you like to use.

If scripts are defined in the repository as well as the classpath, the files in the repository take precedence over the files on the classpath, as mentioned in *Overriding Web Scripts* section.

Step-by-step – retrieving the rating for a whitepaper

Getting a specific rating is roughly the same as getting a whitepaper. A controller searches for ratings and stores them in the model, then two response templates (one for HTML and one for JSON) are used to return the data in the appropriate format.

To create a web script that retrieves a rating for a specific whitepaper, do the following:

1. The descriptor and response templates are very similar to the whitepaper example. Create a new descriptor called `rating.get.desc.xml` in repo | src | main | amp | config | alfresco | extension | templates | webscripts | com | someco | ratings as follows:

```
<webscript>
   <shortname>Get Content Rating</shortname>
   <description>Returns rating data for the specified
      node</description>
   <url>/someco/rating?id={id}&amp;user={user?}</url>
   <url>/someco/rating.json?id={id}&amp;user={user?}</url>
   <url>/someco/rating.html?id={id}&amp;user={user?}</url>
   <format default="json">extension</format>
   <authentication runas="admin">guest</authentication>
   <transaction>none</transaction>
</webscript>
```

2. Retrieving the rating for a whitepaper is a bit easier because of the existing getRating function in rating.js. All the controller has to do is grab the node ID of the whitepaper in question, locate the node, and then call the getRating function. Create a new controller in repo | src | main | amp | config | alfresco | extension | templates | webscripts | com | someco | ratings called rating.get.js, as shown here:

```
<import resource="classpath:alfresco/extension/scripts/rating.js">

    if (args.id == null || args.id.length == 0) {
        logger.log("ID arg not set");
        status.code = 400;
        status.message = "Node ID has not been provided";
        status.redirect = true;
    } else {

        varcurNode =
          search.findNode("workspace://SpacesStore/"+ args.id);
        if (curNode == null) {
            logger.log("Node not found");
            status.code = 404;
            status.message = "No node found for id:" + args.id;
            status.redirect = true;
        } else {
            model.rating = getRating(curNode, args.user);
        }
    }
```

3. Create a response template called rating.get.json.ftl that retrieves rating data from the model and outputs a JSON rating object:

```
{"rating" :
      {
        "average" : "${rating.average}",
        "count" : "${rating.count}",
        "user" : "${rating.user}"
      }
}
```

4. Create a response template called `rating.get.html.ftl`. In a later example, you're going to incorporate a graphical ratings widget into this page. You'll use the HTML page this response template creates to test the widget. For now, just output the ratings data and provide a link to get back to the whitepaper list:

```html
<html>
    <head>
    </head>
    <body>
        <script type="text/javascript">
            function deleteRatings(id) {
              alert("Not yet implemented");
            }
        </script>

        <p>
          <a href="${url.serviceContext}/someco
           /whitepapers.html?guest=true">
           Back to the list</a> of whitepapers</p>
        <p>Node: ${args.id}</p>
        <p>Average: ${rating.average}</p>
        <p># of Ratings: ${rating.count}</p>
        <#if (rating.user> 0)>
           <p>User rating: ${rating.user}</p>
        </#if>
        <p>
           <a href="#" onclick=deleteRatings
           ("${args.id}")>Delete ratings</a>
           for this node
        </p>
    </body>
</html>
```

5. Package, deploy, and test.

Point your browser at the whitepapers web script. Click the **Rating** link. The **Rating** link invokes the web script you just created. You should see this:

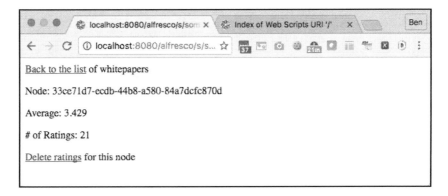

Test out the JSON response by replacing the `html` string in the URL with `json`. The rating service should return something similar to this:

Specifying optional arguments

Did you catch the new twist in the URL declaration for this web script? Here it is again:

```
<url>/someco/rating?id={id}&amp;user={user?}</url>
```

The question mark in the `user` value placeholder declares the argument as optional. Using the optional indicator is, well, optional. Alfresco does not enforce mandatory parameters, and it doesn't care if you provide an argument that isn't declared. You may have noticed that the whitepaper script will show the user's last rating if you pass the `user` argument in, even though you may not have included it in the URL declaration.

At some point, Alfresco may start enforcing that web script calls should match the declared URL. Or it might start generating documentation based on the descriptor. So, you might as well get in the habit of declaring all of your arguments now. Plus, in the absence of automatically generated documentation, the descriptor is what people will use to figure out how to call your web script (no matter how much time you spend crafting documentation elsewhere).

Handling errors

In both the whitepapers example and the ratings example, you probably noticed some error handling code. For example, in the `rating.get.js` file, if the whitepaper node cannot be located, the following code is executed:

```
status.code = 404;
status.message = "No node found for id:" + args.id;
status.redirect = true;
```

The response `code` gets set to `404`, which is the standard HTTP response code for `Not Found`. An error message is set and the `redirect` property is set to `true`, which tells the web script framework to `redirect` the response to the error handling templates.

For example, if you pass a bad node ID to the `rating.html` web script, you'll get a response that looks like this:

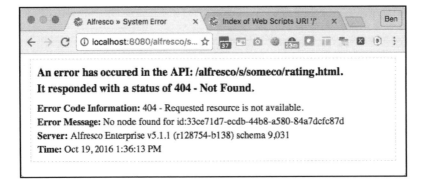

Similarly, if you pass a bad node ID to the `rating.json` web script (the same script with a different response format), the JSON that comes back will be as follows:

```
{
    "status" :
    {
      "code" : 404,
      "name" : "Not Found",
      "description" : "Requested resource is not available."
    },

    "message" : "No node found for id:33ce71d7-ecdb-44b8-a580-84a7dcfc87d",
    "exception" : "",

    "callstack" :
    [

    ],

    "server" : "Enterprise v5.1.1 (r128754-b138) schema 9,031",
    "time" : "Oct 19, 2016 1:36:48 PM"
}
```

Getting an error back in the request response format is nice. The calling code can handle errors more gracefully when it knows the format that will come back, even when exceptions are thrown.

The examples show the standard response template for error codes. Depending on the solution you are building it might make more sense to customize these, whether simply for look-and-feel or because you want to structure the response differently. You can override the standard error templates with your own by creating FreeMarker files that follow a specific naming convention. When an error occurs, the framework attempts to find a template specific to the HTTP method, response format, and error code. If one does not exist, it looks for a more general fit until it ultimately reaches the default `status.ftl`.

The following table shows the naming convention and location for error templates beginning with the most specific case and ending with the most general:

Naming convention	Location	Example	What it does
`<scriptid>.<method>.<format>.<code>.ftl`	Same as descriptor	`whitepapers.get.html.404.ftl`	Displays when a GET request for an HTML response of the whitepapers script returns a 404 error.
`<scriptid>.<method>.<format>.status.ftl`	Same as descriptor	`whitepapers.get.html.status.ftl`	Displays when a GET request for an HTML response of the whitepapers script returns an error.
`<format>.<code>.ftl`	Package hierarchy	`html.404.ftl`	Displays for all HTML responses that return a 404.
`<format>.status.ftl`	Package hierarchy	`html.status.ftl`	Displays for all HTML responses that return any error.
`<code>.ftl`	WEB-INF/classes/alfresco/webscripts	`404.ftl`	Default error template for all 404 errors across all packages, scripts, and response formats.
`status.ftl`	WEB-INF/classes/alfresco/webscripts	`status.ftl`	Default, out-of-the-box error template for all errors.

Error templates have access to the web script model and the FreeMarker API, like any other response template. Error templates in the package hierarchy have access to the `status` root variable.

Writing Java-backed web scripts

You now have a web script that returns all whitepapers, and a web script that returns the rating summary for a specific whitepaper. The next step is to implement a web script that supports the POST method so that people can submit new ratings.

Like all web scripts, the web script that creates ratings will run as the user executing the script. In this case, you are appending guest=true to the URL, but we will use the runAs property in the web script descriptor to run the code using the username admin. Another way to handle this would be to set the web script's minimum authentication level to User, give named users (or one or more groups) write access to the whitepapers folder, and make website users authenticated. But SomeCo doesn't want to set up user accounts for every user who might rate content. Any user ought to be able to rate content whether or not he or she can authenticate with Alfresco as a named user. So, we'll use the runAs option. In this example, you'll use admin as that user. In production, using a user account dedicated to the purpose of creating ratings is a better idea.

 JavaScript or Java controllers? All of the HTTP methods are supported using either API. The JavaScript API is getting more powerful with each release. But in this case, the JavaScript API just doesn't support what's required. Obviously, you can choose what's right for your organization and the task at hand. Some companies choose to standardize on Java controllers across the board. Others prefer the speed of development afforded by JavaScript, using Java only when JavaScript doesn't suffice.

Step-by-step – writing a Java-backed web script to handle ratings posts

Let's write a new web script for ratings that handles the POST method to create new rating objects for a specific whitepaper. Like the web scripts you've seen so far, this is going to involve a FreeMarker template and a descriptor, but instead of using JavaScript for a controller you are going to write a Java class. To let the Web Script Framework know about the Java class, you'll use a new Spring bean configuration file to declare which web script the controller class belongs to.

Follow these steps:

1. First, create the descriptor in `repo | src | main | amp | config | alfresco | extension | templates | webscripts | com | someco | ratings`. This script handles the POST method, so name the descriptor `rating.post.desc.xml` and populate it as follows:

```
<webscript>
    <shortname>Post Content Rating</shortname>
    <description>Sets rating data for the specified
      node</description>
    <url>/someco/rating</url>
    <url>/someco/rating.json</url>
    <url>/someco/rating.html</url>
    <format default="json">extension</format>
    <authenticationrunas="admin">guest</authentication>
    <transaction>requiresnew</transaction>
</webscript>
```

2. The response templates simply echo back the node, rating, and user argument values that were used to create the new rating. Create the HTML response template called `rating.post.html.ftl`:

```
<html>
  <body>
        <p>Successfully added rating:</p>
        <p>Node:${node}</p>
        <p>Rating:${rating}</p>
        <p>User:${user}</p>
        <p><a href="${url.service}?id=${node}">Show rating</a></p>
  </body>
</html>
```

3. Then, create the JSON response template called `rating.post.json.ftl`:

```
{"rating" :
        {
         "node" : "${node}",
         "rating" : "${rating}",
         "user" : "${user}"
        }
}
```

4. Let's start by creating a new `RatingService`. Create the following interface `com.someco.repo.service.RatingService`:

```
package com.someco.repo.service;
public interface RatingService {

}
```

Be aware that Alfresco out-of-the-box proposes as well a rating service. Be careful when you'll create the implementation by referencing the right class in the right package. If you wanted to be extremely careful, you could have renamed your service `SomecoRatingService` instead of `RatingService`.

5. Then, add the `create` method:

```
NodeRef create(NodeRef document, int rating, String user);
```

6. Next, add the following import:

```
import org.alfresco.service.cmr.repository.NodeRef;
```

7. Let's create the implementation in the `com.someco.repo.service.impl.RatingServiceImpl` class that implements the interface that we just created:

```
package com.someco.repo.service.impl;
import org.alfresco.service.cmr.repository.NodeRef;
import com.someco.repo.service.RatingService;
public class RatingServiceImpl implements RatingService {

    @Override
    public NodeRef create(NodeRef document, int rating, String user)
{

      return null;
    }

}
```

8. The Node Service will be injected as a dependency by Spring:

```
private NodeServicenodeService;
```

9. The `create` method should first ask the `nodeService` if the whitepaper already has the rateable aspect. If it does, no action is necessary, otherwise, add the aspect:

```
// add the aspect to this document if it needs it
    if (!nodeService.hasAspect(document,
      SomeCoModel.ASPECT_RATEABLE)) {
        nodeService.addAspect(document,
          SomeCoModel.ASPECT_RATEABLE, null);
    }
```

10. Below the `if` statement, create a new properties map to store the rating and rater properties:

```
Map<QName, Serializable> props
    = new HashMap<QName, Serializable>();
props.put(SomeCoModel.PROP_RATING, rating);
props.put(SomeCoModel.PROP_RATER, user);
```

11. Use the node service to create a new ratings node as a child to the whitepaper, then close out the method:

```
ChildAssociationRefratingAssoc =
    nodeService.createNode(document, SomeCoModel.ASSOC_RATINGS,
    QName.createQName(SomeCoModel.SOMECO_MODEL_URI,
    SomeCoModel.PROP_RATING.getLocalName()
    + new Date().getTime()), SomeCoModel.TYPE_RATING, props);
```

12. Then, change the `return` statement:

```
    return ratingAssoc.getChildRef();
```

13. Complete the class by adding a setter for the `nodeService` and save the class:

```
public void setNodeService(NodeServicenodeService) {
    this.nodeService = nodeService;
    }
```

14. In the `com.someco.repo.common.SomeCoModel`class, just add the following QName for the `Rater` property, if it's missing:

```
public final static QName PROP_RATER
    = QName.createQName(SOMECO_MODEL_URI, "rater");
```

15. Now, we need to define our service in a Spring context file. Open the `repo | src | main | amp | config | alfresco | module | repo | context | service-context.xml` file and add the following bean:

```
<bean id="someco.ratingService"
    class="com.someco.repo.service.impl.RatingServiceImpl" >
  <property name="nodeService" ref="NodeService" />
</bean>
```

16. Next, implement the web script's controller logic. All you have to do is write a Java class that grabs the ID, rating, and rater arguments and then creates the new rating node using the service that we just implemented. To do that, create a new class in `repo | src | main | java` called `com.someco.repo.scripts.PostRating`. The class name isn't significant, but following a descriptive naming convention is helpful, particularly if there will be a large number of Java-backed web scripts. The class must extend `org.springframework.extensions.webscripts.DeclarativeWebScript`. More details on this page: http://docs.alfresco.com/5.1/concepts/ws-and-Java.html.

```
public class PostRating extends DeclarativeWebScript{
```

17. The rating service and the node service will be injected as a dependency by Spring:

```
private NodeServicenodeService;
private RatingServiceratingService;
```

18. The controller logic goes in the `executeImpl()` method. The first thing you need to do after declaring the method is initialize the `ratingValue` variable and grab the ID, rating, and user arguments:

```
@Override
protected Map<String,
 Object>executeImpl(WebScriptRequest req,  Status status) {

    intratingValue = -1;
    String id =  req.getParameter("id");
    String rating = req.getParameter("rating");
    String user = req.getParameter("user");
```

19. Next, attempt to parse the rating value. If an exception is thrown, move forward with the initialized value, which will get caught during the range check:

```
try {
    ratingValue = Integer.parseInt(rating);
} catch (NumberFormatExceptionnfe) {
}
```

20. The parameters are all required. Web scripts do not yet enforce mandatory arguments, so the controller does the checking and sets an error code if there is a problem. If all the arguments have been provided and the rating is in the range, we are just calling the service that we created before:

```
if (id == null || rating == null || rating.equals("0")
   || user == null) {
    logger.debug("ID, rating, or user not set");
    status.setCode(400);
    status.setMessage("Required data has not been provided");
    status.setRedirect(true);
} else if ((ratingValue< 1) || (ratingValue> 5)) {
    logger.debug("Rating out of range");
    status.setCode(400);
    status.setMessage("Rating value must be
       between 1 and 5 inclusive");
    status.setRedirect(true);
} else {
    NodeRefcurNode = new NodeRef("workspace://SpacesStore/"
    + id);
    if (!nodeService.exists(curNode)) {
        logger.debug("Node not found");
        status.setCode(404);
        status.setMessage("No node found for id:" + id);
        status.setRedirect(true);
    } else {
        ratingService.create(curNode, Integer.parseInt(rating),
           user);
    }

}
```

21. The rating data that was passed in needs to set on the model so that it can be echoed back by the response templates:

```
Map<String, Object> model = new HashMap<String, Object>();
  model.put("node", id);
  model.put("rating", rating);
  model.put("user", user);

  return model;
}
```

22. Then, add the logger definition at the top of the class:

```
private Logger logger = Logger.getLogger(PostRating.class);
Be sure to use the following import for the logger:
import org.apache.log4j.Logger;
```

23. Complete the class by adding a setter for the two services that we defined previously, add all the required imports, and save the class:

```
public void setNodeService(NodeServicenodeService) {
   this.nodeService = nodeService;
}
public void setRatingService(RatingServiceratingService) {
   this.ratingService = ratingService;
}
```

24. Save the class.

25. Now you need to let the web script framework know that this new class is the controller for the rating web script. Open the Spring bean configuration file in repo | src | main | amp | config | alfresco | module | repo | context | webscript-context.xml and add the following bean:

```
<bean id="webscript.com.someco.ratings.rating.post"
    class="com.someco.repo.scripts.PostRating" parent="webscript">
        <property name="nodeService" ref="NodeService" />
        <property name="ratingService" ref="someco.ratingService" />
</bean>
```

26. Package, deploy, and test.

Once you get the UI widget wired in, it will be easier to test. For now, verify that your new web script shows up. To navigate to the index for the new web script directly, go to this URL:

`http://localhost:8080/alfresco/s/index/package/com/someco/ratings`

You should see this:

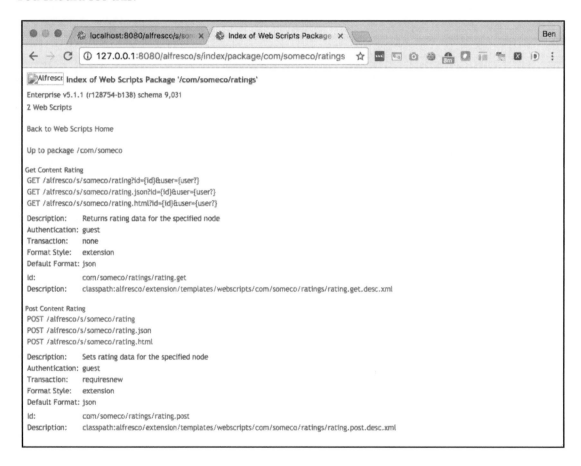

However, if you are too impatient, you can use a tool such as Postman to simulate your call, as shown in the following screenshot:

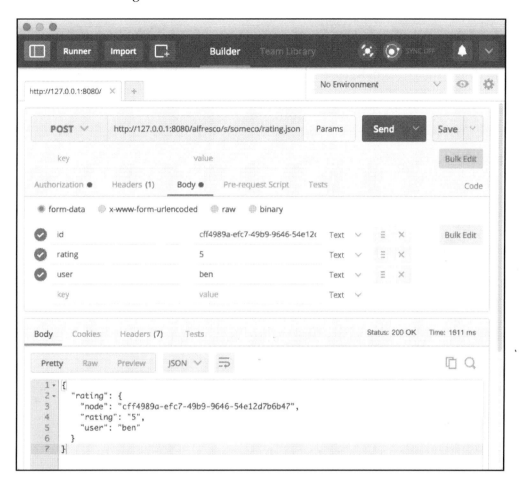

Using the correct ID for Web Script Beans

The web script framework uses the bean's ID to find Java-based web script controllers. The ID follows a naming convention. The convention is as follows:

```
webscript.package.service-id.method
```

In this example, the package is `com.someco.ratings`, the service ID is `rating`, and the HTTP method is `post`. If you don't follow this convention, the bean won't be registered as a controller for the web script. You won't see an error. The code simply fails to get called.

Another potential gotcha is the parent attribute of the bean element. The parent bean is the singular web script here versus the plural web scripts, which is how Data Dictionary web script folders are named. That's an easy one to miss and kind of hard to debug.

Using both Java and JavaScript for controller logic

Using a Java-backed web script doesn't exclude the use of JavaScript for a particular web script. If you have both a Java class and a JavaScript file, the Java class gets executed first followed by the JavaScript. The script has access to everything the Java class put in the model, and can update the model before passing it along to the response template.

This is potentially confusing because people who try to support your web script may see the JavaScript controller and initially assume it is solely responsible for the controller logic. Compounding the problem is the fact that Java beans are wired in via Spring, and the context files are not located near the web scripts. To lessen the potential maintenance headaches, put all of your logic for a given web script either in JavaScript or Java, but not both.

Wiring a web script to UI widgets

SomeCo wants to show a graphical ratings widget on its web page. When the user clicks a star, it should post the corresponding rating to Alfresco. In a subsequent example, you'll see how to leverage the widget on SomeCo's website. For this example, you are going to add the ratings widget to the HTML response for the rating web script. That will let you test both the widget and the rating POST.

 We'll use jQuery in our HTML page. For the ratings widget, it is based on code from the library at `http://rateyo.fundoocode.ninja/`.

You may recall that in the earlier rating example, the HTML response simply showed the rating summary data for a given whitepaper. The goal now is to enhance that response with the rating widget so that the POST can be tested. The following figure shows what the response will look like when you are done. This example whitepaper node has 2 ratings and an average rating of 3:

The purpose of the rating widget is two-fold. First, it graphically displays the average rating for a whitepaper. Second, each star in the widget is hot. When you click one of the rating stars, an asynchronous post is made to someco | rating, which causes a new rating object to get created. The value of the rating posted depends on the star clicked. The person submitting the rating would normally be passed in based on some sort of credential, maybe from a portal session or a cookie. In this example, you are going to add a field to the page so that you can specify any value you want for the rater.

Step-by-step – using a widget to post ratings

Adding the ratings widget to the rating web script HTML is going to involve referencing an external JavaScript library and updating our HTML and JavaScript code by modifying the existing FreeMarker template.

Here are the steps:

1. First, edit the `rating.get.html.ftl` file to add new HTML related to the rater field and the rating widget. Just paste the following code below the `#` of `Ratings` paragraph:

```
<form name="login">
  Rater: <input name="userId"></input>
</form>
<#if (rating.user> 0)>
    <p>User rating: ${rating.user}</p>
</#if>
<p>Rating:</p>
<div id="rating"></div>
```

2. Now work on the JavaScript. The rating widget has an associated JavaScript file that needs to be referenced in the head element. There is also a dependency on the jQuery JavaScript library. Modify the contents as follows:

```
<head>
    <link rel="stylesheet"
      href="//cdnjs.cloudflare.com/ajax/libs
      /rateYo/2.2.0/jquery.rateyo.min.css">
    <script src="//code.jquery.com/jquery-1.12.4.min.js">
    </script>
    <script
      src="//cdnjs.cloudflare.com/ajax/libs
        /rateYo/2.2.0/jquery.rateyo.min.js">
    </script>
</head>
```

3. Now add the following JavaScript code to the existing script section. This code is initializing the star widget, and then bind a function to the *set* event triggered when the user clicks on a star. The method called in the *set* event will send a POST query to Alfresco to save the rating. If the query is a success, it will just refresh the page:

```
$(function () {
  $("#rating").rateYo({
      rating: ${rating.average},
      fullStar: true
  }).on("rateyo.set", function (e, data) {
      var rating = data.rating;
      var user = $("input[name='userId]").val();
  if (user == null || user.length() == 0)
    user = "ben";
  var id = "${args.id}";
  $.post({
      url: "${url.serviceContext}/someco/rating",
      data: {
        rating: rating,
        user: user,
        id: id
      }
  }).success(function() {
    location.reload();
  });
  });
});
```

4. Package, deploy, restart, and test.

You should now be able to invoke the web script to list the whitepapers. From there, you can follow the rating link to see the rating data for a specific whitepaper, which includes the rating widget. The ratings widget should be displaying the number of stars based on the current average rating for the whitepaper. If you click on a star, it should post the appropriate rating to Alfresco.

You will notice that our Freemarker files is using external references to JavaScript libraries and CSS file. It means that you'll need access to the Internet to be sure that it works as expected.

If you use a specific name in the **Rater** field to post a **Rating**, you can see the value of that user's rating by appending the user argument to the URL for either the whitepaper or rating web scripts:

Implementing the delete ratings link

You now know more than enough to implement the **Delete ratings** link on the rating web script HTML response page (`rating.get.html.ftl`) on your own. Here are some hints if you need them:

- In the `rating.get.html.ftl` file, add the AJAX call to the `deleteRatings()` function. The call will be to a new web script you need to write.
- The jQuery library provides the option of sending DELETE queries. The only argument the script needs is the node ID of the whitepaper that needs to have its ratings cleared.
- Set the required authentication level for the new web script to **admin** to keep guests from deleting ratings.
- Decide whether you want to use JavaScript or Java for the controller. If you go the JavaScript route, add a `deleteRatings()` function to the `rating.js` file and call that from your controller. If you go with Java, remember that you'll need to configure the controller as a bean in `someco-scripts-context.xml` and update the interface and the service related to the `RatingService`.
- If you get stuck, look at the source code that accompanies the chapter (be careful, the code provided is covering only the Java option).

When you are done, you'll be able to create, read, update, and delete ratings entirely through web scripts.

Adding the web script calls to SomeCo's whitepaper web page

You now have a RESTful API in place for working with whitepapers and ratings. Now SomeCo's web team can integrate the frontend website with the Alfresco backend by making calls to the web scripts you created. This book isn't about frontend web development. So, rather than having you recreate this code step-by-step, here's a rough outline of the steps the web team went through. At the end of the summary, you can deploy the final product and test it out.

The repo | src | main | amp | web | html | someco.html page is the only HTML page on SomeCo's website at the moment. In this example, we used Bootstrap framework for the user interface, and jQuery for the JavaScript framework.

If you open the HTML file provided to you in the attached code with this chapter, you'll find a DIV element that will populate using JavaScript:

```
<div id="whitepapers"></div>
```

Then, look at the following embedded JavaScript code:

```
var whitepapers = {};
$.get({
url : 'http://localhost:8080/alfresco/s/someco/whitepapers.json?guest=true'
}).success(function(data) {
  for (vari = 0; i<data.whitepapers.length; i++) {
        var wp = data.whitepapers[i];
        var html = "<div class='whitepaper' id='" + wp.id + "'>
            <h4 class='title'>" + wp.title + "</h4></div>
            <div id='rating-" + wp.id + "'></div>";
        $("#whitepapers").append(html);
        $("#rating-" + wp.id).rateYo({
          rating : wp.rating.average,
          readOnly : true
        });
        whitepapers[wp.id] = wp;
        $("#" + wp.id + " .title").click(function() {
            var id = $(this).parent(".whitepaper").attr("id");
            $("#wp-title").html(whitepapers[id].title);
            $("#wp-description").html(whitepapers[id].description);
            $("#wp-download").removeClass("hidden");
```

```
                    $("#wp-download").attr("href", "http://localhost:8080"
                      + whitepapers[id].link);
              });
          }
      });
```

As you can see, we send a GET request to retrieve the list of whitepapers in JSON format. If the query is successful, we browse the results:

- Create a div element for each whitepaper
- Append the generated HTML code to the page
- Call the library to render the star widget. You'll notice that we are using the readOnly attribute, because we can't rate whitepapers from the website
- Finally, bind the click event on the title of the whitepaper that displays the whitepaper details on the right side

At the top of the page, you'll find all dependencies that we require, including jQuery, Bootstrap, and the jQuery rateYo plugin:

```
<script src="https://code.jquery.com/jquery-2.2.4.min.js"
  integrity="sha256-BbhdlvQf/xTY9gja0Dq3HiwQF8LaCRTXxZKRutelT44="
  crossorigin="anonymous"></script>

<link rel="stylesheet"
href="https://maxcdn.bootstrapcdn.com/bootstrap/3.3.7/css/bootstrap.min.css
"
  integrity="sha384-
BVYiiSIFeK1dGmJRAkycuHAHRg32OmUcww7on3RYdg4Va+PmSTsz/K68vbdEjh4u"
  crossorigin="anonymous">

<link rel="stylesheet"
href="https://maxcdn.bootstrapcdn.com/bootstrap/3.3.7/css/bootstrap-theme.m
in.css"
  integrity="sha384-
rHyoN1iRsVXV4nD0JutlnGaslCJuC7uwjduW9SVrLvRYooPp2bWYgmgJQIXwl/Sp"
  crossorigin="anonymous">

<script
  src="https://maxcdn.bootstrapcdn.com/bootstrap/3.3.7/js/bootstrap.min.js"
  integrity="sha384-
Tc5IQib027qvyjSMfHjOMaLkfuWVxZxUPnCJA7l2mCWNIpG9mGCD8wGNIcPD7Txa"
  crossorigin="anonymous"></script>

<link rel="stylesheet"
href="//cdnjs.cloudflare.com/ajax/libs/rateYo/2.2.0/jquery.rateyo.min.css">
```

```
<scriptsrc="//cdnjs.cloudflare.com/ajax/libs/rateYo/2.2.0/jquery.rateyo.min
.js"></script>
```

Making other types of content rateable

You've just created a RESTful API in the Alfresco Repository and you used it to let SomeCo website users rate whitepaper content. What's cool, though, is that none of the rating logic depends on the specific Whitepaper type. Remember that rateable was defined as an aspect. It can get added to any object in the repository. And because the rating web scripts deal with Node IDs, the ratings web scripts and widget will work on anything SomeCo decides to make rateable in the future.

Dealing with the cross-domain scripting limitation

You may have noticed that all the URL examples use localhost. In fact, for development, SomeCo's HTML pages (whitepaper index and whitepaper detail) that make AJAX calls are also on localhost. In real life, however, it is highly likely that the code making AJAX calls to your web scripts will reside on a different host than the one where Alfresco lives. This creates a problem called the cross-domain scripting limitation. The issue is that for security reasons, browsers don't let you open an XMLHttpRequest to a different host than the one serving the page. There are two ways you can handle this depending on your situation:

- Use a proxy servlet. Servers aren't subject to the browser's security constraints. They can make calls to any host they want. You can easily write your own Java servlet that acts as a reverse proxy. AJAX calls go against the proxy servlet hosted on the same domain as the page making the call, and the proxy servlet then invokes the web script on the other domain, and returns the results to the calling client.
- Enable CORS in Alfresco as we already explained in Chapter 6, *Creating an Angular Application*, by deploying the enable-cors-1.0.jar file in the Alfresco Repository.

Handling form data

The rating example makes an AJAX call using the POST method. What if, instead of using AJAX, you were simply posting an HTML form? The web script framework is able to handle form posts, including multi-part forms.

For example, let's implement a new HelloWorld example as a form post instead of passing the name argument in the query string. We can use a static HTML page to render the form, but for the cost of an extra descriptor let's use a web script for both the GET (to render the form) and the POST (to process the form data). To do this, you'll need two descriptors (one for GET and one for POST), two FreeMarker templates, and a JavaScript controller.

Step-by-step – implementing a form-based Hello World

To create a new version of the Hello World web script using a form, do the following:

1. Create a descriptor for the GET called `helloworldform.get.desc.xml` in repo | src | main | amp | config | alfresco | extension | templates | webscripts | com | someco with the following content:

   ```xml
   <webscript>
       <shortname>Hello World Form</shortname>
       <description>Hello world form web script</description>
       <url>/someco/helloworldform</url>
   </webscript>
   ```

2. Create a FreeMarker template for the GET called `helloworldform.get.html.ftl` to present a simple form to capture the name. Add the following content:

   ```html
   <html>
       <body>
           <form action="${url.service}" method="post">
             Name:<input name="name"><br />
               <input type="submit" name="submit" value="Go!">
           </form>
       </body>
   </html>
   ```

3. Now write the web script that handles the POST. Create a POST descriptor called `helloworldform.post.desc.xml` by copying the GET descriptor. The two differ only in name and description:

   ```xml
   <webscript>
           <shortname>Hello World Form Post</shortname>
           <description>Hello world form post web script</description>
           <url>/someco/helloworldform</url>
   </webscript>
   ```

4. Create a JavaScript controller `helloworldform.post.js` to put the name in the model. This isn't strictly necessary. You could just grab the argument from the FreeMarket template, but you're going to add to this controller in the next example:

```
model.name = args.name;
```

5. Last, add a FreeMarker template for the POST that echoes back the field value:

```html
<html>
    <body>
        <p>Hello, ${name}!</p>
    </body>
</html>
```

6. Package, deploy, and test.

When you navigate your browser to
`http://localhost:8080/alfresco/service/someco/helloworldform`, you should see the form returned by the GET FreeMarker template:

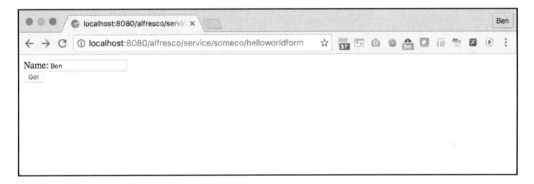

When you specify a value and click **Go!**, the controller for the POST extracts the field value and adds it to the model, so the FreeMarker template for the POST can display it.

Step-by-step – using file upload in a multipart request

Web scripts can handle multipart forms. That means you can add a file upload control to a form and then do something with that file, such as persist it to the repository.

The previous example was not a multipart form-the fields were passed to the controller as part of the `args` array. When using a multipart form, form fields reside in the `formdata` variable. To handle a file upload, all you have to do is know where to get the fields and the file and then do something with it. Let's modify the example you just did to handle a file upload. Follow these steps:

1. Create the `helloworldform2.get.html.ftl` file to change the form to a multipart form, and add a file upload control like this:

```html
<html>
  <body>
    <form action="${url.service}" method="post"
        enctype="multipart/form-data" accept-charset="utf-8">
        Name:<input name="name"><br />
        File:<input type="file" name="file"><br />
        <input type="submit" name="submit" value="Go!">
    </form>
  </body>
</html>
```

2. Create the `helloworldform2.get.desc.xml` file:

```xml
<webscript>
    <shortname>Hello World Form 2</shortname>
    <description>Hello world form web script</description>
    <url>/someco/helloworldform2</url>
    <transaction>none</transaction>
</webscript>
```

3. Create the `helloworldform2.post.desc.xml` file:

```xml
<webscript>
  <shortname>Hello World Form Post 2</shortname>
  <description>Hello world form post web script</description>
  <url>/someco/helloworldform2</url>
  <authentication runas="admin">guest</authentication>
  <transaction>required</transaction>
</webscript>
```

4. Create the `helloworldform2.post.js` controller. Because this is a multipart form, the fields are in the `formdata` variable. The field object named `file` will have special properties for the filename, mime type, and the content. First, add the code to extract these values:

```
for each (field in formdata.fields) {
    if (field.name == "name") {
        model.name = field.value;
    }
    if (field.name == "file" &&field.isFile) {
        filename = field.filename;
        content = field.content;
        mimetype = field.mimetype;
    }
}
```

5. Then, add code that grabs a folder to save the content to, creates the content, sets some properties, and saves the new node:

```
var results = search.luceneSearch("+PATH:"app:company_home/*"
    +TYPE:"cm:folder" +@cm\\:name:"Someco"");

vartargetFolder = results[0];
varnewDoc = targetFolder.createFile(filename);
newDoc.properties.content.write(content);
newDoc.properties.content.mimetype = mimetype;
newDoc.save();
model.node = newDoc;
```

6. Finally, create the Freemarker for the POST request in the `helloworldform2.post.html.ftl` file:

```
<html>
    <body>
        <p>Document Successfully Uploaded: ${node.name}!</p>
    </body>
</html>
```

7. Package, deploy and test.

Before testing, be sure to create a folder called `Someco` in your Alfresco repository. Now when you point your browser to `http://localhost:8080/alfresco/service/someco/helloworldform2`, you will see the new file upload control:

After setting the name, selecting a file, and clicking **Go!**, you'll see a successful message. If you log in to the Alfresco Share and go to the `Someco` folder, you should see the newly persisted file:

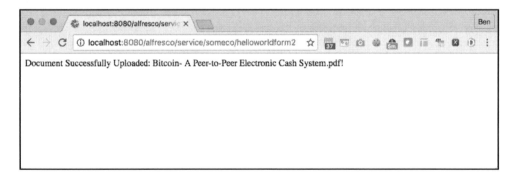

Advanced web scripts

Now that you have the basics under your belt, let's look at a few advanced web script topics.

Dealing with web script authentication

How web scripts authenticate depends on the runtime you are using. HTTP-based web scripts, such as the ones you built to work with whitepapers and ratings, are configured out of the box to use basic authentication. If you invoke a web script that requires a higher level of authentication than what's already taken place, the browser will present a basic authentication login dialog.

If you have Alfresco configured to leverage an SSO provider such as CAS, web scripts will leverage the session created when the user logs in to the centralized login page. The Chapter 10, *Security*, contains instructions for installing CAS and integrating it with Alfresco and Alfresco Share.

If you are writing your own web pages that need to invoke authenticated web scripts, one approach is to use a web service call to get a ticket. The ticket is then added to the request. There is a web script that can give you a ticket based on username and password:
`http://localhost:8080/alfresco/service/api/login?u=admin&pw=admin`

You should receive an XML object like this one:

```
<?xml version="1.0" encoding="URF-8"?>
<ticket>TICKET_0a748bc2543f2b271dc4cb9955c11a042cad72cd</ticket>
```

Be aware that you can ask for a JSON object as well by calling
`http://localhost:8080/alfresco/service/api/login.json?u=admin&pw=admin`
and you'll receive a JSON object like this one:

```
{
    "data":
    {
    "ticket":"TICKET_9306571267d178b130a570be150736b52c0506a3"
    }
}
```

Then, you can call any web script by adding the `alf_ticket` parameter like that:

```
?alf_ticket=TICKET_9306571267d178b130a570be150736b52c0506a3
```

You can find more information on this page:
`http://docs.alfresco.com/5.1/tasks/ws-specify-user-identity.html`.

Controlling web script cache

The web script descriptor includes a `cache` element that can be used to attempt to influence how the web script response is cached. The following snippet shows how the cache is configured by default:

```
<webscript>
...
    <cache>
        <never>true</never>
        <public>false</public>
        <mustrevalidate>true</mustrevalidate>
    </cache>
</webscript>
```

The cache settings are used as follows:

- Setting the `never` element to `true` says that the response should never be cached
- Specifying `false` for the `public` element means that the response should not be stored in a public cache
- Setting the `mustrevalidate` element to `true` indicates that the response contains dynamic content, and that the cache should always check to ensure it has the most up-to-date response

As you can see, by default, web scripts are not configured to be cache-friendly. It is important to remember, however, that the web script runtime may or may not support the cache settings, and that caching the response is not the responsibility of the web script run time. It is handled by the proxy sitting in front of the web script and the client making the request.

In the case of HTTP web scripts, the default settings create the following cache-related HTTP response headers:

```
Cache-Control: no-cache

Pragma: no-cache
```

The most cache-friendly configuration for a web script would look like this:

```
<cache>
    <never>false</never>
    <public>true</public>
    <mustrevalidate>false</mustrevalidate>
</cache>
```

With this configuration in place, the cache-related response headers no longer contain the `pragma` setting, and `Cache-Control` is set to `public`.

Cache settings made in the descriptor can be overridden at runtime by manipulating the `cache` root object from within the `controller`. See the Appendix for a complete list of JavaScript root objects, including the `cache` variable.

Summary

This chapter gave you an introduction to the Alfresco Web Script Framework. You began with a very simple Hello World script and then gradually moved to more complex examples culminating in a REST API for retrieving whitepapers, getting the average rating for a specific whitepaper, posting new ratings for a given whitepaper, and deleting all ratings for a specific whitepaper.

The SomeCo website was able to leverage the web scripts to add a whitepaper list along with a graphical ratings widget. The widget, the web scripts, and the backend model are generic enough to be used for other types of content as well.

Other takeaways from this chapter include the following:

- Web scripts are mainly composed of an XML descriptor, one or more FreeMarker templates (one for each response format), and, optionally, a controller.
- Controllers can be implemented as JavaScript or Java, and have full access to the Alfresco API. Controllers share data with the view via the model, which is essentially a HashMap.
- The URL structure and the arguments a web script accepts are completely up to you.
- The level of authentication (`none`, `guest`, `user`, `admin`) required for a web script is defined in the descriptor. How a web script authenticates depends on the runtime.
- Web scripts can be deployed to either the classpath or the repository. Regardless of where they are deployed, the web script directory can be used to browse and refresh the available web scripts.
- Centralizing business logic into a service is a good practice. In this chapter, you created a rating service that centralized all logic related to creating rating nodes.

Alfresco's Web Script Framework provides an easy way to integrate with the Alfresco repository. It is especially attractive when you are writing frontend code that leverages JavaScript toolkits, because those toolkits heavily utilize REST and AJAX.

8
Advanced Workflow

Every organization has business processes that lend themselves to automation. Often, these business processes are content-centric. In `Chapter 1`, *The Alfresco Platform* you learned that Alfresco provides an embedded workflow engine called Activiti. In this chapter, you'll explore Alfresco's advanced workflow capability provided by this embedded workflow engine. Alfresco provides as well a product called Alfresco Activiti Suite, but this product is out of the scope of this book.

Specifically, in this chapter you will learn:

- What workflow is and why you need a workflow engine
- How to create business process definitions using both a text editor and the Activti Graphical Process Designer
- The steps required to expose a custom business process to Alfresco Share
- How to add logic to workflows using expressions, JavaScript, and Java
- How to create an asynchronous process involving the Activiti Runtime Service, Alfresco Web Scripts, and actions
- How to debug workflows using Alfresco's workflow console and Activiti Explorer
- How to compare Alfresco's two options for workflow (advanced workflows and simple workflows)

What is a workflow?

When Alfresco released version 1.4, it made a huge leap forward in enterprise readiness. That was the release when Alfresco embedded the JBoss jBPM engine into the product, which meant that enterprises could route Alfresco repository content through complex business processes. In 2010, Alfresco launched Activiti to replace JBoss JBPM. Activiti can be used embedded in Alfresco, but also as a standalone. For a while, Alfresco supported both jBPM and Activiti as an embedded workflow engine. However, from the latest 5.x version, jBoss is considered as deprecated and shouldn't be used.

Most content has some sort of process around it. That's why content repositories almost always have a mechanism to streamline, facilitate, and report against the business processes that produce, consume, or transform the content within them.

 The terms `workflow` and `business process` will be used interchangeably throughout this book.

But before geeking out on the wonders of graph-based execution languages, let's agree on what the term **workflow** means. Generically, *workflow may be considered a view or representation of real work. The flow being described may refer to a document, service or product that is being transferred from one step to another.* The term has been around since people started studying the nature of work in the early twentieth century in an effort to streamline manufacturing processes.

In fact, in the world of ECM, it is sometimes helpful to think of an assembly line or manufacturing process when thinking about how content flows through an organization. Content is born of raw material (data), shaped and molded by one or more people (collaboration) or machines (systems), reviewed for quality, and delivered to consumers. Content may go through a single process or many sub processes. Content may take different routes through a process based on certain aspects of that content. The output of an organization or department of knowledge is essentially the content that comes rolling off the assembly line (the collection of workflows that define that organization's business processes).

Although not always formalized or automated, almost everyone in modern society has been involved in a workflow in some way:

- When you submit an insurance claim, you are initiating a workflow.
- If you witness drunk and disorderly conduct on an airline flight and are asked to provide a statement to the airline, you are participating in a workflow. (Seriously, it happens more often than you'd think.)
- When you check on the status of your loan application, you are asking for metadata about a running workflow.
- When someone brings you a capital request that requires your approval because it is over a certain dollar amount, a characteristic of that request (the dollar amount) has triggered a decision within the workflow that routes the capital request to you.
- When you give the final approval for a piece of web content to be published, it is likely that you are completing a workflow.

As varied as these examples are, all of them have a couple of things in common that make them relevant to ECM:

- they are examples of human-to-human and, in some cases, human-to-machine interaction
- they are content- or document-centric

These are two very important characteristics that help clarify the kind of workflow most relevant to the ECM space. There are standalone workflow engines (Activiti is one of them) that can be used to model and execute all sorts of "repeatable patterns of activity" with or without content. But in the world of ECM, patterns involving humans working with content are the focus. Of course, document-centric workflows may include fully automated steps and machine-to-machine interactions. The point is that document-centric workflows in which humans review, approve, or collaborate in some way are in the scope of the discussion, while processes that run lights-out system-to-system orchestration or integration are not.

Workflow options

Some of you are saying, "You're right. Workflows are everywhere. I could really streamline my organization by moving processes currently implemented with e-mail, phone calls, and cubical drive-bys into a more formalized workflow. What are my options?" Let's talk about three: roll your own, standalone workflow engines, and embedded workflow engines.

Roll your own

People are often tempted to meet their workflow requirements with custom code. Very basic systems might be able to get by with a single flag on a record or an object that declares the status of the content such as "Draft", or "In Review", or "Approved". But flags only capture the "state" of a piece of content. If you want to automate how content moves from state to state, the coding and maintenance becomes more complex. Sure, you can write code as part of your application that knows that once draft documents are submitted for review, they need to go to Purchasing first, and then to Finance, if and only if the requested cash outlay is more than $10m. But do you really want to write it?

People intent on rolling their own workflow often realize the maintenance problem this creates. So they create an abstraction used to describe the flow from state to state that keeps them from embedding that logic in compiled code. Once they've done that, they've essentially created their own proprietary workflow engine that no one else in the world knows how to run or maintain. And with all of the open source workflow engines available, this seems like a particularly flagrant waste of resources.

For these reasons, the "roll your own" option is really not recommended for any but the most basic workflow requirements.

Standalone engines

There are a number of standalone workflow engines, both open source and proprietary. They are sometimes more broadly referred to as **BPM (Business Process Management)** systems. These are often extremely robust and scalable solutions that can be used to model, simulate, and execute any process you can think of, from high-volume loan processing to call center queue management. Often, these workflow engines are implemented in conjunction with a rules engine that lets business users have control over complicated if-then-else decision trees.

Standalone engines are most appropriate for extremely high volume or exceedingly complex solutions involving multiple systems. Another good use for standalone engines is when you are developing a custom application that has workflow requirements. Standalone engines can usually talk to any database or content management repository you might have implemented. But they won't be as tightly integrated into the content management system's user interface as the workflow engine built into a CMS. For this reason, for content-centric solutions that operate mostly within the scope of a CMS, it is usually less complicated (and less expensive) to use the workflow engine embedded within the CMS, provided it has enough functionality to meet the workflow requirements of the business.

Embedded workflow engines

Almost every CMS available today, whether open source or proprietary, has a workflow engine of some sort embedded within it. However, the capability of each of these varies widely.

The major benefit of leveraging an embedded workflow engine is the tight level of integration for users as well as developers. Users can initiate and interact with workflows without leaving the CMS client. Typically, developers customizing or extending the CMS can work with workflows using the core CMS API.

Alfresco is an "embedded workflow engine" example. It embeds Activiti, which is an example of a standalone engine.

Creating process definitions

Activiti is an open source, standalone workflow engine. OK, it is more than just a standalone workflow engine. Activiti calls itself a "a light-weight workflow and Business Process Management (BPM) Platform targeted at business people, developers and system admins". Workflow is one of several different domains that can be addressed with a graph-based execution language, but it is the only one this book concerns itself with.

The Activiti engine is responsible for managing deployed processes, instantiating and executing processes, persisting process state and metadata to a relational database and tracking task assignment and task lists.

Activiti is built on the idea that any process can be described as a graph or a set of connected nodes. Workflows are described with "process definitions" using an XML-based language called **Business Process Model and Notation (BPMN)**. BPMN is a standard for modeling business processes. It's one example of a graph-based execution language. Activiti especially works on BPMN 2.0.

In Activiti, each node represents a step in a workflow. Connections between nodes signify the transition from one step to another. Creating a process definition is a matter of creating nodes to represent steps in the process and connecting them with transitions.

Step-by-step – creating a Hello World process definition

Let's get your feet wet by writing a simple process. Conceptually, the process looks like this:

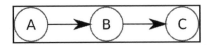

The process has three nodes. Node A and Node C are the Start and Stop nodes. Node B will write a message to the log. For now, you'll implement this process using raw XML and deploy and run it using Alfresco's workflow console. In later examples, you'll use the Activiti Graphical Process Designer to design and deploy the process, and Alfresco Share to instantiate and run the workflow.

To create a simple Hello World process, follow these steps:

1. In your Eclipse project, create a new folder structure called | repo | src | main | amp | config | alfresco | module | repo | workflows.

2. Within the new worfklows folder, create a new XML file called HelloWorldProcess.bpmn20.xml with the following content:

```xml
<?xml version="1.0" encoding="UTF-8"?>
<definitions id="definitions"
    targetNamespace="http://activiti.org/bpmn20"
    xmlns:activiti="http://activiti.org/bpmn"
    xmlns="http://www.omg.org/spec/BPMN/20100524/MODEL">
<process id="helloWorld" name="Hello World Process">
    <startEvent id="theStart" />
    <sequenceFlow id='flow1' sourceRef='theStart'
        targetRef='hello' />
    <serviceTask id="hello" name="Hello Task"
        activiti:class="org.alfresco.repo.workflow
        .activiti.script.AlfrescoScriptDelegate">

    <extensionElements>
        <activiti:field name="script">
            <activiti:string><![CDATA[logger
            .log("Hello World!");]]>
            </activiti:string>
        </activiti:field>
    </extensionElements>
    </serviceTask>
    <sequenceFlow id='flow2' sourceRef='hello'
        targetRef='theEnd' />
```

```
        <endEvent id="theEnd" />
    </process>

    </definitions>
```

3. Save the file.
4. Double-check that in
   `repo|src|main|amp|config|alfresco|module|repo|log4j.properties`
   you've got `log4j.logger.org.alfresco.repo.jscript` set to debug.
5. Package, deploy and restart Tomcat.
6. Log in to the Alfresco Admin Console client as admin
   (`http://localhost:8080/alfresco/s/enterprise/admin/admin-system summary`)
7. Click on the **Workflow Console** menu item in the left.
8. Use the console to deploy the workflow. Type the following command and click
   Execute:

   ```
   deploy activiti alfresco/module/repo
        /workflows/HelloWorldProcess.bpmn20.xml
   ```

   The console should respond with something similar to:

9. Now start a workflow using this process definition. The console already has the newly deployed workflow in context, so type **start** and click **Execute**. The console should respond with something similar to:

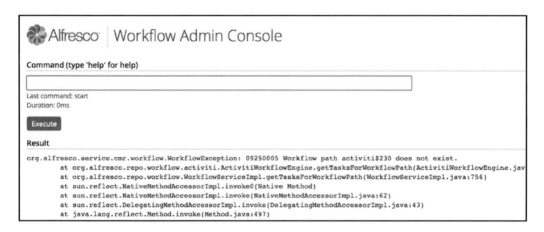

10. As you can see by the console output, you have an exception Worfklow path does not exist, generated by the Java method called getTasksForWorkflowPath. You may think that it failed, so let's check the log file. You should be able to see a trace similar to this one:

```
DEBUG [repo.jscript.ScriptLogger] [http-apr-8080-exec-8]
    Hello World!
```

So, it means that our workflow has been properly executed. Let's explain why we have an error message. Our workflow definition contains one start event, one service task, and one end event. It doesn't include any user task. When the workflow is started, it transitions automatically to the service task and then completes. It's why we have an error message; the console wants to display the current tasks for this workflow instance, but the instance is already completed so the workflow path doesn't exist anymore.

This was almost the simplest process you could possibly define, but you learned that:

- Processes can be defined with plain XML.
- Processes can reside in the Alfresco classpath. In this case, you used the workflows directory located in your module.
- Processes can be deployed and started using the Alfresco workflow console.

Be aware that Alfresco Enterprise also provides another user interface called *Activiti Explorer* or *Activiti Workflow Console*. To open it, click on the menu item **Process Engines**, then click on **Activiti Workflow Console**. If you click on the item **Deployed process definitions**, you should be able to see the *Hello World* process that we deployed:

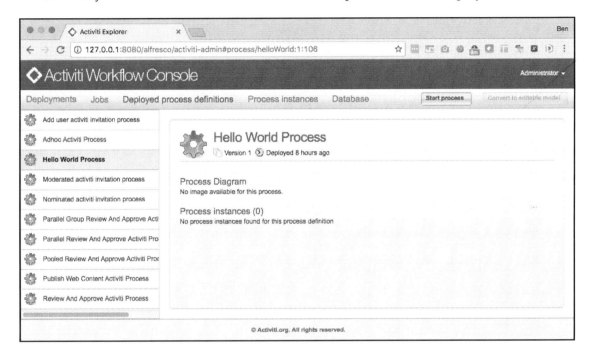

You could have deployed your process definition by clicking on **Deployments, Upload New** in the top menu.

Using the Activiti graphical process designer

One of the nice things about Activiti is that a graphical tool is available as an Eclipse plugin for creating and deploying process definitions, called the **ActivitiDesigner**.

There are people in the business of marketing workflow tools who love to say things such as "Using the graphical process designer, business analysts can create advanced workflows without writing any code!" Graphical process designers are definitely useful, but be realistic. Code has to be written.

The designer is most useful for quickly designing the process, setting node properties, and connecting nodes. Once that's done, you may have to switch over to the XML to finish out the definition.

The Activiti Designer is freely available from `http://www.activiti.org/userguide/#acti` `vitiDesigner`. It installs as an Eclipse plugin. To install the plugin, click on **Help|Install New Software**, then use the update site `http://activiti.org/designer/update/` and select the **Activiti Eclipse BPMN 2.0 Designer**. Click on **Next**, and then **Finish**.

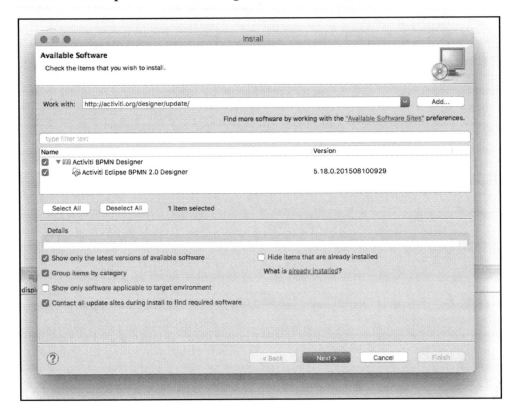

When Eclipse is restarted, if you do **File** | **New** | **Other** and see **Activiti Diagram** as shown in the following screenshot, you've successfully installed the plugin:

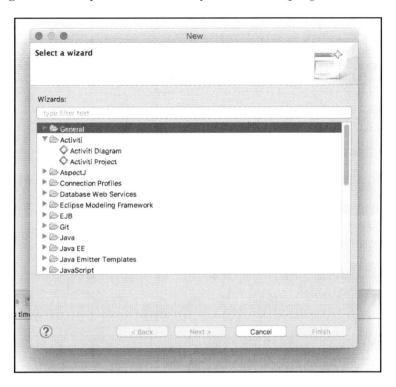

Step-by-Step – using Activiti process designer to create processes

Let's jazz up the process a bit and this time, instead of raw XML, let's use the designer to create and deploy the process definition file.

The HelloWorld process definition had a single path. Execution progressed from node A to node B to node C. In practice, however, most workflows have multiple execution paths. Consider the following figure:

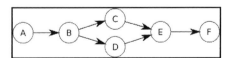

By looking at the transitions, you can see that the path of execution will always be from node A to node B. Node B has two outgoing paths. One path is to node C and the other to node D. The paths converge on node E. Then, it goes to the node F. Note that from the diagram it is impossible to tell which path will be taken. It's also possible that both could be followed simultaneously.

Let's implement the process described by the diagram using the designer. The result of that will be a `HelloWorld2Process.bpmn20.xml` file just like before. But the designer will enable you to create it more quickly than you would be able to by writing the XML from scratch. To do this, follow these steps:

1. In the repo Eclipse project, navigate to the `workflows` directory you created for the Hello World example.

2. Select **File| New| Other| Activiti | Activiti Diagram**. Specify `HelloWorld2Process` as the process name and click **Finish**. You'll notice that the file is called `HelloWorld2Process.bpmn`. You could keep it like that but to keep the same convention name, rename it `HelloWorld2Process.bpmn20.xml`. If you want to rename it, be sure to close it first and then rename it. Otherwise, the Activiti designer may be confused. As well, because the extension will be XML. STS will open the standard XML Editor. You'll need to do a right click on the file, and click on **Open with|Other....** Then, select the **Activiti Diagram Editor**.

3. The **main** tab is used to lay out the process by selecting node types from the palette (such as **StartEvent**, **EndEvent**, **ParallelGateway**, **ExclusiveGateway,UserTask,** and **ServiceTask**) and clicking on the canvas. Add a **StartEvent**, an **EndEvent**, two **ParallelGateway,** and two **AlfrescoScriptTask** to the canvas.

4. Organize the nodes to appear roughly as they do in the node diagram shown earlier in this section.

5. Node properties can be edited using the **Properties** view below the diagram view. Set the names of the two nodes to **Node C** and **Node D** respectively, and set the IDs of the same two nodes to **nodeC** and **nodeD** respectively. If you struggle to find the **Properties** view, you have two options. The first one is to add this view by clicking in the top menu in **Window|Show View|Properties**. Or you can open the Activiti perspective by clicking on **Window|Perspective|Open Perspective|Other...** and select **Activiti**.

6. The **SequenceFlow** item is used to connect the nodes. Connect the nodes to match the node diagram. You have two main options to create a transition. The quickest one is to put your cursor on the task that will be the source of the transition. A menu should appear around the task and you'll be able to click on an arrow icon. The second option is to browse the palette on the right side of the editor and to click on **Connection|SequenceFlow**. When you are done, the process should look like this:

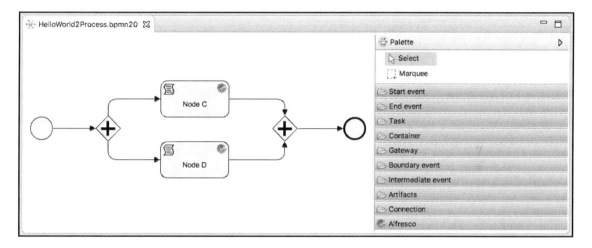

7. Click on the white area, and open the **Properties** view. Update the following attributes:

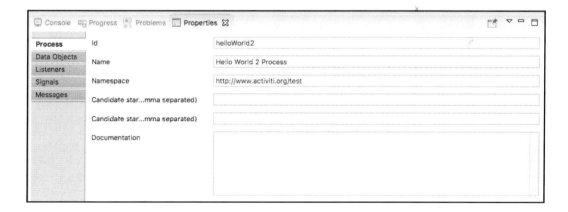

8. Click on each node C and D, open the **Properties** view, select the tab Main config and add the logger statement (be sure to display a different message in node D).

9. Save the file.
10. You could take the process and deploy it right now by re-packaging, and then deploying from the classpath using the workflow console as you did in the HelloWorld example. In this case, we'll use the Activiti Explorer as previously described by clicking on **Deployments | Upload new** in the Activiti Explorer. When it's done, you should see your file listed in the list of deployments:

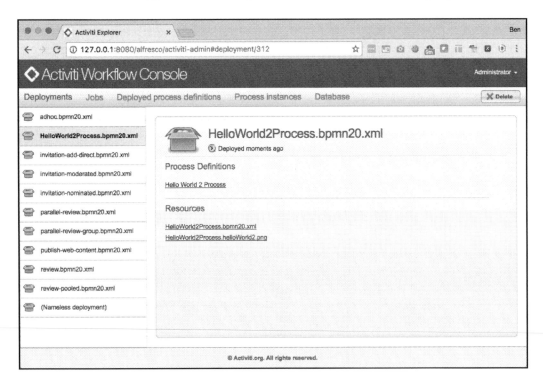

11. If you click on the tab **Deployed process definitions**, you should see as well your new definition with the right diagram:

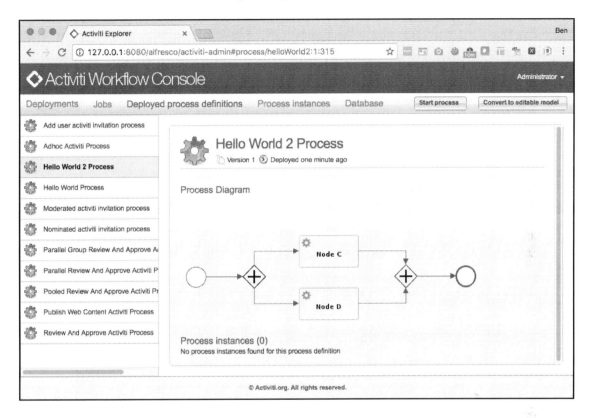

12. Now test out the new process with the workflow console. Log in to the Alfresco Administration Console as admin, and click on the menu item called Workflow Console.

13. Type **show definitions all** and click **Execute**. You should see an entry with the name equals to **activiti$helloWorld2**. Make a note of its ID, which will look something like **activiti$helloWorld2:1:315**.

14. Tell the console you want to work in the context of the **helloWorld2** definition. Type **use definition activiti$helloWorld2:1:315**, replacing **activiti$helloWorld2:1:315** with your specific ID, and then click **Execute.**

15. Start a new workflow. Type **start** and click **Execute**. The console should respond with something similar to the previous example with the error message.

16. Check your log file and you should see the two following messages:

```
DEBUG [repo.jscript.ScriptLogger] [http-apr-8080-exec-3]
Hello World! From Node C!

DEBUG [repo.jscript.ScriptLogger] [http-apr-8080-exec-3]
Hello World! From Node D!
```

Tokens

A token is like the `You Are Here` flag for a process-it points to the execution state. The token moves from node-to-node as the process is executed. But it doesn't move on its own. Tokens only move when they are signaled. Let's look at an example. In the figure, when you initially execute the process, the token is at node **A**. Then the token will take the only path available to it, which is to move to node **B**. From node **B** there are multiple paths available. In our example, we used a parallel gateway. The token spawned two child tokens, one for the path from node **B** to node **C**, and one from node **B** to node **D**. When the paths converge, the child tokens go away and the parent token resumes.

Node types

Nodes are typed (in a Java sense, not in a content sense). A node's type determines how it behaves. You saw in the previous example that both branches in the execution path were executed because both Hello World messages showed up in the log. Why didn't the execution proceed down only in a single path? It was because you used a parallel gateway, which is a special type of node that spawns concurrent paths of execution. The following table summarizes the node types available in Activiti out of the box:

Node Type	Description
Start Event	Only one allowed per process definition. Only outgoing transitions are allowed.
Parallel Gateway	Spawns multiple concurrent paths of execution. This node type is used to fork and to join the execution path.
Exclusive Gateway	Choice between multiple paths of execution. You'll see examples of how to implement the logic for a decision later in the chapter.
User Task	Used to model work that needs to be done by a human actor
Script Task	Represents an automatic activity.
Java Service Task	Used to invoke an external Java class.

Sub Process	Represents a node that contains other nodes which on itself form a process that is part of the bigger process.
Call Activity	Calls an external subprocess (it's different to the previous node that executes an embedded subprocess)
End Event	Marks the end of a process. Only incoming transitions are allowed.

The preceding table contains only the most useful node types. Feel free to check the Activiti documentation that describe all possible node types (`http://www.activiti.org/userguide/`).

Versioning process definitions

When you check in an updated process definition to the Activiti engine, it automatically versions the process. On the workflow console, when you run show definitions all, the response includes every version of every process definition currently deployed.

You may be wondering what happens to running workflow instances when a new version of the process definition is checked in. The answer is that Activiti handles that gracefully. It makes sure that running workflows continue to run with their original process definition. All new workflows will use the most current process definition.

Using alternative deployment methods

So far you've seen how to deploy process definitions to Alfresco through the workflow console and the Activiti Explorer. Processes can also be deployed through Spring.

Of these, the most common in the Alfresco world is through Spring. The following snippet shows how to point to a single process definition. If you have multiple workflows to deploy using this approach, use multiple props elements:

```
<bean id="someco.workflowBootstrap" parent="workflowDeployer">
    <property name="workflowDefinitions">
        <list>
            <props>
                <prop key="engineId">activiti</prop>
                <prop key="location">alfresco/module/repo
                /workflows/HelloWorldProcess.bpmn20.xml</prop>
                <prop key="mimetype">text/xml</prop>
                <prop key="redeploy">true</prop>
            </props>
```

```
          </list>
      </property>
  </bean>
```

The `engineId` **must be set to** `activiti`.

The `location` is any location on the classpath. But to be consistent with how customizations are deployed, I recommend standardizing on the Alfresco extension directory or more specifically in a directory called workflows within your module.

The `mimetype` setting is **text/xml** when deploying the `HelloWorldProcess.bpmn20.xml` file.

The redeploy flag tells Alfresco whether or not it should automatically redeploy the process on startup. During development if you are deploying your processes via Spring, you probably want this to be set to true. Once you get to production, set it to false to avoid needlessly creating new versions of the process definition every time the server is restarted.

Wiring a process to the Alfresco UI

So far you've learned the definition of workflow, specifics around the Activiti engine, and how to deploy processes. But the discussion up to this point hasn't been specific to Alfresco. In Alfresco, users need to:

- Start workflows
- Add one or more pieces of content to a workflow ("Approve an application form", for example)
- Assign tasks to users and/or groups, and work with the tasks assigned to them
- Provide process-specific metadata for a specific workflow such as due dates, priority, special processing instructions, or any other custom metadata you can think of

Activiti is just an engine-it is up to the application embedding the engine to expose the capabilities of the engine to the user interface. Alfresco's already done that work for you. Figuring out how to wire your custom workflows into Alfresco Share is just a matter of following Alfresco's framework.

Alfresco uses the same mechanism to model workflow process data and the corresponding Alfresco Share interface as it does to define custom content models. You learned how to extend Alfresco's content model in `Chapter 3`, *Working with Content Models*. The steps for integrating a custom workflow with Alfresco Share are identical. At a high level it involves:

- Defining a content model for your workflow in which workflow tasks map to content types (Alfresco-provided types, custom types, or both)
- Updating `share-config-custom.xml` to tell Alfresco how to expose the process metadata to Alfresco Share
- Externalizing the strings

Let's see how this works by wiring the Hello World process you created earlier to Alfresco Share. After that, you'll work through a more complex example for SomeCo.

Step-by-step – grabbing the Hello World argument from the user

The Hello World process you created at the start of the chapter didn't require any user involvement other than signaling the start node. Once you did that, it ran to completion. Certainly, you'll have workflows like this. Workflows can be useful for chaining together several automated operations that don't need human involvement. In this example, though, you need to learn how to integrate a custom workflow with the Alfresco Share user interface. So let's modify the Hello World example to say hello to a name specified when the workflow is launched. This will involve creating a custom workflow content model, configuring the Alfresco Share user interface, and modifying the process definition to retrieve the string from the model.

Let's get started. Follow these steps:

1. First, in the workflows folder in your Eclipse project make a copy of the `HelloWorldProcess.bpmn20.xml` process definition. Call the new file `HelloWorldUIProcess.bpmn20.xml`.
2. Now edit the process definition. There are three areas that need to be addressed. First, the process id and name need to change:

```
<process id="helloWorldUI" name="Hello World UI Process">
```

3. Next, the goal is to have the person starting the workflow specify a string when the workflow is launched. To do this, let's update the start event by specifying the content model type that will be used on the start task:

```
<startEvent id="theStart" activiti:formKey
    ="scwf:submitHelloWorldTask" />
```

4. The final change to the process is to read the string that was set by the workflow initiator. The string will be stored in a property as defined in the yet-to-be-created custom workflow content model. All you have to do is declare a variable that matches the property name, and then reference it in the log statement. Note the use of an underscore ("_") instead of a colon (":") to separate the namespace from the property name. Modify the `hello` service task as follows:

```
<serviceTask id="hello" name="Hello Task"
activiti:class="org.alfresco.repo.workflow
.activiti.script.AlfrescoScriptDelegate">
    <extensionElements>
        <activiti:field name="script">
            <activiti:string><![CDATA[logger.log("Hello, "
            + scwf_helloName + "!");]]>

            </activiti:string>
        </activiti:field>
    </extensionElements>
</serviceTask>
```

5. Save the file.
6. When the workflow is launched, the initiator specifies a name string. Alfresco has to know how to handle that data. Alfresco uses a content model to do that. Create a new content model XML file in repo | src | main | amp | config | alfresco | module | repo | model called `scWorkflowModel.xml` with the following content:

```
<?xml version="1.0" encoding="UTF-8"?>
<!-- Definition of new Model -->
<model name="scwf:workflowmodel"
    xmlns="http://www.alfresco.org/model/dictionary/1.0">

<!-- Optional meta-data about the model -->
<description>Someco Workflow Model</description>
<author>BenChevallereau</author>
<version>1.0</version>

<!-- Imports are required to allow references to
```

```
definitions in other models -->
<imports>

<import uri=
   "http://www.alfresco.org/model/dictionary/1.0" prefix="d" />
<import uri="http://www.alfresco.org/model/bpm/1.0"
   prefix="bpm" />
</imports>

<!-- Introduction of new namespaces defined by this model -->
<namespaces>
<namespace uri="http://www.someco.com/model/workflow/1.0"
  prefix="scwf" />
</namespaces>
```

Two important things to notice in the previous XML code. First, you'll notice that we import an Alfresco model defined by the prefix bpm. This model will provide use the basic model elements to configure our workflow like the start task content type that we use below. The second important thing is the creation of a dedicated content model. We could have re-used the same content model to define the document types, and the workflow types. It's more a good practice to organize your types and aspects related to documents in one content model, and to isolate your workflow types and aspects in another content model.

7. Add to it a type that corresponds to the task you created in the start-element, which was called scwf:submitHelloWorldTask. The type only needs one property, which is the name string:

```
<types>
    <type name="scwf:submitHelloWorldTask">
    <parent>bpm:startTask</parent>
    <properties>
        <property name="scwf:helloName">
            <type>d:text</type>
            <mandatory>true</mandatory>
            <multiple>false</multiple>
        </property>
    </properties>
    </type>
</types>
</model>
```

Notice the inheritance with the type bpm:startTask provided by the out-of-the-box Alfresco model.

8. Save the model XML file.

9. Create a new properties file in `repo | src | main | amp | config | alfresco | module | repo | messages` called `scWorkflow.properties`. The properties file for workflows follows a specific syntax. First, add properties related to the custom workflow model. These properties describe the type and the property you added to the model:

```
#
# Hello World UI Workflow
#

# scWorkflowModel related strings
scwf_workflowmodel.type.scwf_submitHelloWorldTask.title
    =Start Hello World UI Workflow
scwf_workflowmodel.type.scwf_submitHelloWorldTask.description
    =Submit a workflow that says hello in the log
scwf_workflowmodel.property.scwf_helloName.title
    =Name
scwf_workflowmodel.property.scwf_helloName.description
    =Say hello to this person
```

10. Then, add properties that relate to the process. In this example, the only process-related properties are used to give the workflow a title and a description. Alfresco will display the title and description in the Start Advanced Workflow wizard:

```
# Workflow related strings
helloWorldUI.workflow.title=Hello World UI
helloWorldUI.workflow.description
    =A simple hello world process using Activiti
```

11. Save the properties file.

12. This time, we'll deploy our process using a Spring bean. In the folder `repo | src | main | amp | config | alfresco | module | repo | context`, create a new file called `workflow-context.xml` and add the following content:

```xml
<?xml version='1.0' encoding='UTF-8'?>
<!DOCTYPE beans PUBLIC '-//SPRING//DTD BEAN//EN'
    'http://www.springframework.org/dtd/spring-beans.dtd'>
<beans>
    <bean id="someco.workflowBootstrap" parent="workflowDeployer">
    <property name="workflowDefinitions">
      <list>
        <props>
          <prop key="engineId">activiti</prop>
          <prop key="location">
```

```
                        alfresco/module/${project.artifactId}
                        /workflows/HelloWorldUIProcess.bpmn20.xml
                </prop>
                <prop key="mimetype">text/xml</prop>
                <prop key="redeploy">true</prop>
            </props>
          </list>
        </property>
        </bean>
    </beans>
```

13. You have to tell Alfresco about the new model. Recall that models are configured in a Spring context bean. Edit the previous context file called `workflow-context.xml` to add a new property with the name equal to models.

```
<property name="models">
  <list>
    <value>

alfresco/module/${project.artifactId}/model/scWorkflowModel.xml
    </value>
  </list>
</property>
```

14. Alfresco also needs to know about the `scWorkflow.properties` file. It makes sense to add it to the same context file. Add a new property with the name equal to `labels`:

```
<property name="labels">
    <list>
        <value>
            alfresco/module/${project.artifactId}/messages/scWorkflow
        </value>
    </list>
</property>
```

15. Save the context file.

16. Then, edit your `module-context.xml` file and add an `import` reference:

```
<import resource="classpath:alfresco/module/
${project.artifactId}/context/workflow-context.xml" />
```

17. Now, we need to configure Alfresco Share. Open the file share | src | main | resources | META-INF | share-config-custom.xml and add the following config element:

```
<config evaluator="string-compare"
  condition="activiti$helloWorldUI">
 <forms>
  <form>
   <field-visibility>
     <show id="bpm:workflowDescription" />
      <show id="packageItems" />
      <show id="scwf:helloName" />
      <show id="transitions" />
      <show id="bpm:status" />
   </field-visibility>
   <appearance>
     <set id="" appearance="title"
     label-id="workflow.set.general" />
     <set id="items" appearance="title"
     label-id="workflow.set.items" />
     <set id="progress" appearance="title"
     label-id="workflow.set.task.progress" />

     <set id="other" appearance="title"
     label-id="workflow.set.other" />
     <field id="bpm:workflowDescription"
       label-id="workflow.field.message">
       <control template="/org/alfresco/components
       /form/controls/textarea.ftl">
       <control-param name="style">width: 95%</control-param>
       </control>
     </field>
     <field id="packageItems" set="items" />
     <field id="scwf:helloName" set="other" />
     <field id="bpm:status" set="progress" />
   </appearance>
  </form>
 </forms>
</config>
```

Let's explain this XML code. First, we can see that we match this form configuration by defining the `condition` field with the Activiti workflow identifier. Then, we configured in the workflow which content type to use for the start task. This is how Alfresco maps this configuration to the content type that we defined for the start task.

Instead of starting from scratch, we just re-used an existing configuration in Alfresco Share. If you open the file `WEB-INF | classes | alfresco | share-workflow-form-config.xml` in the Share web application in Tomcat, you should find a form configuration for the workflow `activiti$activitiAdhoc`. We just removed some out-of-the-box fields and added our custom field.

18. Package, deploy, and test.

To start an advanced workflow in Alfresco Share, you can use the **My Tasks** dashlet. If you don't already have it on your dashboard, you can add it by yourself by clicking on the wheel icon. Just click on the `Start Workflow` action:

You should see your workflow listed as well as the other Hello World workflow examples and the out-of-the-box workflows:

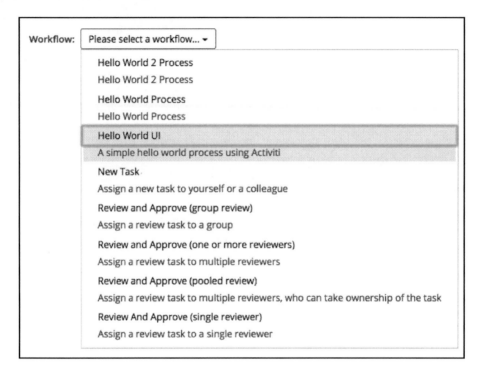

If you select the Hello Word UI, you should see the form that we created, as well as the externalized string for the label:

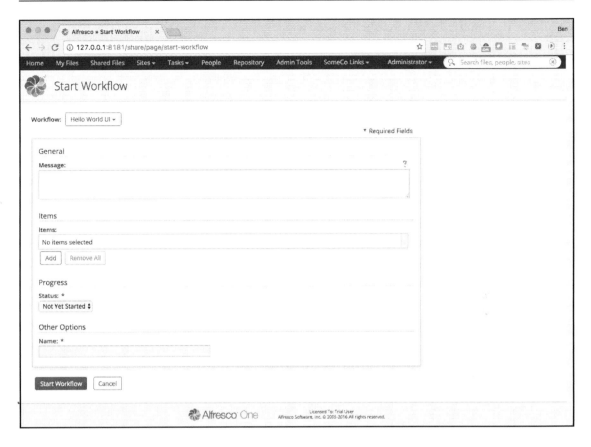

Just populate the **Name** field with your name, and click on **Start Workflow**. Unfortunately, you'll get the same error message when you were using the Workflow Console. And it's for the same reason; we don't have any user task in our process. Don't worry, we are getting to it!

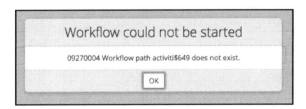

If you check the log file, you should see our new message with the value that you entered:

```
DEBUG [repo.jscript.ScriptLogger] [http-apr-8080-exec-8] Hello, Ben!
```

Understanding workflow-specific content models

The workflow-specific content model defines the data structure for the process. Workflow models use the same fundamental building blocks-types, properties, aspects, and associations-as "normal" Alfresco content model definitions. In fact, if you already have a custom model, you can define your workflow-specific model in the same content model XML file. But to reduce confusion, I recommend you do what you did here and keep your content types separate from your workflow types using at least two different model files.

What is the purpose of the workflow-specific model? Think of it like any other content model. Custom content models are used to define the metadata you want to capture about a piece of content. The metadata (properties) is grouped into types and aspects. By virtue of defining these properties as part of the content model, Alfresco takes care of persisting the data to the underlying database.

Workflow models function in the same way. Suppose you have a process in which three different departments are involved in an approval process. Maybe you'd like the workflow initiator to be able to define which of those departments are required approvers and which are optional or "FYI" reviewers. The workflow model defines how that information is going to be stored.

As in other content models, you don't have to start from scratch. Alfresco ships out of the box with some workflow-specific types already defined. There are two model definition files related to this. One is called bpmModel.xml. It resides in the folder alfresco | model packaged in the JAR file alfresco-repository-5.*.zip deployed in the Alfresco web application root under WEB-INF | lib. The other is called workflowModel.xml and it resides in the same JAR file but in the folder alfresco | workflow.

The BPM model file contains the lowest-level workflow classes such as the base definition for all tasks and the default start task. It also contains important aspects such as a set of "assignee" aspects that define associations between tasks and users or groups.

The workflow model file contains the content model for the out-of-the box process definitions. This model file offers a lot of potential for reuse in your custom processes. For example, if your process starts by allowing the submitter to specify a list of several people to receive a task, you could use the `submitParallelReviewTask`. If you want to base an approval on the percentage of individuals who approve a task, you can use the `submitConcurrentReviewTask`. Of course, just like any model, you are free to use these as is, extend them, or not use them at all.

When users interact with the workflow via Share, Alfresco will use the workflow content model and the `share-config-custom.xml` file to figure out what metadata to expose to the UI, and how to present it just as it does when viewing content properties. Alfresco uses the value of the field `formKey` configured on each task to figure out the appropriate workflow content type. So, all tasks in which there are Alfresco Share user interactions must be given a value that corresponds to the name of a workflow content type.

You may have noticed that the custom type you created (`scwf:startHelloWorldTask`) was a subtype of `bpm:startTask`, that inherits from `bpm:workflowTask`. Doing that added key properties and aspects to your workflow, including the ability to associate content with the workflow. If you look at the `bpmModel.xml` file, you'll see that the `bpm:workflowTask` includes an association called `bpm:package`. That's what is used to relate workflow instances with the content being routed by the workflow.

Assigning tasks to users and groups

A task is a step in a workflow that requires human interaction. Activiti maintains a list of tasks assigned to each participant. How users interact with the task list is up to the application embedding the Activiti engine. In Alfresco Share out-of-the-box, you have two options.

The first one is to use the **My Tasks** that we used previously. The second one is to use the page using the same name **My Tasks**. To open it, click on the top banner to Tasks | My Tasks. It will show a to-do list for the currently logged in user. As users complete their tasks, the tasks are removed from the to-do list. An empty to do list is shown here:

If tasks are steps a human performs, how do tasks get associated with the people who need to perform them? When defining a business process, it is important to understand how the participants in the process will do the work. One specific area that needs to be considered is whether to use *candidates* for a given task, or assign a task directly to a user. Suppose you assigned a task to a group of 10 people. You could iterate through the group and assign a task to each and every member of the group, and then not consider the task complete until all actors have taken action. An alternative is to use candidates. All members of a group are notified of the task. But as soon as one actor takes "ownership" of the task, it is removed from everyone else's to-do list. The owner can then either complete the task or return it to the pool. If it is returned to the pool, all members of the group see the task in their to-do list until another person takes ownership or completes the task. To implement this concept, Activiti is using mainly two attributes:

- `activiti:candidateUsers`: This is used to make a user (or a list of users) a potential candidate for a task
- `activiti:candidateGroups`: This is used to make a group (or a list of groups) a potential candidate for a task

Be aware that those two properties can be used at the same time. And finally, you can use an expression like `${initiator.properties.userName}`. The variable initiator is used to represent the person who started the workflow. Let's say that you want to implement a review process; you want to inform the initiator that the review has been completed. In this case, you'll create a task using this expression as the assignment.

And finally, you have another option to assign a task. You may decide to assign a task directly to a user, and not anymore to candidate users or groups. To achieve that, Activiti is using the property, `activiti:assignee`. It's quite rare that you want to use this property with a real username; you usually want to use it with an expression like the one just described.

Step-by-step – creating the initial Whitepaper submission workflow

In earlier chapters, you created an action item linked to a repository action that enables and disables Whitepapers for publication to the Web. You used an evaluator to show or hide the action item based on whether or not the user was a member of the Publisher group. That approach works fine in cases where the action doesn't require review or approval. But SomeCo wants anyone in the company to be able to submit a Whitepaper for publication to the website, as long as the right people review the document before it is published. This process is well-suited to an advanced workflow.

The Whitepaper needs to be reviewed by the Operations team as well as the Marketing team. It doesn't matter who on the team does the review. SomeCo wants to notify each team and then let one representative from each team "own" the review task.

Either team can reject the Whitepaper. If it is rejected, the person who submitted the Whitepaper can make revisions and resubmit. If both teams approve, the Whitepaper moves on to the next step.

Here are the high-level steps involved in implementing this process:

1. Lay out the process using the Activiti Process Designer.
2. Add user tasks with appropriate assignments.
3. Add two parallel gateways and an exclusive gateway to take a decision.
4. Wire the process to Alfresco Share by updating the SomeCoWorkflow Content Model and modifying the Share configuration.

To get this done, follow these steps:

1. Create a new process in `repo | src | main | amp | config | alfresco | module | repo | workflows` **called** `publishWhitepaper.bpmn20.xml`.
2. Using the Activiti Designer, lay out the process as shown in the diagram that follows:

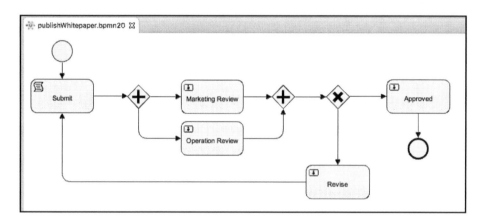

3. Click on the white area and change the process ID and name as displayed in the following screenshot:

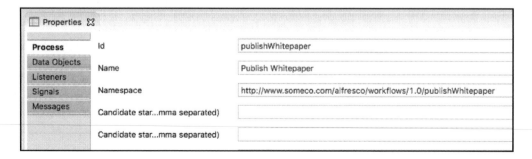

4. Now, let's configure the assignment of the Marketing Review task. Click on the task **Marketing Review** and open the tab **Main config**:
    - Type `GROUP_Marketing` in the **Candidate groups** field;
    - Type `scwf:reviewTask` in the **Form key** field.

It should look like this:

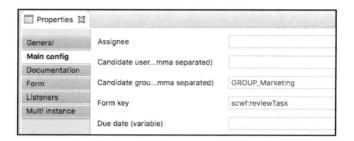

5. Click on the **Revise** task and open the tab **Main config**:
6. Do the same with the Operation Review, but assign it to the group, GROUP_Operation.
    - Type `${initiator.properties.userName}` in the **Assignee** field;
    - Type `wf:adhocTask` in the *Form key* field (which is one of the default forms provided by Alfresco).

It should look like this:

7. Do exactly the same for the **Approved** task.
8. Click on the **Start Event** and populate the **Form key** field with another type provided by Alfresco, bpm:startTask.

9. Finally, click on the **Submit** service task (for the moment, this task is useless, but be patient and you'll see why we created it):

```
logger.log("Submit whitepaper!");
```

10. The shell of the process is now complete. It doesn't do anything special yet, but once you wire in the UI, you'll be able to test that the assignment works as you expect. Now let's integrate the process with Alfresco by defining the content model and updating the Share configuration. Update repo | src | main | amp | config | alfresco | module | repo | model | scWorkflowModel.xml by adding the following types:

```xml
<type name="scwf:reviewTask">
    <parent>wf:activitiReviewTask</parent>
    <overrides>
        <property name="bpm:packageItemActionGroup">
            <default>read_package_item_actions</default>
        </property>
    </overrides>
</type>
```

Don't worry too much about the bpm:packageItemActionGroup, it's explained in the following page. But if you are too curious, you can jump to the *Controlling What Actions Can Be Taken from the Task Management Dialog* section.

11. Finally, add the following import tag in the imports tag already existing:

```xml
<import uri="http://www.alfresco.org/model
    /workflow/1.0" prefix="wf" />
```

12. Now the share-config-custom.xml file. Add the Share configuration for the new workflow types and properties. You can see that although the BPM model defines several properties, you're only exposing the workflow description and comment properties for this particular process:

```xml
<config evaluator="string-compare"
  condition="activiti$publishWhitepaper">
 <forms>
   <form>
     <field-visibility>
       <show id="bpm:workflowDescription" />
       <show id="packageItems" />
       <show id="transitions" />
     </field-visibility>
```

```
<appearance> <set id="" appearance="title"
  label-id="workflow.set.general" />

  <set id="items" appearance="title"
    label-id="workflow.set.items" />

  <set id="progress" appearance="title"
    label-id="workflow.set.task.progress" />

  <field id="bpm:workflowDescription"
    label-id="workflow.field.message">

    <control template="/org/alfresco/components
      /form/controls/textarea.ftl">

      <control-param name="style">
        width: 95%
      </control-param>

    </control>
  </field> <field id="packageItems" set="items" />
</appearance>
</form>
</forms>
</config>

<config evaluator="task-type" condition="scwf:reviewTask">
<forms>
  <form>
    <field-visibility>
      <show id="message" />
      <show id="packageItems" />
      <show id="bpm:comment" />
      <show id="wf:reviewOutcome" />
    </field-visibility>
    <appearance>
      <set id="" appearance="title"
      label-id="workflow.set.task.info" />
      <set id="info" appearance="" template="/org/alfresco
      /components/form/3-column-set.ftl" />
      <set id="progress" appearance="title"
      label-id="workflow.set.task.progress" />
      <set id="items" appearance="title"
      label-id="workflow.set.items" />
      <set id="response" appearance="title"
      label-id="workflow.set.response" />
      <field id="message">
        <control template="/org/alfresco/components
```

```
        /form/controls/info.ftl" />
      </field>
      <field id="packageItems" set="items" />
      <field id="bpm:comment"
      label-id="workflow.field.comment" set="response">
      <control template="/org/alfresco
      /components/form/controls/textarea.ftl">
        <control-param name="saveLineBreaks">true</control-param>
      </control>
    </field>
    <field id="wf:reviewOutcome"
    label-id="workflow.field.outcome" set="response">
        <control template="/org/alfresco/components
        /form/controls/workflow/activiti-transitions.ftl" />
    </field>
  </appearance>
 </form>
</forms>
</config>
```

In the previous XML code, we can see that we define a config element based on the Activiti workflow identifier that will configure the form that you see when you start a new workflow; and another config element based on the type scwf:reviewTask. To summarize, when you want to configure a workflow form, you should use the Activiti workflow identifier for the start task, and the content type that you defined in the **Form Key** attribute for all other user tasks.

13. Then, we need to update the `workflow-context.xml` file and add the definition of our workflow in the list by adding this element to the list tag:

```
<props>
  <prop key="engineId">activiti</prop>
  <prop key="location">alfresco/module
    /${project.artifactId}/workflows
    /publishWhitepaper.bpmn20.xml</prop>
  <prop key="mimetype">text/xml</prop>
  <prop key="redeploy">true</prop>
</props>
```

14. The last step is to externalize the strings. Update `repo | src | main | amp | config | alfresco | module | repo | messages | scWorkflow.properties` with the model-related strings:

```
scwf_workflowmodel.type.scwf_reviewTask.title
 =Whitepaper Review Task
scwf_workflowmodel.type.scwf_reviewTask.description
 =Review documents
publishWhitepaper.workflow.title
 =Publish Whitepaper to SC Web
publishWhitepaper.workflow.description
 =Review and approve SC Whitepaper content
```

15. Save the properties file.
16. Package and deploy the changes and then restart Alfresco. Don't forget to restart Share too if you are using the SDK.
17. Test the process.

To test the process, do the following:

1. If you haven't done so already, create a group called `Operations` and one called `Marketing`. Create a couple of test users for each group.
2. In the repository, create a test Whitepaper in the **Marketing** site, if you don't have any already.
3. Configure the permissions on the Marketing site such that the marketing and operation groups have Collaborator access or higher.
4. Start a workflow by clicking on the action **More...** | **Start Workflow** on your test Whitepaper.

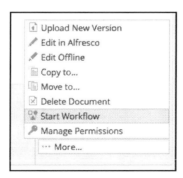

5. You should see the newly-deployed workflow in the list of available workflows:

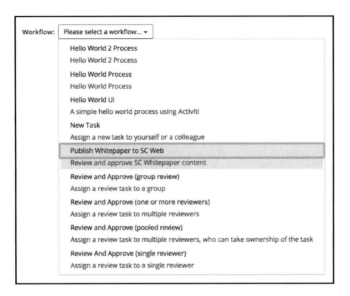

6. Add a message and click on **Start Workflow**:

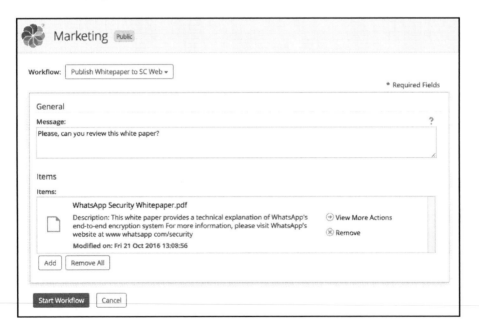

7. Log in as one of your test users. On the user dashboard, you should have the **My Tasks** dashlet (if not, add it by configuring your dashboard):

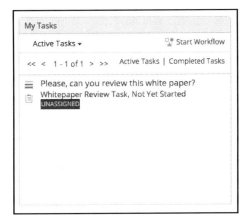

8. You will notice that we see the value that you entered in the **Message** field as a task description. If you didn't populate it, you would have seen the name of the task:

9. You can notice the UNASSIGNED label. It's because this process is designed with candidate users, so any users in the **Marketing** group can complete this task. If you click on the task, either take ownership of the task by clicking on the **Claim** button (the task will disappear off the list of tasks for all other marketing users) or simply **Approve** or **Reject** the task.

10. After you have completed the **Marketing Review** and the **Operation Review**, open the **Activiti Workflow Console**. Open the tab **Process Instances** and locate your workflow instance. You'll see that an **Approved** task is assigned to the user that you used to start the workflow, and is waiting to be completed. You can see as well who completed the **Marketing** and **Operation** Review:

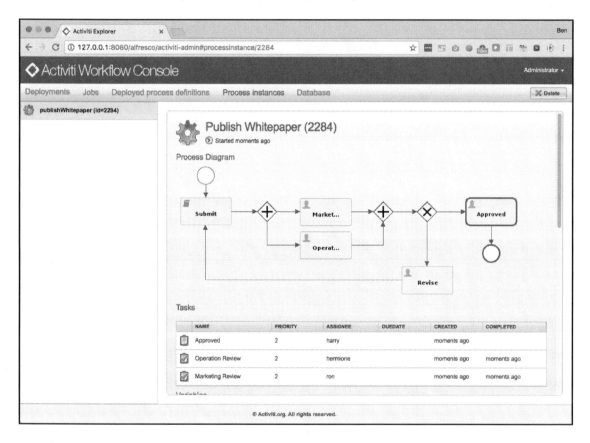

11. Login as the initiator of the workflow, complete the task, and go back to the workflow console. Your process instance should disappear, because it's complete.

In the real world, you'd run several tests as you have to make sure you test every possible path through the workflow. This can be tedious. So if you are doing several complex workflows as part of your project, make sure you allocate enough time to test them adequately. Bumpy workflows are a surefire way to erode user adoption.

If you test this workflow, you'll notice that the workflow always goes to the **Approved** task, even if you click on the **Reject** button on the review tasks. It's because we haven't configured the decision process yet.

Controlling what actions can be taken from the Task Management dialog

The `bpm:packageItemActionGroup` defines what actions are available for working with the content in the workflow at that particular step in the process. The reviewers should not be able to add or remove anything to or from the workflow. The property is set to have read_package_item_actions as the default:

```
<overrides> <property name="bpm:packageItemActionGroup">
<default>read_package_item_actions</default> </property> </overrides>
```

If you login as reviewer and open a task, you should only be able to read the list of documents:

Then, if you login as the initiator of the workflow and open the **Accepted**task, you should be able to add new documents to your process. It's because the default action group is add_package_item_actions:

Other out-of-the box package item action groups include: edit_and_remove_package_item_actions, remove_package_item_actions, and add_package_item_actions.

Enabling the Workflow Initiator to Select Users and Groups

If you have run any of the out-of-the box advanced workflows, you've seen that it is possible to let the workflow initiator select users and/or groups, which are then used to assign tasks. In SomeCo's example, you hardcoded the groups on each task, but doing something user-configurable is easy.

Alfresco's out-of-the box process definitions reside in the JAR file alfresco-repository-5.*.jar located in the web application in the WEB-INF | lib. All process definitions are in the subfolder alfresco | workflow. You'll notice there are a number of processes that don't get deployed out-of-the box although they are defined and ready to use. You can also use the **Activiti Explorer** to get all deployed workflow definitions. Let's look at adhoc.bpmn20.xml to see an example of how initiator-specified user and group assignment works.

There are two things of interest in this file related to how the task assignment works. First, note that the start event is using the form `wf:submitAdhocTask`:

```
<startEvent id="start" activiti:formKey="wf:submitAdhocTask" />
```

You know from the previous examples that there must be a corresponding type in Alfresco's model of the same name. You'll see that soon.

Next, notice that the adhoc **Task** is using an expression. However, instead of using the **Assignee** attribute (as we did before), it's using the `humanPerformer` attribute that is exactly the same thing. The expression will resolve to an association called assignee in the bpm namespace that points to the "person" object being assigned:

```
<userTask id="adhocTask" name="Adhoc Task" activiti:formKey="wf:adhocTask">
<extensionElements> [...] </extensionElements> <humanPerformer>
<resourceAssignmentExpression>
<formalExpression>${bpm_assignee.properties.userName}</formalExpression>
</resourceAssignmentExpression> </humanPerformer> </userTask>
```

Alfresco's workflow model, workflowModel.xml, includes the wf:submitAdhocTask type which includes the aspect bpm:assignee as required aspect. (The association to a user, also called bpm:assignee, lives in the BPM model.)

```
<type name="wf:submitAdhocTask"> <parent>bpm:startTask</parent> ...
<mandatory-aspects> <aspect>bpm:assignee</aspect> </mandatory-aspects>
</type>
```

Step-by-step – use dynamic user assignment

We are going to update our process by allowing the initiator to select a user that will be assigned when the workflow is initiated. Then, the **Approved** task will be assigned to this user.

1. Open the workflow definition with the Activiti Designer.
2. Click on the **Start Event**, open the **Properties** view, open the **Main config** tab and change the value of the **Form key** field with wf:submitReviewTask that contains as well the **bpm:assignee** aspect.
3. Then, click on the **Approved** task, open the **Properties** view, open the **Main config** tab, and change the value of the **Assignee** field with ${bpm_assignee.properties.userName}.

   Save the workflow definition.

   Edit the share-config-custom.xml file, and replace the **config** element with the property **condition** equal to activiti$publishWhitepaper with the following element. The difference between the previous configuration and this one is the displaying of the association bpm:assignee.

```
<config evaluator="string-compare"
    condition="activiti$publishWhitepaper">
<forms>
 <form>
   <field-visibility>
     <show id="bpm:workflowDescription" />
     <show id="bpm:assignee" />
     <show id="packageItems" />
     <show id="transitions" />
   </field-visibility>
   <appearance>
     <set id="" appearance="title"
```

```
        label-id="workflow.set.general" />

    <set id="items" appearance="title"
      label-id="workflow.set.items" />

    <set id="assignee" appearance="title"
      label-id="workflow.set.assignee" />

    <set id="progress" appearance="title"
      label-id="workflow.set.task.progress" />

    <field id="bpm:workflowDescription"
        label-id="workflow.field.message">

      <control template="/org/alfresco/components
        /form/controls/textarea.ftl">

      <control-param name="style">width: 95%</control-param>
      </control>
    </field>
    <field id="bpm:assignee"
      label-id="workflow.field.assign_to" set="assignee" />
    <field id="packageItems" set="items" />
  </appearance>
  </form>
 </forms>
</config>
```

4. Package, deploy, and restart Alfresco.

To test the process, do the following:

1. Login and starts a new workflow on one test Whitepaper.

   You should be able to see a new field called **Assignee** at the bottom of the screen. Click on **Select** and search for one user, and select it:

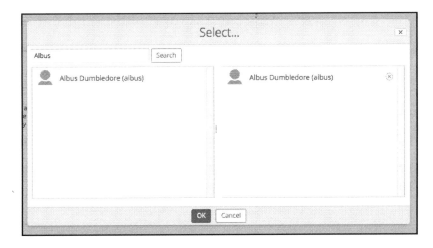

2. Click on **Start Workflow**, and then complete the two review tasks. Then, if you open the **Activiti Explorer**, you'll notice that the **Approved** task is now assigned to the username, **albus** in our case:

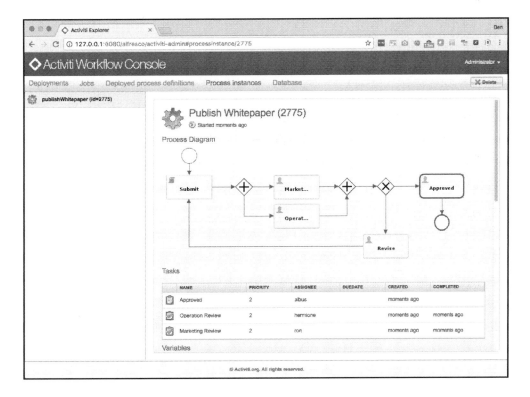

You can set up user and group selection in your own process definitions by following the same pattern.

Adding Logic to Workflows with Listeners and Process Variables

So far you've seen that a process can be modeled as a collection of nodes connected via paths or transitions. A common requirement is to be able to execute some code or business logic at certain points within the process. For example, maybe you want to send an e-mail or want to increment a counter that keeps track of how many times a node has been executed. We already used the concept of service tasks to execute some codes, but now we are going to use event listeners.

An event mechanism has been introduced in Activiti to get notified when various events occur within the engine. In our use case, we are going to focus on the **Task Listener**. A task *listener* is used to execute custom Java logic or an expression upon the occurrence of a certain task-related event. Using the Activiti Designer, you can create listeners on user tasks where you'll be able to configure:

- The event nature: create, assignment, complete, or all.
- The event type: Java class, expression, delegate expression, Alfresco execution script, or Alfresco task script.

We are going to discover some of them in the next section.

Storing Data in Process Variables

Often, there is metadata about a process that needs to be tracked. A due date or a priority flag are two examples. A due date isn't really a property of the content being routed through the workflow-it's a property of the process. Activiti gives us the ability to store this kind of data as part of the running process through process variables.

Process variables are name-value pairs that get persisted with the rest of the process state. To keep it simple, a process instance can have variables (called *process variables*) and user tasks can have variables too. Then, there is a mapping between the properties defined in the content model and Activiti variables. If you look at the out-of-the-box workflow definition adhoc.bpmn20.xml, you'll notice the use of multiple variables related to the content model such as bpm_workflowDueDate, bpm_workflowPriority or wf_notifyMe. All these variables are created automatically by Alfresco and are matched to the values stored by the content model.

Some other variables are provided by Alfresco that you can find on this page http://docs.alfresco.com/5.1/concepts/wf-process-def-node-objects.html. One very important one is the variable called bpm_package. This variable contains associations to the document(s) attached to the current workflow instance. So, you can easily update some properties on attached document along the process.

In the following example, the script element sets an execution variable called scwf_tempCnt equal to 0 when the token enters the node:

```
<extensionElements>
<activiti:taskListener event="create"
class="org.alfresco.repo.workflow.activiti.tasklistener.ScriptTaskListener"
>
<activiti:field name="script"> <activiti:string>
<![CDATA[execution.setVariable('scwf_tempCnt', 0);]]> </activiti:string>
</activiti:field> </activiti:taskListener> </extensionElements> Elsewhere
in the process, you can read the value of the variable with an expression
like: ${scwf_tempCnt}
```

You'll use this kind of syntax on condition in a workflow when you want to implement an exclusive gateway.

Step-by-step – adding logic to the Whitepaper submission workflow

The process you've built so far assigns tasks to the appropriate groups. But you should have noticed during your test that whether the marketing or operations users approved or rejected the content, the workflow always routed to the Approved node. That's because you have yet to add any logic to the process definition. The workflow was simply taking the default transitions.

We didn't configure conditions on any transitions going out from the exclusive gateway, so the first transition defined in the XML file is used. The logic that makes that decision will depend on a process variable. When someone approves the Whitepaper, a counter will get incremented. The condition will check the value. If the counter is equal to 2, both approvals have been received and the workflow can continue down the "happy path". Otherwise, a revision is necessary and so the content should be routed back to the initiator.

The other thing that still needs to be resolved is that once an approval is given, the document needs to be enabled for the Web. In an earlier chapter you wrote an action that sets the web flag and publication date. Now you can benefit from encapsulating that operation into an action by reusing it here. The approved node will use the Alfresco JavaScript API to execute the action.

Implementing this logic involves adding expressions and Alfresco JavaScript to the appropriate events and transitions in the process, and then re-deploying the process definition for testing. To do this, follow these steps:

1. Edit the publishWhitepaper.bpmn20.xml file. You're going to use a counter to keep track of the number of approvals received. You need to be careful to initialize the counter to 0 because it's possible that a Whitepaper may go through several review cycles. The Submit node is a convenient place to do the initialization. Just edit the existing script:

   ```
   logger.log("Submit whitepaper!");
   execution.setVariable("scwf_approveCount", 0);
   ```

   In this case, we create a variable called scwf_approveCount, but we don't define it in our content model. It's not required to prefix it in this case, it's just best practice to prefix all your variables by your custom model prefix.

2. Now you need to increment the counter when the user clicks on **Approve**. By checking the worklowModel.xml file, if you look for the type wf:activitiReviewTask, you'll notice the property,wf:reviewOutcome. This property contains a constraint that allows only the values, **Approve** and **Reject**. It's what drives the displaying of the buttons in Share. We need to create a new listener on the **Marketing Review** task on **complete**. Click on the task, open the **Properties** view, select the tab **Listeners** and click on the button **New**. This script will increment the counter if the user clicked on the **Approve** button:

```
if (task.getVariable('wf_reviewOutcome') == 'Approve')
{
  var newApproveCount= scwf_approveCount+ 1;
  execution.setVariable("scwf_approveCount", newApproveCount);
}
if (newApproveCount>= 2)
{
  execution.setVariable("validated", true);
}
else
{
  execution.setVariable("validated", false);
}
```

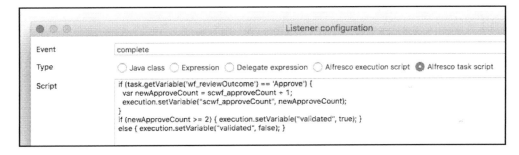

In the previous code, we used the variable validated without prefixing it with scwf. It's something arguable and we could have prefixed it to keep the same convention for all workflow variables that we define.

3. Do the same for the **Operation Review** node.

4. With the counter logic in place, click on the transition between the exclusive gateway and the **Approved** task. Then, open the `Properties` view, open the `Main config` tab, and the following expression to the `Condition` field:

```
${validated}
```

Populate the same field with the following value on the transition between the exclusive gateway and the **Revise** task:

```
${!validated}
```

5. When a Whitepaper is approved, it should have the sc:webable aspect added to it and the isActive and published properties set. The set-web-flag action you wrote in an earlier chapter does just that. So all you have to do is tell the process to execute it for each piece of content in the workflow package using Alfresco JavaScript. We are going to create a new listener on the **Approved** task that will update all attached document. To achieve that, we'll execute the following script on the complete event:

```
var setWebFlagAction = actions.create("set-web-flag");
setWebFlagAction.parameters["active"] = true;
for (var i= 0; i<bpm_package.children.length; i++)
{
    logger.log("Approving whitepaper:"
    + bpm_package.children[i].nodeRef);

    setWebFlagAction.execute(bpm_package.children[i]);
}
```

6. Save the `publishWhitepaper.bpmn20.xml` file. Use the Activiti Explorer to deploy the updated process, and then test it out.

To test out the updated process, start a workflow on a Whitepaper that does not have its isActive flag set to true. In your test, if both approvers approve the content, the workflow should complete successfully and the flag should be set to true. Otherwise, the initiator will get a chance to make revisions or abort the workflow.

Getting access to the content in the workflow

If you open the out-of-the-box `workflowModel.xml`, you should find the `wf:submitReviewTask` type has an ancestor type that adds an association called `bpm:package`. That's what allows the JavaScript in the `Approved` node to iterate over the content that is being routed through the workflow. Always remember that unless you've done something to prevent it, the workflow initiator can add multiple files to a workflow.

Using multi-instances

In the SomeCo example, you created two explicit review task nodes in your process: The `MarketingReview` node's task was assigned to the `Marketing` group and the `OperationsReview` node's task was assigned to the `Operation` group.

But what if, instead, the workflow initiator was able to pick as many actors as thought necessary? There are two out-of-the box processes that show an example of this: `parallel-review-group.bpmn20.xml` and `parallel-review.bpmn20.xml`(the former is for groups, while the latter is for individual users).

These processes use an Activiti concept called multi-instance. A multi-instance *activity* is a way of defining repetition for a certain step in a business process. In programming concepts, a multi-instance matches the **for each** construct. A counter is then used to track how many approvals are obtained, similar to the counter used in the SomeCo example.

Looking at `parallel-review-group.bpmn20.xml`, you can see that the `foreach` is iterating over each person in the selected group. The person will be in a process variable called `reviewAssignee`:

```
<multiInstanceLoopCharacteristicsisSequential="false">
  <loopDataInputRef>wf_groupMembers</loopDataInputRef>
  <inputDataItem name="reviewAssignee" />

  <completionCondition>
    ${wf_actualPercent>= wf_requiredApprovePercent
       || wf_requiredApprovePercent> (100 - wf_actualRejectPercent)}
  </completionCondition>
</multiInstanceLoopCharacteristics>
```

The `reviewTask` user task makes an assignment using the value of the reviewer process variable. When this process is actually running, there will be one task for each person in the group.

```
<humanPerformer>
  <resourceAssignmentExpression>
    <formalExpression>${reviewAssignee}</formalExpression>
  </resourceAssignmentExpression>
</humanPerformer>
```

If the approve transition is taken, the counter will be incremented as well as the approval percentage:

```
<activiti:taskListener event="complete"
class="org.alfresco.repo.workflow.activiti
  .tasklistener.ScriptTaskListener">

  <activiti:field name="script">
    <activiti:string>
      if(task.getVariableLocal('wf_reviewOutcome') == 'Approve')
        {
          var newApprovedCount=wf_approveCount + 1;
          var newApprovedPercentage
            =(newApprovedCount/wf_reviewerCount)*100;
          execution.setVariable('wf_approveCount', newApprovedCount);
          execution.setVariable('wf_actualPercent', newApprovedPercentage);
        }
      else
        {
          var newRejectCount=wf_rejectCount + 1;
          var newRejectPercentage=(newRejectCount / wf_reviewerCount) *
100;
          execution.setVariable('wf_rejectCount', newRejectCount);
          execution.setVariable('wf_actualRejectPercent',
            newRejectPercentage);
        }
    </activiti:string>
  </activiti:field>
</activiti:taskListener>
```

Then, the transition between the exclusive gateway and the **Approved** task will be taken only if the approval percentage is higher than the required approval percentage:

```
<sequenceFlow id='flow3' sourceRef='reviewDecision' targetRef='approved'>
    <conditionExpressionxsi:type="tFormalExpression">
        ${wf_actualPercent>= wf_requiredApprovePercent}
    </conditionExpression>
</sequenceFlow>
```

The use of multi-instance activity is not limited to dealing with assignments. It is a generic construct that could be used any time you need to spawn parallel flows based on a list.

Using the Activiti API

In the previous example, the logic was easily handled by either expressions or JavaScript within the business process. However, there may be cases when Activiti actions are better implemented in Java. For example, there might be an API readily available in Java that isn't available in JavaScript. Or suppose you want to manipulate workflows from outside a business process. Maybe you want to complete tasks, add items to a workflow, or start a workflow from an action, a web script, or a custom dialog. You can use the Activiti Java services or the Alfresco Workflow Service. In our case, we'll use the first option.

The next example gives you a chance to try out both of these scenarios. In one, you're going to write a custom Activti Task Listener. In the other, you are going to use the ActivitiRuntimeService to signal a process.

SomeCo would like to update the Whitepaper submission workflow to optionally include review by an external third party. The third party might be a SomeCo partner, for example, that does not have login credentials for Alfresco, but still needs to be able to approve or reject content. You will give external third parties the ability to approve or reject a task via a URL by writing a web script that uses Alfresco's Workflow Service to signal the node to take the appropriate approve or reject transition.

The third party needs to know they need to review content. Alfresco has a mail action available out-of-the box that could be called from JavaScript. But Java is better suited for grabbing everything needed for the body of the e-mail. So you'll write a custom ActivitiTaskListener class, and then invoke the out-of-the box mail action from there.

Step-by-step – implementing third-party review

Someday there will be an out-of-the box mechanism for exposing business processes to external parties. Until then, you can roll your own using the out-of-the box mail action and web scripts. There are two pieces required to make this work. First, you need a web script that signals the node to take either the approve or reject transition. Second, when the token arrives in the **ThirdPartyReview** node, an e-mail should go to the third party with **approve** and **reject** links. The recipient will open the e-mail and click on either the **approve** link or the **reject** link. Both links are calls to the
same web script-the path that needs to be taken is passed as an argument to the web script.

Implementing this is going to involve:

1. Updating the process definition to include two new exclusive gateways to define if we need a third-party review, and if this review is accepted or rejected. We'll need as well a new task for this external review that we'll design with a **Receive Task**.

2. Updating the workflow model to include a new aspect representing "third-party reviewable" metadata, and a new type for the start task. This also requires corresponding updates to the `share-config-custom.xml` file and the `scWorkflow.properties` file.

3. Writing a web script that figures out the appropriate workflow and then uses the ActivitiRuntimeService from a Java-based controller to take the appropriate transition. This includes configuring the controller as a Spring bean.

4. Writing an ActivitiJavaListener class to compose the email body, and then send it to the third-party recipient using the out-of-the box e-mail action via Alfresco's Action Service.

At the end of this example, SomeCo will be able to involve third parties who know nothing about Alfresco in an Alfresco-managed business process using everyone's favorite knowledge management and collaboration application: e-mail.

To put this in place, follow these steps:

1. First, update the `publishWhitepaper.bpmn20.xml` process definition to include two new exclusive gateways and a new `ReceiveTasknode`. A receive task is a simple task that waits for the arrival of a certain message. The third-party review is optional. The reason we design it like that is that you don't want to bother the third party with a review task if the internal reviewers aren't going to approve the content. Organize the two new gateways and the new receive task following this schema:

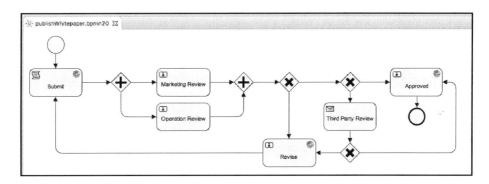

2. Save the process definition for now. You'll return to add logic to the new node in a minute.
3. Edit the
    src | **main** | **amp** | config | alfresco | module | repo | model | scWorkflowModel.xml file. Add the following aspect to track the e-mail address of the third party (be careful, the tag `aspects` needs to be defined after the tag types in the content model, otherwise your model will be invalid):

```xml
<aspects>
  <aspect name="scwf:thirdPartyReviewable">
    <title>Someco Third Party Reviewable</title>
    <properties>
      <property name="scwf:reviewerEmail">
        <type>d:text</type>
        <mandatory>false</mandatory>
        <multiple>false</multiple>
      </property>
    </properties>
  </aspect>
</aspects>
```

4. In the same model, create a new type for the start event that will re-use the aspect defined just previously:

```
<type name="scwf:submitReviewTask">
  <parent>wf:submitReviewTask</parent>
    <mandatory-aspects>
      <aspect>scwf:thirdPartyReviewable</aspect>
    </mandatory-aspects>
</type>
```

5. Now, you need to update your Activiti workflow to match the start event to this new type that we just created. Open the workflow file publishWhitepaper.bpmn20.xml, click on the start event, open the **Properties** view, open the **Main config** tab and specify the type name for the form key:

6. Save the scWorkflowModel.xml file.

7. Edit the repo|src|main|config|alfresco|module|repo|messages|scWorkflow.p roperties file. Add the following model-related strings:

```
scwf_workflowmodel.type.scwf_submitReviewTask.title
=Submit Whitepaper Review Task

scwf_workflowmodel.type.scwf_submitReviewTask.description
=Submit Whitepaper Review Task

scwf_workflowmodel.property.scwf_reviewerEmail.title
=Reviewer email

scwf_workflowmodel.property.scwf_reviewerEmail.description
=Third-party reviewer email address
```

8. Save the scWorkflow.properties file.

9. Edit `share|src|main|resources|META-INF|share-config-custom.xml` and change the `config` tag with the property **condition** equals to `activiti$publishWhitepaper`. In this case, we just add the displaying of the field `scwf:reviewerEmail`:

```xml
<config evaluator="string-compare"
 condition="activiti$publishWhitepaper">
<forms>
  <form>
    <field-visibility>
      <show id="bpm:workflowDescription" />
      <show id="scwf:reviewerEmail" />
      <show id="bpm:assignee" />
      <show id="packageItems" />
      <show id="transitions" />
    </field-visibility>
    <appearance>
      <set id="" appearance="title"
        label-id="workflow.set.general" />
      <set id="items" appearance="title"
        label-id="workflow.set.items" />
      <set id="assignee" appearance="title"
        label-id="workflow.set.assignee" />
      <set id="progress" appearance="title"
        label-id="workflow.set.task.progress" />

      <field id="bpm:workflowDescription"
        label-id="workflow.field.message">

      <control template="/org/alfresco/components
        /form/controls/textarea.ftl">

      <control-param name="style">width: 95%</control-param>
      </control>
    </field>
    <field id="bpm:assignee"
      label-id="workflow.field.assign_to" set="assignee" />

    <field id="scwf:reviewerEmail" set="assignee" />
    <field id="packageItems" set="items" />
  </appearance>
  </form>
</forms>
</config>
```

10. Save the `share-config-custom.xml` file.

11. Now implement the web script. Create a descriptor in `repo|src|main|amp|config|alfresco|extension|templates|webscripts|com|someco|bpm` called `review.get.desc.xml` with the following content:

```
<webscript>
 <shortname>BPM Review</shortname>
 <description>Review and approve a BPM task</description>
 <url>
    /someco/bpm/review?id={idArgument}&amp;action= {transArgument}
 </url>
 <format default="html">extension</format>
 <authentication>guest</authentication>
 <transaction>none</transaction>
</webscript>
```

12. Create a FreeMarker template in the same directory named review.get.html.ftl with HTML that simply echoes back the arguments that were passed in (obviously, SomeCo is going to want to make this a bit friendlier at some point):

```
<html>
 <body>
    <p>Signaled ${args.id} for transition ${args.action}</p>
 </body>
</html>
```

13. Now write the Java controller. Create a new class called `com.someco.repo.scripts.GetReview`. The class extends `DeclarativeWebScript` and has a dependency that will be passed in via Spring, which is the `activitiProcessEngine` bean:

```
package com.someco.repo.scripts;
import java.util.HashMap;
import java.util.Map;
import org.activiti.engine.ProcessEngine;
import org.alfresco.repo.security.authentication
  .AuthenticationUtil;
import org.alfresco.repo.security.authentication
  .AuthenticationUtil.RunAsWork;
import org.apache.log4j.Logger;
import org.springframework.extensions.webscripts
  .DeclarativeWebScript;
import org.springframework.extensions.webscripts.Status;
import org.springframework.extensions.webscripts.WebScriptRequest;
public class GetReview extends DeclarativeWebScript
{
```

```
private ProcessEngine activitiProcessEngine;
private Logger logger = Logger.getLogger(GetReview.class);
protected Map<String, Object>
  executeImpl(WebScriptRequest req, Status status) { }
public void setActivitiProcessEngine(ProcessEngine
  activitiProcessEngine)
{
        this.activitiProcessEngine = activitiProcessEngine;

}
}
```

14. The `executeImpl()` method reads the arguments, then uses the ActivitiRuntimeService to update the value of the execution variable called `scwf_3rdPartyOutcome`, and then signals the workflow. So, for example, if someone were to invoke `http://localhost:8080/alfresco/service/someco/bpm/review?id=1234&action=Approve&guest=true`, the controller would locate the Activiti workflow instance with the ID1234, and then update the variable with the value specified in the **action** parameter, and finally signal the process instance to be able to continue. You'll notice that the `AuthenticationUtil.runAs` method is being used to allow guests to successfully execute the action. Populate the `executeImpl` method with the following code:

```
final String id = req.getParameter("id");
final String action = req.getParameter("action");
if (id == null || action == null)
{
    status.setCode(400);
    status.setMessage("Required data has not been provided");
    status.setRedirect(true);
}
Map<String, Object> model = new HashMap<String, Object>();
model.put("response",
    AuthenticationUtil.runAs(new RunAsWork<String>()
{
    public String doWork() throws Exception
    {
        logger.debug("About to update execution id:"
          + id + " with transition:" + action);

        // Update the variable
        activitiProcessEngine.getRuntimeService()
          .setVariable(id, "scwf_3rdPartyOutcome", action);

        // Signal the execution
        activitiProcessEngine.getRuntimeService().signal(id);
```

```
                    logger.debug("Signal sent."); return "Success";
            }
    }, "admin"));
    return model;
```

15. Save the controller.

16. Java controllers need to be configured as Spring beans. Use the existing `repo|src|main|amp|config|alfresco|module|repo|context|webscript s-context.xml` file to add the bean:

```
    <bean id="webscript.com.someco.bpm.review.get"
      class="com.someco.repo.scripts.GetReview" parent="webscript">

        <property name="activitiProcessEngine"
        ref="activitiProcessEngine" />
    </bean>
```

17. Let's implement the task listener that we'll use on the third-party review task to send the e-mail. Create a new class called `com.someco.repo.bpm.ExternalReviewNotification` that implements `ExecutionListener`. Begin the class as:

```
    package com.someco.repo.bpm;
    import java.io.Serializable;
    import java.util.HashMap;
    import java.util.Map;
    import org.activiti.engine.delegate.DelegateExecution;
    import org.activiti.engine.delegate.ExecutionListener;
    import org.activiti.engine.impl.cfg.*;
    import org.activiti.engine.impl.context.Context;
    import org.alfresco.repo.action.executer.MailActionExecuter;
    import org.alfresco.repo.workflow.activiti.ActivitiConstants;
    import org.alfresco.service.ServiceRegistry;
    import org.alfresco.service.cmr.action.Action;
    import org.alfresco.service.cmr.action.ActionService;
    import org.alfresco.util.UrlUtil;

    public class ExternalReviewNotification
       implements ExecutionListener
    {
        private static final String FROM_ADDRESS = "alfresco@localhost";
        private static final String SUBJECT = "Workflow task requires
action";
        private static final String RECIP_PROCESS_VARIABLE =
"scwf_reviewerEmail";
        @Override public void notify(DelegateExecution execution) throws
Exception
```

```
        {
        }
    }
```

18. The first method that we are going to implement is to get the Alfresco service registry. Basically, it's the entry point to be able to use all Java services provided by Alfresco out-of-the-box. To summarize, you are going to load the process engine configuration (defined in the bean identified by the id `activitiProcessEngineConfiguration` in the file `alfresco|activiti-context.xml` bundled in the `alfresco-repository-5.x.jar`), then we are retrieving a map of services identified in the property beans.

```
protected ServiceRegistry getServiceRegistry()
{
    ProcessEngineConfigurationImpl config
      = Context.getProcessEngineConfiguration();
    if (config != null)
    {
        ServiceRegistry registry =
          (ServiceRegistry) config.getBeans()
          .get(ActivitiConstants.SERVICE_REGISTRY_BEAN_KEY);

        if (registry == null)
        {
            throw new RuntimeException("Service-registry not
present "

            + "in ProcessEngineConfiguration beans, "
            + "expected ServiceRegistry with key"
            + ActivitiConstants.SERVICE_REGISTRY_BEAN_KEY);
        }
        return registry;
    }
    throw new IllegalStateException("No ProcessEngineConfiguration
"

    + "found in active context"); }
```

19. Let's populate the `notify` method. The first thing that you need to do is to retrieve the e-mail address:

```
String recipient = (String)
execution.getVariable(ExternalReviewNotification
    .RECIP_PROCESS_VARIABLE);
```

20. Then, we need to create the mail action provided by Alfresco:

```
ActionService actionService =
   getServiceRegistry().getActionService();

Action mailAction = actionService
   .createAction(MailActionExecuter.NAME);
```

21. We'll use Freemarker to generate the e-mail body. To accomplish that, we need to create a model object that will be passed to the Freemarker template file:

```
Map<String, String> model = new HashMap<String, String>();
model.put("taskName", execution.getCurrentActivityName());
model.put("executionId", execution.getId());
model.put("shareUrl",UrlUtil.getShareUrl(
   getServiceRegistry().getSysAdminParams()));
model.put("alfrescoUrl", UrlUtil.getAlfrescoUrl(
   getServiceRegistry().getSysAdminParams()));
```

You can notice that the method **getSysAdminParams()** is deprecated. We decided to keep it like that. But if you wanted to make it perfectly clean. You'll have extended the `util:map` defined with the id `activitiBeanRegistry` defined in the `activiti-context.xml` and add a new entry to get the service sysAdminParams defined in the file `alfresco|subsystems|sysAdmin|default|sysadmin-parameter-context.xml` in the `alfresco-repository-5.x.jar`.

22. Finally, we have all the required information to send the e-mail:

```
mailAction.setParameterValue(MailActionExecuter.PARAM_SUBJECT,
ExternalReviewNotification.SUBJECT);

mailAction.setParameterValue(MailActionExecuter
.PARAM_TO, recipient);

mailAction.setParameterValue(MailActionExecuter.PARAM_FROM,
   ExternalReviewNotification.FROM_ADDRESS);
```

```
mailAction.setParameterValue(MailActionExecuter.PARAM_TEMPLATE,
"alfresco/module/repo/resources
   /thirdpartyreview-notification.html.ftl");

mailAction.setParameterValue( MailActionExecuter
   .PARAM_TEMPLATE_MODEL, (Serializable) model);

actionService.executeAction(mailAction, null);
```

23. Let's create the Freemarker template. We are not going to be very orginal and re-use one of Alfresco e-mail notification that you can find in theData Dictionary | Email Templates folder. We are not going to display the entire HTML code in the book, but you can find the entire code in the code associated with this chapter. Create a new file called `thirdpartyreview-notification.html.ftl` in the folder `repo | src | main | amp | config | alfresco | module | repo | resources`. The core HTML code looks like the following code. You will notice the re-use of the variables that we defined in the model created in the Java controller:

```
<table cellpadding="0" cellspacing="0" border="0">
   <tr>
    <td>
      <imgsrc="${shareUrl}/res/components/images/task-64.png"
        alt="" width="64" height="64" border="0"
        style="padding-right: 20px;" />
    </td>
    <td>
      <div style="font-size: 22px; padding-bottom: 4px;">
        You have been assigned a task
      </div>
    </td>
   </tr>
</table>
<div style="font-size: 14px; margin: 12px 0px 24px 0px;
  padding-top: 10px; border-top: 1px solid #aaaaaa;">
<p>Hi, </p>
<p>You have been assigned the following task:</p>
<p><b>"${taskName}"</b></p>
<p>Take the appropriate action by clicking one of the
    links below:<p>
<ul>
   <li>
      <a href="${alfrescoUrl}/service/someco/bpm
        /review?id=${executionId}&action=Approve&guest=true">
        Approve
      </a>
```

```
      </li>
      <li>
        <a href="${alfrescoUrl}/service/someco/bpm
        /review?id=${executionId}&action=Reject&guest=true">

          Reject
        </a>
      </li>
    </ul>
    <p>Sincerely,<br /> Alfresco</p>
    </div>
```

24. The last step is to make final updates to the process definition. The first required change is to create a *start* listener on the **Third Party Review** task by referencing the ExternalReviewNotification Java class that we implemented as shown in the following screenshot:

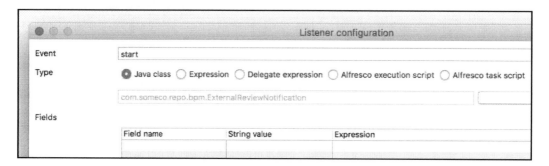

25. Then, we need to add a condition between the exclusive gateway at the exit of the **Third Party Review** task, and the Approved task by using the following condition:

```
${scwf_3rdPartyOutcome == 'Approve'}
```

26. Add another condition to the transition that goes from the same exclusive gateway to the Revise task:

```
${scwf_3rdPartyOutcome == 'Reject'}
```

27. Finally, we need to add more conditions to execute or not the **Third Party Review** task. Click on the transition between the exclusive gateway that goes into the **Third Party Review** task and configure the following condition:

```
${scwf_reviewerEmail!=""}
```

28. Add another condition from the same exclusive gateway to the Approved task:

```
${scwf_reviewerEmail==""}
```

29. Save the process definition.

30. To be able to test, you need first to configure an SMTP server. You can override default properties in your `alfresco-global.properties` file. You can find out all the available properties at `http://docs.alfresco.com/5.1/concepts/email -outboundsmtp-props.html`. However, if you use Alfresco Enterprise, you can use the Administration Console `http://localhost:8080/alfresco/s/enterprise/admin/admin-outboun demail` and update the properties dynamically and test it. Be aware that if you use this tool, the values will be persisted and will take precedence over any values specified in alfresco-global.properties. It can be quite challenging sometimes to keep consistent the Administration console and the property file. If you are a bit confused about which values you should use, you can find the right configuration for GMail, Yahoo, or Zimbra at `https://community.alfresco.com /docs/DOC-4799-outbound-e-mail-configuration`.

31. Package, deploy, and test.

To test this out, launch the workflow on a test Whitepaper. You should be able to configure an e-mail address (if you don't provide any, it will behave as before):

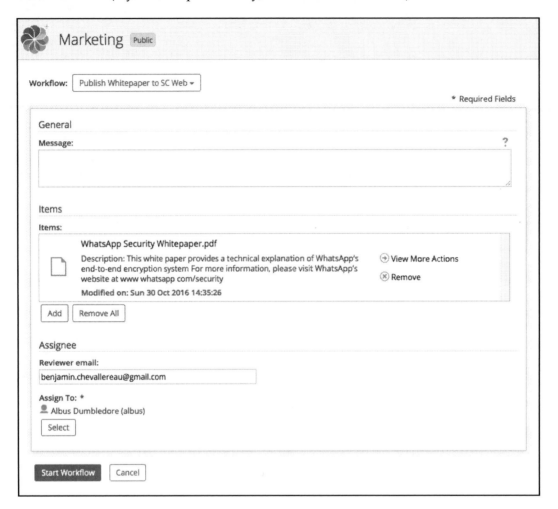

Then, mark both Marketing and Operation reviews as approved. If all goes well, you should get an e-mail that looks like this:

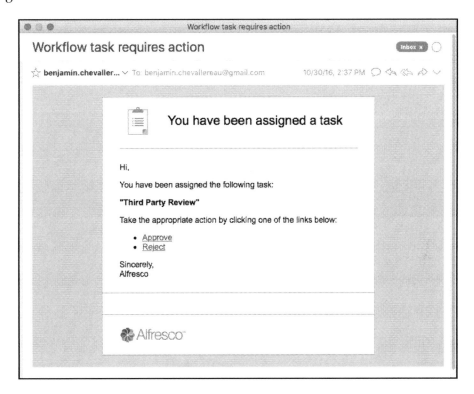

If you open the Activiti Explorer on the relevant workflow instance, you can see that the workflow instance is waiting on the **Third Party Review** task:

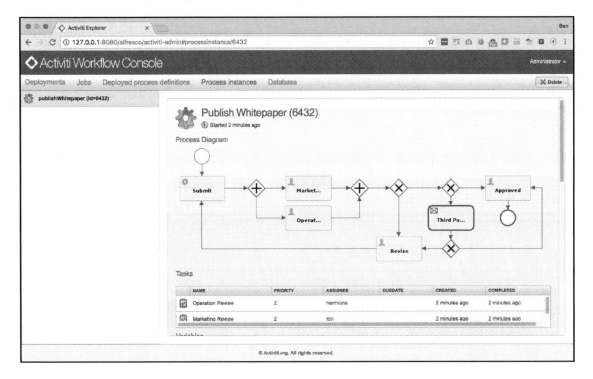

If you click on a link, it should signal the workflow and it should continue on the appropriate path.

Making the third-party review more robust

The third-party review is a good example of wait-state behavior in a process, and shows how web scripts can interact with workflows via the ActivitiJava Service. But there are a few open items that would need to be addressed before you use it in production. Some of these issues include:

- The e-mail recipient doesn't get a copy of the documents being reviewed. One way to address this would be to have the notification action create a ZIP of the documents in the workflow package and then attach that ZIP to the e-mail that gets sent. If you are not a big fan of email attachment, Alfresco can provide a unique URL that anyone can use (no need to authenticate) to access to a document. This URL could be sent in the email body. Another option would be to write additional web scripts to implement a mini-workflow task management user interface that third-party recipients could use to review content and assigned tasks. But then you've moved beyond the simple e-mail interaction into custom client land.
- It'd be really easy for an unauthorized person to signal any node in the system because the controller class doesn't do any validation whatsoever.

In production, you'd want to check that:

- The person making the request is the person assigned to the task
- That the task is still active
- A shared secret of some kind was generated, stored as process metadata, and passed back in as an argument in the URL for validation
- The web script response should be a lot friendlier.

Most of these shortcomings have very little to do with advanced workflows specifically, so they are left up to you to address on your own.

Using timers

Timers are a common requirement for business processes. The most common functionality is around doing something if someone doesn't respond to a task fast enough. That something might be reassigning the task or sending a nasty e-mail to the assignee's boss. Another use might be to purposefully postpone all or part of a process until a specific day and time occurs.

Timer events are events which are triggered by a defined timer. They can be used as a start event, intermediate event, or boundary event. A timer start event is used to create a process instance at given time. A timer boundary event acts as a stopwatch and alarm clock. A timer intermediate event acts as a stopwatch.

Step-by-step – adding a timer to the third-party review

In the previous example, you added the ability for the website submission workflow to incorporate an external third party in the process. SomeCo is glad that its partners will be involved in the process, but it doesn't want them to become an unnecessary bottleneck. To address this, you are going to add a timer to the **Third Party Review** node so that if there is no response after a certain period of time has elapsed, an assumed approval will take place.

Adding a timer is really simple. It involves updating the process definition with the timer tag and redeploying the process. Follow these steps:

1. Edit the `publishWhitepaper.bpmn20.xml` file. After 10 minutes (man, SomeCo has its partners on a short leash!), all attached documents will be automatically considered as approved. Drag and drop `TimerBoundaryEvent` to the **Third Party Review** task as shown in the following figure:

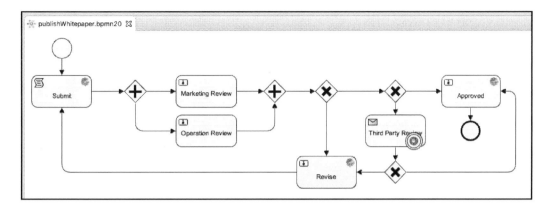

2. Then, create a transition between the timer and the **Approved** task:

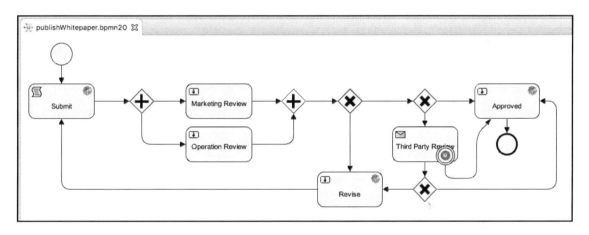

3. Finally, click on the timer and configure the **Time duration** to PT10M. This is a duration syntax using the ISO8601 standard.
4. Save the process, redeploy it using the Activiti Explorer, and then test.

To test the updated process, start a workflow making sure to specify the third-party reviewer e-mail address to trigger the third-party review. After 10 minutes, the approve transition should be taken automatically.

If you prefer not to wait for the countdown to verify that your timer was set correctly, log in to the Alfresco Administration Console, go to the Workflow Console, then type show timers all,and click **Execute**. You should see a response like:

```
id: activiti$7340 , name: 7340 , due date: Sun Oct 30 19:19:37 UTC 2016 ,
path: activiti$7339 , node: thirdParty Review , process: activiti$7199
```

If you don't want to use the **Workflow Console**, you can use the Activiti Explorer too by clicking on the **Jobs** tab. You should notice the same timer job:

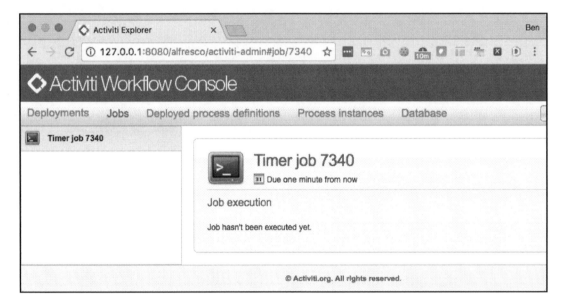

If you select the job and click on the **Execute** button in the top banner, the timer will be considered as expired and the transition to the **Approved** task will be taken.

Debugging workflows

If something goes wrong or you just want to get up close and personal with the execution of a process, you can use the workflow console. The following table shows some common commands and what they do:

Command	What it does
showworkflowsall	Shows all running workflows.
use workflow <workflow id> where <workflow id> is something like activiti$7199	Makes all subsequent commands happen in the context of the specified workflow.
show transitions	Shows all leaving transitions for the current workflow.
signal <path id><transition> where<path id> is something like activiti$71 and <transition> is the name of the leaving transition you want to take. Leave off the transition to take the default.	Signals the token. Good when your workflow is stuck on a node or when you want to take a transition without going through the task management UI.
desc path <path id> where <path id> is something like activiti$71	Dumps the current context. Great for debugging process variables.
end workflow <workflow id>	Cancels the specified workflow.
show definitions all	Shows the current deployed workflow definitions.
undeploy definition <workflow id> or undeploy definition name <workflow name>	Undeploys the specified workflow and stops any workflows running with that definition. The <workflow id> variant undeploys a specific version of a workflow.

These are a subset of the commands available. Type **help** and click **Submit** to see the full list of commands.

Other debug aids include using `logger.log` statements in Alfresco JavaScript actions (with `log4j.logger.org.alfresco.repo.jscript` set to `DEBUG`). You can as well just use logger.warm and you won't have to change the log level.

As mentioned in `Chapter 2`, *Getting Started with Alfresco*, the Eclipse remote debugger is very helpful when trying to troubleshoot Java-based nodes and Java-based listeners.

Comparing Alfresco workflow options

You have now seen how Alfresco leverages the embedded Activiti engine to provide advanced workflow capability. Let's take a look at how advanced workflows compare to simple workflows, so you can make good decisions about which one is more appropriate in a given situation.

Simple workflows are nice end-user tools. Simple workflows use folders and a "forward step/backward step" model to implement serial processes. When a piece of content is dropped in a folder, a rule is triggered that associates a forward step and a backward step (one or the other or both) with the content. These steps are tied to Alfresco actions such as **Set a property** or **Move the content to a specified folder**. End users can then click on the appropriate step for a given piece of content.

For example, suppose there are requirements for a simple submit-review-approve process in which content is submitted, then reviewed, and then approved or rejected. One way to implement this with simple workflows is to use three folders. Let's say they are called **Draft**, **In Review**, and **Approved**, each of which has a rule set that applies a simple workflow. The workflow for content in the **Draft** folder would have a single forward step labeled **Submit**, and its action would move content to the **In Review** folder and send an e-mail to the approver group. The **In Review** folder would have a workflow in which the forward step would be labeled **Approve**, and it would copy the content to an **Approved** folder. The backward step would be labeled **Reject**, and its action would move the content back to the **Drafts** folder.

You can see that simple workflows are useful, but limited with regard to the complexity of the business processes they can handle. A summary of the differences between simple workflows and advanced workflows appears in the following table:

Alfresco simple workflows:	Alfresco advanced workflows:
• Are configurable by non-technical end users via Alfresco Share • Leverage rules, folders, and actions • Can only handle processes with single-step forward and/or backward, or serial flows • Do not support decisions, splits, joins, or parallel flows • Do not maintain state or metadata about the process (you could achieve that using rules and properties, but you'll split the logic in different places)	• Are defined by business analysts and developers via a graphical Eclipse plugin or by writing XML • Leverage the power of the embedded Activiti workflow engine • Can model any business process including decisions, splits, joins, parallel flows, subprocesses, wait states, and timers • Can include business logic written either in JavaScript or Java, either of which can access the Alfresco API (you could simulate that in simple workflows by adding rules on folders) • Maintain state and process variables (metadata) about the process

At the end of the day, simple workflow can be used when you only need to run one workflow on a node at a time and the flow has very little complexity. As the complexity of the process increases the pressure to move to the more full featured BPMN Activiti Engine.

Summary

In this chapter, you learned the following:

- A workflow is a business process and Alfresco embeds the Activiti workflow engine to execute advanced workflows.
- Business process definitions can be created using a text editor or the Activiti Designer.
- Logic can be added to workflows using expressions, JavaScript, and Java.

- Workflows are well suited to long-running processes and can include asynchronous steps triggered by external programs. In the example, you used the ActivitiRuntimeService, Alfresco web scripts, and actions to implement a process involving non-Alfresco users via e-mail.
- Timers can be added to a process using relative or absolute dates. Alfresco's workflow console and Activiti Explorer are handy debugging tools.
- Alfresco's simple workflows are configurable by end users but aren't as powerful or flexible as advanced workflows.

When setting up an advanced workflow for the first time, there are a lot of steps involved because you have to do all the work from mapping the process to custom workflow types. Once the model and Share configuration are in place, additional development iterations on the process tend to move quickly.

The following summarizes the advanced workflow implementation steps:

1. Model the process using the Activiti Designer. Just get the process right-don't worry about node names, listeners, or actions just yet.
2. Add tasks, conditions, and any other necessary assignment logic.
3. Define a workflow content model. If you use a new content model file, remember to update the custom `model-context.xml` file to point to the new content model definition XML file.
4. Update `share-config-custom.xml` to expose workflow tasks to Alfresco Share.
5. Create or update a workflow-specific properties file to externalize the strings in both the workflow model and the process definition.
6. Add logic to gateways, listeners, and transitions using expressions, Alfresco JavaScript, or Java classes.
7. Deploy the process definition using either the Activiti Explorer or by copying the process definition to your module and deploying with a Spring bean configuration file.

9

Amazing Extensions

In this chapter, we are going to cover some extensions, as well as configuration that will show you some amazing capabilities of the Alfresco platform. Be aware that some of them are only available in Alfresco Enterprise. We won't go very deeply into each item, because we just want to open your eyes to Alfresco and let you imagine what you can achieve using it.

Specifically, in this chapter you will learn:

- What the Search Manager is and how you can configure the search result screen by adding your own metadata
- How to use and to configure Smart Folders
- Discover the different methods provided by Alfresco to create your own mobile application
- Create your first application with Appcelerator

Configure and use the search manager

If you do a search in Alfresco Share, using the top right search bar or using the advanced search page, you'll land into the same result page. If you take a look, the search result page displays a left panel with facets. If you click on a value, the list of results will be filtered. By default, this page allows you to filter on:

- Creator
- File Type
- Creation Date
- File Size

- Modifier
- Modification Date

 What's faceted search? Faceted search, also called faceted navigation or faceted browsing, is a technique for accessing information organized according to a faceted classification system, allowing users to explore a collection of information by applying multiple filters. A faceted classification system classifies each information element along multiple explicit dimensions, called facets, enabling the classifications to be accessed and ordered in multiple ways rather than in a single, pre-determined, taxonomic order. (Source: `https://en.wikipedia.org/wiki/Faceted_search`)

Be aware that you can add facets based on your custom content model. If you look at your SomeCo content model, in the `sc:marketingDoc` type, we defined a property called `sc:campaign`, limited by the value constraint `sc:campaignList`. As we may have already discussed, using a constraint to define the campaign list is maybe not the best idea. If you need to add a new campaign, you'll need to change your content model, repackage your module, and redeploy. But it will be enough for our use case.

1. First, we need to change our SomeCo content model to change the indexing of this property. By default, string values are tokenized and then indexed. We won't go into too much detail. For our use case, we want to have a filter listing the complete values, and not partial words. Open your custom content model, `scModel.xml` and locate the `sc:campaignproperty`. Replace the definition with this one (where we specify that we don't want to tokenize the value):

```xml
<property name="sc:campaign">
   <type>d:text</type>
   <multiple>true</multiple>
   <index enabled="true">
       <atomic>true</atomic>
       <stored>false</stored>
       <tokenised>false</tokenised>
       <facetable>true</facetable>
   </index>
   <constraints>
       <constraint ref="sc:campaignList" />
   </constraints>
</property>
```

This kind of change has to be done very carefully. We are changing the way how this property is going to be indexed. If you already have your project in production, you need to clearly understand the impact of this change. In our case, we don't really care because we are still in the development phase.

2. Stop Alfresco, package, and redeploy, but don't restart yet.
3. We just changed the indexing configuration. So, we need to re-index the document already indexed. First, we are going to delete the indexes. Login to your console and execute the following command:

```
rm -rf /opt/alfresco-one/alf_data/solr4/index
```

4. Then, we are going to delete the copy of the model that Solr is storing. It will force Solr to refresh its list of models:

```
rm -rf /opt/alfresco-one/alf_data/solr4/model/*.xml
```

5. Restart Alfresco.
6. Login to Alfresco Share as **Search Manager**. By default, the user admin is a search manager. If you want to give this role to other users, add them to the ALFRESCO_SEARCH_ADMINISTRATORS populate the form with the group.
7. Type the * character in the search field in the top banner, and then **Enter**. You will be redirected to the search result page.

8. Click on **Search Manager**. You should have access to the following page:

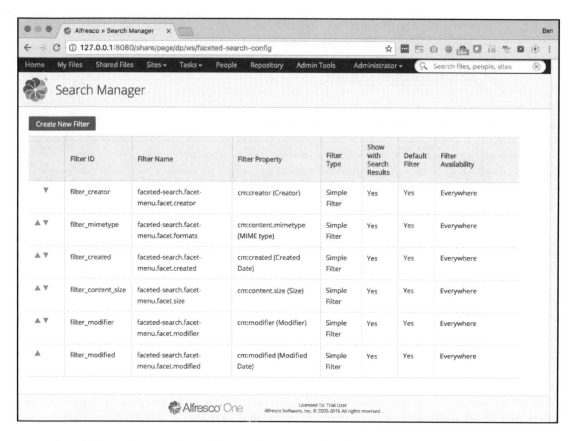

9. Click on **Create New Filter** and populate the form with the following values:

- **Filter ID**: `filter_campaign`
- **Filter Name**: `Campaign`
- **Filter Property**: `sc:campaign`
- **Filter Availability**: `Marketing site`

Filter Availability: `Marketing site` is optional. We assume that all our Marketing documents are in the Marketing site, so we don't want to display this filter to the Operation team.

10. Then, click on the upward triangle to the left of our new facet repeatedly until it is the top item.
11. To be able to test, open the Marketing site, type something in the search field, and type on **Enter**.
12. When the search results page appears, you should see the **Campaign** filter at the top of the list as shown below:

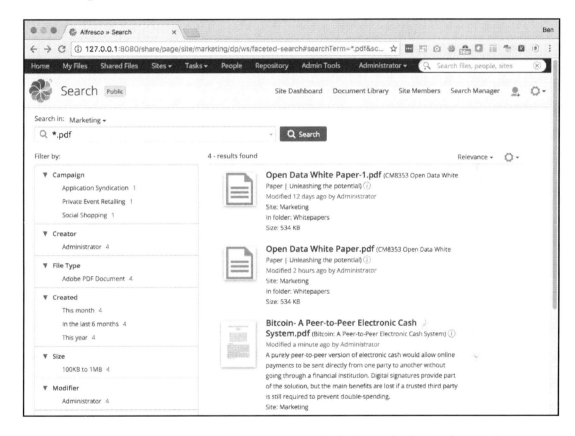

Facet searches are very appreciated by users. It really helps to find the relevant documents using a combination of full text search (or advanced search) and multiple filters. As you can see, this configuration is extremely easy to apply.

Configure and use the Smart Folders

Alfresco provides a way to do smart virtual classification. **Smart Folders** organize all your documents and folders to be able to view them based on types, properties, or document type. Smart Folders are bundled as a core element of Alfresco, so there is no need to install any separate AMP in your instance. Using Smart Folders in this way helps you to manage your information; for example, where you have a number of sources of information in a variety of folders. Content that might be related to, but not directly involved in your work is also retrieved, depending on the search criteria. Let's discover some terms that you need for fully understanding how it works:

- **Filing rule**: Defined in a Smart Folder template and defines in which physical folder a document will be moved when a user attempts to upload a document to a Smart Folder. The rule specifies the type and aspects to apply with all relevant property values as well.
- **Smart Folder**: Displays the result of a search query using the same view as the traditional browse capabilities. A smart folder can contain child smart folders.
- **Smart Folder Template**: A JSON file stored in the Alfresco repository in the `Repository | DataDictionary | Smart Folder Templates` folder.

Let's jump to the configuration and see what we can do.

1. Even if this mechanism is included in Alfresco out-of-the-box, it's disabled by default. Stop Alfresco, and edit your `alfresco-global.properties` file located in the `opt | alfresco-one | tomcat | shared | classes` folder and change the property called `smart.folders.enabled`:

   ```
   smart.folders.enabled=true
   ```

2. Restart Alfresco, login to **Alfresco Share** and upload some documents using different file types.

3. Let's add some categories to some documents. To do that for a few documents, click on the **Manage Aspects** action and add the **Classifiable (cm:generalclassifiable)** aspect. When it's done, click on **Edit Properties**. You should now be able to link your document with the out-of-the-box categories bundled in Alfresco:

4. Finally, add the tag **Confidential** to some documents as well. Then, your documents should look like this one after having attached categories and tags:

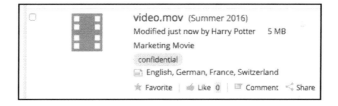

5. Click on **My Files** in the top banner, create a folder called **Documents**, click on **Manage Aspects** and add the **System Smart Folder (smf:systemConfigSmartFolder)** aspect.

6. Now, you need to attach this folder to a **Smart Folder Template**. For the moment, we are going to use the only default one provided by Alfresco. On the newly created folder, click on **Edit Properties**, click on **All Properties...** Be sure that you select the `smartFoldersExample.json` file in the **Smart Folder Template** field:

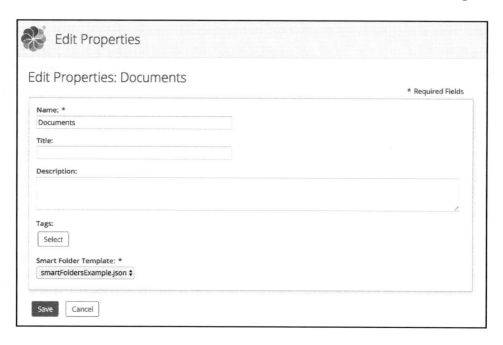

7. Open the **Documents** folder, you should see a sub-folder called **My Content**. This is a **Smart Folder** and you can confirm it because the icon contains a magnifying glass. If you expand this folder, you'll see the full hierarchy:

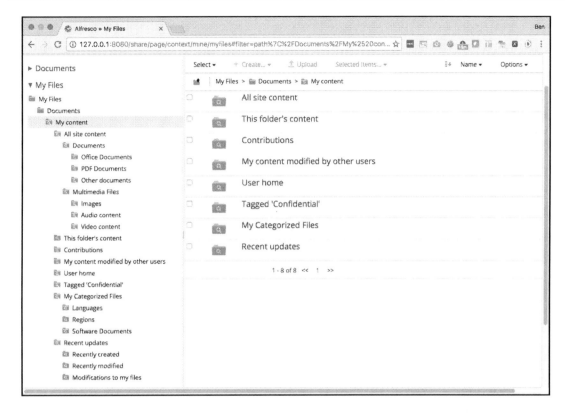

8. I'm not going to explain the goal of each folder because the folder names are quite self-explanatory. So, let's open the `smartFoldersExample.json` file stored in the `Data Dictionary | Smart Folder Templates` repository folder. The first thing that you notice is that you can define a strong hierarchy not based on any query:

```
{
  "name": "Virtual Folders Example",
  "nodes": [
    {
      "id": "1",
      "name": "My content",
      "description": "My files in this repository",
      "nodes": [
        {
          "id": "11",
          "name": "All site content",
          "description":
            "My files in all sites by file & media-type
```

```
             - no upload",
        "nodes": [
          {
            "id": "111",
            "name": "Documents",
            "description": "My documents by mimetype",
            "nodes": [
                ...
            ]
          },
          {
            "id": "112",
            "name": "Multimedia Files",
            "description": "My media files by mediatype",
            "nodes": [
                ...
            ]
          }
        ]
      },
      {
        "id": "12",
        "name": "This folder's content",
        "description":
          "My files in this site or folder tree by file
          & media-type - no upload",
        "nodes": [
          {
            "id": "121",
            "name": "Documents",
            "description": "My documents by mimetype",
            "nodes": [
                ...
            ]
          },
          {
            "id": "122",
            "name": "Multimedia Files",
            "description": "My media files by mediatype",
            "nodes": [
                ...
            ]
          }
        ]
      },
      {
        "id": "17",
        "name": "My Categorized Files",
```

```
        "description":
          "My files in category or a sub category - no upload",
        "nodes": [
          ...
        ]
      },
      {
        "id": "18",
        "name": "Recent updates",
        "description": "Files added or updated in the
          past 7 days",
        "nodes": [
          ...
        ]
      }
    ],
    ...
  }
  ]
}
```

9. Then, let's look at a node where a query is executed. Here is the node that displays all Office Documents stored in sites with the current user as modifier or creator. You can see the use of the %CURRENT_USER% variable that makes the query dynamic for each user:

```
{
  "id": "1111",
  "name": "Office Documents",
  "search": {
    "language": "fts-alfresco",
    "query": "(PATH:'/app:company_home/st:sites//*')
      AND (=cm:content.mimetype:application/ms* OR
          =cm:content.mimetype:application/vnd.ms* OR
          =cm:content.mimetype:application/vnd.openxmlformats*)
      AND (=cm:modifier:%CURRENT_USER% OR
        =cm:creator:%CURRENT_USER%)"
  }
}
```

10. If you tested by yourself, you can see that you have another folder called Office Documents as a subfolder of This folder's content. This folder categorizes only documents stored in the Documents folder that you created manually. Let's check its definition. You can seethe use of the %ACTUAL_PATH% variable that makes the query dynamic for each folder:

```
{
  "id": "1211",
  "name": "Office Documents",
  "search": {
    "language": "fts-alfresco",
    "query": "(PATH:'%ACTUAL_PATH%//*')
      AND (=cm:content.mimetype:application/ms* OR
        =cm:content.mimetype:application/vnd.ms* OR
        =cm:content.mimetype:application/vnd.openxmlformats*)
      AND (=cm:modifier:%CURRENT_USER% OR
        =cm:creator:%CURRENT_USER%)"
  }
}
```

11. I'll let you check node with the id attribute equals to 16 by yourself to see how we use tags, and the nodes 171, 172, and 173 to check how we use categories in the queries. Let's focus on node 181 that shows the Recently Created documents for the current user. You can see that you can do some date/time manipulation to make your queries dynamic:

```
{
  "id": "181",
  "name": "Recently created",
  "description": "Files I recently created",
  "search": {
      "language": "fts-alfresco",
      "query": "+TYPE:'cm:content'
    AND =cm:creator:%CURRENT_USER%
    AND +cm:created:[NOW/DAY-7DAYS TO NOW/DAY+1DAY]"
  }
}
```

12. Before creating our own template, let's talk about one last element. You may have noticed that the upload capabilities (the upload button and the drag and drop) are disabled on all smart folders in this example, except one which is `Documents | MyContent | Contributions`. The corresponding rule is the same as the node executing the query but a filling rule is defined in the `filling` object. The filling rule specifies where the document should be physically stored. In this case, it's using the `%ACTUAL_PATH%` variable. It means that the uploaded documents will be stored in the `Documents` folder. Then, we have a `classification` object describing which content type and aspects should be applied to the new document. And finally, we have a `properties` object listing all metadata that should be assigned to the new document:

```
{
  "id": "13",
  "name": "Contributions",
  "description": "My 'dublin core' contributions
    - add new files here to contribute",
  "search": {
    "language": "fts-alfresco",
    "query": "+ASPECT:'cm:dublincore'
        AND (=cm:creator:%CURRENT_USER% OR
        =cm:modifier:%CURRENT_USER%)"
  },
  "filing": {
    "path": "%ACTUAL_PATH%",
    "classification": {
        "type": "cm:content",
        "aspects": [
          "cm:dublincore"
        ]
      },
    "properties": {
        "cm:contributor": "%CURRENT_USER%",
        "cm:rights": "Alfresco",
        "cm:publisher": "Alfresco"
    }
  }
}
```

If you upload a document and you check the properties, you'll see the properties dynamically assigned:

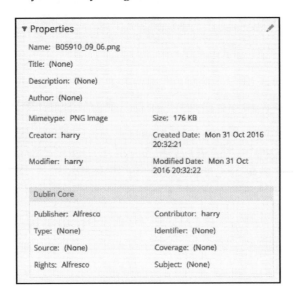

Step-by-step – create your own Smart Folder template

If you remember, all SomeCo Marketing documents can be attached to one or more campaign, and the SomeCo whitepaper type inherits from this content type. Then, we worked on making whitepaper active or not, with a publication date. Finally, we worked on whitepaper ratings. We are going to use all those elements to create a custom Smart Folder Template.

1. Create a file called `SomeCoWhitepapers.json`. You can create it anywhere, because we'll upload it later in the repository. We created a copy of it in the `repo | src | main | amp | config | alfrescp | module | repo | resources` folder. Let's start with the main structure:

```
{
    "name": "SomeCo Marketing Virtual Folders",
    "nodes": [
    ]
}
```

2. For the next steps, we'll add all virtual folders to the `nodes` array. The first one will just list all whitepapers in the containing folder:

```
{
  "id": "1",
  "name": "All Whitepapers",
  "description": "List all whitepapers in this folder",
  "search": {
    "language": "fts-alfresco",
    "query": "(PATH:'%ACTUAL_PATH%//*') AND TYPE:'sc:whitepaper'"
  }
},
```

3. Then, we'll create a folder called `By Campaign` and create a subnode for each campaign listed in the content model:

```
{
  "id": "2",
  "name": "By Campaign",
  "description": "Whitepapers by campaign",
  "nodes": [
    {
      "id": "21",
      "name": "Application Syndication",
      "search": {
        "language": "fts-alfresco",
        "query": "(PATH:'%ACTUAL_PATH%//*')
        AND TYPE:'sc:whitepaper'
        AND sc:campaign:'Application Syndication'"
      }
    },
    {
      "id": "22",
      "name": "Private Event Retailing",
      "search": {
        "language": "fts-alfresco",
        "query": "(PATH:'%ACTUAL_PATH%//*')
        AND TYPE:'sc:whitepaper'
        AND sc:campaign:'Private Event Retailing'"
      }
    },
    {
      "id": "23",
      "name": "Social Shopping",
      "search": {
        "language": "fts-alfresco",
        "query": "(PATH:'%ACTUAL_PATH%//*')
```

```
            AND TYPE:'sc:whitepaper'
            AND sc:campaign:'Social Shopping'"
        }
      }
   ]
},
```

4. The following folder is to find whitepapers by status:

```
{
  "id": "3",
  "name": "By Status",
  "description": "Whitepapers by status",
  "nodes": [
    {
      "id": "31",
      "name": "Published",
      "search": {
        "language": "fts-alfresco",
        "query": "(PATH:'%ACTUAL_PATH%//*')
        AND TYPE:'sc:whitepaper' AND sc:isActive:true"
      }
    },
    {
      "id": "32",
      "name": "Not Published",
      "search": {
        "language": "fts-alfresco",
        "query": "(PATH:'%ACTUAL_PATH%//*')
            AND TYPE:'sc:whitepaper'
            AND ( sc:isActive:false OR ISNULL:'sc:isActive' )"
      }
    }
  ]
},
```

5. As we discovered in the default example in Alfresco, we can use filters on dates. We'll use that to create filters on the publication date:

```
{
  "id": "4",
  "name": "By Publication Date",
  "description": "Whitepapers by publication date",
  "nodes": [
    {
      "id": "41",
      "name": "Yesterday",
      "search": {
```

```
              "language": "fts-alfresco",
              "query": "(PATH:'%ACTUAL_PATH%//*')
           AND TYPE:'sc:whitepaper'
           AND sc:isActive:true
           AND sc:published:[NOW/DAY-1DAY TO NOW/DAY+1DAY]"
         }
       },
       {
         "id": "42",
         "name": "Last Week",
         "search": {
           "language": "fts-alfresco",
           "query": "(PATH:'%ACTUAL_PATH%//*')
           AND TYPE:'sc:whitepaper'
           AND sc:isActive:true
           AND sc:published:[NOW/DAY-7DAYS TO NOW/DAY+1DAY]"
         }
       },
       {
         "id": "43",
         "name": "Last 2 Weeks",
         "search": {
           "language": "fts-alfresco",
           "query": "(PATH:'%ACTUAL_PATH%//*')
           AND TYPE:'sc:whitepaper'
           AND sc:isActive:true
           AND sc:published:[NOW/DAY-14DAYS TO NOW/DAY+1DAY]"
         }
       }
     ]
   },
```

6. And finally, the last one is about user ratings:

```
   {
     "id": "5",
     "name": "By Rate",
     "description": "Whitepapers by rate",
     "nodes": [
       {
         "id": "51",
         "name": "Between 0 and 1",
         "search": {
           "language": "fts-alfresco",
           "query": "(PATH:'%ACTUAL_PATH%//*')
             AND TYPE:'sc:whitepaper'
             AND sc:isActive:true
             AND sc:averageRating:[0 TO 1]"
```

```
          }
        },
        {
          "id": "52",
          "name": "Between 1 and 2",
          "search": {
            "language": "fts-alfresco",
            "query": "(PATH:'%ACTUAL_PATH%//*')
              AND TYPE:'sc:whitepaper'
              AND sc:isActive:true
              AND sc:averageRating:[1 TO 2]"
          }
        },
        {
          "id": "53",
          "name": "Between 2 and 3",
          "search": {
            "language": "fts-alfresco",
            "query": "(PATH:'%ACTUAL_PATH%//*')
            AND TYPE:'sc:whitepaper'
            AND sc:isActive:true
            AND sc:averageRating:[2 TO 3]"
          }
        },
        {
          "id": "54",
          "name": "Between 3 and 4",
          "search": {
            "language": "fts-alfresco",
            "query": "(PATH:'%ACTUAL_PATH%//*')
              AND TYPE:'sc:whitepaper'
              AND sc:isActive:true
              AND sc:averageRating:[3 TO 4]"
          }
        },
        {
          "id": "55",
          "name": "Between 4 and 5",
          "search": {
            "language": "fts-alfresco",
            "query": "(PATH:'%ACTUAL_PATH%//*')
            AND TYPE:'sc:whitepaper'
            AND sc:isActive:true
            AND sc:averageRating:[4 TO 5]"
          }
        }
      ]
    }
```

7. We are done with our JSON file and it is now complete. Upload this file in the `Data Dictionary | Smart Folder Templates` repository folder. Click on this document and change the type to **Smart Folder Template**.

8. I've been a bit messy and stored all my whitepapers in a folder called Whitepapers in my **Marketing** site. But this is the perfect occasion to demonstrate the use of Smart Folders. Add the **System Smart Folder (smf:systemConfigSmartFolder)** aspect to the `Whitepapers` folder. Update properties and select the JSON file that we created:

9. Expand the folder and you should discover all virtual folders that we defined:

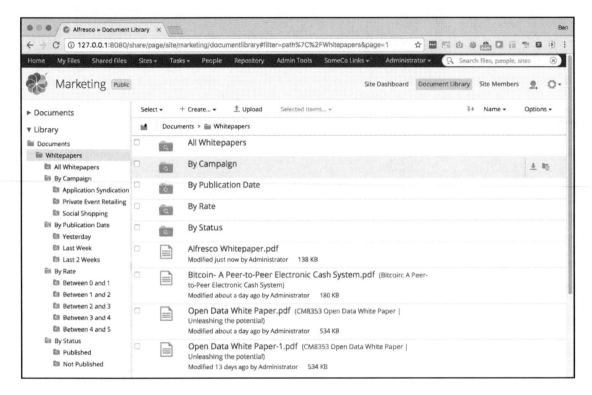

10. You'll notice that all upload capabilities are disabled. It's because we didn't define any filling rules. The first one that we'll create is on the node with the `id` property equals to `1`. The filling rule will change the type and add some aspects. This is not really required because we already have a rule on the folder. If you want to be sure that it works, you can remove these actions from the rule. The filling rule should look like this one and be added as a sibling of the `search` object (don't forget the comma):

```
"filing": {
  "path": "%ACTUAL_PATH%",
  "classification": {
    "type": "sc:whitepaper",
    "aspects": [
        "sc:webable",
        "sc:rateable"
    ]
  }
}
```

11. Then, we are going to add a filling rule for each campaign. The only difference is that we populate the `sc:campaign` property. This is the rule for the Application Syndication**campaign**:

```
"filing": {
  "path": "%ACTUAL_PATH%",
  "classification": {
    "type": "sc:whitepaper",
    "aspects": [
        "sc:webable",
        "sc:rateable"
      ]
  },
  "properties": {
    "sc:campaign": "Application Syndication"
  }
}
```

12. Now, you should be able to add the filing rule for the other two campaigns.

13. Save the JSON file and upload the new version in Alfresco Share.

14. That's it. You can now test by yourself.

Smart Folder is a very powerful tool for creating a dynamic folder hierarchy, and helps users find their documents more easily. Using the JSON structure, it's very easy to add or remove virtual folders and it's completely dynamic. Be aware that Smart Folders can use metadata inheritance. In our example, we defined the value of each campaign in the filing rule. In some use cases, you want to get the value from the physical folder (in our case the folder Marketing). If you are looking for more information, you can check the following page:

```
http://docs.alfresco.com/5.1/concepts/sf-intro.html
```

Alfresco mobile

Accessing documents on the go becomes more and more vital for a lot of companies. Providing a web application is not enough anymore, assuming that employees will use their laptop connected to Internet. Now, we need to access information or to interact with the repository directly from smartphones or tablets.

Alfresco already provides an iOS app and an Android app completely free. But some clients want to customize their application completely. From the logo, or the app name, to the type of documents that can be seen, or the possible actions, everything should be customizable. Alfresco provides you a lot of options to achieve that:

- **Alfresco Mobile SDK for Android**: Includes a set of APIs and samples that will simplify the development of your own app. Using these artifacts, you can build an application that connects to your Alfresco instance on-premises or Alfresco Cloud.
  (`http://docs.alfresco.com/mobile_sdk/android/concepts/mobile-sdk-android-intro.html`)

- **Alfresco Mobile SDK for iOS**: Alfresco provides the same facility if you want to develop an iOS application.
  (`http://docs.alfresco.com/mobile_sdk/ios/concepts/mobile-sdk-ios-intro.html`)

If you don't want to start from scratch, you can use samples provided in each SDK, but if you just want to make a slight change in the existing app, you can obtain the source code for the Android and iOS apps on GitHub:

- `https://github.com/Alfresco/alfresco-android-app`
- `https://github.com/Alfresco/alfresco-ios-app`

Finally, Alfresco provides another SDK for Appcelerator (`http://www.appcelerator.com/`). This is an open source framework allowing the development of mobile applications in JavaScript and then package them for iOS, Android, or Windows Phone. We are going to use this framework in this tutorial to create our first Application.
(`http://docs.alfresco.com/mobile_sdk/appcelerator/concepts/mobile-sdk-appcelerator-intro.html`)

The next section will be based on MAC OS Sierra. It means that some screens, instructions, and folders may be different if you use a different OS. You'll need a Mac if you want to build iOS applications, if you are working on another OS, just stick to Android. If you use a Mac, you'll need to have Xcode installed on your computer. Refer to the Alfresco documentation if you have any questions by following the link above.

Step-by-step – import and run the Alfresco Sample UI

In this section, we are going to discover the Appcelerator development environment and how to configure it with the Alfresco SDK. Then, we'll import the sample application provided by Alfresco and run it on an iPhone.

1. The first thing that we need to do is to download **Appcelerator Studio**. You'll need to sign up to Appcelerator if you don't have an account yet (`http://www.appcelerator.com/signup/`). When you are logged in, you should access this page:

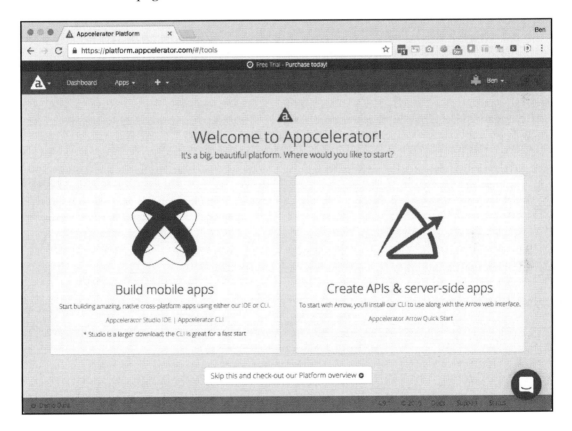

2. Click on **Appcelerator Studio IDE** in the **Build mobile apps**panel. Download the right version depending on your operating system.

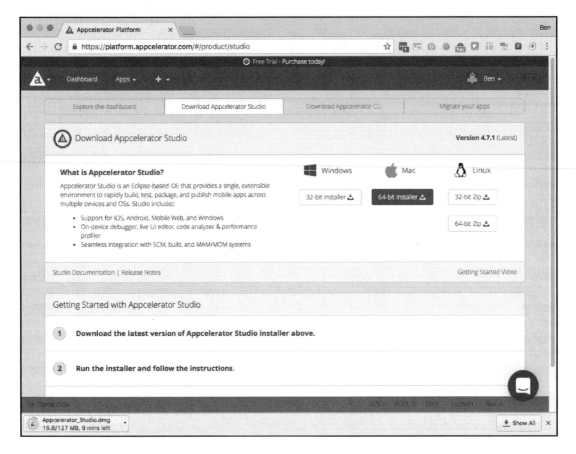

3. Then, follow the relevant instructions depending on your operating system:
   http://docs.appcelerator.com/platform/latest/#!/guide/Installing_Studi
   o

4. When it's installed, start **Appcelerator Studio**. Please note that the screens may be slightly different if you don't use the same operating system. These instructions are based on MAC OS Sierra. The first task is to decide where you want to store your project by selecting a workspace folder:

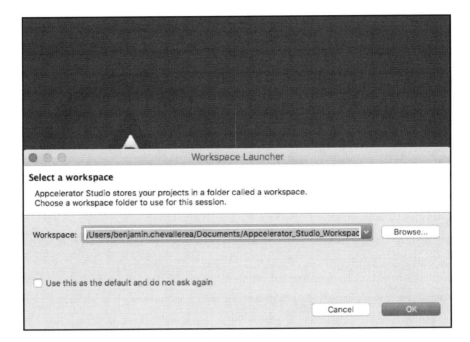

5. Authenticate your Appcelerator account. Then, you'll receive an e-mail with an authorization code. Use this code when Appcelerator asks for it after the authentication.

6. At the first startup of the studio, you may have a window asking you to install the **Titanium SDK**. This is required for us to be able to create our application. Click on **Install**:

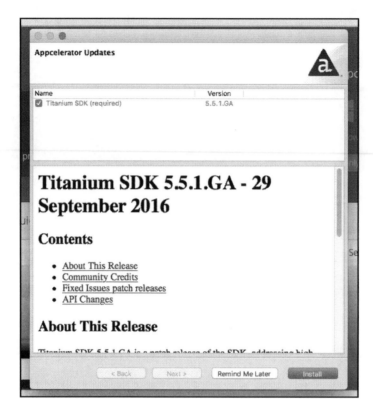

7. When the SDK is installed, you need to download the sample project provided by Alfresco. Open the following URL:
   `https://github.com/Alfresco/alfresco-appcelerator-sdk`. Click on **Clone or download**, and then click on **Download ZIP**:

8. When it's downloaded, unzip this file wherever you want. You should notice a folder called **AlfrescoUI**. This is the folder that contains the sample project. Open Appcelerator Studio, and click on **File** | **Import**. Then, select **Appcelerator** | **Existing Mobile Project**:

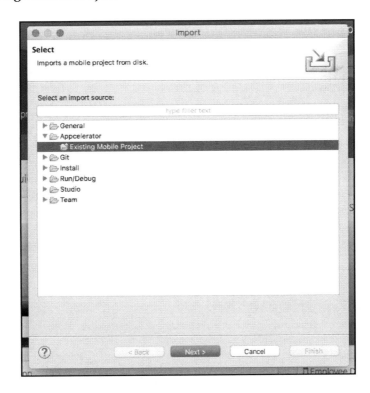

9. In the **Project directory** field, look for the **AlfrescoUI** folder that we extracted in the previous step. Click on **Finish**. You should have a new project in the **Project Explorer** view:

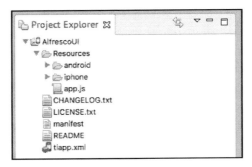

10. Before you are able to run this project, you need to install the SDK on your system. Open the following URL: https://github.com/Alfresco/alfresco-appcelerator-sdk/releases, and download the SDK for Android and iOS. The current release at the time of writing is 1.2. Download the `com.alfresco.appcelerator.module.sdk-android-1.2.zip` and `com.alfresco.appcelerator.module.sdk-iphone-1.2.zip` ZIP files.

11. After downloading these two modules, you need to install them in Appcelerator. Click on **Help** | **Install Mobile Menu…** Select each ZIP file, and then pick**Titanium SDK** as Output Location. Finally, click on **OK**. Follow the same procedures for both ZIP files.

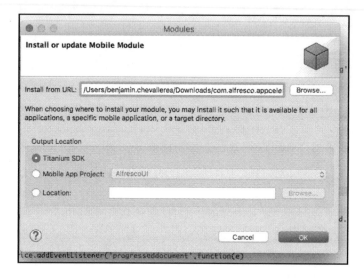

12. We need to define an icon for our application. Of course, you can use any icon. Appcelerator recommends using a 1024 x 1024 pixels image. If you have no idea, just go to `https://www.iconfinder.com/`, and look for free icons or get the Alfresco logo here–`https://devproducts.alfresco.com/images/alfresco-icon.png`. The maximum resolution on this website is 512 x 512 pixels. Just download a free icon in PNG format using the maximum resolution. Save the icon at the root of the project, and name it `DefaultIcon.png`.

13. Now, you are ready to run the project. Right-click on the **AlfrescoUI** project, and click on **Run As**. Then, select the target platform that you want to test. We are selecting **iPhone 6**. You may have the following error message, if this is the case, start **XCode** and accept the license.

```
[ERROR] :Xcode EULA has not been accepted.
[ERROR] :  Launch Xcode and accept the license.
```

14. First, you may need to zoom out by clicking on **Window** | **Scale**. Then, you should see something like this simulator:

15. If your Vagrant machine is up and running, click on **Log in**. You should see the list of folders and documents at the root of your repository:

16. Finally, if you browse to the folder that contains your whitepapers (for example `Sites` | `marketing` | `Whitepapers`). You should be able to see all your documents and folders, as well as all virtual folders that we created in the previous section:

In this section, we discovered how to install Appcelerator studio, import the two SDKs provided by Alfresco, import the Sample UI application developed by Alfresco, and run it in a simulator. But we want to go a bit further than that and build our own application. Our application is going to be quite simple and allows everyone to access published whitepapers. Of course, this is not a book about Appcelerator or mobile development. We just want to show you how to use the `SearchService` available in the Alfresco SDK and develop your own app.

Step-by-step – create SomeCo mobile application

The `SampleUI` application is what we call a *classic* mobile application in the Appcelerator Studio. It means that the entire application is built from the JavaScript file called `app.js`. It contains the logic as well as the code that builds the UI. The Titanium SDK introduced a new framework called **Alloy**. Using it, you separate UI rendering and logic. You can build your UI using XML and a CSS-like syntax called TSS for style. Your JavaScript code contains only the logic of your application. To summarize, Alloy is a very useful framework for implementing a MVC (Model-View-Controller) approach. Don't forget that, even if you use XML and TSS, the SDK will compile everything in JavaScript, as you would do without using Alloy.

1. Let's create your new project. Click on **File** | **New** | **Mobile App Project**. Select **Alloy** on the left side, and pick **Default Alloy Project**. Then, click on **Next**:

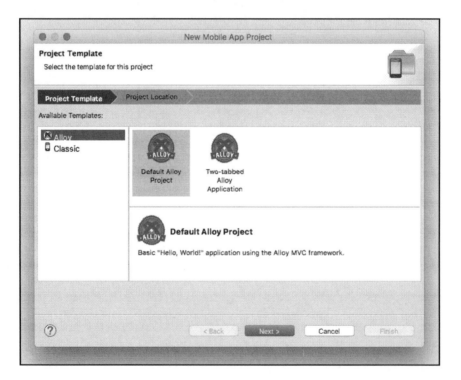

2. Specify `SomeCoWhitepapers` as **Project Name**, and `com.someco.whitepapers` for the **App Id**. Then, just leave all other options at the defaults and click on **Finish**:

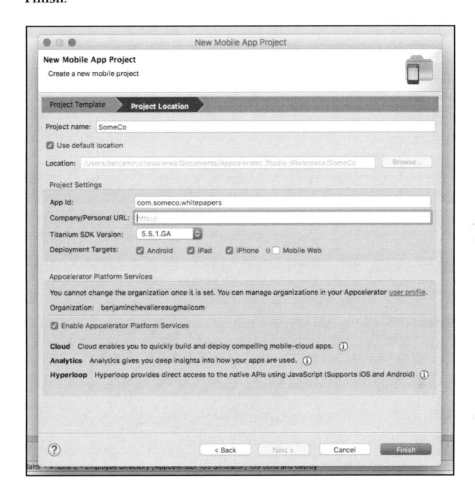

3. It should open the `tiapp.xml` file automatically. The first action is to add the Alfresco SDK module in our project. In the top-right corner, you should find a panel called **Modules** containing all registered modules in this project. By default, there is only `ti.cloud` module. Click on the Plus icon, and look for `*alfresco*`:

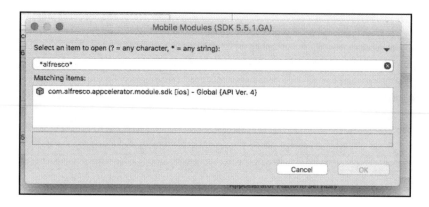

4. Select the Alfresco SDK, click on **OK** and save your file.
5. Another file should be opened by default after the creation of the project called `app | views | index.xml`. So far, it should just contain a Hello World label. We want to implement a list of items that contains all whitepapers. Replace the content with this code:

```
<Alloy>
  <Window class="container">
    <ListView id="elementsList"
      defaultItemTemplate="elementTemplate">
      <Templates>
        <ItemTemplate name="elementTemplate" height="80">
          <View id="documentProperties">
            <Label bindId="name" id="name" />
            <View id="secondLine">
              <Label class="line2 fieldLabel" text="Date: " />
              <Label class="line2" bindId="date" id="date" />
            </View>
          </View>
        </ItemTemplate>
      </Templates>
      <ListSection name="elements"></ListSection>
    </ListView>
  </Window>
</Alloy>
```

6. Let's add some styling in the app | styles | index.tss file and replace the content with this code:

```
".container": {
backgroundColor: "white",
  top: 25
}

"#documentProperties": {
  top: 0,
  left: 10,
  right: 0,
  bottom: 0,
  layout: "vertical",
verticalAlign: Ti.UI.TEXT_VERTICAL_ALIGNMENT_CENTER
}

"#name": {
  left: 0,
  top: 4,
  height: 55,
  color: "black",
textAlign: Ti.UI.TEXT_ALIGNMENT_LEFT,
  font: {
fontSize: 16
  }
}

"#secondLine": {
  left: 0,
  right: 0,
  layout: "horizontal"
}

".fieldLabel": {
  color: "#999"
}

".line2": {
  font: {
    fontSize: 10
  }
}
```

7. We have completed the UI design of our application. Now, we need to develop our controller. Open the app | controllers | index.js file and remove all content. Then, we need to get the module, and create a session to connect to Alfresco. Change the properties if you want to connect to another Alfresco instance:

```
var SDKModule = require('com.alfresco.appcelerator.module.sdk');
var properties = {
  serverUrl : "http://localhost:8080/alfresco",
  serverUsername : "admin",
  serverPassword : "admin"
};
var repoSession = SDKModule.createRepositorySession(properties);
```

8. Then, let's define the variable that will contain details about the available whitepapers:

```
var items = [];
```

9. Finally, we are creating two event listeners for when we'll create the session to connect to Alfresco. The error listener will just display a message to the user. The success listener is empty for the moment, but we'll populate it in the next step. Then, we connect to Alfresco and display the main UI:

```
repoSession.addEventListener('error', function(e) {
alert("ERROR: Cannot connect to server (" + e.errorcode + "): "
 + e.errorstring);
});
repoSession.addEventListener('success', function(e) {

});
repoSession.connect();
$.index.open();
```

10. Now, we need to populate the success event listener. The first step is to retrieve the Alfresco Search service and add an error listener that will display a message:

```
Ti.API.info("Connected to server: " + e.servername);
var searchService = SDKModule.createSearchService();
searchService.initialiseWithSession(repoSession);
searchService.addEventListener('error', function(e) {
  alert(e.errorstring);
});
```

11. We need to create another listener that populates the items variable. This event will be called when a search is done and a new document will be found:

```
searchService.addEventListener('documentnode', function(e) {
var doc = e.document;
items.push({
name : {
text : doc.name
    },
date : {
    text :String.formatDate(doc.modifiedAt, "long")
    }
  });
$.elementsList.sections[0].setItems(items);
});
```

12. The final step is to actually send the query. We'll use CMIS to get all whitepapers with the `isActive` property equal to `true`:

```
var query = "SELECT * "
  + "FROM sc:whitepaper AS wp"
  + " JOIN sc:webable AS web"
  + " ON wp.cmis:objectId = web.cmis:objectId"
  + " WHERE web.sc:isActive = true";
searchService.searchWithStatement(query);
```

13. And you are done! Run the application in the same way as the previous section. You should be able to see a similar screen to the following:

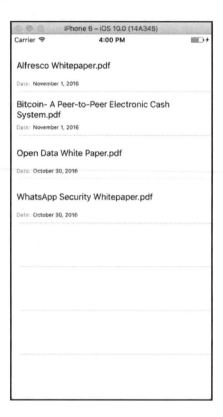

In this section, you discovered how to create a new mobile application using the Alloy framework. We used the search service provided by the Alfresco SDK to execute a CMIS query and list all documents in a `ListView` component. This app is very basic and could be greatly improved:

- By changing the displaying of documents, adding a thumbnail for each document, displaying the description of each document instead of the document name
- By adding new features like download or rate
- By displaying a new screen to add feedback on each whitepaper

However, the goal of this section is not to build a full app from scratch but just show you how to use this Alfresco SDK, and more specifically, the search service. You can download the full HTML documentation at

`https://github.com/Alfresco/alfresco-appcelerator-sdk/releases` to see all available services and methods provided.

Summary

In this chapter, you learned how the Search Manager can be configure to customize the search results screen. You discover how you can add new facets based on your custom content model, and they can be displayed depending on the context: entire repository or specific site.

Then, you discovered the concept of Smart Folders and how they can be used to create virtual classification based on metadata. You investigated the sample of smart folder JSON configuration provided by Alfresco. And then you created your own smart folder classification based on search queries.

Finally, you learned that Alfresco provides you many ways to create your own mobile application. And you used the Appcelerator SDK to create your own application in JavaScript and package it for iOS.

10
Security

This chapter is all about security from both an authentication and an authorization perspective. By the end of this chapter, you'll know how to configure Alfresco to authenticate against LDAP, how to set up Single Sign-On (SSO), and how to work with Alfresco's security services. Specifically, you are going to learn how to:

- Install a basic OpenLDAP implementation
- Configure Alfresco to authenticate against LDAP, including "chaining" LDAP with Alfresco authentication
- Configure LDAP synchronization
- Install and configure a popular open source SSO solution from JA-SIG called CAS
- Establish SSO between Alfresco and two of Tomcat's sample servlets
- Create users and groups with the Alfresco API
- Understand the out-of-the-box permissions
- Define a custom permission group or role, which you will then leverage to refactor how the SomeCo Web Enable/Disable links work

Authenticating and synchronizing with LDAP

Most production Alfresco implementations use something other than Alfresco to authenticate. That's because many enterprises already have a central user directory, and it makes a lot of sense to have Alfresco take advantage of that. There are almost as many different approaches to authentication as there are applications. Microsoft shops will often run NTLM or Kerberos authentication, both of which are supported by Alfresco. Most of the time, though, companies store users in one or more LDAP directories and then configure applications to authenticate against those directories.

In this chapter, the directions refer to OpenLDAP. There are other open source LDAP servers available such as Fedora Directory Server and Apache Directory. Proprietary directory servers also work with Alfresco. The most common one is Microsoft Active Directory, but others such as Sun ONE Directory Server and Novell eDirectory are known to work with Alfresco as well.

Step-by-step – setting up a local OpenLDAP server

When testing out authentication against LDAP, you will want a local LDAP directory so that you can have full knowledge and control of the schema and other settings. We are lucky enough to be running CentOS, installing OpenLDAP is very easy.

1. Login to your virtual machine, and authenticate as `root`:

   ```
   sudo su -
   ```

2. Then, install OpenLDAP:

   ```
   yum -y install *openldap*
   ```

3. Create the new database configuration:

   ```
   cp /usr/share/openldap-servers/DB_CONFIG.example
       /var/lib/ldap/DB_CONFIG
       chown ldap. /var/lib/ldap/DB_CONFIG
   ```

4. Start LDAP:

   ```
   systemctl start slapd
   systemctl enable slapd
   ```

5. Create an LDAP root password for administration purposes (in our case, I'll use the password `admin`):

   ```
   [root@localhost ~]# slappasswd
   New password: admin
   Re-enter new password: admin
   {SSHA}OcpQhMt6yOZHOTr5gCVH3/pWu2B8jatF
   ```

6. The generated password in the previous step will be used in this step. Create a file called `chrootpw.ldif` (the location is not important) by typing:

```
nano chrootpw.ldif
```

7. And type the following content (replace the password in the last line with the value generated in the step 5):

```
dn: olcDatabase={0}config,cn=config
changetype: modify
add: olcRootPW
olcRootPW: {SSHA}OcpQhMt6yOZHOTr5gCVH3/pWu2B8jatF
```

8. Then, save by typing CTRL+X, confirm by typing Y, and finally type on the *Enter* key to validate the filename.

9. And, finally, type the following command that will apply the current file that we defined above:

```
ldapadd -Y EXTERNAL -H ldapi:/// -f chrootpw.ldif
```

You should get these messages:

```
SASL/EXTERNAL authentication started
SASL username: gidNumber=0+uidNumber=0,
  cn=peercred,cn=external,cn=auth
SASL SSF: 0
modifying entry "olcDatabase={0}config,cn=config"
```

10. Let's import some basic schemas provided by OpenLDAP by typing these three following commands:

```
ldapadd -Y EXTERNAL -H ldapi:/// -f \
/etc/openldap/schema/cosine.ldif
ldapadd -Y EXTERNAL -H ldapi:/// -f \
/etc/openldap/schema/nis.ldif
ldapadd -Y EXTERNAL -H ldapi:/// -f \
   /etc/openldap/schema/inetorgperson.ldif
```

The directory is now configured, but we need to create our domain for SomeCo. The easiest way to get things into and out of LDAP is by using LDIF files, as we already did in the previous steps to configure our OpenLDAP instance. An LDIF file is a plain-text file that follows a specific format. Once you create an LDIF file you can import it from the command line using `ldapadd`.

11. Let's create a new password for the LDAP domain manager (in our case, we'll use secret):

```
[root@localhost ~]# slappasswd
New password: secret
Re-enter new password: secret
{SSHA}M4ZY3SXKeyR9W+xwB0U2dEmtvdLTZCzu
```

12. Create a new `chdomain.ldif` using `nano` and write this content (be sure to replace the `olcRootPW` with the value that you generated in the step above):

```
dn: olcDatabase={1}monitor,cn=config
changetype: modify
replace: olcAccess
olcAccess: {0}to * by dn.base="gidNumber=0+uidNumber=0,
cn=peercred,cn=external,cn=auth"
  read by dn.base="cn=Manager,dc=someco,dc=com" read by * none

dn: olcDatabase={2}hdb,cn=config
changetype: modify
replace: olcSuffix
olcSuffix: dc=someco,dc=com

dn: olcDatabase={2}hdb,cn=config
changetype: modify
replace: olcRootDN
olcRootDN: cn=Manager,dc=someco,dc=com

dn: olcDatabase={2}hdb,cn=config
changetype: modify
add: olcRootPW
olcRootPW: {SSHA}M4ZY3SXKeyR9W+xwB0U2dEmtvdLTZCzu

dn: olcDatabase={2}hdb,cn=config
changetype: modify
add: olcAccess
olcAccess: {0}to attrs=userPassword,
shadowLastChange by
  dn="cn=Manager,dc=someco,dc=com"
write by anonymous auth by self write by * none
olcAccess: {1}to dn.base="" by * read
olcAccess: {2}to * by dn="cn=Manager,dc=someco,
    dc=com" write by * read
```

13. Then, apply this LDIF file:

```
ldapmodify -Y EXTERNAL -H ldapi:/// -f chdomain.ldif
```

You should get these messages:

```
SASL/EXTERNAL authentication started
SASL username: gidNumber=0+uidNumber=0,cn=peercred,
cn=external,cn=auth
SASL SSF: 0
modifying entry "olcDatabase={1}monitor,cn=config"
modifying entry "olcDatabase={2}hdb,cn=config"
modifying entry "olcDatabase={2}hdb,cn=config"
modifying entry "olcDatabase={2}hdb,cn=config"
modifying entry "olcDatabase={2}hdb,cn=config"
```

We created the manager account, but it needs some data before it can be used. It needs:

- A root entry under which all other entries will be stored. The root entry will be called dc=someco, dc=com.
- A place to store SomeCo employees. It is common to call this people, so the entry will be named ou=people, dc=someco, dc=com.
- A place to store groups. Keeping it simple, the groups will live under an entry named ou=groups, dc=someco, dc=com.

This structure isn't required for the directory to work with Alfresco-your production directory is probably very different. In fact, trying to wrangle a directory that has grown in fits and starts, over time, like an unkempt hedgerow, is where you'll spend most of your time getting Alfresco to work against your real-life LDAP directory.

Populate the root directory entry, the people and group entries, and some test users by following these steps:

1. Create an LDIF file called root.ldif with the following content using the nano command as we did before:

```
dn: dc=someco,dc=com
dc: someco
description: Root LDAP entry for someco.com
objectClass: dcObject
objectClass: organizationalUnit
ou: rootobject
```

```
dn: ou=people,dc=someco,dc=com
ou: people
description: All people in organization
objectClass: organizationalUnit

dn: ou=groups,dc=someco,dc=com
ou: groups
description: All groups in organization
objectClass: organizationalUnit
```

2. Import it into the LDAP directory using `ldapadd` as follows:

```
ldapadd -x -f root.ldif -Dcn=Manager,dc=someco,
dc=com -wsecret
```

You should get these messages:

```
adding new entry "dc=someco,dc=com"
adding new entry "ou=people,dc=someco,dc=com"
adding new entry "ou=groups,dc=someco,dc=com"
```

3. Now create a new LDIF file called `test-users.ldif` with the following content, repeating (and modifying) the block to create as many test users as you want (be careful, you'll need to add one blank line between each block):

```
dn: uid=tuser1,ou=people,dc=someco,dc=com
cn: tuser1
sn: User1
givenName: Test
objectclass: top
objectclass: person
objectclass: organizationalPerson
objectclass: inetOrgPerson
ou: People
l: London
uid: tuser1
mail: tuser1@email.com
userpassword: password
```

4. Again, use `ldapadd` to import the `test-users.ldif` file into the directory:

```
ldapadd -x -f test-users.ldif -Dcn=Manager,
dc=someco,dc=com -wsecret
```

You should get this message:

```
adding new entry "uid=tuser1,ou=people,dc=someco,dc=com"
```

5. Now query the directory using `ldapsearch` to verify that you can find one of your test users. For example, the command to search for `tuser7` is shown below. The `-LLL` flag specifies that the results should be returned in LDIF format, which gives you a nice way to export data from the directory in a format that can be easily shared:

```
ldapsearch -x -LLL -Dcn=Manager,dc=someco,
dc=com -wsecret -b "ou=people,dc=someco,dc=com" "uid=tuser1"
```

You should get this output:

```
dn: uid=tuser1,ou=people,dc=someco,dc=com
cn: tuser1
sn: User1
givenName: Test
objectClass: top
objectClass: person
objectClass: organizationalPerson
objectClass: inetOrgPerson
ou: People
l: London
uid: tuser1
mail: tuser1@email.com
userPassword:: cGFzc3dvcmQ=
```

The command-line tools `ldapadd`, `ldapdelete`, `ldapsearch`, and `ldapmodify` are common, quite easy-to-use tools for doing things such as validating an LDAP query, inspecting an attribute, or exporting directory data. If you don't have these, or you'd just rather use a GUI, there are several open source, graphical LDAP clients available. One of them is Apache Directory Studio, which can optionally run as an Eclipse plug-in and can talk to other LDAP-compliant directories. It isn't restricted to Apache Directory Server.

6. Finally, import a test group. Create a new LDIF file called `test-groups.ldif`. Use the following example to create as many test groups as you'd like:

```
dn: cn=Test Group 1,ou=groups,dc=someco,dc=com
objectClass: top
objectClass: groupOfNames
cn: Test Group 1
member: uid=tuser1,ou=people,dc=someco,dc=com
```

7. Then import the LDIF file using `ldapadd` just like you've done in the previous steps:

```
ldapadd -x -f test-groups.ldif -Dcn=Manager,dc=someco,dc=com -wsecret
```

You should get this message:

```
adding new entry "cn=Test Group 1,ou=groups,dc=someco,dc=com"
```

Assuming your data was loaded OK, you've now got a working directory server with a set of test users and a test group. Using an LDAP server in development can be helpful. For example, if you need a large number of test users, it is a lot easier to generate an LDIF file using a Perl script or something similar and then import that into LDAP, rather than either manually creating the users or using the Alfresco API to do it.

 For more information on working with OpenLDAP, take a look at *Mastering OpenLDAP: Configuring, Securing and Integrating Directory Services*, by Matt Butcher, Packt Publishing.

Step-by-step – configuring Alfresco to authenticate against LDAP

Pointing Alfresco at LDAP is pretty easy. It involves modifying some properties in your `alfresco-global.properties` file. Even if we are doing this example using LDAP, you can obviously use other authentication mechanisms:

- `external`: This is used to delegate the authentication to an external system
- `alfrescoNtlm`: Performs authentication based on user and password information stored in Alfresco
- `passthru`: Allows connection to the Windows domain controller
- `ldap` and `ldap-ad`: Allows connection to LDAP or ActiveDirectory systems
- `kerberos`: Used to connect to systems using the Kerberos protocol

Then, you can configure your Alfresco instance with only one server, but you may need to connect to multiple servers using multiple authentication systems. To cover this requirement, Alfresco is using the concept of authentication chain. It is a priority-ordered list of authentication subsystem instances and respects the following syntax (comma separated list):

```
instance_name1:type1,...,instance_namen:typen
```

Let's take a look at the default authentication chain in Alfresco. Open the JAR library `alfresco-repository-5.x.jar` located in the `WEB-INF|lib` folder of the Alfresco web application. If you unzip this JAR file, and open the file `alfresco|repository.properties`, you should find the following property:

```
# The default authentication chain
authentication.chain=alfrescoNtlm1:alfrescoNtlm
```

As you can see, the default value of the authentication is defining only one instance called `alfrescoNtlm1` and using the authentication system `alfrescoNtlm`. Let's go a little bit deeper and understand how these authentication systems are defined and configured. In the expanded JAR file, you can open the folder `alfresco|subsystems|Authentication`. This folder contains all available authentication subsystems. It's the first time that we talk about a subsystem. In the Alfresco world, a subsystem is a configurable module responsible for a sub-part of Alfresco functionality. Below this folder, you can find all authentication subsystems and the list of available properties. Some key points about subsystems:

- They can be stopped/started without stopping/starting the whole repository.
- They are used when there are several implementations of some functionality. Like authentication providers or search subsystems (Lucene, Solr1, Solr4, Solr6…)

It's a good idea to get non-chained LDAP working first, and then modify the configuration to set up chaining. That way, if it doesn't go as planned, you can tell whether it is your LDAP server settings or the chaining configuration that's the culprit. To configure Alfresco to authenticate against LDAP, do this:

1. Stop Alfresco and edit the `alfresco-global.properties` file:

```
nano /opt/alfresco-one/tomcat/shared
    /classes/alfresco-global.properties
```

2. Add the following property at the end of the file to replace the default authentication chain:

```
### Authentication ###
authentication.chain=ldap1:ldap
```

3. Save the file.

4. Create a subfolder structure like this one
   `subsystems|Authentication|ldap|ldap1` in `|opt|alfresco-one|tomcat|shared|classes|alfresco|extension`.

5. Create a new file called `ldap-authentication.properties` in `ldap1` and paste the content from the file of the same name located in `alfresco|subsystems|Authentication|ldap` from the expanded JAR file. This file contains all properties that you can configure.

6. Edit your newly created file `ldap-authentication.properties` and update the format of the usernames in the directory:

   ```
   ldap.authentication.userNameFormat=uid=%s,
   ou=people,dc=someco,dc=com
   ```

7. Specify the host name and port of the LDAP directory:

   ```
   # The URL to connect to the LDAP server
   ldap.authentication.java.naming.provider.url
     =ldap://localhost:389
   ```

8. Specify the **Domain Name (DN)** of a user entry that can read people and groups. This will be used later when you configure synchronization. It isn't used for authentication. Alfresco binds as the authenticating user when attempting to authenticate:

   ```
   # The default principal to use (only used for LDAP sync)
   ldap.synchronization.java.naming.security
     .principal=cn=Manager,dc=someco,dc=com
   ```

9. Specify the password of the user provided in the previous step:

   ```
   # The password for the default principal
   (only used for LDAP sync)
   ldap.synchronization.java.naming.security.credentials=secret
   ```

10. Update the group search base:

    ```
    # The group search base restricts the LDAP group query
    # to a sub section of tree on the LDAP server.
    ldap.synchronization.groupSearchBase=ou=Groups,
    dc=someco,dc=com
    ```

11. Update the user search base:

```
# The user search base restricts the LDAP user query
#to a sub section of tree on the LDAP server.
ldap.synchronization.userSearchBase=ou=People,
dc=someco,dc=com
```

12. Save the properties file.
13. Restart Alfresco.

To test the setup, attempt to log in. Unless you set up an `admin` entry in your LDAP directory, you won't be able to log in as `admin`. You'll fix that shortly. Instead, try one of the test users you imported in the LDIF file.

If you check the log file, you should see that Alfresco started the `ldap1` authentication subsystem:

```
Starting 'Authentication' subsystem, ID: [Authentication, managed, ldap1]
Startup of 'Authentication' subsystem, ID: [Authentication, managed, ldap1]
complete
```

You probably noticed that the LDAP authentication subsystem includes two subcomponents: authentication and synchronization. They are both active by default (you can change these settings by modifying your property file). By checking the log file, you should see messages like these ones:

```
Starting 'Synchronization' subsystem, ID: [Synchronization, default]
Synchronizing users and groups with user registry 'ldap1'
Retrieving all groups from user registry 'ldap1'
Synchronization,Category=directory,id1=ldap1,id2=1 Group Analysis:
Commencing batch of 1 entries
Synchronization,Category=directory,id1=ldap1,id2=1 Group Analysis:
Processed 1 entries out of 1. 100% complete. Rate: 16 per second. 0
failures detected.
Synchronization,Category=directory,id1=ldap1,id2=1 Group Analysis:
Completed batch of 1 entries
Synchronization,Category=directory,id1=ldap1,id2=3 Group Creation and
AssociatiSynchronization,Category=directory,id1=ldap1,id2=3 Group Creation
and Association Deletion: Completed batch of 1 entries
Retrieving all users from user registry 'ldap1'
Synchronization,Category=directory,id1=ldap1,id2=6 User Creation and
Association: Commencing batch of 2 entries
Synchronization,Category=directory,id1=ldap1,id2=6 User Creation and
Association: Processed 2 entries out of 2. 100% complete. Rate: 0 per
second. 0 failures detected.
Synchronization,Category=directory,id1=ldap1,id2=6 User Creation and
```

```
Association: Completed batch of 2 entries
Finished synchronizing users and groups with user registry 'ldap1'
1 user(s) and 1 group(s) processed
```

It means that all available users in your LDAP server have been created in Alfresco. This synchronization job is executed every night at midnight. It's managed by the subsystem **Synchronization** that you can also find in your expanded JAR file. You may ask why it's executed when I start my Alfresco instance. If you open the file `default-synchronization.properties` located in `alfresco|subsystems|Synchronization|default` in your expanded JAR file, you should find:

```
synchronization.syncOnStartup=true
```

You can do an additional, quick experiment. Now that Alfresco is started, use LDIF to add a new user in LDAP. If you log in with an existing user and look for it, you won't be able to find it. However, if you try to log in to Alfresco with this new user, you are able to log in. Additionally, if you check the Alfresco log file, you can see that a synchronization job has been started. If you look at the same property file listed above, you should see the following property:

```
synchronization.syncWhenMissingPeopleLogIn=true
```

This setting allows synchronization of users if a new user is trying to login but it's not created yet in Alfresco, because the nightly job has not been executed yet, so the user is not created yet in Alfresco.

Step-by-step – configuring chaining

With LDAP authentication turned on, you are no longer able to log in as `admin`. That's because you essentially swapped out Alfresco's out of the box authentication component for an LDAP authentication component, and `admin` doesn't exist in LDAP.

Sometimes, there is a requirement to configure Alfresco to try one authentication source and, if it fails, try another. Suppose, for example, that SomeCo's operational staff has a tight grip on the LDAP directory. The Alfresco team might need to troubleshoot a problem and would like to use test IDs, but the turnaround time on getting new entries added to LDAP is too lengthy. Plus, the directory team would rather not pollute the production server with a bunch of fake users named after characters from your favorite movies. One solution is to chain LDAP authentication to Alfresco's authentication so that if a user isn't found in LDAP, Alfresco will attempt to find a matching entry in its own repository.

Of course, there are other reasons to use chaining. Maybe in your organization, users aren't all centrally managed-some might be in LDAP, while others are in some other proprietary store.

Let's set up SomeCo to chain LDAP to Alfresco. Here are the steps:

1. Stop Alfresco and edit the `alfresco-global.properties` file:

   ```
   nano /opt/alfresco-one/tomcat/shared/classes
   /alfresco-global.properties
   ```

2. Update your authentication chain with the following configuration. This configuration will try to authenticate the user against LDAP first, and then we'll try against Alfresco if the first authentication didn't work:

   ```
   authentication.chain= ldap1:ldap,alfrescoNtlm1:alfrescoNtlm
   ```

3. Save the file.
4. Restart Alfresco.

You should now be able to log in using admin, one of the test users you created in a previous chapter, or one of the test users in LDAP.

Setting up Single Sign-On (SSO)

If multiple applications in the enterprise use the same LDAP server to authenticate, why force your users to re-enter the same username and password just because they are moving from one application to another? The answer, as usual, is time and money. However, implementing a Single Sign-On (SSO) solution and configuring Alfresco to leverage it may be easier than you think.

There are many SSO providers available and specific implementations can vary dramatically from company to company. In the next exercise, you'll install an open source SSO server called CAS from JA-SIG, and then configure Alfresco to use it. This should give you just enough of a taste of SSO to determine if it makes sense in your organization and what might be involved for a full production rollout, whether using CAS or some other SSO package.

Step-by-step – implementing SSO

This exercise involves downloading, installing, and configuring a base install of CAS, then installing and configuring Apache, and then configuring Alfresco. When that's done, you'll be able to visit Alfresco and other CAS-protected web applications without requiring more than one login. In a traditional architecture, Apache and CAS will be installed on a dedicated server to be re-usable by many applications. But in our case, to keep it simple, we'll install everything in the same virtual machine that we have.

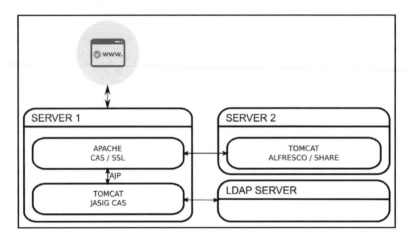

To install CAS and configure Alfresco for SSO, follow these steps:

1. You're going to install CAS in a separate application server from Alfresco. We'll set up another Tomcat instance in the VM. You'll need to change its HTTP, SSL, and shutdown ports. We'll use 8081, 8444, and 8006 respectively in this example. We'll also use Apache to handle SSL and CAS, so we need to open the HTTP ports 1080 and 1443. The first action is to update our Vagrant file to open the HTTP and SSL ports of Tomcat and Apache. Let's first suspend our virtual machine by typing the following from the folder vms|vagrant:

    ```
    vagrant suspend
    ```

2. Then, edit the file Vagrantfile and these four rules:

    ```
    # Redirect CAS HTTP port
    config.vm.network "forwarded_port", guest: 8081, host: 8081
    # Redirect CAS SSL port
    config.vm.network "forwarded_port", guest: 8444, host: 8444
    # Redirect Apache HTTP port
    config.vm.network "forwarded_port", guest: 1080, host: 1080
    ```

```
# Redirect Apache SSL port
config.vm.network "forwarded_port", guest: 1443, host: 1443
```

3. Finally, let's reload your virtual machine:

```
vagrant reload --provision
```

You should see the following messages confirming that the new forwarding rules are added:

```
==> default: Forwarding ports...
    default: 8080 => 8080 (adapter 1)
    default: 8000 => 8000 (adapter 1)
    default: 9000 => 9000 (adapter 1)
    default: 8081 => 8081 (adapter 1)
    default: 8444 => 8444 (adapter 1)
    default: 1080 (guest) => 1080 (host) (adapter 1)
    default: 1443 (guest) => 1443 (host) (adapter 1)
    default: 22 => 2222 (adapter 1)
```

4. Log back to your virtual machine by typing `vagrant ssh`

5. Log in as root by typing: `sudo su -`

6. Let's start by setting up a new Tomcat instance:

```
cd /opt
wget http://archive.apache.org/dist/tomcat/
  tomcat-6/v6.0.39/bin/apache-tomcat-6.0.39.zip
unzip apache-tomcat-6.0.39.zip
mv apache-tomcat-6.0.39 cas
```

7. Let's change the default port used by Tomcat to avoid being in conflict with the Tomcat instance used by Alfresco. Edit the file |opt|cas|conf|server.xml. Change line 22 defining the shutdown port to the following line:

```
<Server port="8006" shutdown="SHUTDOWN">
```

Change line 90 defining the AJP port to the following line:

```
<Connector port="8010"
  protocol="AJP/1.3"
  redirectPort="8444"
  enableLookups="false"
/>
```

Change lines `69-71` defining the connector on the port `8080` to the following lines:

```
<Connector port="8081" maxHttpHeaderSize="8192"
  maxThreads="150"
  minSpareThreads="25"
  maxSpareThreads="75"
  enableLookups="false"
  redirectPort="8444"
  acceptCount="100"
  connectionTimeout="20000"
  disableUploadTimeout="true" />
```

And finally add the following SSL connector below the previous connector:

```
<Connector port="8444" protocol="HTTP/1.1"
  SSLEnabled="true"
  maxThreads="150"
  scheme="https"
  secure="true"
  keystoreFile="/opt/cas/conf/keystore"
  keystorePass="secret"
  clientAuth="false"
  sslProtocol="TLS" />
```

8. We need to check if the `JAVA_HOME` environment variable is properly set. Just type:

```
echo $JAVA_HOME
```

If it returns nothing, you need to configure it. Just edit or create the file `|etc|profile.d|java.sh` by typing:

```
nano /etc/profile.d/java.sh
```

And add the following two lines:

```
export JAVA_HOME=/opt/alfresco-one/java
export PATH=$PATH:$JAVA_HOME/bin
```

This file will be automatically loaded at the next session so you can logout and log back in. Or you can just ask to load this file:

```
source /etc/profile.d/java.sh
```

If you retype the `echo` command, you should get:

```
/opt/alfresco-one/java/
```

9. Create the SSL key for your machine using Java's **keytool** program:

```
cd /opt/cas/conf
keytool -keystore keystore -genkey
 -alias tomcat -keyalg RSA
```

It will ask you for a password to protect your keystore. As you can see above, we used `secret` as the password:

```
Enter keystore password:  secret
Re-enter new password: secret
```

Then, it will ask for your first name and last name, you need to use the name of the machine running the CAS Tomcat server. In our case, it's `localhost`:

```
What is your first and last name?
  [Unknown]:  localhost
```

Then, you can keep `Unknown` for the other questions:

```
What is the name of your organizational unit?
  [Unknown]:
What is the name of your organization?
  [Unknown]:
What is the name of your City or Locality?
  [Unknown]:
What is the name of your State or Province?
  [Unknown]:
What is the two-letter country code for this unit?
  [Unknown]:
    It will ask you to confirm, be sure to type yes:
Is CN=localhost, OU=Unknown, O=Unknown,
L=Unknown, ST=Unknown, C=Unknown correct?
  [no]:  yes
```

The last question is asking you if you want to set up another password for this certificate. In this case, we don't, so just type ENTER:

```
Enter key password for <tomcat>
   (RETURN if same as keystore password):
```

10. Let's start this Tomcat instance and validate that we have the basics properly configured. Before starting Tomcat, we need to make all scripts executable:

```
cd /opt/cas/bin
chmod +x *.sh
```

Then, we can start Tomcat:

```
sh startup.sh
```

11. If you open your browser to the URL `http://localhost:8081/`, you should get the following page:

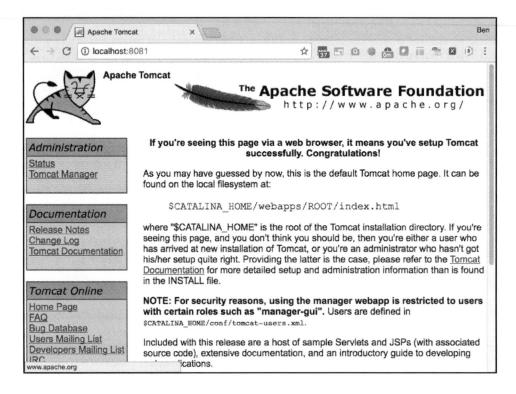

12. Then, you can check if HTTPS is working properly by opening
`https://localhost:8444/`. If you use Google Chrome, you'll have a screen
like this one. It's because we use a self-signed certificate. You just need to click on
ADVANCED, and then **Proceed.**

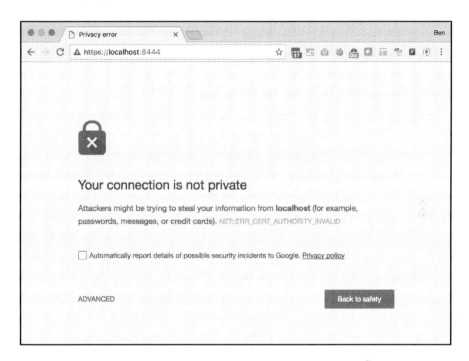

13. We confirmed that Tomcat is properly set up, so we can stop it:

```
sh /opt/cas/bin/shutdown.sh
```

14. Let's download and install the CAS server:

```
cd /opt/cas/webapps/
wget http://central.maven.org/maven2/org/jasig
   /cas/cas-server-webapp/3.6.0/cas-server-webapp-3.6.0.war
mv cas-server-webapp-3.6.0.war cas.war
```

15. Restart Tomcat:

```
sh /opt/cas/bin/startup.sh
```

You should be able to see the login screen by pointing your browser to `https://localhost:8444/cas`.

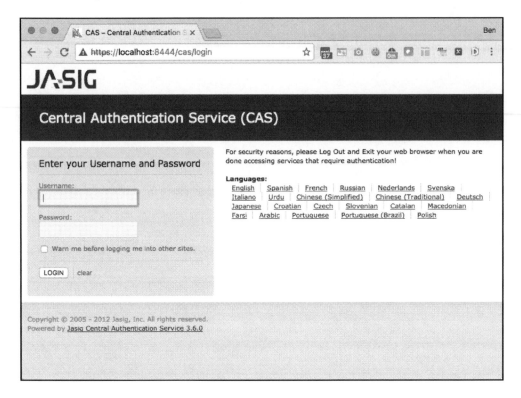

16. We didn't configure any authentication provider. If you check the log file, you should a message like this one:

```
WARN
[org.jasig.cas.authentication.handler.support
  .SimpleTestUsernamePasswordAuthenticationHandler] –
<org.jasig.cas.authentication.handler.support
  .SimpleTestUsernamePasswordAuthenticationHandler is only
  to be used in a testing environment.
  NEVER enable this in a production environment.>
```

It means that you can connect using any username/password combination where the password is the username. If you try with `test/test`, you should get a screen confirming that the login was successful:

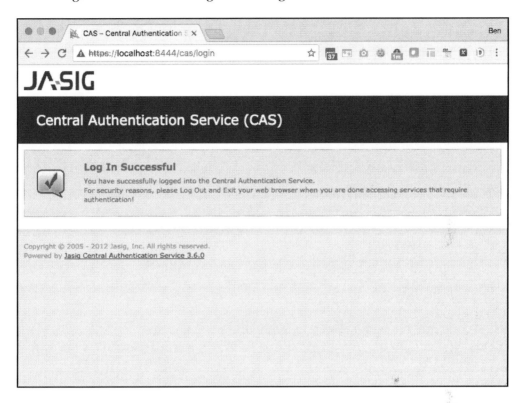

17. Be aware that the configuration of the SSL port of the Tomcat used by CAS is not necessary in our case because we'll use Apache to handle SSL. However, it's a required step if you decide not to use Apache.

18. Now, we can start to install Apache. We'll use three important modules called `mod_ssl` to handle HTTPS, `mod_proxy_ajp` to redirect queries to CAS and Alfresco using the AJP protocol, and `mod_auth_cas` to manage the authentication between the web applications. The first ones are easily installable, but there are multiple versions of the last one and some of them are not compatible with the installation. We need to install the module from EPEL (Extra Packages for Enterprise Linux):

```
yum -y install epel-release
yum clean all
```

19. We can install Apache with all required modules:

```
yum install -y httpd mod_ssl httpd-devel apr
apr-devel apr-util apr-util-devel mod_auth_cas
```

20. When Apache is installed, we are going to change the listening ports. First, we need to change the default HTTP listening port 80 to 1080. Edit the file |etc|httpd|conf|httpd.conf, identify the Listen directive and change it to:

```
Listen 1080
```

Then, identify the ServerName directive (that should be commented), uncomment it and change it to:

```
ServerName localhost:1080
```

21. We also need to change the SSL listening port 443 to 1443. Edit the file |etc|httpd|conf.d|ssl.conf, identify the Listen directive and change it to:

```
Listen 1443 https
```

Then, identify the VirtualHost configuration and change it to:

```
<VirtualHost _default_:1443>
```

We need to configure the mod_auth_cas module. Create the file |etc|httpd|conf.d|mod_auth_cas.conf. The first lines added are to configure how Apache can connect to CAS, and where it can find the certificates that we'll generate in a later step:

```
CASLoginURL https://localhost:1443/cas/login
CASValidateURL https://localhost:1443/cas/serviceValidate
CASCertificatePath /etc/pki/tls/certs
```

Then, we create the configuration for the alfresco web application, but we disable the CAS authentication for some path like scripts, css or images:

```
<LocationMatch ^/alfresco/(?!service/|service$
 |webdav/|webdav$|s/|s$|scripts/|css/|images/).*>
    AuthType CAS
    AuthName "CAS"
    require valid-user
    CASScope /alfresco
    CASAuthNHeader X-Alfresco-Remote-User
</LocationMatch>
We add as well the configure for the share web application:
```

```
<Location /share>
    AuthType CAS
    AuthName "CAS"
     require valid-user
    CASScope /share
    CASAuthNHeader X-Alfresco-Remote-User
</Location>
```

And finally, for testing purposes, we want to protect the out-of-the-box examples web application provided by Tomcat:

```
<Location /examples>
 AuthType CAS
 AuthName "CAS"
 require valid-user
 CASScope /examples
</Location>
```

We need to configure the `mod_proxy_ajp` module that will redirect the queries between Apache and the two Tomcat instances that we have using the AJP protocol. Create the file `|etc|httpd|conf.d|mod_proxy_ajp.conf`. First, we add a redirection on queries using `/alfresco` or `/share` to the Tomcat containing our Alfresco web applications (configured with the default AJP port 8009):

```
ProxyPass /alfresco ajp://localhost:8009/alfresco
ProxyPassReverse /alfresco ajp://localhost:8009/alfresco
ProxyPass /share ajp://localhost:8009/share
ProxyPassReverse /share ajp://localhost:8009/share
```

And then, we add a redirection on queries using `/cas` to the Tomcat containing the CAS web application that we installed (configured with port 8010 in step 7):

```
ProxyPass /cas ajp://localhost:8010/cas
ProxyPassReverse /cas ajp://localhost:8010/cas
```

Finally, for testing purposes, we redirect queries on `/examples` to the CAS Tomcat:

```
ProxyPass /examples ajp://localhost:8010/examples
ProxyPassReverse /examples ajp://localhost:8010/examples
```

Then, we need to do the same thing for the SSL port. Edit the file
|etc|httpd|conf.d|ssl.conf and add the following lines before the final VirtualHost
closing tag:

```
ProxyPass /cas ajp://localhost:8010/cas
ProxyPassReverse /cas ajp://localhost:8010/cas
ProxyPass /examples ajp://localhost:8010/examples
ProxyPassReverse /examples ajp://localhost:8010/examples
SSLVerifyClient optional
SSLCACertificatePath /etc/pki/tls/certs/
SSLOptions +StdEnvVars +ExportCertData
```

Apache is now configured. We just need to generate the certificates that will be used
between Alfresco, CAS, and Apache. Create the self-signed certificates:

```
touch /etc/pki/CA/index.txt
echo 01 > /etc/pki/CA/serial
cd /etc/pki/CA/
openssl genrsa -out private/cakey.pem -des3 2048
```

And use the passphrase secret:

```
Generating RSA private key, 2048 bit long modulus
.................................+++
.........+++
e is 65537 (0x10001)
Enter pass phrase for private/cakey.pem:secret
Verifying - Enter pass phrase for private/cakey.pem:secret
```

Then, type the following command and use the same pass phrase secret:

```
openssl req -new -x509 -days 365
-key private/cakey.pem -out cacert.pem -subj
'/CN=localhost'
```

We need to configure Apache to trust this self-signed certificate:

```
cp cacert.pem /etc/pki/tls/certs/
cd /etc/pki/tls/certs/
ln -s cacert.pem `openssl x509 -hash -noout
-in cacert.pem`.0
```

Replace the HTTP server's test certificate with the certificate issued by Alfresco CA by
typing:

```
openssl req -nodes -new -out localhost.csr
-keyout ../private/localhost.key
```

And then, reply to the questions following this template:

```
Generating a 2048 bit RSA private key
......................+++
................................+++
writing new private key to '../private/localhost.key'
-----
You are about to be asked to enter information that will be incorporated
into your certificate request.
What you are about to enter is what is called a Distinguished Name or a DN.
There are quite a few fields but you can leave some blank
For some fields there will be a default value,
If you enter '.', the field will be left blank.
-----
Country Name (2 letter code) [XX]:UK
State or Province Name (full name) []:Greater London
Locality Name (eg, city) [Default City]:London
Organization Name (eg, company) [Default Company Ltd]:SomeCo Ltd
Organizational Unit Name (eg, section) []:
Common Name (eg, your name or your server's hostname) []:localhost
Email Address []:

Please enter the following 'extra' attributes
to be sent with your certificate request
A challenge password []:
An optional company name []:
```

Then, sign the client certificate with our certificate:

```
openssl x509 -req -days 365 -in localhost.csr -CA /etc/pki/CA/cacert.pem -
CAkey /etc/pki/CA/private/cakey.pem -set_serial 01 -out localhost.crt
```

And use the pass phrase secret:

```
Signature ok
subject=/C=UK/ST=Greater London/L=London/O=SomeCo Ltd/CN=localhost
Getting CA Private Key
    Enter pass phrase for /etc/pki/CA/private/cakey.pem:secret
```

The next step is creating the certificates that will be used between Share and the Alfresco repository:

```
openssl genrsa -des3 -out ../private/alfresco-system.key 1024
```

---

[465]

And use the pass phrase `secret`:

Generating RSA private key, 1024 bit long modulus

```
........................++++++
.......++++++
e is 65537 (0x10001)
Enter pass phrase for ../private/alfresco-system.key:secret
Verifying - Enter pass phrase for ../private/alfresco-system.key:secret
```

And generate the CSR certificate and use the pass phrase `secret`:

```
openssl req -new -key ../private/alfresco-system.key -out alfresco-
system.csr -subj '/CN=alfresco-system'
```

Sign the client certificate and use the pass phrase `secret`:

```
openssl x509 -req -days 365 -in alfresco-system.csr -CA
/etc/pki/CA/cacert.pem -CAkey /etc/pki/CA/private/cakey.pem -set_serial 02
-out alfresco-system.crt
```

Package the certificate in the P12 format:

```
openssl pkcs12 -export -out alfresco-system.p12 -in alfresco-system.crt -
inkey ../private/alfresco-system.key -certfile /etc/pki/CA/cacert.pem
```

And use the pass phrase `secret` too:

```
Enter pass phrase for ../private/alfresco-system.key:secret
Enter Export Password:secret
Verifying - Enter Export Password:secret
```

Copy the P12 certificate into Share:

```
cp alfresco-system.p12 /opt/alfresco-
one/tomcat/shared/classes/alfresco/web-extension/
```

Finally, generate the truststore that will be used by Alfresco Share:

```
keytool -importcert -alias alfresco-system -keystore /opt/alfresco-
one/tomcat/shared/classes/alfresco/web-extension/ssl-truststore -file
/etc/pki/CA/cacert.pem
```

Use the same pass phrase `secret`:

```
Enter keystore password: secret
Re-enter new password:secret
```

And finally, confirm that you want to add the certificate to the truststore:

```
Trust this certificate? [no]:  yes
Certificate was added to keystore
```

We configured Apache and the Tomcat instance containing CAS. The last step is to configure the Alfresco repository and Share. First, stop Alfresco if it is running:

```
service alfresco stop
```

Then, we need to disable the authentication on the AJP port. Edit the file |opt|alfresco-one|tomcat|conf|server.xml and add a new attribute tomcatAuthentication to the AJP connector using the value false. You should have:

```
<Connector port="8009" protocol="AJP/1.3" redirectPort="8443"
tomcatAuthentication="false" />
```

Alfresco needs to be configured to use the external authentication subsystem instead of the default alfrescoNtlm subsystem, or the ldap subsystem that you may have configured previously. In this example, we'll configure the subsystem by listing all properties in the same file. You can see the property, external.authentication.proxyHeader, it contains the header name that will be used to pass information between Apache and Alfresco. Edit the file |opt|alfresco-one|tomcat|shared|classes|alfresco-global.properties and use the following properties (be sure that you have only one property, authentication.chain):

```
authentication.chain=external1:external
external.authentication.proxyUserName=
external.authentication.enabled=true
external.authentication.defaultAdministratorUserNames=admin
external.authentication.proxyHeader=X-Alfresco-Remote-User
```

1. Share needs to be configured too. Edit the file |opt|alfresco-one|tomcat|shared|classes|alfresco|web-extension|share-config-custom.xml. Locate a config element with the condition attribute equal to Remote. Be careful, you may have more than one. So, find the one that is commented. It should look like the following code. Uncomment it, you should have this XML code containing six sub elements that we are going to explain:

```
<config evaluator="string-compare" condition="Remote">
  <remote>
    [...]
  </remote>
</config>
```

2. The first element included in the remote tag is the SSL configuration. Be sure to update the path and the password for the keystore and the truststore:

```
<ssl-config>
  <keystore-path>/opt/alfresco-one/tomcat/shared
    /classes/alfresco/web-extension/alfresco-system.p12
  </keystore-path>
  <keystore-type>pkcs12</keystore-type>
  <keystore-password>secret</keystore-password>
  <truststore-path>/opt/alfresco-one/tomcat/shared
    /classes/alfresco/web-extension/ssl-truststore
  </truststore-path>
  <truststore-type>JCEKS</truststore-type>
  <truststore-password>secret</truststore-password>
  <verify-hostname>true</verify-hostname>
</ssl-config>
```

3. Then, we have the two connectors. Only change is required. Be sure to specify the right header name in the `userHeader` tag:

```
<connector>
  <id>alfrescoCookie</id>
  <name>Alfresco Connector</name>
  <description>Connects to an Alfresco instance
using cookie-based authentication</description>
  <class>org.alfresco.web.site.servlet
    .SlingshotAlfrescoConnector</class>
</connector>

<connector>
  <id>alfrescoHeader</id>
  <name>Alfresco Connector</name>
  <description>Connects to an Alfresco instance using
    header and cookie-based authentication</description>
  <class>org.alfresco.web.site.servlet
    .SlingshotAlfrescoConnector</class>
  <userHeader>X-Alfresco-Remote-User</userHeader>
</connector>
```

4. Finally, we can configure the three endpoints. The only difference with the configuration in the file is that we configure the three endpoints to use the `alfrescoHeader` **connector** in the tag `connector-id`:

```
<endpoint>
  <id>alfresco</id>
  <name>Alfresco - user access</name>
  <description>Access to Alfresco Repository WebScripts
```

```
      that require user authentication</description>
    <connector-id>alfrescoHeader</connector-id>
    <endpoint-url>http://localhost:8080/alfresco/wcs</endpoint-url>
    <identity>user</identity>
    <external-auth>true</external-auth>
  </endpoint>

  <endpoint>
    <id>alfresco-feed</id>
    <parent-id>alfresco</parent-id>
    <name>Alfresco Feed</name>
    <description>Alfresco Feed - supports basic HTTP
      authentication via the EndPointProxyServlet</description>
    <connector-id>alfrescoHeader</connector-id>
    <endpoint-url>http://localhost:8080/alfresco/wcs</endpoint-url>
    <identity>user</identity>
    <external-auth>true</external-auth>
  </endpoint>

  <endpoint>
    <id>alfresco-api</id>
    <parent-id>alfresco</parent-id>
    <name>Alfresco Public API - user access</name>
    <description>Access to Alfresco Repository Public API
      that require user authentication.
  This makes use of the authentication that is provided
      by parent 'alfresco' endpoint.</description>
    <connector-id>alfrescoHeader</connector-id>
    <endpoint-url>http://localhost:8080/alfresco/api</endpoint-url>
    <identity>user</identity>
    <external-auth>true</external-auth>
  </endpoint>
```

It's now time to start everything and to test:

```
service alfresco start
service httpd start
sh /opt/cas/bin/startup.sh
```

First, you can test that Apache works as expected by opening the URL
`https://localhost:1443/`. And you should see the following page:

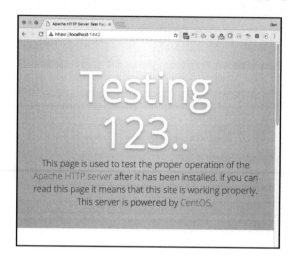

Now, start a new navigator in incognito mode. By doing that, when you close the window,
it will delete all cookies stored in your browser. Open the URL
`https://localhost:1443/examples/servlets/servlet/HelloWorldExample`, you
should see the CAS login page and authenticate using any username and password (but be
sure to provide a password equal to the username). Then you should be allowed to access
it:

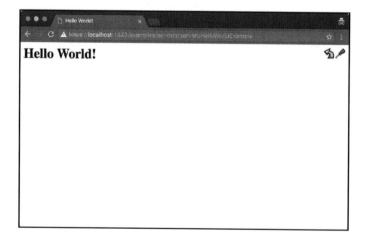

Finally, try to open the following URL: `https://localhost:1443/share/`, and you'll access Alfresco Share and you'll be authenticated using the username that you used in CAS. You'll notice that you can use any username and it will authenticate you. It's because we use the standard CAS web application that just validates that the username matches the password. The next step is to configure CAS to validate the authentication against LDAP.

Logging Out

You'll notice that the Logout link disappeared from Share because we enabled SSO. You may want to recreate this link. You just need to create a new menu item as we already did in the previous chapter redirecting to the CAS logout page. It will invalidate the session, and the user will have to re-login if he wants to access Alfresco Share.

Step-by-step – configuring CAS to use LDAP for authentication

This really has nothing to do with Alfresco, but it completes the picture. At this point, CAS is letting in anyone who specifies a username that matches their password. What it needs to do is use the same `OpenLDAP` directory for authentication we pointed Alfresco to earlier. This involves creating a new WAR file with LDAP dependencies, and then changing the LDAP configuration.

To get CAS working with LDAP, do this:

1. First, we need to install Maven:

   ```
   cd /opt
   wget http://mirrors.ukfast.co.uk/sites
   /ftp.apache.org/maven/maven-3/3.3.9/binaries
   /apache-maven-3.3.9-bin.zip
   unzip apache-maven-3.3.9-bin.zip
   ln -s apache-maven-3.3.9 maven
   ```

2. Then, we need to set up some environment variables. Create the file |etc|profile.d|maven.sh and add the following content:

   ```
   #!/bin/bash
   MAVEN_HOME=/opt/maven
   PATH=$MAVEN_HOME/bin:$PATH
   export PATH MAVEN_HOME
   ```

3. Because we don't want to restart our VM, we are just going to reload our file:

```
source /etc/profile.d/maven.sh
```

4. Double-check that Maven is installed by typing:

```
mvn -v
```

You should get a trace like this one:

```
Apache Maven 3.3.9 (bb52d8502b132ec0a5a3f4c09453c07478323dc5;
2015-11-10T16:41:47+00:00)
Maven home: /opt/maven
Java version: 1.8.0_65, vendor: Oracle Corporation
Java home: /opt/alfresco-one/java
Default locale: en_US, platform encoding: UTF-8
OS name: "linux", version: "3.10.0-327.el7.x86_64",
arch: "amd64", family: "unix"
```

5. We can build our own CAS web application. The first step is to create the required folder structure:

```
cd /root
mkdir -p custom-cas-server/src/main/webapp/WEB-INF/
cd custom-cas-server
```

6. Let's create the file pom.xml in the current folder. This file will define what we need to create our custom CAS web application. Let's create the main structure:

```
<?xml version="1.0"?>
<project xmlns="http://maven.apache.org/POM/4.0.0"
xmlns:xsi="http://www.w3.org/2001/XMLSchema-instance"
xsi:schemaLocation="http://maven.apache.org/POM/4.0.0
http://maven.apache.org/maven-v4_0_0.xsd">
  <modelVersion>4.0.0</modelVersion>
  <groupId>com.someco.cas</groupId>
  <artifactId>someco-cas</artifactId>
  <version>1.0-SNAPSHOT</version>
   <packaging>war</packaging>
  <name>SomeCo CAS webapp</name>
  <organization>
    <name>SomeCo</name>
    <url>http://www.someco.com</url>
  </organization>
  <description>SomeCo's configuration of the
    JA-SIG CAS server.</description>
</project>
```

7. Then, in the `project` element, we'll add the following `dependencies` elements. We have three dependencies: (1) the main WAR file containing the web application; (2) the main CAS library; (3) the library to use LDAP:

```
<dependencies>
  <dependency>
    <groupId>org.jasig.cas</groupId>
    <artifactId>cas-server-webapp</artifactId>
    <version>3.6.0</version>
    <type>war</type>
  </dependency>
  <dependency>
    <groupId>org.jasig.cas</groupId>
    <artifactId>cas-server-core</artifactId>
    <version>3.6.0</version>
  </dependency>
  <dependency>
    <groupId>org.jasig.cas</groupId>
    <artifactId>cas-server-support-ldap</artifactId>
    <version>3.6.0</version>
  </dependency>
</dependencies>
```

8. Then, we need to customize the building of the WAR file by specifying, for example, the name of the WAR file that we want:

```
<build>
  <finalName>cas</finalName>
  <plugins>
    <plugin>
      <artifactId>maven-compiler-plugin</artifactId>
      <version>3.0</version>
      <configuration>
        <source>1.5</source>
        <target>1.5</target>
      </configuration>
    </plugin>
  </plugins>
</build>
```

9. And, we finally need to configure this file to specify where the CAS dependencies should be downloaded:

```
<repositories>
  <repository>
    <id>jasig-repository</id>
    <name>JA-SIG Maven2 Repository</name>
```

```
    <url>http://developer.ja-sig.org/maven2</url>
  </repository>
</repositories>
```

10. The Maven file is now ready. However, we still have one last step. Create the file deployerConfigContext.xml in the folder |root|custom-cas-server|src|main|webapp|WEB-INF. The file is a bit lengthy but you can find it in the code attached to this chapter. Let's start by creating the bean that handles the authentication handlers:

```xml
<?xml version="1.0" encoding="UTF-8"?>
<beans xmlns="http://www.springframework.org/schema/beans"
xmlns:xsi="http://www.w3.org/2001/XMLSchema-instance"
 xmlns:p="http://www.springframework.org/schema/p"
xmlns:tx="http://www.springframework.org/schema/tx"
xmlns:sec="http://www.springframework.org/schema/security"
xsi:schemaLocation="http://www.springframework.org/schema/beans
http://www.springframework.org/schema/beans/spring-beans-3.1.xsd
 http://www.springframework.org/schema/tx
http://www.springframework.org/schema/tx/spring-tx-3.1.xsd
http://www.springframework.org/schema/security
http://www.springframework.org/schema/security
/spring-security-3.1.xsd">
<bean id="authenticationManager"
class="org.jasig.cas.authentication.AuthenticationManagerImpl">
  <property name="credentialsToPrincipalResolvers">
    <list>
      <bean
        class="org.jasig.cas.authentication.principal
        .UsernamePasswordCredentialsToPrincipalResolver">
        <property name="attributeRepository"
        ref="attributeRepository"/>
      </bean>
      <bean
        class="org.jasig.cas.authentication.principal
        .HttpBasedServiceCredentialsToPrincipalResolver"/>
    </list>
  </property>
  <property name="authenticationHandlers">
    <list>
      <bean
        class="org.jasig.cas.authentication.handler
        .support.HttpBasedServiceCredentialsAuthenticationHandler"
        p:httpClient-ref="httpClient"/>
      <bean class="org.jasig.cas.adaptors.ldap
      .BindLdapAuthenticationHandler">
        <property name="filter" value="uid=%u"/>
```

```
        <property name="searchBase"
        value="ou=People,dc=someco,dc=com"/>
        <property name="contextSource" ref="contextSource"/>
    </bean>
  </list>
</property>
</bean>
</beans>
```

11. Then, let's add the bean that defines how to connect to our local LDAP instance:

```
<bean id="contextSource"
class="org.springframework.ldap.core.support.LdapContextSource">
  <property name="pooled" value="true"/>
  <property name="urls">
    <list>
      <value>ldap://localhost:389/</value>
    </list>
  </property>
  <property name="userDn" value="cn=Manager,dc=someco,dc=com"/>
  <property name="password" value="secret"/>
  <property name="baseEnvironmentProperties">
    <map>
      <entry>
        <key>
          <value>java.naming.security.authentication</value>
        </key>
        <value>simple</value>
      </entry>
    </map>
  </property>
</bean>
```

12. Finally, we need to add some other beans required by CAS:

```
<user-service id="userDetailsService">
  <user name="admin" password="notused"
    authorities="ROLE_ADMIN"/>
</user-service>
<bean id="attributeRepository"
    class="org.jasig.services.persondir
    .support.StubPersonAttributeDao">
  <property name="backingMap">
    <map>
      <entry key="uid" value="uid"/>
      <entry key="eduPersonAffiliation"
        value="eduPersonAffiliation"/>
      <entry key="groupMembership" value="groupMembership"/>
```

```
          </map>
        </property>
      </bean>
      <bean id="serviceRegistryDao"
      class="org.jasig.cas.services.InMemoryServiceRegistryDaoImpl">
        <property name="registeredServices">
          <list>
            <bean class="org.jasig.cas.services.RegexRegisteredService">
              <property name="id" value="0"/>
              <property name="name" value="HTTP and IMAP"/>
              <property name="description"
              value="Allows HTTP(S) and IMAP(S) protocols"/>
              <property name="serviceId" value="^(https?|imaps?)://.*"/>
              <property name="evaluationOrder" value="10000001"/>
            </bean>
          </list>
        </property>
      </bean>
      <bean id="auditTrailManager"
      class="com.github.inspektr.audit.support
      .Slf4jLoggingAuditTrailManager"/>
      <bean id="healthCheckMonitor"
      class="org.jasig.cas.monitor.HealthCheckMonitor">
        <property name="monitors">
          <list>
            <bean class="org.jasig.cas.monitor.MemoryMonitor"
              freeMemoryWarnThreshold="10"/>
            <bean class="org.jasig.cas.monitor.SessionMonitor"
              ticketRegistry-ref="ticketRegistry"
              serviceTicketCountWarnThreshold="5000"
              sessionCountWarnThreshold="100000"/>
          </list>
        </property>
      </bean>
```

13. We are ready to package our custom CAS web application. Go to the
   |root|custom-cas-server folder and type:

   ```
   mvn clean package
   ```

   It will download all required artifacts and that may take a few minutes. Then
   you should get a trace like this one:

   ```
   [INFO] --- maven-war-plugin:2.2:war
   (default-war) @ someco-cas ---
   [INFO] Packaging webapp
   [INFO] Assembling webapp [someco-cas] in
    [/root/custom-cas-server/target/cas]
   ```

```
[INFO] Processing war project
[INFO] Copying webapp resources
 [/root/custom-cas-server/src/main/webapp]
[INFO] Processing overlay
 [ id org.jasig.cas:cas-server-webapp]
[INFO] Webapp assembled in [2066 msecs]
[INFO] Building war:
 /root/custom-cas-server/target/cas.war
[INFO] WEB-INF/web.xml already added, skipping
[INFO] -----------------------------------
[INFO] BUILD SUCCESS
[INFO] -----------------------------------
[INFO] Total time: 7.713 s
[INFO] Finished at: 2016-11-26T18:35:58+00:00
[INFO] Final Memory: 11M/58M
[INFO] -----------------------------------
```

14. Stop the Tomcat instance containing CAS:

    ```
    sh /opt/cas/bin/shutdown.sh
    ```

15. Remove the existing CAS web application:

    ```
    rm -rf /opt/cas/webapps/cas*
    ```

16. Then, move our custom web application to Tomcat:

    ```
    mv target/cas.war /opt/cas/webapps/
    ```

17. Now restart your CAS Tomcat server and attempt to log in. You should be able to log in using any of the test users you loaded into LDAP.

    ```
    sh /opt/cas/bin/startup.sh
    ```

You now have SSO working between Alfresco and two other webapps, and CAS is using your OpenLDAP directory for authentication. You can now try to log in to CAS using the user that you defined in your LDAP instance.

Working with security services

The first part of this chapter was about authentication, or knowing who the user is. This section is about authorization, which is about specifying what the user can do once he/she is authenticated. First, you'll see how to secure the admin user and give additional users admin rights. Then you'll learn how to use Alfresco's security services classes to create users and groups with the API. And finally, you'll see how to declare your own custom permission groups when the out-of-the-box permission groups don't meet your needs.

Securing the admin user

As you and everyone else in the world knows, the default password for Alfresco's admin account is `admin`. If you use the installer, it will prompt you for a password. If you are using Alfresco for authentication (and even if you aren't), you should change the password for the admin user after you set up your Alfresco instance. If you use LDAP or some other source for authentication and create an entry in the directory for `admin`, change the password for the admin user in that system. The admin is the all-powerful super user, and so securing the admin account is an important step.

Granting additional users admin rights

Most organizations have more than one person helping support the Alfresco infrastructure. You could share the admin password with whoever needs it, but a better practice is to assign admin rights to specific users.

You have two main ways to grant administration rights to a user. The first one is to add a user to the special group called `ALFRESCO_ADMINISTRATORS`:

1. Log in to Alfresco Share as Administrator and click on **Admin Tools** in the top banner.
2. Click on **Groups** in the left menu bar.
3. Type **ALFRESCO** in the search bar, and click on **Browse.**

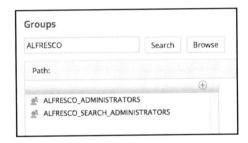

4. Click on the group `ALFRESCO_ADMINISTRATORS`. You'll notice three available actions: (1) Create a new subgroup; (2) Add an existing group; (3) Add an existing user. If you already have an LDAP group with all your administrators, you can just add this group as a subgroup. Update LDAP and when it's resynchronized with Alfresco, it will automatically give administrator privileges to the new LDAP group members.

In our case, we are just clicking on the **Add User** icon. Search for the user you are looking for:

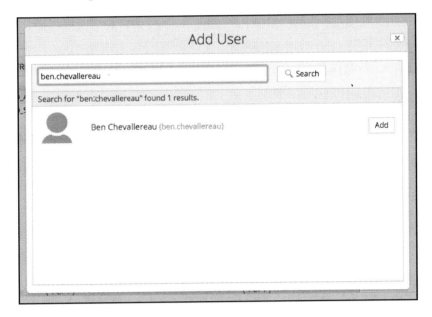

5. Click on **Add.**

The previous steps explain how to grant privilege access to a user using Alfresco Share. It's possible to configure this information at the configuration level. To achieve that, you need to update the `alfresco-global.properties` file located in `<TOMCAT_HOME>|shared|classes`. However, the property that you can use is different depending on the authentication subsystem that you use, and some subsystems don't provide it:

- NTLM: Not available
- External: `external.authentication.defaultAdministratorUserNames`
- * Kerberos: `kerberos.authentication.defaultAdministratorUserNames`
- LDAP: `ldap.authentication.defaultAdministratorUserNames`
- Passthru: `passthru.authentication.defaultAdministratorUserNames`

You can just re-define one of these properties in your file and override it with a comma separated list of usernames that should be configured as Alfresco administrator.

Creating users and Groups Programmatically

The easiest way to load users into Alfresco, if you don't have any use registry as LDAP, is to upload a CSV file as explained on this page: `http://docs.alfresco.com/5.1/tasks/admintools-upload-users.html`. But there may be times when you need to create users or groups dynamically with the API. For example, you might be writing a custom client that enables a user or group management. Or, you may need to create a bunch of service accounts used by different American states.

First, you should understand how users are stored. Every Alfresco user, whether or not Alfresco is handling authentication, is stored in the `SpacesStore` as a `cm:person` object. You can see these objects by using the node browser to navigate to System/People:

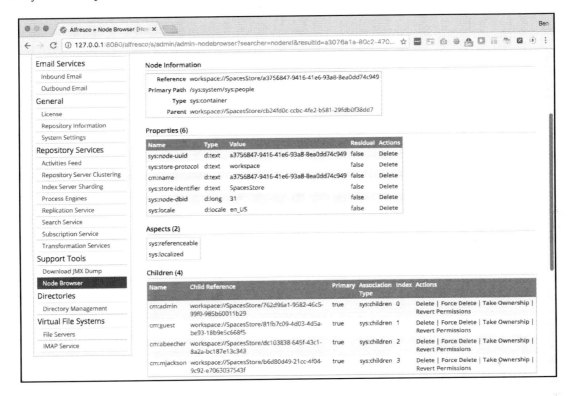

Users managed by Alfresco (where Alfresco is the authentication source) are stored in the `alfrescoUserStore` as `usr:user` objects under System/People. Again, using the node browser you can see these objects:

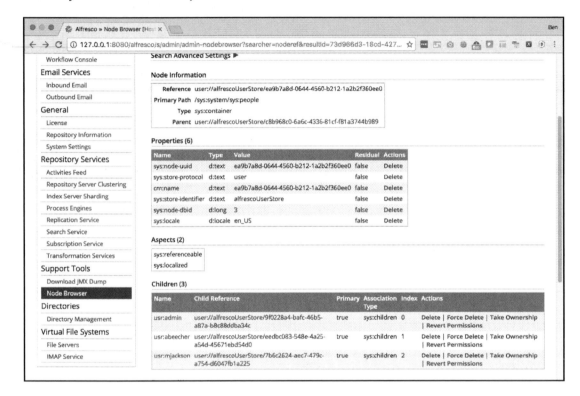

Groups are stored in `SpacesStore` as well as under System/Authorities as `cm:authorityContainer`. The node browser for the Alfresco administrators group looks like this:

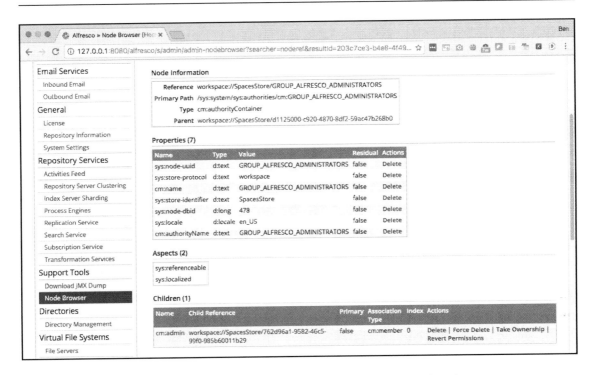

You may have taken a look at the `userModel.xml` model packaged in the `org|alfresco|repo|security|authentication` folder within the `alfresco-repository-*.jar` available in the `WEB-INF|lib`folder of your Alfresco installation (you'll notice that this model is not located with all the other ones in `alfresco|model` of the same JAR file). As you can tell by inspecting the model file, the `usr:user` type inherits from `usr:authority`. If you look at the `contentModel.xml` (located in `alfresco|model`), groups aren't called groups at all. They are `cm:authorityContainer`, which inherit from `cm:authority` and have an association to other authority objects (groups can contain both users and other groups).

Knowing where and how users and groups are stored is important for troubleshooting and administrative tasks. It also explains why, when you create users through the API and if you are creating an Alfresco user (that is, Alfresco manages the user instead of LDAP), you have to create both the `usr:user` object and the `cm:person` object. As you'll see in the next exercise, the `AuthenticationService` manages `usr:user` objects while the `PersonService` is in charge of `cm:person` objects.

Step-by-step – creating users and groups through the Java services

In this section, we are going to create users and groups in a Java-backed webscript that will generate an HTML output to review what the webscript accomplished. We'll quickly go through creating the webscript skeleton that we covered in Chapter 7, *Exposing Content through a RESTful API with Web Scripts,* but we'll spend more time on how we create a user and group in Java. We'll focus on creating users and groups based on American states.

We could discuss the advantage of implementing this feature in a webscript. It's possible to use another way called bootstrap in Alfresco to import users and groups as explained on this page: http://docs.alfresco.com/5.1/references/dev-extension-points-bootstrap.html. As you can see, it consists of writing some XML documents representing the data that you want to import, and then a Spring bean to ask Alfresco to load this data at startup. This capability can be very useful but it means that you can't execute it on demand. Let's assume that you want to deliver the first version of your application for only five American states. But then, you need to give access to five new states, so you'll need to follow the same process by defining a bunch of XML documents again. By using a webscript, you can run it whenever and wherever you want and will just create the missing groups or users.

1. Let's start by creating a new folder in your repo project
   `src|main|amp|config|alfresco|extension|templates|webscripts|com|someco|data`.

2. Then, create the definition file, `init.get.desc.xml`:

   ```
   <webscript>
     <shortname>Initialize the repository
       for the SomeCo project</shortname>
     <url>/someco/init</url>
     <format default="html">extension</format>
     <authentication>admin</authentication>
     <transaction>required</transaction>
   </webscript>
   ```

3. Then, just copy the HTML Freemarker file, `init.get.html.ftl` from the code attached to this chapter. The most interesting part is the `body` element that displays all messages provided by the Java code:

   ```
   <body>
     <div class="index">
       <div class="title">
         <h1>Alfresco Artifacts Intialisation</h1>
   ```

```
    </div>
    <div class="index-list">
      <#list messages as message>
        <p>${message}</p>
      </#list>
    </div>
  </div>
</body>
```

4. Update the `webscript-context.xml` fileto create the association between the webscript definition and the Java class by adding the following bean:

```
<bean id="webscript.com.someco.data.init.get"
class="com.someco.repo.scripts.InitializeRepository"
 parent="webscript">
  <property name="serviceRegistry" ref="ServiceRegistry" />
  <property name="alfrescoGlobalProperties"
    ref="global-properties" />
</bean>
```

5. Open `alfresco-global.properties` in `src|main|amp|config|alfresco|module|repo` and add the following properties:

```
someco.groups=AL,AK,AZ,AR,CA,CO,CT,DE,FL,GA,HI,ID,
    IL,IN,IA,KS,KY,LA,ME,MD,MA,MI,MN,MS,MO,MT,NE,NV,
    NH,NJ,NM,NY,NC,ND,OH,OK,OR,PA,RI,SC,SD,
    TN,TX,UT,VT,VA,WA,WV,WI,WY
someco.groupDisplayName.AL=Alabama
someco.groupDisplayName.AK=Alaska
someco.groupDisplayName.AZ=Arizona
someco.groupDisplayName.AR=Arkansas
someco.groupDisplayName.CA=California
someco.groupDisplayName.CO=Colorado
someco.groupDisplayName.CT=Connecticut
someco.groupDisplayName.DE=Delaware
someco.groupDisplayName.FL=Florida
someco.groupDisplayName.GA=Georgia
someco.groupDisplayName.HI=Hawaii
someco.groupDisplayName.ID=Idaho
someco.groupDisplayName.IL=Illinois
someco.groupDisplayName.IN=Indiana
someco.groupDisplayName.IA=Iowa
someco.groupDisplayName.KS=Kansas
someco.groupDisplayName.KY=Kentucky
someco.groupDisplayName.LA=Louisiana
someco.groupDisplayName.ME=Maine
```

```
someco.groupDisplayName.MD=Maryland
someco.groupDisplayName.MA=Massachusetts
someco.groupDisplayName.MI=Michigan
someco.groupDisplayName.MN=Minnesota
someco.groupDisplayName.MS=Mississippi
someco.groupDisplayName.MO=Missouri
someco.groupDisplayName.MT=Montana
someco.groupDisplayName.NE=Nebraska
someco.groupDisplayName.NV=Nevada
someco.groupDisplayName.NH=New Hampshire
someco.groupDisplayName.NJ=New Jersey
someco.groupDisplayName.NM=New Mexico
someco.groupDisplayName.NY=New York
someco.groupDisplayName.NC=North Carolina
someco.groupDisplayName.ND=North Dakota
someco.groupDisplayName.OH=Ohio
someco.groupDisplayName.OK=Oklahoma
someco.groupDisplayName.OR=Oregon
someco.groupDisplayName.PA=Pennsylvania
someco.groupDisplayName.RI=Rhode Island
someco.groupDisplayName.SC=South Carolina
someco.groupDisplayName.SD=South Dakota
someco.groupDisplayName.TN=Tennessee
someco.groupDisplayName.TX=Texas
someco.groupDisplayName.UT=Utah
someco.groupDisplayName.VT=Vermont
someco.groupDisplayName.VA=Virginia
someco.groupDisplayName.WA=Washington
someco.groupDisplayName.WV=West Virginia
someco.groupDisplayName.WI=Wisconsin
someco.groupDisplayName.WY=Wyoming
```

6. It's now time to create the
   `com.someco.repo.scripts.InitializeRepository` Java class that will
   handle the creation of the users and the groups. We won't go into the details of
   the Java class as you already know how to do that. The first method that we add
   is to create a root group that calls another method:

```
private List<String>checkGroup(String groupName,
     String groupDisplayName) {
   return checkGroup(groupName, groupDisplayName, null);
}
```

7. Then, we create the method (called by the previous one) that creates a group in a parent group:

```
private List<String> checkGroup(String groupName,
String groupDisplayName, String parentName) {
  Set<String> zones = Collections.singleton("APP.DEFAULT");
  List<String> messages = new ArrayList<String>();

  AuthorityService authorityService
    = serviceRegistry.getAuthorityService();

  if (authorityService.authorityExists(
    "GROUP_" + groupName.toUpperCase()))
messages.add("The group " + groupName + " already exists.");
    else {
      String groupInfo = authorityService.createAuthority(
      AuthorityType.GROUP,
      groupName.toUpperCase(),
      groupDisplayName, zones);
      if (parentName != null)
        authorityService.addAuthority(
          "GROUP_" + parentName.toUpperCase(),
          "GROUP_" + groupName.toUpperCase());
        messages.add("The group " + groupInfo
            + " has been created.");
    }
    return messages;
}
```

The first element that you notice is the creation of the zones variable. Zones are used in Alfresco to partition authorities. For example, Alfresco uses zones to record from which LDAP the users and groups are synchronized. Zones are used to hide groups from the administration pages in Alfresco Share. Then, we check if the authority already exists. If it doesn't exist, we create the new group and assign it to a parent group if one has been provided.

1. Then, in the executeImpl method, after defining the variables that we'll need:

```
PersonService personService = serviceRegistry.getPersonService();
AuthorityService authorityService =
    serviceRegistry.getAuthorityService();
MutableAuthenticationService authenticationService =
serviceRegistry.getAuthenticationService();
List<String> messages = new ArrayList<String>();
Map<String, Object> model = new HashMap<String, Object>();
```

2. And we create the root SomeCo group:

```
messages.addAll(checkGroup("SOMECO", "Someco User Group"));
```

3. We get the variable containing all groups that we want to create. For each of them, we retrieve the display name and we create the group in the root group that we created in the previous step:

```
if (alfrescoGlobalProperties.containsKey("someco.groups")) {
String[] groupNames = alfrescoGlobalProperties.getProperty(
"someco.groups").split(",");
  for (String groupName : groupNames) {
    String groupDisplayName =
alfrescoGlobalProperties.getProperty(
"someco.groupDisplayName." + groupName);
messages.addAll(
checkGroup(groupName, groupDisplayName, "SOMECO"));
[...]
  }
}
```

4. After creating the group for each state, we just need to add below the creation of a user. For the username, we just add the underscore character at the end and at the beginning of the group name:

```
String username = "_" + groupName + "_";
if (personService.personExists(username)) {
messages.add("The user " + username + " already exists.");
} else {
  [...]
}
```

5. If the user doesn't exist, we create it, configure the password to be the same as the username and we add it to the relevant group:

```
// Create the user
HashMap<QName, Serializable> properties =
new HashMap<QName, Serializable>();
properties.put(ContentModel.PROP_USERNAME, username);
properties.put(ContentModel.PROP_FIRSTNAME, "Service Account");
properties.put(ContentModel.PROP_LASTNAME, groupName);
properties.put(ContentModel.PROP_ORGANIZATION, "SomeCo");
personService.createPerson(properties);
// Create the authentication
authenticationService.createAuthentication(username,
username.toCharArray());
authenticationService.setAuthenticationEnabled(username, true);
```

```
// Add the user to the group
authorityService.addAuthority("GROUP_" + groupName.toUpperCase(),
username);
messages.add("The user " + username + " has been created.");
```

6. Package, deploy, and test.

If you open the URL: `http://127.0.0.1:8080/alfresco/s/someco/init`, you should get a screen that looks like this where you can see which user and group have been created:

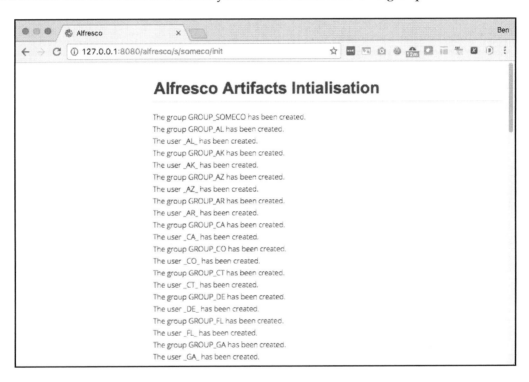

Feel free to refresh the page and you'll see different messages telling you that all users and groups already exist. Then, you can delete random groups or users, run the webscript again to be sure that everything is all right. You should now have a basic idea about how to work with the three main security services: `AuthenticationService`, `AuthorityService`, and `PersonService`.

Understanding permission definitions

Alfresco's out-of-the-box permission definitions are stored in
`alfresco|model|permissionDefinitions.xml` bundled in the JAR file `alfresco-repository-5.x.jar`. If you've ever wondered what the difference is between a Contributor and Editor, this is the file that holds the answer. As you may already observe, there are specific roles for Share sites as well. Those roles are in the `sitePermissionDefinitions.xml` file contained in the folder than `permissionDefinitions.xml`.

Like just about everything else in Alfresco, the permission definitions can be extended. This can be really helpful when the out-of-the-box permissions don't give you exactly what you need. You'll work through such an example in a bit. But first, let's take a peek at how the five permission groups or "roles" you see in Share are defined, and then we'll take a look at the specific site roles.

Permission groups

Permission Groups roll up other Permission Group(s) and Permission(s) into higher-level concepts that make sense to people who have to deal with permissions. In Alfresco Share, these are labeled "roles", although technically they are permission groups.

In Alfresco, users are assigned to groups. Groups are assigned to roles for specific folders and objects. Individual users can also be assigned roles, but using groups is a much better practice. When an individual changes job roles, it is much easier to simply change his/her group membership than updating every object where he/she has been given individual access.

Suppose Caroline is in a group called "HR Administrators", which is given the role of **Contributor** on the "resume" folder. Using the following diagram, let's figure out what Caroline can do:

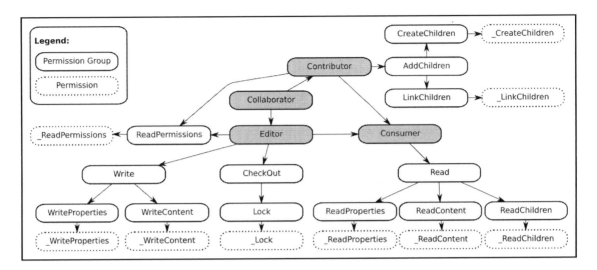

The diagram shows that **Contributor** is a permission group that includes the **Consumer**, **AddChildren**, and **ReadPermissions** permission groups. Each of these permission groups includes others, eventually leading to the following list of low-level permissions for a **Contributor**:

- _ReadProperties
- _ReadChildren
- _ReadContent
- _CreateChildren
- _LinkChildren
- _ReadPermissions

So, Caroline can read the resume folder's properties, can see the children listed in the folder, and can even read the content of the folder object. She can add new files to the folder and can read the permissions of the folder. But Caroline can't change anything she doesn't own because she lacks _**WriteProperties** and _**WriteContent** permissions.

The "can't change anything she doesn't own" caveat is important to understand. Owners have full control over their content. An owner can be explicitly set or can be implicitly based on the creator of the content. So in this case, even though Caroline is just a **Contributor**, she'd still be able to change anything she created unless the ownership of those objects is changed.

Because Caroline is in a group, if she were to move to a different department and be back-filled by another person-Justin, for example-it would be easy to simply remove Caroline from the group and add Justin. Now Caroline would no longer be able to add content to the folder, but Justin would. Unless the ownership is changed, though, she will continue to be able to make changes to any content she owns unless a script is run to change the ownership to Justin or someone else.

Permissions

As shown in the diagram, at some point, permission groups stop including additional permission groups. In other words, you get to the lowest level in the tree. How, then, do permission groups get tied to actual, low-level permissions? Each permission is granted to a permission group, sometimes conditionally. In the diagram, the **_Lock** permission is only granted to the **Lock** permission group when the user also has **Write** permission on that node:

```
<permission name="_Lock" requiresType="false" expose="false">
    <grantedToGroup permissionGroup="Lock" />
    <requiredPermission on="node" type="sys:base"  name="Write"/>
</permission>
```

Permission sets

Permission sets are collections of permission groups specific to an Alfresco type. For example, the permission groups applicable to a `cm:folder` object are:

- Coordinator
- Collaborator
- Contributor
- Editor
- Consumer
- RecordsAdministrator (not exposed to the UI out-of-the-box)

On the other hand, the permission groups relevant to a `st:site` (an Alfresco Share site) listed in the file `sitePermissionDefinitions.xml` are:

- SiteManager
- SiteCollaborator
- SiteContributor
- SiteConsumer

Permission sets can also be tied to aspects. For example, when an object has the `cm:ownable` aspect applied, one of the things you can do is take ownership of that object (that is, set the "owner" attribute). But you have to have a specific permission level to do that. So, there is a permission set tied to the `cm:ownable` aspect called `TakeOwnership` that includes the permission group `SetOwner`:

```
<permissionSet type="cm:ownable" expose="selected">
    <permissionGroup name="TakeOwnership" requiresType="false"
    expose="false">
        <includePermissionGroup permissionGroup="SetOwner"
        type="cm:ownable" />
    </permissionGroup>
    <permissionGroup name="SetOwner" requiresType="false"
    expose="false"/>
        <permission name="_SetOwner" expose="false" requiresType="false">
        <grantedToGroup permissionGroup="SetOwner" />
        <requiredPermission on="node" type="sys:base"
        name="_WriteProperties" />
    </permission>
</permissionSet>
```

Step-by-step – setting up a publisher custom role

In Chapter 5, *Customizing Alfresco Share*, you implemented action evaluator classes that made sure only members of the Publisher group would see the action items related to setting the flag that determines if a piece of content should show up on the portal or not. It worked fine at the time, but now that you know about customizing the out-of-the-box permissions, you can do better. First, here are some of the issues with the original approach:

- The group name was hardcoded in the Spring configuration file share-slingshot-application-context.xml.
- It assumed that the list of people who were allowed to use the action links was the same across the entire organization. If, for example, Sales wanted to use the action to publish something on the portal as well as Marketing, individuals from both teams would have to be added to the Publisher group (or groups within that group) meaning they could publish or un-publish each other's content.
- It assumed that if you had Write permissions on the node, you should see the link. The evaluator then performed the group check. So users still had to belong to the Publisher group, even if they had Write permission. But because not everyone who has Write is in the Publisher group, it is a bit inefficient.

- People who can publish content to the portal can also change the content. Let's suppose that SomeCo wants more fine-grained control. Thus, people who are only supposed to enable or disable the web flag should not be able to actually change any content.

You can address these issues by implementing a custom role. Let's call it `SitePublisher`. Instead of having an evaluator check for membership in a particular group, groups can be assigned to the `SitePublisher` role. The action can then check to see if the current user has that role, and hide the link if he/she doesn't.

This also has the advantage of being able to split up responsibilities more granularly. In one site, the Sales group could be assigned to `SitePublisher`, while in another site the Marketing group could have that role.

Because it is a custom role, you have more control over what people with that permission can do. In this case, a `SitePublisher` should be able to read everything but edit only the properties. (They have to be able to edit the properties because the `sc:isActive` flag is a property on the object.)

Finally, this gives your administrator accounts access to the action items. In the old approach, you had to remember to add `admin` to the Publisher group. Because administrators get all permissions, when the action item checks to see if the administrator has `SitePublisher` permissions, it will return true and the link will be displayed (subject to the logic in the evaluator classes).

Now that you're convinced this is a great idea, go do it. This is going to involve defining a new permission group (`EnableFlag`), and another one for sites (`SitePublisher`) in a new permission definitions file, externalizing the role name, changing the permission required to see the action item, and refactoring the evaluator definition to use the new permission.

Here are the steps:

1. Copy the out-of-the-box `permissionDefinitions.xml` file into your project under `src|main|amp|config|alfresco|module|repo|model`.
2. Rename the file to `scPermissionDefinitions.xml`.
3. Modify `scPermissionDefinitions.xml` to include your custom permission. The first thing to do is locate the permission group `ChangePermissions`. Add below this group, the following permission group:

   ```
   <permissionGroup name="EnableFlag" expose="true"
   allowFullControl="false" />
   ```

4. Save the `scPermissionDefinitions.xml` file.

5. Copy the out-of-the-box `sitePermissionDefinitions.xml` file into your project under `src|main|amp|config|alfresco|module|repo|model`.

6. Rename the file to `scSitePermissionDefinitions.xml`.

7. You want users to be able to grant people the `SitePublisher` permission on Share sites. Add a new permission group `SitePublisher` that includes the `EnableFlag` permission group defined above in the permission set for `st:site`:

```
<permissionGroup name="SitePublisher"
allowFullControl="false" expose="true">
  <includePermissionGroup permissionGroup="Consumer"
    type="cm:cmobject" />
  <includePermissionGroup permissionGroup="ReadPermissions"
    type="sys:base" />
  <includePermissionGroup permissionGroup="WriteProperties"
    type="sys:base" />
  <includePermissionGroup permissionGroup="EnableFlag"
    type="sys:base" />
</permissionGroup>
```

8. Save the `scSitePermissionDefinitions.xml` file.

9. Create a new context file `permission-context.xml` in `src|main|amp|config|alfresco|module|repo|context`:

```
<?xml version='1.0' encoding='UTF-8'?>
<!DOCTYPE beans PUBLIC '-//SPRING//DTD BEAN//EN'
'http://www.springframework.org/dtd/spring-beans.dtd'>
<beans>
[...]
</beans>
```

10. Override the out-of-the-box `permissionsModelDAO` bean with your own to point to the custom permissions definition file you were just modifying:

```
<bean id='permissionsModelDAO'
class="org.alfresco.repo.security
    .permissions.impl.model.PermissionModel" init-method="init">
  <property name="model">
    <value>alfresco/module/${project.artifactId}/model
    /scPermissionDefinitions.xml</value>
  </property>
  <property name="dtdSchema">
    <value>alfresco/model/permissionSchema.dtd</value>
  </property>
  <property name="nodeService">
```

```
      <ref bean="nodeService" />
    </property>
    <property name="dictionaryService">
      <ref bean="dictionaryService" />
    </property>
  </bean>
```

11. Override the out-of-the-box siteService_permissionBootstrap bean with your own to point to the new permissions definition file for the Share site:

```
<bean id="siteService_permissionBootstrap"
  parent="permissionModelBootstrap">
<property name="model">
    <value>alfresco/module/${project.artifactId}/model
    /scSitePermissionDefinitions.xml</value>
</property>
</bean>
```

12. The last bean that we need to add is the overriding of the baseJsonConversionComponent bean. We need to update it to make the new permission group EnableFlag available in the Share configuration file:

```
<bean id="baseJsonConversionComponent" abstract="true">
  <property name="nodeService" ref="NodeService" />
  <property name="publicServiceAccessService"
    ref="PublicServiceAccessService" />
  <property name="namespaceService" ref="NamespaceService" />
  <property name="fileFolderService" ref="FileFolderService" />
  <property name="lockService" ref="LockService" />
  <property name="permissionService" ref="PermissionService" />
  <property name="contentService" ref="ContentService" />
  <property name="userPermissions">
    <list>
      <value>Unlock</value>
      <value>CancelCheckOut</value>
      <value>ChangePermissions</value>
      <value>CreateChildren</value>
      <value>Delete</value>
      <value>Write</value>
      <value>EnableFlag</value>
    </list>
  </property>
</bean>
```

13. We have now completed the configuration on the Alfresco side. The first thing that we need to configure on the Share side is the messages. Edit the file, `share|src|main|amp|config|alfresco|web-extension|messages|share.properties` and add the following lines:

```
role.SitePublisher=SomeCo Publisher
role.SitePublisher.description=has view-only
rights in a site but can enable/disable the published flag.
group.SitePublisher=SomeCo Publishers
```

14. We need to change the evaluators that use the group membership to show/hide the flag related actions. Edit the file `share|src|main|amp|config|alfresco|web-extension|share-slingshot-application-context.xml` and locate the evaluator `evaluator.doclib.action.isSomecoPublishable`. Remove the reference to the evaluator `evaluator.doclib.action.isSomecoPublisher`:

```xml
<bean id="evaluator.doclib.action.isSomecoPublishable"
parent="evaluator.doclib.action.chainedMatchAll">
  <property name="evaluators">
    <list>
      <ref bean="evaluator.doclib.action.isSomecoWhitepaper" />
      <ref bean="evaluator.doclib.action.isSomecoWebable" />
      <ref bean="evaluator.doclib.action.isSomecoWebInactive" />
    </list>
  </property>
</bean>
```

15. Do the same for the evaluator `evaluator.doclib.action.isSomecoUnpublishable`:

```xml
<bean id="evaluator.doclib.action.isSomecoUnpublishable"
  parent="evaluator.doclib.action.chainedMatchAll">
  <property name="evaluators">
    <list>
      <ref bean="evaluator.doclib.action.isSomecoWhitepaper" />
      <ref bean="evaluator.doclib.action.isSomecoWebable" />
      <ref bean="evaluator.doclib.action.isSomecoWebActive" />
    </list>
  </property>
</bean>
```

16. Finally, we need to change the definition of the actions in
`share|src|main|resources|META-INF|share-config-custom.xml`. Locate
the actions `someco-web-enable` and `someco-web-disable` and change the
`permissions` tag to use the new `EnableFlag` permission group:

```
<permissions>
  <permission allow="true">EnableFlag</permission>
</permissions>
```

17. Save the changes you made everywhere.
18. Package, deploy your changes, and then restart Alfresco.

To test out your changes, log in to Alfresco Share as Site Manager of the Marketing site. Go
to the dashboard of the site and click on **Site Members**. Click on **Add User** and search for a
new user. You should be able to select the new **SomeCo Publisher** role:

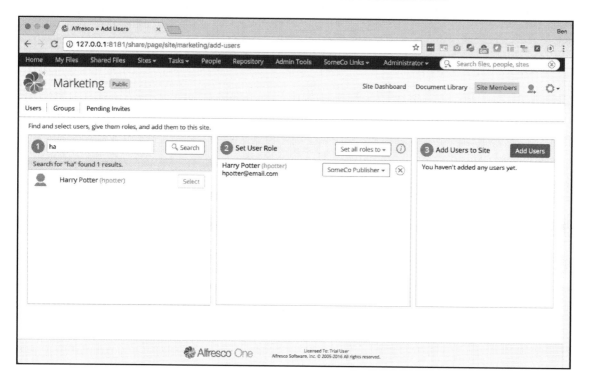

By going back to the dashboard, you should see your new user as **SomeCo Publisher** in the **Site Members** dashlet:

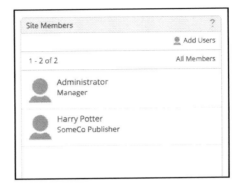

When you log out and log in again as the user you just granted the publisher role, you should see, and be able to successfully execute, the enable and disable actions, as well as all out-of-the-box *Consumer* actions:

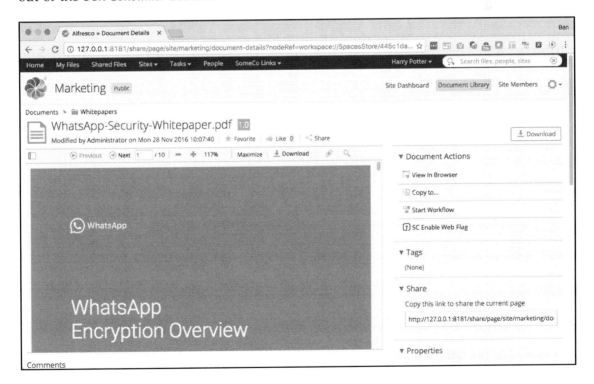

Global Permissions

The last section in the `permissionDefinitions.xml` file is a set of global permissions. Global permissions, as the name implies, apply to everything and supersede any other permissions that might be set on the object. The list of global permissions is short:

- Those belonging to the Administrator role always have full control
- Content owners (people belonging to the Owner role for a particular piece of content) always have full control
- Lock owners (people belonging to the Lock Owner role for a particular piece of content) always have Unlock, CheckIn, and Cancel Checkout permissions

Mapping Permissions to Methods

The names of the low-level permissions are pretty descriptive, but you might be wondering how these permissions are hooked in to the Alfresco API. As mentioned earlier in the chapter, Alfresco uses Spring Security. Spring Security bean configurations map methods in Alfresco's service classes to permissions. You can see the mapping in `alfresco|public-services-security-context.xml` packaged in the JAR file `alfresco-repository-5.x.jar`. Following is a portion of the mapping for the NodeService with methods requiring the `ReadProperties` permission highlighted, as an example:

```
<bean id="NodeService_security"
class="org.alfresco.repo.security.permissions.impl.acegi.MethodSecurityInte
rceptor">
    <property name="authenticationManager"><ref
bean="authenticationManager"/></property>
    <property name="accessDecisionManager"><ref
local="accessDecisionManager"/></property>
    <property name="afterInvocationManager"><ref
local="afterInvocationManager"/></property>
    <property name="objectDefinitionSource">
    <value>
        org.alfresco.service.cmr.repository.NodeService.
          getStores=ACL_ALLOW,AFTER_ACL_NODE.sys:base.ReadProperties
        org.alfresco.service.cmr.repository.NodeService
          .createStore=ACL_METHOD.ROLE_ADMINISTRATOR
        org.alfresco.service.cmr.repository.NodeService
          .exists=ACL_ALLOW
        org.alfresco.service.cmr.repository.NodeService
          .getNodeStatus=ACL_NODE.0.sys:base.ReadProperties
        org.alfresco.service.cmr.repository.NodeService
          .getNodeRef=AFTER_ACL_NODE.sys:base.ReadProperties
        org.alfresco.service.cmr.repository.NodeService
```

```
.getAllRootNodes=ACL_NODE.0.sys:base.ReadProperties,AFTER_ACL_NODE.sys:base
.ReadProperties
        org.alfresco.service.cmr.repository.NodeService
          .getRootNode=ACL_NODE.0.sys:base.ReadProperties
        org.alfresco.service.cmr.repository.NodeService
          .createNode=ACL_NODE.0.sys:base.CreateChildren
        org.alfresco.service.cmr.repository.NodeService

.moveNode=ACL_NODE.0.sys:base.DeleteNode,ACL_NODE.1.sys:base.CreateChildren
        org.alfresco.service.cmr.repository.NodeService
          .setChildAssociationIndex=ACL_PARENT.0.sys:base.WriteProperties
        org.alfresco.service.cmr.repository.NodeService
          .getType=ACL_ALLOW
            ...
```

If you develop your own services, you can follow the same pattern to secure your methods using the same set of permission definitions.

Summary

When you started out the chapter, you had an Alfresco server that only knew about the users stored in its repository. By now, your server is not only authenticating against an external LDAP directory, but can also share a session with other web applications through the magic of Single Sign-On (SSO).

You saw some sample code for working with three of Alfresco's security services classes (AuthenticationService, AuthorityService, and PersonService) and also learned where Alfresco keeps its permission definitions (and how to extend them).

Specifically, you learned how to:

- Install a basic OpenLDAP implementation
- Configure Alfresco to authenticate against LDAP, including "chaining" LDAP with Alfresco authentication
- Configure LDAP synchronization
- Install and configure a popular open source SSO solution from JA-SIG called CAS

- Establish SSO between Alfresco and two of Tomcat's sample servlets
- Create users and groups with the Alfresco API
- Understand the out-of-the-box permissions
- Define a custom permission group or role, which you then leveraged to refactor how the SomeCo Web Enable/Disable links work

Index

Printed in Great Britain
by Amazon